Instructor's Resource Manual to acco

ELECTRONIC DEVICES, Fifth Edition
and
ELECTRONIC DEVICES:
ELECTRON-FLOW VERSION, Third Edition

Thomas L. Floyd

Prentice Hall
Upper Saddle River, New Jersey   Columbus, Ohio

Cover Photo: Copyright © Photosynthesis/International Stock
Editor: Linda Ludewig
Production Editor: Rex Davidson
Design Coordinator: Karrie M. Converse
Cover Designer: Brian Deep
Production Manager: Patricia A. Tonneman
Marketing Manager: Ben Leonard

This book was printed and bound by Victor Graphics. The cover was printed by Victor Graphics.

© 1999 by Prentice-Hall, Inc.
Simon & Schuster/A Viacom Company
Upper Saddle River, New Jersey 07458

All rights reserved. No part of this book may be reproduced, in any form or by any means, without permission in writing from the publisher.

Printed in the United States of America

10 9 8 7 6 5 4 3 2 1

ISBN: 0-13-080025-2

Prentice-Hall International (UK) Limited, *London*
Prentice-Hall of Australia Pty. Limited, *Sydney*
Prentice-Hall Canada Inc., *Toronto*
Prentice-Hall Hispanoamericana, S. A., *Mexico*
Prentice-Hall of India Private Limited, *New Delhi*
Prentice-Hall of Japan, Inc., *Tokyo*
Simon & Schuster Asia Pte. Ltd., *Singapore*
Editora Prentice-Hall do Brasil, Ltda., *Rio de Janeiro*

Table of Contents

Solutions for End-of-Chapter Problems

Chapter 1	2
Chapter 2	4
Chapter 3	16
Chapter 4	24
Chapter 5	33
Chapter 6	46
Chapter 7	62
Chapter 8	70
Chapter 9	81
Chapter 10	88
Chapter 11	103
Chapter 12	110
Chapter 13	117
Chapter 14	124
Chapter 15	130
Chapter 16	138
Chapter 17	143
Chapter 18	148

Selected Results for System Applications	153
Electronics Workbench Tutorial	162
Summary of EWB Example Circuit Files Results	200
Summary of EWB Troubleshooting Circuit Files Results	210
PSpice Tutorial	216
Summary of PSpice Example Circuit Files Results	222
Summary of PSpice Troubleshooting Circuit Files Results	231
Test Item File	237
Transparency Masters	335

Chapter 1
Introduction to Semiconductors

Section 1-1 Atomic Structure

1. An atom with an atomic number of 6 has **6 electrons** and **6 protons**.

2. The M shell of an atom can have $2n^2 = 2(3)^2 = 18$ **electrons**

Section 1-2 Semiconductors, Conductors, and Insulators

3. The materials represented in Figure 1-42 are
   (a) Insulator   (b) Semiconductor   (c) Conductor

4. An atom with four valence electrons is a **semiconductor**.

Section 1-3 Covalent Bonds

5. In a silicon crystal, each atom forms **four** covalent bonds.

Section 1-4 Conduction in Semiconductors

6. When heat is added to silicon, more free electrons and holes are produced.

7. Current is produced in silicon at the **conduction** band and the **valence** band.

Section 1-5 N-type and P-type Semiconductors

8. Doping is the carefully controlled addition of trivalent or pentavalent atoms to pure (intrinsic) semiconductor material for the purpose of increasing the number of majority carriers (free electrons or holes).

9. Antimony is a pentavalent (donor) material used for doping to increase free electrons. Boron is a trivalent (acceptor) material used for doping to increase the holes.

Section 1-6 The PN Junction

10. The electric field across the pn junction is created by donor atoms in the n region losing free electrons to acceptor atoms in the p region. This creates positive ions in the n-region near the junction and negative ions in the p region near the junction. A field is then established between the ions.

11. The barrier potential of a pn junction represents an energy gradient that must be overcome by conduction electrons and produces a voltage drop, not a source of energy.

Chapter 1

Section 1-7 Biasing the PN Junction

12. To forward bias a pn junction, the positive terminal of a voltage source must be connected to the **p-region.**

13. A series resistor is needed to **limit the current** through a forward biased pn junction to a value which will not damage the junction because the junction itself has very little resistance.

Section 1-8 Current-Voltage Characteristic of a PN Junction

14. To generate the forward bias portion of the characteristic curve, connect a voltage source across the pn junction for forward bias, and place an ammeter in series with the diode and a voltmeter across the pn junction. Slowly increase the voltage from zero and plot the current vs the forward voltage.

15. A temperature increase would cause the barrier potential to decrease from 0.7 V to 0.6 V.

Section 1-9 The Diode

16. (a) The diode is reverse biased (b) The diode is forward biased
    (c) The diode is forward biased (d) The diode is forward biased

17. (a) $V_R = \left(\dfrac{50 \text{ M}\Omega}{50 \text{ M}\Omega + 10 \text{ }\Omega}\right)(5 \text{ V} - 8 \text{ V}) \cong -3 \text{ V}$
    (b) $V_F = 0.3 \text{ V}$
    (c) $V_F = 0.3 \text{ V}$
    (d) $V_F = 0.3 \text{ V}$

18. (a) Since $V_D = 25 \text{ V} = 0.5 V_S$, the diode is **open**.
    (b) The diode is forward biased but since $V_D = 15 \text{ V} = V_S$, the diode is **open.**
    (c) The diode is reverse biased but since $V_R = 2.5 \text{ V} = 0.5 V_S$, the diode is **shorted**.
    (d) The diode is reverse biased and $V_R = 0 \text{ V}$. The diode is **operating properly**.

19. $V_A = V_{S1} = \mathbf{+25 \text{ V}}$
    $V_B = V_{S1} - 0.7 \text{ V} = 25 \text{ V} - 0.7 \text{ V} = \mathbf{+24.3 \text{ V}}$
    $V_C = V_{S2} + 0.7 \text{ V} = 8 \text{ V} + 0.7 \text{ V} = \mathbf{+8.7 \text{ V}}$
    $V_D = V_{S2} = \mathbf{+8.0 \text{ V}}$

Chapter 2
Diodes and Applications

Section 2-1 Half-Wave Rectifiers

1. See Figure 2-1.

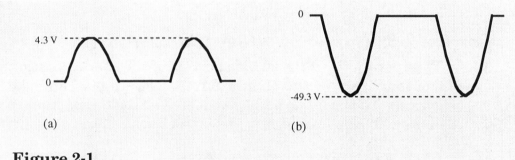

Figure 2-1

2. (a) $I_F = \dfrac{V_{(p)in} - 0.7\text{ V}}{R} = \dfrac{5\text{ V} - 0.7\text{ V}}{47\text{ }\Omega} = \dfrac{4.3\text{ V}}{47\text{ }\Omega} = \mathbf{91.5\text{ mA}}$

   (b) $I_F = \dfrac{V_{(p)in} - 0.7\text{ V}}{R} = \dfrac{50\text{ V} - 0.7\text{ V}}{3.3\text{ k}\Omega} = \dfrac{49.3\text{ V}}{3.3\text{ k}\Omega} = \mathbf{14.9\text{ mA}}$

3. $V_{sec} = \left(\dfrac{1}{5}\right)V_{pri} = \left(\dfrac{1}{5}\right)115\text{ V} = \mathbf{23\text{ V}}\text{ rms}$

4. $V_s = \left(\dfrac{N_2}{N_1}\right)115\text{ V} = \left(\dfrac{1}{2}\right)115\text{ V} = 57.5\text{ V rms}$

   $V_{p(sec)} = 1.414(57.5\text{ V}) = 81.3\text{ V}$

   $V_{avg(sec)} = \dfrac{V_{p(sec)}}{\pi} = \dfrac{81.3\text{ V}}{\pi} = 25.9\text{ V}$

   $P_{L(p)} = \dfrac{\left(V_{p(sec)} - 0.7\text{ V}\right)^2}{R_L} = \dfrac{(80.6\text{ V})^2}{220\text{ }\Omega} = \mathbf{29.5\text{ W}}$

   $P_{L(avg)} = \dfrac{\left(V_{avg(sec)}\right)^2}{R_L} = \dfrac{(25.9\text{ V})^2}{220\text{ }\Omega} = \mathbf{3.05\text{ W}}$

Chapter 2

Section 2-2 Full-Wave Rectifiers

5. (a) $V_{avg} = \dfrac{V_p}{\pi} = \dfrac{5\text{ V}}{\pi} = \mathbf{1.59\text{ V}}$

(b) $V_{avg} = \dfrac{2V_p}{\pi} = \dfrac{2(100\text{ V})}{\pi} = \mathbf{63.7\text{ V}}$

(c) $V_{avg} = \dfrac{2V_p}{\pi} + 10\text{ V} = \dfrac{2(10\text{ V})}{\pi} + 10\text{ V} = \mathbf{16.4\text{ V}}$

(d) $V_{avg} = \dfrac{2V_p}{\pi} - 15\text{ V} = \dfrac{2(40\text{ V})}{\pi} - 15\text{ V} = \mathbf{10.5\text{ V}}$

6. (a) Center-tapped full-wave rectifier

(b) $V_{p(sec)} = \left(\dfrac{1}{4}\right)(1.414)110\text{ V} = \mathbf{38.9\text{ V}}$

(c) $\dfrac{V_{p(sec)}}{2} = \dfrac{38.9\text{ V}}{2} = \mathbf{19.4\text{ V}}$

(d) See Figure 2-2. $V_{RL} = 19.4\text{ V} - 0.7\text{ V} = \mathbf{18.7\text{ V}}$

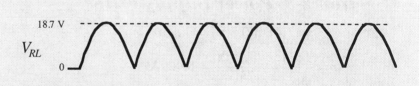

Figure 2-2

(e) $I_F = \dfrac{\dfrac{V_{p(sec)}}{2} - 0.7\text{ V}}{R_L} = \dfrac{18.7\text{ V}}{1\text{ k}\Omega} = \mathbf{18.7\text{ mA}}$

(f) PIV = 19.4 V + 18.7 V = **38.1 V**

7. $V_{avg} = \dfrac{110\text{ V}}{2} = 55\text{ V}$ for each half

$V_{avg} = \dfrac{V_p}{\pi}$

$V_p = \pi V_{avg} = \pi(55\text{ V}) = \mathbf{172.8\text{ V}}$

Chapter 2

8. See Figure 2-3.

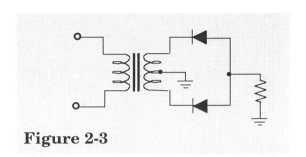

Figure 2-3

9. $\text{PIV} = V_p = \dfrac{\pi V_{avg(out)}}{2} = \dfrac{\pi(50\text{ V})}{2} = $ **78.5 V**

10. $\text{PIV} = V_{p(out)} = 1.414(20\text{ V}) = $ **28.3 V**

11. See Figure 2-4.

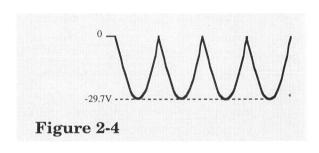

Figure 2-4

Section 2-3 Power Supply Filters

12. $V_{r(pp)} = (1.414)(0.5\text{ V}) = 707\text{ mV pp}$

$r = \dfrac{V_{r(pp)}}{V_{dc}} = \dfrac{707\text{ mV}}{75\text{ V}} = $ **0.00943**

13. $V_{r(pp)} = \dfrac{V_{p(in)}}{fR_LC} = \dfrac{30\text{ V}}{(120\text{ Hz})(600\text{ }\Omega)(50\text{ }\mu\text{F})} = $ **8.33 V pp**

$V_{DC} = \left(1 - \dfrac{1}{2fR_LC}\right)V_{p(in)} = \left(1 - \dfrac{1}{(240\text{ Hz})(600\text{ }\Omega)(50\text{ }\mu\text{F})}\right)30\text{ V} = $ **25.8 V**

14. $\%r = \left(\dfrac{V_{r(pp)}}{V_{dc}}\right)100 = \left(\dfrac{8.33\text{ V}}{25.8\text{ V}}\right)100 = $ **32.3 %**

15. $V_{r(pp)} = (0.01)(18\text{ V}) = 180\text{ mV}$

$V_{r(pp)} = \left(\dfrac{1}{fR_LC}\right)V_{p(in)}$

$C = \left(\dfrac{1}{fR_LV_r}\right)V_{p(in)} = \left(\dfrac{1}{(120\text{ Hz})(1.5\text{ k}\Omega)(180\text{ mV})}\right)18\text{ V} = $ **556 μF**

Chapter 2

16. $V_{r(pp)} = \dfrac{V_{p(in)}}{fR_LC} = \dfrac{80\text{ V}}{(120\text{ Hz})10\text{ k}\Omega)(10\text{ μF})} = 6.67\text{ V}$

$V_{DC} = \left(1 - \dfrac{1}{2fR_LC}\right)V_{p(in)} = \left(1 - \dfrac{1}{(240\text{ Hz})(10\text{ k}\Omega)(10\text{ μF})}\right)80\text{ V} = 46.7\text{ V}$

$r = \dfrac{V_{r(pp)}}{V_{DC}} = \dfrac{6.67\text{ V}}{46.7\text{ V}} = \mathbf{0.143}$

17. $V_{p(in)} = (12\text{ V})(1.414)(3) = 49.5\text{ V}$
$V_{r(in)} = (49.5\text{ V})(0.308) = 15.2\text{ V}$

$V_{dc(in)} = \dfrac{2V_{p(in)}}{\pi} = 31.5\text{ V}$

$X_L = 2\pi fL = 2\pi(120\text{ Hz})(200\text{ mH}) = 151\text{ }\Omega$

$X_C = \dfrac{1}{2\pi fC} = \dfrac{1}{2\pi(120\text{ Hz})(100\text{ μF})} = 13.3\text{ }\Omega$

$V_{r(out)} = \left(\dfrac{X_C}{X_L - X_C}\right)V_{r(in)} = \left(\dfrac{13.3\text{ }\Omega}{137.7\text{ }\Omega}\right)15.2\text{ V} = \mathbf{1.47\text{ V}}$

$V_{dc(out)} = \left(\dfrac{R_L}{R_W + R_L}\right)V_{dc(in)} = \left(\dfrac{3.3\text{ k}\Omega}{3.4\text{ k}\Omega}\right)31.5\text{ V} = \mathbf{30.6\text{ V}}$

18. $V_{p(sec)} = 1.414(12\text{ V})(3) = 50.9\text{ V}$
See Figure 2-5.

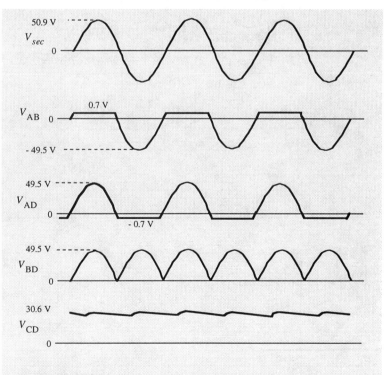

Figure 2-5

Chapter 2

Section 2-4 Diode Limiting and Clamping Circuits

19. See Figure 2-6.

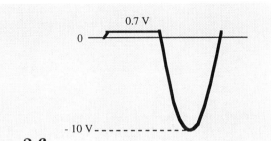

Figure 2-6

20. Apply Kirchhoff's law at the peak of the postive half cycle:

(b) 25 V = $V_R + V_R$ + 0.7 V

$2V_R$ = 24.3 V

$V_R = \dfrac{24.3 \text{ V}}{2}$ = 12.15 V

$V_{out} = V_R$ + 0.7 V = 12.15 V + 0.7 V = 12.85 V

See Figure 2-7(a).

(c) $V_R = \dfrac{11.3 \text{ V}}{2}$ = 5.65 V

$V_{out} = V_R$ + 0.7 V = 5.65 V + 0.7 V = 6.35 V

See Figure 2-7(b).

(d) $V_R = \dfrac{4.3 \text{ V}}{2}$ = 2.15 V

$V_{out} = V_R$ + 0.7 V = 2.15 V + 0.7 V = 2.85 V

See Figure 2-7(c).

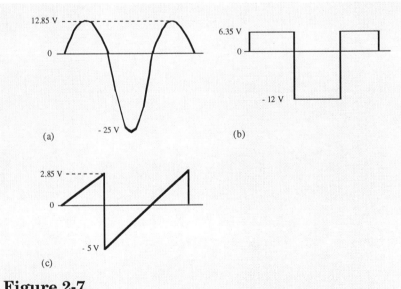

Figure 2-7

Chapter 2

21. See Figure 2-8.

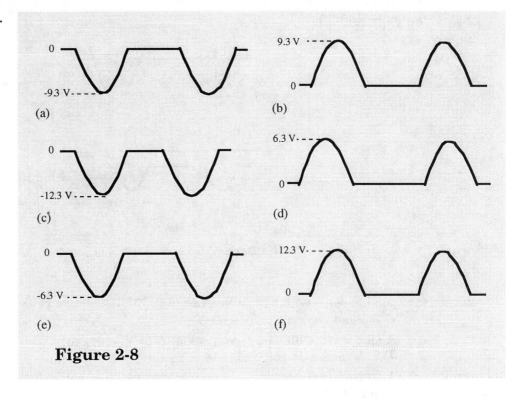

Figure 2-8

22. See Figure 2-9.

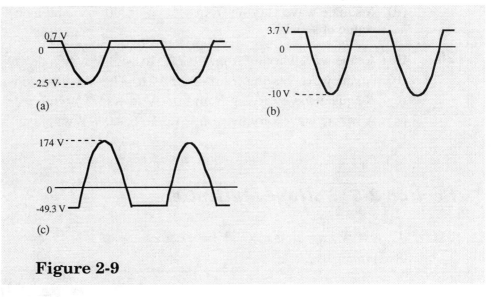

Figure 2-9

23. See Figure 2-10

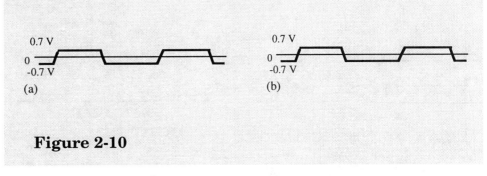

Figure 2-10

Chapter 2

24. See Figure 2-11.

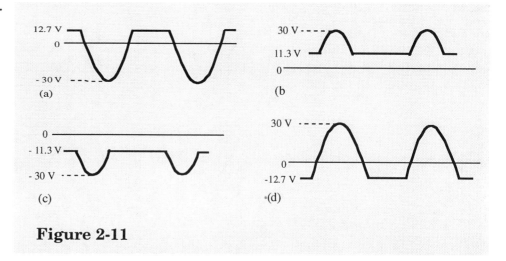

Figure 2-11

25. (a) A sine wave with a positive peak at 0.7 V, a negative peak at -7.3 V, and a dc value of -3.3 V.
  (b) A sine wave with a positive peak at 29.3 V, a negative peak at -0.7 V, and a dc value of + 14.3 V.
  (c) A square wave varying from + 0.7 V to - 15.3 V with a dc value of - 7.3 V.
  (d) A square wave varying from + 1.3 V to - 0.7 V with a dc value of + 0.3 V.

26. (a) A sine wave varying from - 0.7 V to +7.3 V with a dc value of + 3.3 V.
  (b) A sine wave varying from - 29.3 V to +7.3 V with a dc value of + 14.3 V.
  (c) A square wave varying from - 0.7 V to + 15.3 V with a dc value of + 7.3 V.
  (d) A square wave varying from - 1.3 V to + 0.7 V with a dc value of - 0.3 V.

Section 2-5 Voltage Multipliers

27. $V_{OUT} = 2V_{p(in)} = 2(1.414)(20\ V) = $ **56.6 V**
See Figure 2-12.

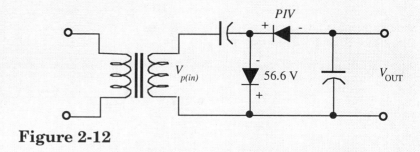

Figure 2-12

Chapter 2

28. $V_{OUT(trip)} = 3V_{p(in)} = 3(1.414)(20\text{ V}) = \textbf{84.8 V}$
$V_{OUT(quad)} = 4V_{p(in)} = 4(1.414)(20\text{ V}) = \textbf{113 V}$
See Figure 2-13.

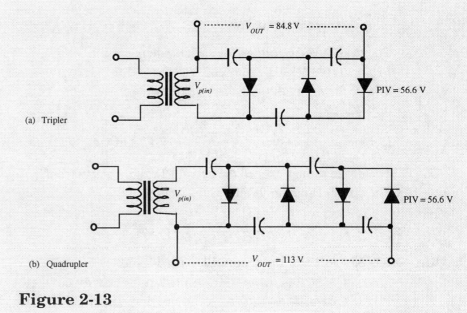

Figure 2-13

Section 2-6 The Diode Data Sheet

29. The PIV is specified as the peak repetitive reverse voltage = **50 V**.

30. The PIV is specified as the peak repetitive reverse voltage = **400 V**.

31. Use the specified $I_{FSM} = 800$ A.

$R_{surge(min)} = \dfrac{50\text{ V}}{800\text{ A}} = \textbf{62.5 m}\boldsymbol{\Omega}$

Section 2-7 Troubleshooting

32. If a bridge rectifier diode opens, the output becomes a half-wave voltage resulting in an increased ripple at 60 Hz.

33. $V_{avg} = \dfrac{2V_p}{\pi} = \dfrac{2(115\text{ V})(1.414)}{\pi} \cong 104\text{ V}$

The output of the bridge is correct. However, the 0 V output from the filter indicates that the **coil is open** or that the **capacitor is shorted**.

34. (a) Correct
(b) Incorrect. Open diode.
(c) Correct
(d) Incorrect. Open diode.

11

Chapter 2

35.
$$V_{sec} = \frac{115 \text{ V}}{5} = 23 \text{ V rms}$$

$V_{p(sec)} = 1.414(23 \text{ V}) = 32.5 \text{ V}$

The peak voltage for each half of the secondary is

$$\frac{V_{p(sec)}}{2} = \frac{32.5 \text{ V}}{2} = 16.3 \text{ V}$$

The peak inverse voltage for each diode is
PIV = 2(16.3 V) + 0.7 V = 33.2 V
The peak current through each diode is

$$I_p = \frac{\frac{V_{p(sec)}}{2} - 0.7 \text{ V}}{R_L} = \frac{16.3 \text{ V} - 0.7 \text{ V}}{330 \text{ }\Omega} = 47.3 \text{ mA}$$

The diode ratings exceed the actual PIV and peak current.
The circuit should not fail.

Section 2-8 System Application

36. (a) No voltage between TP1 and TP2:
   Possible causes: fuse blown or power cord not plugged in.
   Corrective action: check fuse and power plug. Replace fuse or insert plug.

   (b) No voltage between TP3 and TP4, 110 V from TP1 to TP2:
   Possible causes: open primary or shorted secondary.
   Corrective action: check windings with ohmmeter. Replace transformer.

   (c) 50 V between TP3 and TP4, input voltage correct:
   Possible causes: partially shorted primary or wrong turns ratio.
   Corrective action: check primary winding and transformer rating. Replace transformer.

   (d) 25 V between TP3 and TP4, input voltage correct:
   Possible causes: partially shorted secondary or wrong turns ratio.
   Corrective action: check secondary winding and transformer rating. Replace transformer.

   (e) Full-wave voltage with peak of 50 V from TP7 to ground :
   Possible cause: Filter capacitor open.
   Corrective action: check capacitor with ohmmeter. Replace capacitor.

   (f) Excessive 120 Hz ripple at TP7:
   Possible causes: leaky filter capacitor or excessive loading.
   Corrective action: check capacitor and load. Replace capacitor or correct load condition.

   (g) 60 Hz ripple at TP7:
   Possible cause: open diode in bridge.
   Corrective action: check diodes with ohmmeter and replace defective one.

   (h) No voltage at TP7:
   Possible causes: open surge resistor, blown fuse, open winding, shorted C.
   Corrective action: check all and replace defective component.

Chapter 2

37. Something must be causing a diode to open. Check all the diodes for opens this time. You will most likely find one. The PIV or the maximum surge current must have been exceeded. Excessive PIV could be caused by some shorted priimary windings which would produce an excessive secondary voltage. If caused by excessive surge current, a small limiting resistor will have to be placed in series with C_1.

38. If the top diode in Figure 2-92 were reversed, two forward biased diodes would be placed in series across the secondary during the negative half cycle which, most likely, would blow the diodes open and result in no voltage at TP8.

Advanced Problems

39.
$$V_r = \left(\frac{1}{fR_LC}\right)V_{p(in)}$$

$$C = \left(\frac{1}{fR_LV_r}\right)V_{p(in)} = \left(\frac{1}{(120\text{ Hz})(3.3\text{ k}\Omega)(0.5\text{ V})}\right)35\text{ V} = \mathbf{177\ \mu F}$$

40.
$$V_{DC} = \left(1 - \frac{1}{2fR_LC}\right)V_{p(in)}$$

$$\frac{V_{DC}}{V_{p(in)}} = \left(1 - \frac{1}{2fR_LC}\right)$$

$$\frac{1}{2fR_LC} = 1 - \frac{V_{DC}}{V_{p(in)}}$$

$$\frac{1}{2fR_L\left(1 - \frac{V_{DC}}{V_{p(in)}}\right)} = C$$

$$C = \frac{1}{(240\text{ Hz})(1\text{ k}\Omega)(1 - 0.933)} = \frac{1}{(240\text{ Hz})(1\text{ k}\Omega)(0.067)} = \mathbf{62.2\ \mu F}$$

Then
$$V_r = \left(\frac{1}{fR_LC}\right)V_{p(in)} = \left(\frac{1}{(120\text{ Hz})(1\text{ k}\Omega)(62.2\ \mu F)}\right)15\text{ V} = \mathbf{2\ V}$$

41. The capacitor input voltage is
$$V_{p(in)} = (1.414)(24\text{ V}) - 1.4\text{ V} = 32.5\text{ V}$$

$$R_{surge} = \frac{V_{p(in)}}{I_{surge}} = \frac{32.5\text{ V}}{50\text{ A}} = \mathbf{651\ m\Omega}$$

The nearest standard value is 680 mΩ

Chapter 2

42. See Figure 2–14.

The voltage at point A with respect to ground is
$V_A = 1.414(9 \text{ V}) \text{ m} = 12.7 \text{ V}$
Therefore
$V_B = 12.7 \text{ V} - 0.7 \text{ V} = 12 \text{ V}$
$V_r = 0.05 V_B = 0.05(12 \text{ V}) = 0.6 \text{ V peak to peak}$

$$C = \left(\frac{1}{fR_L V_r}\right) V_B = \left(\frac{1}{(120 \text{ Hz})(680 \text{ }\Omega)(0.6 \text{ V})}\right) 12 \text{ V} = 245 \text{ }\mu\text{F}$$

The nearest standard value is 270 µF
Let $R_{surge} = 1 \text{ }\Omega$
$I_{surge(max)} = \dfrac{12 \text{ V}}{1 \text{ }\Omega} = 12 \text{ A}$
$I_O = \dfrac{12 \text{ V}}{680 \text{ }\Omega} = 17.6 \text{ mA}$
$PIV = 2V_{p(out)} + 0.7 \text{ V} = 24.7 \text{ V}$

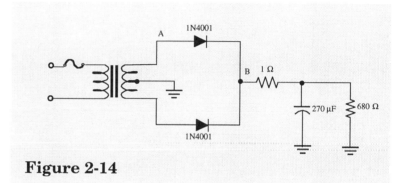

Figure 2-14

43. See Figure 2–15.

$I_{L(max)} = 100 \text{ mA}$
$R_L = \dfrac{9 \text{ V}}{100 \text{ mA}} = 90 \text{ }\Omega$
$V_r = 1.414(0.25 \text{ V}) = 0.354 \text{ V}$
$V_r = 2(0.35 \text{ V}) = 0.71 \text{ V peak to peak}$

$$V_r = \left(\frac{1}{(120 \text{ Hz})(90 \text{ }\Omega)C}\right) 9 \text{ V}$$

$$C = \frac{9 \text{ V}}{(120 \text{ Hz})(90 \text{ }\Omega)(0.71 \text{ V})} = 1174 \text{ }\mu\text{F}$$

Use $C = 1200 \text{ }\mu\text{F}$

Each half of the supply uses identical components. 1N4001 diodes are feasible since the average current is $(0.318)(100 \text{ mA}) = 31.8 \text{ mA}$.

$R_{surge} = 1 \text{ }\Omega$ will limit the surge current to an acceptable value.

Chapter 2

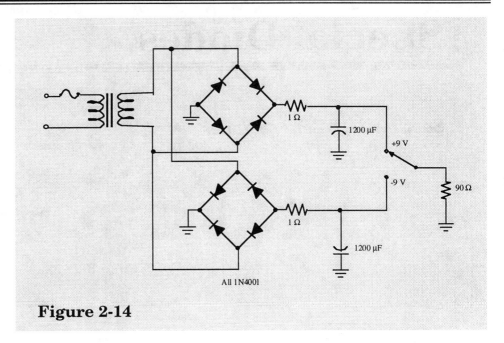

Figure 2-14

44. Both positive and negative limiting of a sinusoidal voltage is not achievable with a single dc source.

45. $V_{C1} = (1.414)(110 \text{ V}) - 0.7 \text{ V} = 156 \text{ V} - 0.7 \text{ V} = \mathbf{155.3 \text{ V}}$
$V_{C2} = 2(1.414)(110 \text{ V}) - 2(0.7 \text{ V}) = 312 \text{ V} - 1.4 \text{ V} = \mathbf{310.6 \text{ V}}$

Chapter 3
Special Diodes

Section 3-1 Zener Diodes

1. See Figure 3-1.

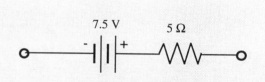

Figure 3-1

2. $I_{ZK} \cong 3$ mA
   $V_Z \cong -8.5$ V

3. $R_Z = \dfrac{\Delta V_Z}{\Delta I_Z} = \dfrac{5.65 \text{ V} - 5.6 \text{ V}}{30 \text{ mA} - 20 \text{ mA}} = \dfrac{0.05 \text{ V}}{10 \text{ mA}} = 5\,\Omega$

4. $\Delta I_Z = 50$ mA $- 25$ mA $= 25$ mA
   $\Delta V_Z = \Delta I_Z R_Z = (+25 \text{ mA})(15\,\Omega) = +0.375$ V
   $V_Z = V_{ZT} + \Delta V_Z = 4.7$ V $+ 0.375$ V $= \mathbf{5.08\ V}$

5. $\Delta T = 70\,°C - 25\,°C = 45\,°C$
   $V_Z = 6.8 \text{ V} + \dfrac{(6.8 \text{ V})(0.0004/°C)}{45\,°C} = 6.8 \text{ V} + 0.12 \text{ V} = \mathbf{6.92\ V}$

Section 3-2 Zener Diode Applications

6. $V_{IN(min)} = V_Z + I_{ZK}R = 14 \text{ V} + (1.5 \text{ mA})(560\,\Omega) = \mathbf{14.8\ V}$

7. $\Delta V_Z = (I_{ZT} - I_{ZT})R_Z = (28.5 \text{ mA})(20\,\Omega) = 0.57$ V
   $V_{OUT} = V_{ZT} - \Delta V_Z = 14 \text{ V} - 0.57 \text{ V} = 13.43$ V
   $V_{IN(min)} = I_{ZK}R + V_{OUT} = (1.5 \text{ mA})(560\,\Omega) + 13.43 \text{ V} = \mathbf{14.3\ V}$

8. $\Delta V_Z = I_Z R_Z = (40 \text{ mA} - 30 \text{ mA})(30\,\Omega) = 0.3$ V
   $V_Z = 12 \text{ V} + \Delta V_Z = 12 \text{ V} + 0.3 \text{ V} = 12.3$ V
   $R = \dfrac{V_{IN} - V_Z}{40 \text{ mA}} = \dfrac{18 \text{ V} - 12.3 \text{ V}}{40 \text{ mA}} = \mathbf{143\,\Omega}$

Chapter 3

9. $V_Z \cong 12 \text{ V} + 0.3 \text{ V} = 12.3 \text{ V}$
See Figure 3-2

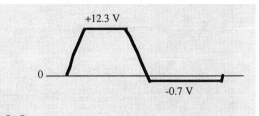

Figure 3-2

10. $V_{Z(min)} = V_Z - \Delta I_Z R_Z = 5.1 \text{ V} - (35 \text{ mA} - 1\text{mA})(12 \text{ }\Omega)$
$= 5.1 \text{ V} - (34 \text{ mA})(12 \text{ }\Omega) = 5.1 \text{ V} - 0.41 \text{ V} = 4.69 \text{ V}$
$V_R = 8 \text{ V} - 4.69 \text{ V} = 3.31 \text{ V}$
$I_T = \dfrac{V_R}{R} = \dfrac{3.31 \text{ V}}{22 \text{ }\Omega} = 151 \text{ mA}$
$I_{L(max)} = 151 \text{ mA} - 1 \text{ mA} = \textbf{150 mA}$
$V_{Z(max)} = 5.1 \text{ V} + (70 \text{ mA} - 35 \text{ mA})(12 \text{ }\Omega) = 5.1 \text{ V} + 0.42 \text{ V} = 5.52 \text{ V}$
$V_R = 8 \text{ V} - 5.52 \text{ V} = 2.48 \text{ V}$
$I_T = \dfrac{2.48 \text{ V}}{22 \text{ }\Omega} = 113 \text{ mA}$
$I_{L(min)} = 113 \text{ mA} - 70 \text{ mA} = \textbf{43 mA}$

11. % Load Regulation $= \dfrac{V_{Z(max)} - V_{Z(min)}}{V_{Z(min)}} \times 100\% = \dfrac{5.52 \text{ V} - 4.69 \text{ V}}{4.69 \text{ V}} \times 100\% = \textbf{17.7 \%}$

12. With no load and $V_{IN} = 6$ V:
$I_Z \cong \dfrac{V_{IN} - V_Z}{R + R_Z} = \dfrac{6 \text{ V} - 5.1 \text{ V}}{34 \text{ }\Omega} = 26.5 \text{ mA}$
$V_{OUT} = V_Z - \Delta I_Z R_Z = 5.1 \text{ V} - (35 \text{ mA} - 26.5 \text{ mA})(12 \text{ }\Omega) = 5.1 \text{ V} - 0.1 \text{ V} = 5 \text{ V}$
With no load and $V_{IN} = 12$ V:
$I_Z \cong \dfrac{V_{IN} - V_Z}{R - R_Z} = \dfrac{12 \text{ V} - 5.1 \text{ V}}{34 \text{ }\Omega} = 203 \text{ mA}$
$V_{OUT} = V_Z + \Delta I_Z R_Z = 5.1 \text{ V} + (202.9 \text{ mA} - 35 \text{ mA})(12 \text{ }\Omega) = 5.1 \text{ V} + 2.01 \text{ V} = 7.11 \text{ V}$
% Line Regulation $= \dfrac{\Delta V_{OUT}}{\Delta V_{IN}} \times 100\% = \dfrac{7.11 \text{ V} - 5 \text{ V}}{12 \text{ V} - 6 \text{ V}} \times 100\% = \textbf{35.2 \%}$

13. % Load Regulation $= \dfrac{V_{NL} - V_{FL}}{V_{FL}} \times 100\% = \dfrac{8.23 \text{ V} - 7.98 \text{ V}}{7.98 \text{ V}} \times 100\% = \textbf{3.13 \%}$

Chapter 3

14. % Line Regulation $= \dfrac{\Delta V_{OUT}}{\Delta V_{IN}} \times 100\% = \dfrac{0.2 \text{ V}}{10 \text{ V} - 5 \text{ V}} \times 100\% = $ **4 %**

15. % Load Regulation $= \dfrac{V_{NL} - V_{FL}}{V_{FL}} \times 100\% = \dfrac{3.6 \text{ V} - 3.4 \text{ V}}{3.4 \text{ V}} \times 100\% = $ **5.88 %**

Section 3-3 Varactor Diodes

16. At 5 V, $C = 20$ pF
At 20 V, $C = 10$ pF
$\Delta C = 20$ pF $- 10$ pF $=$ **10 pF** (decrease)

17. From the graph, $V_R = $ **3 V** @ 25 pF

18. $f_r = \dfrac{1}{\sqrt{2\pi L C_T}}$

$C_T = \dfrac{1}{4\pi^2 L f_r^2} = \dfrac{1}{4\pi^2 (2 \text{ mH})(1 \text{ MHz})^2} = 12.7 \text{ pF}$

Since they are in series, each varactor must have a capacitance of
$2C_T = $ **25.4 pF**

19. Each varactor has a capacitance of 25.4 pF. Therefore, from the graph
$V_R \cong $ **2.5 V**

Section 3-4 Optical Diodes

20. Assuming $V_F = 1.2$ V
$I_F = \dfrac{24 \text{ V} - 1.2 \text{ V}}{680 \text{ }\Omega} = 33.5 \text{ mA}$

From the graph, the radiant power is approximately **80 mW**.

21. See Figure 3–3
$R = \dfrac{5 \text{ V} - 0.7 \text{ V}}{30 \text{ mA}} = 143 \text{ }\Omega$

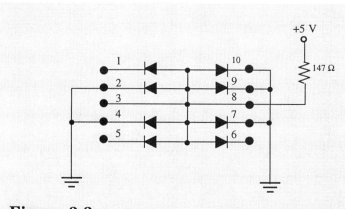

Figure 3-3

Chapter 3

22. $I_R = \dfrac{10\text{ V}}{200\text{ k}\Omega} = 50\text{ }\mu\text{A}$

23. (a) $R = \dfrac{V_S}{I} = \dfrac{3\text{ V}}{100\text{ }\mu\text{A}} = 30\text{ k}\Omega$

(b) $R = \dfrac{V_S}{I} = \dfrac{3\text{ V}}{350\text{ }\mu\text{A}} = 8.57\text{ k}\Omega$

(c) $R = \dfrac{V_S}{I} = \dfrac{3\text{ V}}{510\text{ }\mu\text{A}} = 5.88\text{ k}\Omega$

24. The microammeter reading will increase.

Section 3-5 Other Types of Diodes

25. $R = \dfrac{\Delta V}{\Delta I} = \dfrac{125\text{ mV} - 200\text{ mV}}{0.25\text{ mA} - 0.15\text{ mA}} = \dfrac{-75\text{ mV}}{0.10\text{ mA}} = -750\text{ }\Omega$

26. Tunnel diodes are used in oscillators.

27. The reflective ends cause the light to bounce back and forth, thus increasing the intensity of the light. The partially reflective end allows a portion of the reflected light to be emitted.

Section 3-6 Troubleshooting

28. (a) All voltages are correct.
(b) V_3 should be 12 V. Zener is open.
(c) V_1 should be 110 V. Fuse is open.
(d) Capacitor C_1 is open.
(e) Transformer winding open.

29. (a) With D_5 open, $V_{OUT} \cong 30$ V
(b) With R_1 open, $V_{OUT} = 0$ V
(c) With C_1 leaky, V_{OUT} has excessive 120 Hz ripple limited to 12 V
(d) With C_1 open, V_{OUT} is full wave rectified voltage limited to 12 V
(e) With D_3 open, V_{OUT} has 60 Hz ripple limited to 12 V
(f) With D_2 open, V_{OUT} has 60 Hz ripple limited to 12 V
(g) With T_1 open, $V_{OUT} = 0$ V
(h) With F_1 open, $V_{OUT} = 0$ V

30. The voltage reading is too low. Inspection of the circuit board reveals that the second diode from the top is connected backwards.

Chapter 3

31. The input voltage is correct but there is 0 V at the rectifier output. Possible causes are open fuse, open transformer, or open resistor. Cannot be isolated further with given measurements.

32. The LED (D_6) will not light when any of the following faults occur:
D_6 open, R_1 open, R_2 open, fuse blown, transformer winding open, D_5 shorted, or C_1 shorted.

33. The photodiode D_1 will not respond when there is:
No dc voltage
R_1 open
D_1 open
A short in the threshold, counter, and display circuits
Step 1: Check for 5.1 V dc.
Step 2: Check for a dc voltage at the D_1 cathode.

Data Sheet Problems

34. From the data sheet of Figure 3–7
(a) @ 25 °C: $P_{D(max)} = $ **1.0 W** for a 1N4738
(b) For a 1N4751:
@ 70 °C; $P_{D(max)} = 1.0$ W $- (6.67$mW $/$ °C$)(20$°C$) = 1.0$ W $- 133$ mW $=$ **867 mW**
@ 100 °C; $P_{D(max)} = 1.0$ W $- (6.67$mW $/$ °C$)(50$°C$) = 1.0$ W $- 333$ mW $=$ **667 mW**
(c) $I_{ZK} = $ **0.5 mA** for a 1N4738
(d) @ 25 °C: $I_{ZM} = 1$W $/ 27$ V $= $ **37.0 mA** for a 1N4750
(e) $\Delta Z_Z = 700 \: \Omega - 7.0 \: \Omega = $ **693 Ω** for a 1N4740
(f) @ 25 °C: $V_{ZMAX} = 6.8$ V $+ (4$ mV/°C$)(25$°C$) = 6.8$ V $+ 100$ mV $= $ **6.9 V** for a 1N4736
(g) @ 75 °C: $V_{ZMIN} = 20$ V $+ (15$ mV/°C$)(50$°C$)) = 20$ V $+ 750$ mV $= $ **20.8 V** for a 1N4747

35. From the data sheet of Figure 3–22
(a) $V_{R(max)} = $ **60 V** for a 1N4738
(b) For a 1N5141
@ 60 °C; $P_{D(max)} = 400$ mW $- (2.67$ mW $/$ °C$)(35$°C$) = 400$ mW $- 93.5$ mW $= $ **307 mW**
(c) For a 1N5148
@ 80 °C; $P_{D(max)} = 2.0$ W $- (13.3$ mW $/$ °C$)(55$°C$) = 2.0$ W $- 732$ mW $= $ **1.27 W**
(d) $C_D \cong $ **21 pF** for a 1N4750
(e) For maximum figure of merit a **1N5139** is best
(f) For $V_R = 60$ V, $C_D = 13.5$ pF/2.8 $= $ **4.82 pF** for a 1N5142

Chapter 3

36. From the data sheet of Figure 3–31
 (a) 9 V cannot be applied in reverse across an MLED81
 (b) When 5.1 V is used to forward bias the MLED81 for $I_F = 100$ mA, $V_F \cong 1.42$ V
 $$R = \frac{5.1 \text{ V} - 1.42 \text{ V}}{100 \text{ mA}} = \frac{3.68 \text{ V}}{100 \text{ mA}} = \mathbf{36.8 \ \Omega}$$
 (c) At 45°C max imum power dissipation is
 100 mW – (2.2 mW / °C)(20°C) = 100 mW – 44 mW = 56 mW
 If $V_F = 1.5$ V and $I_F = 50$ mA, $P_D = 75$ mW. The power rating is **exceeded**
 (d) For $I_F = 30$ mA, max imum axial radiant intensity is approximately **4.3 mW / sr**
 (e) For $I_F = 20$ mA and $\theta = 20°$, radiant intensity is 90% or max imum or
 (0.9)(20 mW / sr) = **18 mW / sr**

37. From the data sheet of Figure 3–36
 (a) With no incident light and a 10 kΩ series resistor, the voltage across an MRD821 is approximately equal to the **reverse bias source voltage.**
 (b) Reverse current is greatest at about **940 nm**.
 (c) At $T_A \cong 60°C$, dark current is about **40 nA**
 (d) Sensitivity is maximum for $\lambda = $ **940 nm**
 (e) At 900 nm the sensitivity is about 80% of maximum
 (0.8)(50 µA/mW/cm²) = **40 µA/mW/cm²**
 (f) For $\lambda = 900$ nm, $\theta = 40°$ and an irradience of 3 mW/cm²
 $I_D = (0.8)(0.87)(50$ µA/mW/cm²$)(3$ mW/cm²$) = $ **104 µA**

Advanced Problems

38. See Figure 3-4

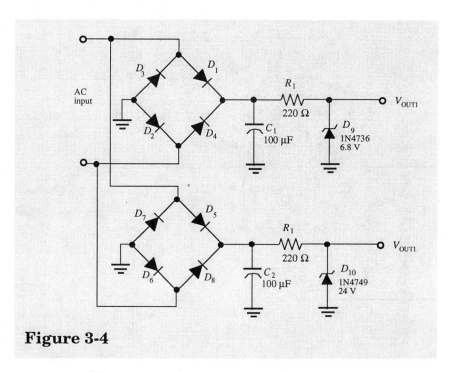

Figure 3-4

Chapter 3

39. $V_{OUT1} \cong \mathbf{6.8\ V}$, $V_{OUT2} \cong \mathbf{24\ V}$

40. For a 1 kΩ load on each output:
$I_{OUT(1)} \cong \dfrac{6.8\ V}{1\ k\Omega} = 6.8\ mA$
$I_{OUT(2)} \cong \dfrac{24\ V}{1\ k\Omega} = 24\ mA$
$I_{Z1} \cong 37\ mA$ for V_{ZT}
$I_{Z2} \cong 10.5\ mA$ for V_{ZT}
$I_T = 6.8\ mA + 24\ mA + 37\ mA + 10.5\ mA = 78.3\ mA$
The fuse rating should be 100 mA or **1/8 A**

41. See Figure 3–5.
Use a 1N4738 zener
$I_T = 35\ mA + 31\ mA = 66\ mA$
$R = \dfrac{24\ V - 8.2\ V}{66\ mA} = 239\ \Omega$

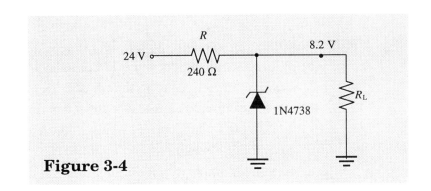

Figure 3-4

42. Use a 1N5148 varactor diode.
From the graph in Figure 3–22, the maximum and minimum varactor capacitances are roughly
$C_{max} \cong 80\ pF$ @ 1 V and $C_{min} \cong 12\ pF$ @ 60 V
Use these capacitance values to calculate an inductance range for 350 kHz and 850 kHz:
$L_{max} = \left(\dfrac{1}{2\pi f_{min}\sqrt{C_{min}}}\right)^2 = 2.92\ mH$
$L_{min} = \left(\dfrac{1}{2\pi f_{max}\sqrt{C_{max}}}\right)^2 = 2.58\ mH$
Choose $L = 2.7\ mH$ and calculate required C_{min} and C_{max}:
$C_{min} = \left(\dfrac{1}{2\pi f_{max}\sqrt{L}}\right)^2 = 13\ pF$
$C_{max} = \left(\dfrac{1}{2\pi f_{min}\sqrt{L}}\right)^2 = 77\ pF$

Chapter 3

42. *Continued*

From the graph in Figure 3–22, the reverse voltages for these capacitance values are approximately:

$V_{R(max)} \cong 50$ V for 13 pF

$V_{R(min)} \cong 1.2$ V for 77 pF

Let $V_{BIAS} = 100$ V

$$V_{R(min)} = \left(\frac{R_3}{R_2 + R_3 + R_4 + R_5}\right) V_{BIAS}$$

$$V_{R(max)} = \left(\frac{R_3 + R_4}{R_2 + R_3 + R_4 + R_5}\right) V_{BIAS}$$

Let $R_2 + R_3 + R_4 + R_5 = 100$ kΩ

$$R_3 = \frac{V_{R(min)}(R_2 + R_3 + R_4 + R_5)}{V_{BIAS}} = \frac{1.2 \text{ V}(100 \text{ k}\Omega)}{100 \text{ V}} = 1.2 \text{ k}\Omega$$

$$R_4 = \frac{V_{R(max)}(R_2 + R_3 + R_4 + R_5)}{V_{BIAS}} - R_3 = \frac{50 \text{ V}(100 \text{ k}\Omega)}{100 \text{ V}} - 1.2 \text{ k}\Omega = 49 \text{ k}\Omega$$

Use $R_4 = 50$ kΩ

$R_2 + R_5 = 100$ kΩ $- 50.2$ kΩ $= 49.8$ kΩ

Let $R_5 = 1.2$ kΩ

$R_2 = 49.8$ kΩ $- 1.2$ kΩ $= 48.6$ κΩ

Use $R_2 = 47$ kΩ

All other component values are same as in Figure 3–24.

43. See Figure 3-6.

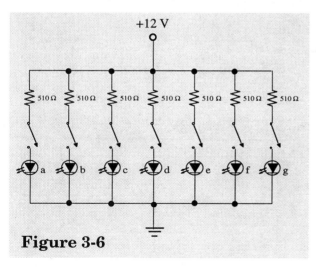

Figure 3-6

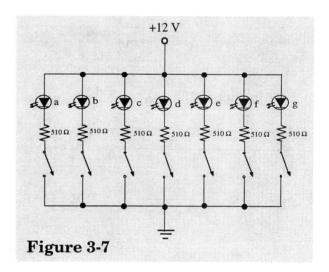

Figure 3-7

44. See Figure 3-7.

Chapter 4
Bipolar Junction Transistors

Section 4-1 Transistor Construction

1. Majority carriers in the base region of an npn transistor are **holes.**

2. Because of the narrow base region, the minority carriers invading the base region find a limited number of partners for recombination and, therefore, move across the junction into the collector region rather than out of the base lead.

Section 4-2 Basic Transistor Operation

3. The base is thin and lightly doped so that a recomination (base) current is generated that is small compared to the collector current.

4. $I_B = 0.02 I_E = 0.02(30 \text{ mA}) = 0.6 \text{ mA}$
   $I_C = I_E - I_B = 30 \text{ mA} - 0.6 \text{ mA} = \textbf{29.4 mA}$

5. The base must be positive with respect to the collector and negative with respect to the emitter.

6. $I_C = I_E - I_B = 5.34 \text{ mA} - 475 \text{ μA} = \textbf{4.87 mA}$

Section 4-3 Transistor Characteristics and Parameters

7. $\alpha_{DC} = \dfrac{I_C}{I_E} = \dfrac{8.23 \text{ mA}}{8.69 \text{ mA}} = \textbf{0.947}$

8. $\beta_{DC} = \dfrac{I_C}{I_B} = \dfrac{25 \text{ mA}}{200 \text{ μA}} = \textbf{125}$

9. $\beta_{DC} = \dfrac{\alpha_{DC}}{1 - \alpha_{DC}} = \dfrac{0.96}{1 - 0.96} = \textbf{24}$

10. $\alpha_{DC} = \dfrac{\beta_{DC}}{\beta_{DC} + 1} = \dfrac{30}{31} = \textbf{0.968}$

11. $I_C = \alpha_{DC} I_E = 0.96(9.35 \text{ mA}) = \textbf{8.98 mA}$

12. $I_C = \dfrac{V_{RC}}{R_C} = \dfrac{5 \text{ V}}{1 \text{ k}\Omega} = 5 \text{ mA}$

    $\beta_{DC} = \dfrac{I_C}{I_B} = \dfrac{5 \text{ mA}}{50 \text{ μA}} = \textbf{100}$

Chapter 4

13. $\alpha_{DC} = \dfrac{\beta_{DC}}{\beta_{DC} + 1} = \dfrac{100}{101} = \mathbf{0.99}$

14. $I_B = \dfrac{V_{BB} - V_{BE}}{R_B} = \dfrac{4\text{ V} - 0.7\text{ V}}{4.7\text{ k}\Omega} = \dfrac{3.3\text{ V}}{4.7\text{ k}\Omega} = \mathbf{702\ \mu A}$

$I_C = \dfrac{V_{CC} - V_{CE}}{R_C} = \dfrac{24\text{ V} - 8\text{ V}}{470\ \Omega} = \mathbf{34\text{ mA}}$

$I_E = I_C + I_B = 34\text{ mA} + 702\ \mu A = \mathbf{34.7\text{ mA}}$

$\beta_{DC} = \dfrac{I_C}{I_B} = \dfrac{34\text{ mA}}{702\ \mu A} = \mathbf{48.4}$

15. (a) $V_{BE} = \mathbf{0.7\text{ V}}$

$I_B = \dfrac{V_{BB} - V_{BE}}{R_B} = \dfrac{4.3\text{ V}}{3.9\text{ k}\Omega} = 1.1\text{ mA}$

$I_C = \beta_{DC} I_B = 50(1.1\text{ mA}) = 55\text{ mA}$

$V_{CE} = V_{CC} - I_C R_C = 15\text{ V} - (55\text{ mA})(180\ \Omega) = \mathbf{5.10\text{ V}}$

$V_{BC} = V_{BE} - V_{CE} = 0.7\text{ V} - 5.10\text{ V} = \mathbf{-4.40\text{ V}}$

(b) $V_{BE} = \mathbf{-0.7\text{ V}}$

$I_B = \dfrac{V_{BB} - V_{BE}}{R_B} = \dfrac{-3\text{ V} - (-.07\text{ V})}{27\text{ k}\Omega} = \dfrac{-2.3\text{ V}}{27\text{ k}\Omega} = -85.2\ \mu A$

$I_C = \beta_{DC} I_B = 125(-85.2\ \mu A) = -10.7\text{ mA}$

$V_{CE} = V_{CC} - I_C R_C = -8\text{ V} - (-10.7\text{ mA})(390\ \Omega) = \mathbf{-3.83\text{ V}}$

$V_{BC} = V_{BE} - V_{CE} = -0.7\text{ V} - (-3.83\text{ V}) = \mathbf{3.13\text{ V}}$

16. (a) $I_{C(sat)} = \dfrac{V_{CC}}{R_C} = \dfrac{15\text{ V}}{180\ \Omega} = 83.3\text{ mA}$

$I_B = \dfrac{V_{BB} - V_{BE}}{R_B} = \dfrac{5\text{ V} - 0.7\text{ V}}{3.9\text{ k}\Omega} = 1.1\text{ mA}$

$I_C = \beta_{DC} I_B = 50(1.1\text{ mA}) = 55\text{ mA}$

$I_C < I_{C(sat)}$

Therefore, the transistor is **not saturated**.

(b) $I_{C(sat)} = \dfrac{V_{CC}}{R_C} = \dfrac{8\text{ V}}{390\ \Omega} = 20.5\text{ mA}$

$I_B = \dfrac{V_{BB} - V_{BE}}{R_B} = \dfrac{3\text{ V} - 0.7\text{ V}}{27\text{ k}\Omega} = 85.2\ \mu A$

$I_C = \beta_{DC} I_B = 125(85.2\ \mu A) = 10.7\text{ mA}$

$I_C < I_{C(sat)}$

Therefore, the transistor is **not saturated**.

Chapter 4

17. $V_B = 2$ V

$V_E = V_B - V_{BE} = 2$ V $- 0.7$ V $= 1.3$ V

$I_E = \dfrac{V_E}{R_E} = \dfrac{1.3 \text{ V}}{1 \text{ k}\Omega} = \textbf{1.3 mA}$

$I_C = \alpha_{DC} I_E = (0.98)(1.3 \text{ mA}) = \textbf{1.27 mA}$

$\beta_{DC} = \dfrac{\alpha_{DC}}{1 - \alpha_{DC}} = \dfrac{0.98}{1 - 0.98} = 49$

$I_B = \dfrac{I_C}{\beta_{DC}} = \dfrac{1.27 \text{ mA}}{49} = \textbf{26 }\boldsymbol{\mu}\textbf{A}$

18. (a) $V_B = V_{BB} = \textbf{10 V}$

$V_C = V_{CC} = \textbf{20 V}$

$V_E = V_B - V_{BE} = 10$ V $- 0.7$ V $= \textbf{9.3 V}$

$V_{CE} = V_C - V_E = 20$ V $- 9.7$ V $= \textbf{10.7 V}$

$V_{BE} = \textbf{0.7 V}$

$V_{BC} = V_B - V_C = 10$ V $- 20$ V $= \textbf{- 10 V}$

(b) $V_B = V_{BB} = \textbf{- 4 V}$

$V_C = V_{CC} = \textbf{-12 V}$

$V_E = V_B - V_{BE} = -4$ V $- (- 0.7$ V$) = \textbf{- 3.3 V}$

$V_{CE} = V_C - V_E = -12$ V $- (- 3.3$ V$) = \textbf{- 8.7 V}$

$V_{BE} = \textbf{- 0.7 V}$

$V_{BC} = V_B - V_C = -4$ V $- (- 12$ V$) = \textbf{8 V}$

19. For $\beta_{DC} = 100$:

$I_E = \dfrac{V_B - V_{BE}}{R_E} = \dfrac{10 \text{ V} - 0.7 \text{ V}}{10 \text{ k}\Omega} = 930 \text{ }\mu\text{A}$

$\alpha_{DC} = \dfrac{\beta_{DC}}{1 + \beta_{DC}} = \dfrac{100}{101} = 0.990$

$I_C = \alpha_{DC} I_E = (0.990)(930 \text{ }\mu\text{A}) = 921 \text{ }\mu\text{A}$

For $\beta_{DC} = 150$:

$I_E = 930 \text{ }\mu\text{A}$

$\alpha_{DC} = \dfrac{\beta_{DC}}{1 + \beta_{DC}} = \dfrac{150}{151} = 0.993$

$I_C = \alpha_{DC} I_E = (0.993)(930 \text{ }\mu\text{A}) = 924 \text{ }\mu\text{A}$

$\Delta I_C = 924 \text{ }\mu\text{A} - 0.921 \text{ }\mu\text{A} = \textbf{3 }\boldsymbol{\mu}\textbf{A}$

Chapter 4

20. $P_{D(max)} = V_{CE}I_C$

$$V_{CE(max)} = \frac{P_{D(max)}}{I_C} = \frac{1.2 \text{ W}}{50 \text{ mA}} = \mathbf{24 \text{ V}}$$

21. $P_{D(max)} = 0.5 \text{ W} - (75\ °\text{C})(1 \text{ mW}/°\text{C}) = 0.5 \text{ W} - 75 \text{ mW} = \mathbf{425 \text{ mW}}$

Section 4-4 The Transistor as an Amplifier

22. $V_{out} = A_v V_{in} = 50(100 \text{ mV}) = \mathbf{5 \text{ V}}$

23. $A_v = \dfrac{V_{out}}{V_{in}} = \dfrac{10 \text{ V}}{300 \text{ mV}} = \mathbf{33.3}$

24. $A_v = \dfrac{R_C}{r'_e} = \dfrac{560 \text{ }\Omega}{10 \text{ }\Omega} = 56$

$V_c = V_{out} = A_v V_{in} = 56(50 \text{ mV}) = \mathbf{2.8 \text{ V}}$

Section 4-5 The Transistor as a Switch

25. $I_{C(sat)} = \dfrac{V_{CC}}{R_C} = \dfrac{5 \text{ V}}{10 \text{ k}\Omega} = \mathbf{500 \text{ }\mu\text{A}}$

$I_{B(min)} = \dfrac{I_{C(sat)}}{\beta_{DC}} = \dfrac{500 \text{ }\mu\text{A}}{150} = \mathbf{3.33 \text{ }\mu\text{A}}$

$I_{B(min)} = \dfrac{V_{IN(min)} - 0.7 \text{ V}}{R_B}$

$R_B I_{B(min)} = V_{IN(min)} - 0.7 \text{ V}$

$V_{IN(min)} = R_B I_{B(min)} + 0.7 \text{ V} = (3.33 \text{ }\mu\text{A})(1 \text{ M}\Omega) + 0.7 \text{ V} = \mathbf{4.03 \text{ V}}$

26. $I_{C(sat)} = \dfrac{15 \text{ V}}{1.2 \text{ k}\Omega} = 12.5 \text{ mA}$

$I_{B(min)} = \dfrac{I_{C(sat)}}{\beta_{DC}} = \dfrac{12.5 \text{ mA}}{50} = 250 \text{ }\mu\text{A}$

$R_{B(min)} = \dfrac{V_{IN} - 0.7 \text{ V}}{I_{B(min)}} = \dfrac{4.3 \text{ V}}{250 \text{ }\mu\text{A}} = \mathbf{17.2 \text{ k}\Omega}$

$V_{IN(cutoff)} = \mathbf{0 \text{ V}}$

Chapter 4

Section 4-6 Transistor Packages and Terminal Identification

27. See Figure 4-1

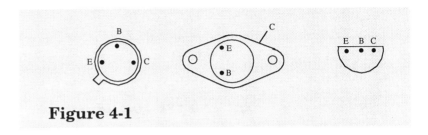

Figure 4-1

28. (a) Small-signal
(b) Power
(c) Power
(d) Small-signal
(e) RF

Section 4-7 Troubleshooting

29. With the positive probe on the emitter and the negative probe on the base,
the ohmmeter indicates an **open**, since this reverse biases the base-emitter junction.
With the positive probe on the base and the negative probe on the emitter,
the ohmmeter indicates a **very low resistance**, since this forward biases the base-collector junction.

30. (a) Transistor's collector junction or terminal is open.
(b) Collector resistor is open.
(c) Operating properly.
(d) Transistor's base junction or terminal open (no base or collector current).

31. (a) $I_B = \dfrac{5\text{ V} - 0.7\text{ V}}{68\text{ k}\Omega} = 63.2\text{ }\mu\text{A}$

$I_C = \dfrac{9\text{ V} - 3.2\text{ V}}{3.3\text{ k}\Omega} = 1.76\text{ mA}$

$\beta_{DC} = \dfrac{I_C}{I_B} = \dfrac{1.76\text{ mA}}{63.2\text{ }\mu\text{A}} = \mathbf{27.8}$

(b) $I_B = \dfrac{4.5\text{ V} - 0.7\text{ V}}{27\text{ k}\Omega} = 141\text{ }\mu\text{A}$

$I_C = \dfrac{24\text{ V} - 16.8\text{ V}}{470\text{ }\Omega} = 15.3\text{ mA}$

$\beta_{DC} = \dfrac{I_C}{I_B} = \dfrac{15.3\text{ mA}}{141\text{ }\mu\text{A}} = \mathbf{109}$

Chapter 4

Section 4-8 System Application

32. With the remote switches closed, Q_1 should be on and Q_2 should be off, keeping the relay contacts (pins 10 and 11) open. When a remote switch opens, Q_1 should turn off and Q_2 should trun on, energizing the relay and closing the contacts. If the Q_1 collector or base is open, such that Q_1 is off all the time, Q_2 will stay on all the time, so this is not the problem. Most likely, Q_2 has failed so that it remains off all the time or R_3, or R_4, could be open. Also, the relay could be faulty.

33. With the remote switches closed, Q_1 and Q_3 should be on and Q_2 and Q_4 should be off keeping the relay contacts (pins 10 and 11) open. When a remote switch opens, Q_1 (or Q_3) should turn off and Q_2 (or Q_4) should turn on, thus energizing the relay and closing the contacts (pins 10 and 11). If the Q_1 (or Q_3) collector or base is open, such that Q_1 (or Q_3) is off all the time, Q_2 (or Q_4) will stay on all the time. Most likely, either Q_2 (or Q_4) or its associated circuitry is faulty such that it remains on all the time. An internally open junction in Q_1 or Q_3 or an open resistor (R_1 or R_6 could cause this problem. Also, the relay may be faulty.

34. The constant 0.1 V at pin 9 indicates that Q_6 is saturated. Most likely Q_5 has failed such that it always acts as an open switch keeping Q_6 saturated. First look for obvious problems such as a burned resistor (R_{11}) or a bad contact. Next check the Q_5 collector with pin 7 connected to pin 6. You should see approximately 0.1 V at the Q_5 collector. If Q_5 is open you will see approximately 3.6 V at the collector.

Data Sheet Problems

35. From the data sheet of Figure 4–19:
    (a) For a 2N3903, $V_{CEO(max)}$ = **40 V**
    (b) For a 2N3904, $I_{C(max)}$ = **200 mA**
    (c) For a 2N3903 @ 25°C, $P_{D(max)}$ = **625 mW**
    (d) For a 2N3904 @ T_C = 25°C, $P_{D(max)}$ = **1.5 W**
    (e) For a 2N3903 with I_C = 1 mA, $h_{FE(min)}$ = **35**

36. For a 2N3904 with T_A = 65°C:
    $P_{D(max)}$ = 625 mW – (65°C – 25°C)(5.0 mW/°C)
    = 625 mW – 40°C(5.0 mW/°C) = 625 mW – 200 mW = **425 mW**

37. For a 2N3903 with T_C = 45°C:
    $P_{D(max)}$ = 1.5 W – (45°C – 25°C)(12 mW/°C)
    = 1.5 W – 20°C(12 mW/°C) = 1.5 W – 240 mW = **1.26 W**

Chapter 4

38. For the circuits of Figure 4–57:
(a) $I_B = \dfrac{3\text{ V} - 0.7\text{ V}}{330\ \Omega} = \dfrac{2.3\text{ V}}{330\Omega} = 6.97\text{ mA}$

$h_{FE} = 15$,

$I_C = 15(6.97\text{ mA}) = 105\text{ mA}$

$V_C = 30\text{ V} - (105\text{ mA})(270\ \Omega) = 30\text{ V} - 28.2\text{ V} = 1.8\text{ V}$

$V_{CE} = 1.8\text{ V} - 0.7\text{ V} = 1.1\text{ V}$

$P_D = (1.1\text{ V})(105\text{ mA}) = 112\text{ mW}$

At 50°C, $P_{D(max)} = 625\text{ mW} - (50°\text{C} - 25°\text{C})(5.0\text{ mW/°C}) = 500\text{ mW}$

No parameter is exceeded.

(b) $V_{CEO} = 45\text{ V}$ which **exceeds** $V_{CEO(max)}$.

39. For the circuits of Figure 4–58:
(a) $I_B = \dfrac{5\text{ V} - 0.7\text{ V}}{10\text{ k}\Omega} = \dfrac{4.3\text{ V}}{10\text{ k}\Omega} = 4.30\ \mu\text{A}$

$h_{FE(max)} = 150$,

$I_C = 150(4.30\ \mu\text{A}) = 64.5\text{ mA}$

$I_{C(sat)} = \dfrac{9\text{ V}}{1\text{ k}\Omega} = 9\text{ mA}$

The transistor is saturated.

(b) $I_B = \dfrac{3\text{ V} - 0.7\text{ V}}{100\text{ k}\Omega} = \dfrac{2.3\text{ V}}{100\text{ k}\Omega} = 23\ \mu\text{A}$

$h_{FE(max)} = 300$,

$I_C = 300(23\ \mu\text{A}) = 6.90\text{ mA}$

$I_{C(sat)} = \dfrac{12\text{ V}}{560\ \Omega} = 21.4\text{ mA}$

The transistor is not saturated.

40. $I_{B(min)} = \dfrac{I_C}{h_{FE(max)}} = \dfrac{10\text{ mA}}{150} = \mathbf{66.7\ \mu\text{A}}$

$I_{B(max)} = \dfrac{I_C}{h_{FE(min)}} = \dfrac{10\text{ mA}}{50} = \mathbf{200\ \mu\text{A}}$

Chapter 4

41. For the circuits of Figure 4–59:

(a) $I_B = \dfrac{8\text{ V} - 0.7\text{ V}}{68\text{ k}\Omega} = \dfrac{7.3\text{ V}}{68\text{ k}\Omega} = 107\ \mu\text{A}$

$h_{FE} = 150$,

$I_C = 150(107\ \mu\text{A}) = 16.1\text{ mA}$

$V_C = 15\text{ V} - (16.1\text{ mA})(680\ \Omega) = 15\text{ V} - 10.95\text{ V} = 4.05\text{ V}$

$V_{CE} = 4.05\text{ V} - 0.7\text{ V} = 3.35\text{ V}$

$P_D = (3.35\text{ V})(16.1\text{ mA}) = 53.9\text{ mW}$

At 40°C, $P_{D(max)} = 360\text{ mW} - (40°\text{C} - 25°\text{C})(2.06\text{ mW/°C}) = 329\text{ mW}$

No parameter is exceeded.

(b) $I_B = \dfrac{5\text{ V} - 0.7\text{ V}}{4.7\text{ k}\Omega} = \dfrac{4.3\text{ V}}{4.7\text{ k}\Omega} = 915\ \mu\text{A}$

$h_{FE} = 300$,

$I_C = 300(915\ \mu\text{A}) = 274\text{ mA}$

$I_{C(sat)} \cong \dfrac{35\text{ V} - 0.3\text{V}}{470\ \Omega} = 73.8\text{ mA}$

The transistor is in hard saturation. Assuming $V_{CE(sat)} = 0.3\text{ V}$

$P_D = (0.3\text{ V})(73.8\text{ mA}) = 22.1\text{ mW}$

No parameter is exceeded.

Advanced Problems

42. $\beta_{DC} = \dfrac{\alpha_{DC}}{1 - \alpha_{DC}}$

$\beta_{DC} - \beta_{DC}\alpha_{DC} = \alpha_{DC}$

$\beta_{DC} = \alpha_{DC}(1 + \beta_{DC})$

$\alpha_{DC} = \dfrac{\beta_{DC}}{(1 + \beta_{DC})}$

43. $I_C = 150(500\ \mu\text{A}) = \mathbf{75\text{ mA}}$

$V_{CE} = 15\text{ V} - (180\ \Omega)(75\text{ mA}) - 0.7\text{ V} = \mathbf{0.8\text{ V}}$

Since $V_{CE(sat)} = 0.3\text{ V}$ @ $I_C = 50\text{ mA}$, the transistor comes out of saturation, although marginally.

44. From the data sheet, $\beta_{DC(min)} = 15$ (for $I_C = 100\text{ mA}$)

$I_{B(max)} = \dfrac{150\text{ mA}}{15} = 10\text{ mA}$

$R_{B(min)} = \dfrac{3\text{ V} - 0.7\text{ V}}{10\text{ mA}} = \dfrac{2.3\text{ V}}{10\text{ mA}} = 230\ \Omega$

Use the standard value of 240 Ω for R_B.

To avoid saturation, the load resistance cannot exceed about

$\dfrac{9\text{ V} - 1\text{ V}}{150\text{ mA}} = 53.3\ \Omega$

See Figure 4–2.

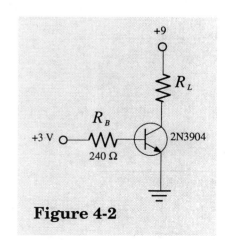

Figure 4-2

Chapter 4

45. Since $I_B = 10$ mA for $I_C = 150$ mA,
$$R_{B(min)} = \frac{9\text{ V} - 0.7\text{ V}}{10\text{ mA}} = \frac{8.3\text{ V}}{10\text{ mA}} = 830\text{ }\Omega$$
Use 910 Ω. The load cannot exceed 53.3 Ω
See Figure 4–3.

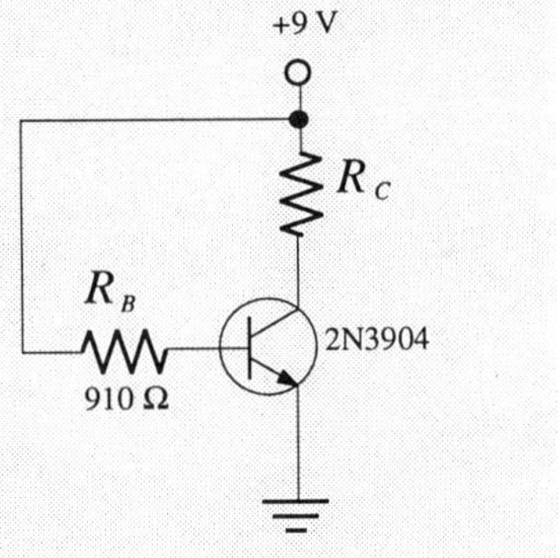

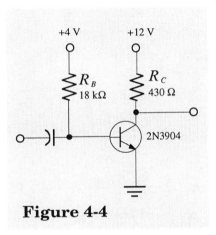

Figure 4-3

46. $R_{C(min)} = A_v r'_e = 50(8\text{ }\Omega) = 400\text{ }\Omega$ (Use 430 Ω)
$$I_C = \frac{12\text{ V} - 5\text{ V}}{430\text{ }\Omega} = 16.3\text{ mA}$$
Assuming $h_{FE} = 100$,
$$I_B = \frac{16.3\text{ mA}}{100} = 163\text{ }\mu\text{A}$$
$$R_{B(max)} = \frac{4\text{ V} - 0.7\text{ V}}{163\text{ }\mu\text{A}} = 20.3\text{ k}\Omega \text{ (Use 18 k}\Omega\text{)}$$
See Figure 4–4.

Figure 4-4

Chapter 5
Transistor Bias Circuits

Section 5-1 The DC Operating Point

1. The transistor is biased too close to saturation.

2. $I_C = \beta_{DC}I_B = 75(150\ \mu A) = 11.3$ mA
   $V_{CE} = V_{CC} - I_CR_C = 18$ V $- (11.3$ mA$)(1$ k$\Omega) = 18$ V $- 11.3$ V $= 6.75$ V
   Q point : $V_{CEQ} = $ **6.75 V**, $I_{CQ} = $ **11.3 mA**

3. $I_{C(sat)} \cong \dfrac{V_{CC}}{R_C} = \dfrac{18\ V}{1\ k\Omega} = $ **18 mA**

4. $V_{CE(cutoff)} = $ **18 V**

5. Horizontal intercept (cutoff):
   $V_{CE} = V_{CC} = $ **20 V**
   Vertical intercept (saturation):
   $I_{C(sat)} = \dfrac{V_{CC}}{R_C} = \dfrac{20\ V}{10\ k\Omega} = $ **2 mA**

6. $I_B = \dfrac{V_{BB} - 0.7\ V}{R_B}$
   $V_{BB} = I_BR_B + 0.7$ V $= (20\ \mu A)(1$ M$\Omega) + 0.7$ V $= $ **20.7 V**
   $I_C = \beta_{DC}I_B = 50(20\ \mu A) = $ **1 mA**
   $V_{CE} = V_{CC} - I_CR_C = 20$ V $- (1$ mA$)(10$ k$\Omega) = $ **10 V**

7. See Figure 5-1.
   $V_{CE} = V_{CC} - I_CR_C$
   $R_C = \dfrac{V_{CC} - V_{CE}}{I_C} = \dfrac{10\ V - 4\ V}{5\ mA} = \dfrac{6\ V}{5\ mA} = $ **1.2 kΩ**
   $I_B = \dfrac{I_C}{\beta_{DC}} = \dfrac{5\ mA}{100} = 0.05$ mA
   $R_B = \dfrac{10\ V - 0.7\ V}{0.05\ mA} = $ **186 kΩ**
   $P_{D(min)} = V_{CE}I_C = (4\ V)(5\ mA) = $ **20 mW**

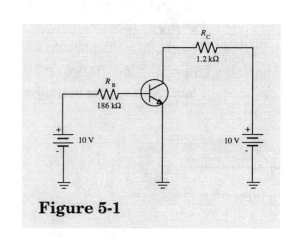

Figure 5-1

Chapter 5

8.
$$I_B = \frac{V_{BB} - V_{BE}}{R_B} = \frac{1.5 \text{ V} - 0.7 \text{ V}}{10 \text{ k}\Omega} = 80 \text{ μA}$$

$$I_{C(sat)} = \frac{V_{CC}}{R_C} = \frac{8 \text{ V}}{390 \text{ }\Omega} = 20.5 \text{ mA}$$

$$I_C = \beta_{DC}I_B = 75(80 \text{ μA}) = 6 \text{ mA}$$

The transistor is biased in the linear region because
$0 < I_C < I_{C(sat)}$

Section 5-2 Base Bias

9. $V_{BB} = V_{CC}$; $V_E = 0$ V

$$I_B = \frac{V_{CC} - 0.7 \text{ V}}{R_B} = \frac{12 \text{ V} - 0.7 \text{ V}}{22 \text{ k}\Omega} = \frac{11.3 \text{ V}}{22 \text{ k}\Omega} = 514 \text{ μA}$$

$$I_C = \beta_{DC}I_B = 90(514 \text{ μA}) = \mathbf{46.3 \text{ mA}}$$

$$V_{CE} = V_{CC} - I_C R_C = 12 \text{ V} - (46.3 \text{ mA})(100 \text{ }\Omega) = \mathbf{7.37 \text{ V}}$$

10. $I_{CQ} = 180(514 \text{ μA}) = \mathbf{92.5 \text{ mA}}$

$V_{CEQ} = 12 \text{ V} - (92.5 \text{ mA})(100 \text{ }\Omega) = \mathbf{2.75 \text{ V}}$

11. I_C changes in the circuit with a common V_{CC} and V_{BB} supply because a change in V_{CC} causes I_B to change which, in turn, changes I_C.

12.
$$I_B = \frac{V_{BB} - V_{BE}}{R_B} = \frac{9 \text{ V} - 0.7 \text{ V}}{15 \text{ k}\Omega} = 553 \text{ μA}$$

$$I_{C(sat)} = \frac{V_{CC}}{R_C} = \frac{9 \text{ V}}{100 \text{ }\Omega} = 90 \text{ mA}$$

For $\beta_{DC} = 50$:
$I_C = \beta_{DC}I_B = 50(553 \text{ μA}) = 27.7 \text{ mA}$
$V_{CE} = V_{CC} - I_C R_C = 9 \text{ V} - (27.67 \text{ mA})(100 \text{ }\Omega) = 6.23 \text{ V}$

For $\beta_{DC} = 125$:
$I_C = \beta_{DC}I_B = 125(553 \text{ μA}) = 69.2 \text{ mA}$
$V_{CE} = V_{CC} - I_C R_C = 9 \text{ V} - (69.2 \text{ mA})(100 \text{ }\Omega) = 2.08 \text{ V}$

Since $I_C < I_{C(sat)}$ for the range of β_{DC}, the circuit remains **biased in the linear region**.

Chapter 5

13.
$$I_{C(sat)} = \frac{V_{CC}}{R_C} = \frac{9\text{ V}}{100\text{ }\Omega} = 90\text{ mA}$$

At 0° C:

$\beta_{DC} = 110 - 110(0.5) = 55$

$$I_B = \frac{V_{CC} - V_{BE}}{R_B} = \frac{9\text{ V} - 0.7\text{ V}}{15\text{ k}\Omega} = 553\text{ }\mu\text{A}$$

$I_C = \beta_{DC}I_B = 55(553\text{ }\mu\text{A}) = 30.4\text{ mA}$

$V_{CE} = V_{CC} - I_C R_C = 9\text{ V} - (30.4\text{ mA})(100\text{ }\Omega) = 5.96\text{ V}$

At 70° C:

$\beta_{DC} = 110 + 110(0.75) = 193$

$I_B = 553\text{ }\mu\text{A}$

$I_C = \beta_{DC}I_B = 193(553\text{ }\mu\text{A}) = 107\text{ mA}$

$I_C > I_{C(sat)}$, therefore the transistor is in saturation at 70° C.

$\Delta I_C = I_{C(sat)} - I_{C(0°)} = 90\text{ mA} - 30.4\text{ mA} = \mathbf{59.6\text{ mA}}$

$\Delta V_{CE} \cong V_{CE(0°)} - V_{CE(sat)} = 5.96\text{ V} - 0\text{ V} = \mathbf{5.96\text{ V}}$

Section 5-3   Emitter Bias

14.   *Assuming* $V_B \cong 0\text{ V}$

$V_E \cong V_B - V_{BE} = 0\text{ V} - 0.7\text{ V} = -0.7\text{ V}$

$$I_E \cong \frac{V_E - V_{EE}}{R_E + R_B/\beta_{DC}} = \frac{-0.7\text{ V} - (-5\text{ V})}{2.2\text{ k}\Omega + 22\text{ k}\Omega/100} = \frac{4.3\text{ V}}{2.42\text{ k}\Omega} = 1.78\text{ mA}$$

$I_C \cong I_E$

$$I_B = \frac{1.78\text{ mA}}{100} = 17.8\text{ }\mu\text{A}$$

$V_B = (17.8\text{ }\mu\text{A})(22\text{ k}\Omega) = \mathbf{-391\text{ mV}}$

$V_E = -391\text{ mV} - 0.7\text{ V} = \mathbf{-1.10\text{ V}}$

$V_C = V_{CC} - I_C R_C = 5\text{ V} - (1.78\text{ mA})(1\text{ k}\Omega) = \mathbf{3.22\text{ V}}$

15.   Assume that at saturation, $V_{CE} \cong 0\text{ V}$

Since $V_E = -1.10\text{ V}$ and $V_{C(sat)} \cong V_{E(sat)}$

$$I_{C(sat)} = \frac{V_{CC} - V_{C(sat)}}{R_C} = \frac{5\text{ V} - (-1.10\text{ V})}{1\text{ k}\Omega} = 6.1\text{ mA}$$

$$R_{E(min)} \cong \frac{V_{RE}}{I_{C(sat)}} = \frac{3.9\text{ V}}{6.1\text{ mA}} = \mathbf{639\text{ }\Omega}$$

Chapter 5

16. At 100° C:
$V_{BE} = 0.7 \text{ V} - (2.5 \text{ mV/°C})(75° \text{ C}) = 0.513 \text{ V}$

$I_E = \dfrac{V_{EE} - V_{BE}}{R_E + R_B/\beta_{DC}} = \dfrac{5 \text{ V} - 0.513 \text{ V}}{2.42 \text{ k}\Omega +} = 1.85 \text{ mA}$

At 25° C:

$I_E = \dfrac{5 \text{ V} - 0.7 \text{ V}}{2.42 \text{ k}\Omega} = \dfrac{4.3 \text{ V}}{2.42 \text{ k}\Omega} = 1.78 \text{ mA}$

$\Delta I_E = 1.85 \text{ mA} - 1.78 \text{ mA} = \textbf{0.07 mA}$

17. A change in β_{DC} does not affect the circuit when

$R_E \gg \dfrac{R_B}{\beta_{DC}}$

Since

$I_E = \dfrac{V_{EE} - V_{BE}}{R_E + R_B/\beta_{DC}}$

In the equation, if R_B/β_{DC} is much smaller than R_E, the affect of β_{dc} is negligible.

A change in β_{DC} does not affect the circuit when

$R_E \gg \dfrac{R_B}{\beta_{DC}}$

Since

$I_E = \dfrac{V_{EE} - V_{BE}}{R_E + R_B/\beta_{DC}}$

In the equation, if R_B/β_{DC} is much smaller than R_E, the effect of β_{DC} is negligible.

18. *Assume* $\beta_{DC} = 100$

$I_C \cong I_E = \dfrac{V_{EE} - V_E}{R_E} = \dfrac{10 \text{ V} - 0.7 \text{ V}}{470 \text{ }\Omega + 10 \text{ k}\Omega/100} = \textbf{16.3 mA}$

$V_{CE} = V_{EE} - V_{CC} - I_C(R_C + R_E) = 20 \text{ V} - 13.1 \text{ V} = \textbf{- 6.95 V}$

Section 5-4 Voltage-Divider Bias

19. $\beta_{DC(min)}R_E = 10R_2$

$\beta_{DC(min)} = \dfrac{10R_2}{R_E} = \dfrac{47 \text{ k}\Omega}{680 \text{ }\Omega} = \textbf{69.1}$

Chapter 5

20. $I_{C(sat)} = \dfrac{V_{CC}}{R_C + R_E} = \dfrac{15 \text{ V}}{2.18 \text{ k}\Omega} = 6.88 \text{ mA}$

$V_{E(sat)} = I_{C(sat)}R_E = (6.88 \text{ mA})(680 \text{ }\Omega) = 4.68 \text{ V}$

$V_B = V_{E(sat)} + 0.7 \text{ V} = 4.68 \text{ V} + 0.7 \text{ V} = 5.38 \text{ V}$

$\left(\dfrac{R_2 \| \beta_{DC}R_E}{R_1 + R_2 \| \beta_{DC}R_E}\right)15 \text{ V} = 5.38 \text{ V}$

$\left(R_2 \| \beta_{DC}R_E\right)(15 \text{ V}) = (5.38 \text{ V})\left(R_1 + R_2 \| \beta_{DC}R_E\right)$

$\left(R_2 \| \beta_{DC}R_E\right)(15 \text{ V}) - \left(R_2 \| \beta_{DC}R_E\right)(5.38 \text{ V}) = R_1(5.38 \text{ V})$

$\left(R_2 \| \beta_{DC}R_E\right)(15 \text{ V} - 5.38 \text{ V}) = (22 \text{ k}\Omega)(5.38 \text{ V})$

$R_2 \| \beta_{DC}R_E = \dfrac{(22 \text{ k}\Omega)(5.38 \text{ V})}{15 \text{ V} - 5.38 \text{ V}} = 12.3 \text{ k}\Omega$

$\dfrac{1}{R_2} + \dfrac{1}{\beta_{DC}R_E} = \dfrac{1}{12.3 \text{ k}\Omega}$

$\dfrac{1}{R_2} + \dfrac{1}{102 \text{ k}\Omega} = \dfrac{1}{12.3 \text{ k}\Omega}$

$\dfrac{1}{R_2} = 71.5 \text{ }\mu\text{S}$

$R_2 = \mathbf{14 \text{ k}\Omega}$

21. $V_B = \left(\dfrac{R_2}{R_1 + R_2}\right)V_{CC} = \left(\dfrac{2 \text{ k}\Omega}{24 \text{ k}\Omega}\right)15 \text{ V} = 1.25 \text{ V}$

$V_E = 1.25 \text{ V} - 0.7 \text{ V} = 0.55 \text{ V}$

$I_E = \dfrac{V_E}{R_E} = \dfrac{0.55 \text{ V}}{680 \text{ }\Omega} = 809 \text{ }\mu\text{A}$

$I_C \cong \mathbf{809 \text{ }\mu\text{A}}$

$V_{CE} = V_{CC} - I_C R_C - V_E = 15 \text{ V} - (809 \text{ }\mu\text{A})(1.5 \text{ k}\Omega + 680 \text{ }\Omega) = \mathbf{13.2 \text{ V}}$

22. $V_B = \left(\dfrac{R_2 \| \beta_{DC}R_E}{R_1 + R_2 \| \beta_{DC}R_E}\right)V_{CC} = \left(\dfrac{15 \text{ k}\Omega \| (110)(1 \text{ k}\Omega)}{47 \text{ k}\Omega + 15 \text{ k}\Omega \| (110)(1 \text{ k}\Omega)}\right)9 \text{ V} = \mathbf{1.97 \text{ V}}$

$V_E = V_B - 0.7 \text{ V} = 1.97 \text{ V} - 0.7 \text{ V} = \mathbf{1.27 \text{ V}}$

$I_C \cong I_E = \dfrac{V_E}{R_E} = \dfrac{1.27 \text{ V}}{1 \text{ k}\Omega} = 1.27 \text{ mA}$

$V_C = V_{CC} - I_C R_C = 9 \text{ V} - (1.27 \text{ mA})(2.2 \text{ k}\Omega) = \mathbf{6.21 \text{ V}}$

23. See Figure 5-2.

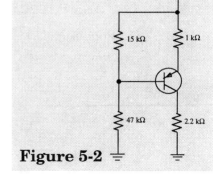

Figure 5-2

Chapter 5

24. (a) $R_{IN(base)} = \beta_{DC}R_E = 50(560\ \Omega) = 28\ k\Omega$

$$V_B = \left(\frac{5.6\ k\Omega\ \|\ 28\ k\Omega}{33\ k\Omega + 5.6\ k\Omega\ \|\ 28\ k\Omega}\right)(-12\ V) = \left(\frac{4.67\ k\Omega}{37.7\ k\Omega}\right)(-12\ V) = -1.49\ V$$

(b) $R_{IN(base)} = 50(1120\ \Omega) = 56\ k\Omega$

$$V_B = \left(\frac{56\ k\Omega\ \|\ 5.6\ k\Omega}{33\ k\Omega + 56\ k\Omega\ \|\ 5.6\ k\Omega}\right)(-12\ V) = \left(\frac{5.09\ k\Omega}{38.1\ k\Omega}\right)(-12\ V) = -1.6\ V$$

25. (a) $V_{EQ} = V_B + 0.7\ V = -1.49\ V + 0.7\ V = -0.79\ V$

$$I_{CQ} \cong I_E = \frac{V_E}{R_E} = \frac{-0.79\ V}{560\ \Omega} = -1.41\ mA$$

$V_{CQ} = V_{CC} - I_C R_C = -12\ V - (-1.41\ mA)(1.8\ k\Omega) = -9.46\ V$

$V_{CEQ} = V_{CQ} - V_{EQ} = -9.46\ V - (-0.79\ V) = -8.67\ V$

(b) $P_{D(min)} = I_{CQ}V_{CEQ} = (-1.41\ mA)(-8.67\ V) = 12.2\ mW$

Section 5-5 Collector Feedback Bias

26. $V_B = 0.7\ V$

$$I_C = \frac{V_{CC} - V_{BE}}{R_C + R_B/\beta_{DC}} = \frac{3\ V - 0.7\ V}{1.8\ k\Omega + 33\ k\Omega/90} = 1.06\ mA$$

$V_C = V_{CC} - I_C R_C = 3\ V - (1.06\ mA)(1.8\ k\Omega) = 1.09\ V$

27. $I_C = 1.06\ mA$ from Problem 26.

$I_C = 1.06\ mA - (0.25)(1.06\ mA) = 0.795\ mA$

$$I_C = \frac{V_{CC} - V_{BE}}{R_C + R_B/\beta_{DC}}$$

$$R_C = \frac{V_{CC} - V_{BE} - I_C R_B/\beta_{DC}}{I_C} = \frac{3\ V - 0.7\ V - (0.795\ mA)(33\ k\Omega)/90}{0.795\ mA} = 2.53\ k\Omega$$

28. $I_C = 0.795\ mA$ from Problem 27.

$V_{CE} = V_{CC} - I_C R_C = 3\ V - (0.795\ mA)(2.53\ k\Omega) = 0.989\ V$

$P_{D(min)} = V_{CE}I_C = (0.989\ V)(0.795\ mA) = 786\ \mu W$

Chapter 5

29. See Figure 5-3.

$$I_C = \frac{V_{CC} - V_{BE}}{R_C + R_B/\beta_{DC}} = \frac{12\text{ V} - 0.7\text{ V}}{1.2\text{ k}\Omega + 47\text{ k}\Omega/200} = \textbf{7.87 mA}$$

$$V_C = V_{CC} - I_C R_C = 12\text{ V} - (7.87\text{ mA})(1.2\text{ k}\Omega) = \textbf{2.56 V}$$

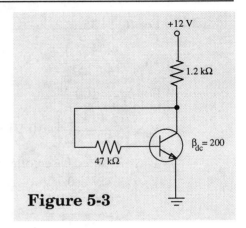

Figure 5-3

Section 5-6 Troubleshooting

30. $V_1 = \textbf{0.7 V}, \quad V_2 = \textbf{0 V}$

$$I_B = \frac{8\text{ V} - 0.7\text{ V}}{33\text{ k}\Omega} - \frac{0.7\text{ V}}{10\text{ k}\Omega} = 221\text{ μA} - 70\text{ μA} = 151\text{ μA}$$

$$I_C = 200(151\text{ μA}) = 30.2\text{ mA}$$

$$I_{C(sat)} = \frac{8\text{ V}}{2.2\text{ k}\Omega} = 3.64\text{ mA, so } V_C \cong V_E = \textbf{0 V}$$

If the problem is corrected:

$$V_1 = \left(\frac{10\text{ k}\Omega}{10\text{ k}\Omega + 33\text{ k}\Omega}\right) 8\text{ V} = \textbf{1.86 V}$$

$$V_2 = V_E = 1.86\text{ V} - 0.7\text{ V} = \textbf{1.16 V}$$

$$I_E = \frac{1.16\text{ V}}{1\text{ k}\Omega} = 1.16\text{ mA}$$

$$V_3 = V_C = 8\text{ V} - (1.16\text{ mA})(2.2\text{ k}\Omega) = \textbf{5.45 V}$$

31. (a) Open collector.
(b) No problems.
(c) Transistor shorted from collector to emitter.
(d) Open emitter.

Chapter 5

32. For $\beta_{DC} = 35$:

$$V_B = \left(\frac{4.5 \text{ k}\Omega}{14.5 \text{ k}\Omega}\right)(-10 \text{ V}) = -3.1 \text{ V}$$

For $\beta_{DC} = 100$:

$$V_B = \left(\frac{5.17 \text{ k}\Omega}{15.17 \text{ k}\Omega}\right)(-10 \text{ V}) = -3.4 \text{ V}$$

The measured base voltage at point 4 is within the correct range.
$V_E = -3.1 \text{ V} + 0.7 \text{ V} = -2.4 \text{ V}$

$$I_C \cong I_E = \frac{-2.4 \text{ V}}{680 \text{ }\Omega} = -3.53 \text{ mA}$$

$V_C = -10 \text{ V} - (-3.53 \text{ mA})(1 \text{ k}\Omega) = -6.47 \text{ V}$

Allowing for some variation in V_{BE} and for resistor tolerances, the measured collector and emitter voltages are correct.

33. (a) The 680 Ω resistor open
Meter 1: **10 V**
Meter 2: **floating**
Meter 3: $V_B = \left(\dfrac{5.6 \text{ k}\Omega}{15.6 \text{ k}\Omega}\right)(-10 \text{ V}) = \mathbf{-3.59 \text{ V}}$
Meter 4: **10 V**

(b) The 5.6 kΩ resistor open.

$$I_B = \frac{9.3 \text{ V}}{10 \text{ k}\Omega + 35(680 \text{ }\Omega)} = 275 \text{ }\mu\text{A}$$

$I_C = 35(275 \text{ }\mu\text{A}) = 9.6 \text{ mA}$

$$I_{C(sat)} = \frac{10 \text{ V}}{1680 \text{ }\Omega} = 5.95 \text{ mA}$$

The transistor is saturated.
Meter 1: **10 V**
Meter 2: (5.95 mA)(680 Ω) = **4.05 V**
Meter 3: 4.05 V + 0.7 V = **4.75 V**
Meter 4: 10 V − (5.95 mA)(1 kΩ) = **4.05 V**

(c) The 10 kΩ resistor is open. The transistor is off.
Meter 1: **10 V**
Meter 2: **0 V**
Meter 3: **0 V**
Meter 4: **10 V**

Chapter 5

    (d) The 1 kΩ resistor open. Collector current is zero.
        Meter 1: **10 V**
        Meter 3: $\left(\dfrac{5.6\ \text{k}\Omega\ \|\ 680\ \Omega}{10\ \text{k}\Omega + 5.6\ \text{k}\Omega\ \|\ 680\ \Omega}\right)(10\ \text{V}) + 0.7\ \text{V} = 0.57\ \text{V} + 0.7\ \text{V} = \mathbf{1.27\ V}$
        Meter 2: 1.27 V – 0.7 V = **0.57 V**
        Meter 4: **floating**

    (e) A short from emitter to ground.
        Meter 1: **10 V**
        Meter 2: **0 V**
        Meter 3: **0.7 V**
        $I_B \cong \dfrac{10\ \text{V} - 0.7\ \text{V}}{10\ \text{k}\Omega} = \dfrac{9.3\ \text{V}}{10\ \text{k}\Omega} = 0.93\ \text{mA}$
        $I_{C(\text{min})} = 35(0.93\ \text{mA}) = 32.6\ \text{mA}$
        $I_{C(\text{sat})} = \dfrac{10\ \text{V}}{1\ \text{k}\Omega} = 10\ \text{mA}$
        The transistor is saturated.
        Meter 4: $\cong \mathbf{0\ V}$

    (f) An open base–emitter junction. The transistor is off.
        Meter 1: **10 V**
        Meter 2: **0 V**
        Meter 3: $\left(\dfrac{5.6\ \text{k}\Omega}{15.6\ \text{k}\Omega}\right)(10\ \text{V}) = \mathbf{3.59\ V}$
        Meter 4: **10 V**

Section 5-7 System Application

34. With R_1 shorted:
$V_B = \mathbf{0\ V}$, $V_E = \mathbf{0\ V}$, $V_C = V_{CC} = \mathbf{9.1\ V}$

35. Faults that will cause the transistor of Figure 5–36 to go into cutoff:
R_1 **open**, R_2 **shorted**, base lead or BE junction **open**

36. $R_{\text{IN(base)}} = 70(470\ \Omega) = 32.9\ \text{k}\Omega$
$R_{\text{IN}} = 2.7\ \text{k}\Omega\ \|\ 32.9\ \text{k}\Omega = 2.50\ \text{k}\Omega$
$V_B = \left(\dfrac{2.50\ \text{k}\Omega}{2.50\ \text{k}\Omega + 5.6\ \Omega}\right)5.1\ \text{V} = \left(\dfrac{2.50\ \text{k}\Omega}{8.10\ \Omega}\right)5.1\ \text{V} = 1.57\ \text{V}$
$V_E = 1.57\ \text{V} - 0.7\ \text{V} = \mathbf{0.872\ V}$
So, $I_C \cong I_E = \dfrac{0.872\ \text{V}}{470\ \Omega} = \mathbf{1.86\ mA}$
$V_C = 5.1\ \text{V} - (1.86\ \text{mA})(1\ \text{k}\Omega) = \mathbf{3.24\ V}$

Chapter 5

37. The following measurments would indicate an open CB junction:
$V_C = V_{CC} = +9.1\ V$
V_B **normal**
$V_E \cong \mathbf{0\ V}$

Data Sheet Problems

38. For $T = 45°C$ and $R_2 = 2.7\ k\Omega$:
$R_{IN(base)} = 2.7\ k\Omega \parallel (30)(470\ \Omega) = 2.7\ k\Omega \parallel 14.1\ k\Omega = 2.27\ k\Omega$ min
$R_{IN(base)} = 2.7\ k\Omega \parallel (300)(470\ \Omega) = 2.7\ k\Omega \parallel 141\ k\Omega = 2.65\ k\Omega$ max
$V_{B(min)} = \left(\dfrac{2.27\ k\Omega}{2.27\ k\Omega + 5.6\ k\Omega}\right) 9.1\ V = \left(\dfrac{2.27\ k\Omega}{7.87}\right) 9.1\ V = \mathbf{2.62\ V}$
$V_{E(min)} = 2.62\ V - 0.7\ V = \mathbf{1.92\ V}$
So, $I_C \cong I_E = \dfrac{1.92\ V}{470\ \Omega} = 4.09\ mA$
$V_{C(max)} = 9.1\ V - (4.09\ mA)(1\ k\Omega) = \mathbf{5.01\ V}$
$V_{B(max)} = \left(\dfrac{2.65\ k\Omega}{2.65\ k\Omega + 5.6\ k\Omega}\right) 9.1\ V = \left(\dfrac{2.65\ k\Omega}{8.25\ k\Omega}\right) 9.1\ V = \mathbf{2.92\ V}$
$V_{E(max)} = 2.92\ V - 0.7\ V = \mathbf{2.22\ V}$
So, $I_C \cong I_E = \dfrac{2.22\ V}{470\ \Omega} = 4.73\ mA$
$V_{C(min)} = 9.1\ V - (4.73\ mA)(1\ k\Omega) = \mathbf{4.37\ V}$

For $T = 55°C$ and $R_2 = 1.24\ k\Omega$:
$R_{IN(base)} = 1.24\ k\Omega \parallel (30)(470\ \Omega) = 1.24\ k\Omega \parallel 14.1\ k\Omega = 1.14\ k\Omega$ min
$R_{IN(base)} = 1.24\ k\Omega \parallel (300)(470\ \Omega) = 1.24\ k\Omega \parallel 141\ k\Omega = 1.23\ k\Omega$ max
$V_{B(min)} = \left(\dfrac{1.14\ k\Omega}{1.14\ k\Omega + 5.6\ k\Omega}\right) 9.1\ V = \left(\dfrac{1.14\ k\Omega}{6.74\ k\Omega}\right) 9.1\ V = \mathbf{1.54\ V}$
$V_{E(min)} = 1.54\ V - 0.7\ V = \mathbf{0.839\ V}$
So, $I_C \cong I_E = \dfrac{0.839\ V}{470\ \Omega} = 1.78\ mA$
$V_{C(max)} = 9.1\ V - (1.78\ mA)(1\ k\Omega) = \mathbf{7.32\ V}$
$V_{B(max)} = \left(\dfrac{1.23\ k\Omega}{1.23\ k\Omega + 5.6\ k\Omega}\right) 9.1\ V = \left(\dfrac{1.23\ k\Omega}{6.83\ k\Omega}\right) 9.1\ V = \mathbf{1.64\ V}$
$V_{E(max)} = 1.64\ V - 0.7\ V = \mathbf{0.938\ V}$
So, $I_C \cong I_E = \dfrac{0.938\ V}{470\ \Omega} = 2.0\ mA$
$V_{C(min)} = 9.1\ V - (2.0\ mA)(1\ k\Omega) = \mathbf{7.10\ V}$

39. At $T = 45°C$ for minimum β_{DC}
$P_{D(max)} = (5.01\ V - 1.92\ V)(4.09\ mA) = (3.09\ V)(4.09\ mA) = 12.6\ mW$
At $T = 55°C$ for minimum β_{DC}
$P_{D(max)} = (7.32\ V - 0.839\ V)(1.78\ mA) = (6.48\ V)(1.78\ mA) = 11.5\ mW$
For maximum beta values, the results are comparable and nowhere near the the maximum:
$P_{D(max)} = 625\ mW - (5.0\ m/°C)(30\ °C) = 475\ mW$
No ratings are exceeded.

Chapter 5

40. For the data sheet of Figure 5–57:
(a) For a 2N2222A, $I_{C(max)} = \mathbf{800mA}$ continuous
(b) For a 2N2118, $V_{BE(max)} = \mathbf{5.0\ V}$ for reverse breakdown or $V_{BE(max)} = \mathbf{2.6\ V}$ for saturation

41. *For a 2N2222 @ $T = 100°C$:*
$P_{D(max)} = 0.8\ W - (4.57\ mW/°C)(100°C - 25°C) = 0.8\ W - 343\ mW = \mathbf{457\ mW}$

42. If I_C changes from 1 mA to 500 mA in a 2N2219, the percentage change in β_{DC} is
$\Delta\beta_{DC} = \left(\dfrac{30-50}{50}\right)100\% = \mathbf{-40\%}$

Advanced Problems

43. See Figure 5–4.
$R_C = \dfrac{V_{CC} - V_{CEQ}}{I_{CQ}} = \dfrac{15\ V - 5\ V}{5\ mA} = 2\ k\Omega$
Assume $\beta_{DC} = 100$.
$I_{BQ} = \dfrac{I_{CQ}}{\beta_{DC}} = \dfrac{5\ mA}{100} = 50\ \mu A$
$R_B = \dfrac{V_{CC} - V_{BE}}{I_{BQ}} = \dfrac{15\ V - 0.7\ V}{50\ \mu A} = 2.86\ k\Omega$

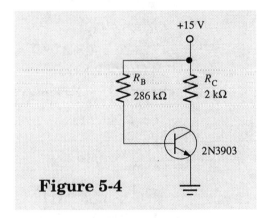

Figure 5-4

44. See Figure 5–5.
Assume $\beta_{DC} = 200$
$I_{BQ} = \dfrac{I_{CQ}}{\beta_{DC}} = \dfrac{10\ mA}{200} = 50\ \mu A$
Let $R_B = 1\ k\Omega$
$R_E = \dfrac{12\ V - (50\ \mu A)(1\ k\Omega) - 0.7\ V}{10\ mA} = \dfrac{11.3\ V}{10\ mA} = 1.13\ k\Omega$
$R_C = \dfrac{12\ V - (-12\ V - 11.3\ V - 4\ V)}{10\ mA} = \dfrac{8.7\ V}{10\ mA} = 870\ \Omega$
870 Ω and 1.13 kΩ are not standard values. $R_C = 820\ \Omega$ and $R_E = 1.2\ k\Omega$
give $I_{CQ} \cong 9.38\ mA$, $V_{CEQ} \cong 5.05\ mA$

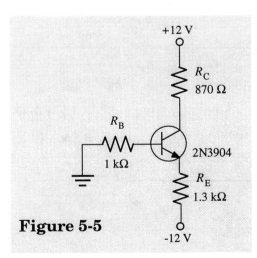

Figure 5-5

Chapter 5

45. See Figure 5–6.

$\beta_{DC(min)} \cong 70$. Let $R_E = 1\ k\Omega$

$V_E = I_E R_E = 1.5\ mA(1\ k\Omega) = 1.5\ V$

$V_B = 1.5\ V + 0.7\ V = 2.2\ V$

$R_C = \dfrac{V_{CC} - V_{CEQ} - V_E}{I_{CQ}} = \dfrac{9\ V - 1.5\ V - 3\ V}{1.5\ mA} = 3\ k\Omega$

$R_1 + R_2 = \dfrac{V_{CC}}{I_{CC(max)} - I_{CQ}} = \dfrac{9\ V}{5\ mA - 1.5\ mA} = 2.57\ k\Omega$ min

Assuming $\beta_{DC} R_E \gg R_2$

$\dfrac{R_1}{R_2} = \dfrac{6.8\ V}{2.2\ V} = 3.09$

$R_1 = 3.09 R_2$

$R_1 + R_2 = R_2 + 3.09 R_2 = 2.57\ k\Omega$

$4.09 R_2 = 2.57\ k\Omega$

$R_2 = \dfrac{2.57\ k\Omega}{4.09} = 628\ \Omega$

So, $R_2 \cong 620$ and $R_2 = 1.92\ k\Omega \cong 2\ k\Omega$

From this,

$R_{IN(base)} = 70(1\ k\Omega) = 70\ k\Omega \gg R_2$

so, $V_B = \left(\dfrac{620\ \Omega}{2.62\ k\Omega}\right) 9\ V = 2.13\ V$

$V_E = 2.13\ V - 0.7\ V = 1.43\ V$

$I_{CQ} \cong I_E = \dfrac{1.43\ V}{1\ k\Omega} = 1.43\ mA$

$V_{CEQ} = 9\ V - (1.43\ mA)(1\ k\Omega + 3\ k\Omega) = 3.28\ V$

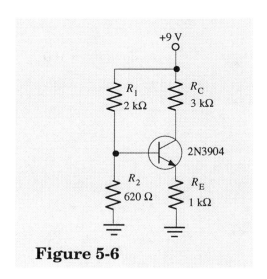

Figure 5-6

46. See Figure 5–7.

$\beta_{DC} \cong 75$.

$I_{BQ} = \dfrac{10\ mA}{75} = 133\ \mu A$

$R_C = \dfrac{V_{CC} - V_{CE}}{I_{CQ}} = \dfrac{5\ V - 1.5\ V}{10\ mA} = 350\ \Omega$ (use 360 Ω)

$R_B = \dfrac{V_{CE} - 0.7\ V}{I_{BQ}} = \dfrac{1.55\ V - 0.7\ V}{133\ \mu A} = 6\ k\Omega$ (use 6.2 $k\Omega$)

$I_{CQ} = \dfrac{5\ V - 0.7\ V}{360\ \Omega + 6.2\ k\Omega/75} = 9.71\ mA$

$V_{CEQ} = V_C = 5\ V - (9.71\ mA)(360\ \Omega) = 1.50\ V$

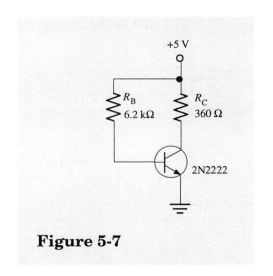

Figure 5-7

Chapter 5

47. The 2N3904 in Figure 5–55 **can be replaced** with a 2N2222 and maintain the same voltage range from 45°C to 55°C because the voltage divider circuit is essentially β independent and the β_{DC} parameters of the two transistors are comparable.

48. For the 2N2222 using the data sheet of Figure 5–57 and Figure 5–58 at $I_c = 150$ mA and $V_{CE} = 1.0$ V:
At $T = -55°C$, $h_{FE(min)} = (0.45)(50) = $ **22.5**
At $T = 25°C$, $h_{FE(min)} = (0.63)(50) = $ **31.5**
At $T = 175°C$, $h_{FE(min)} = (0.53)(50) = $ **26.6**

49. If the ADC loading of the temperature conversion circuit changes from 100 kΩ to 10 kΩ, the Q–point will have a reduced V_{CEQ} because the current through R_C will consist of the same I_C and a larger I_L. I_{CQ} is unaffected in the sense that the transistor collector current is the same, although the collector resistance current is larger. The transistor saturates sooner so that lower temperatures do not register as well, if at all.

Chapter 6
Small Signal Bipolar Amplifiers

Section 6-1 Small-Signal Amplifier Operation

1. Approximately **1 mA**

2. From the graph of Figure 6–3, the highest value of dc collector current is about **6 mA**.

Section 6-2 Transistor AC Equivalent Circuits

3. (a) $h_{ie} = \dfrac{V_b}{I_b} = \dfrac{0.67 \text{ V}}{5 \text{ mA}} = \mathbf{134 \ \Omega}$

   (b) $h_{re} = \dfrac{V_b}{V_c} = \dfrac{0.5 \text{ mV}}{5 \text{ V}} = \mathbf{0.0001}$

   (c) $h_{fe} = \dfrac{I_b}{I_b} = \dfrac{2.2 \text{ mA}}{15 \ \mu\text{A}} = \mathbf{147}$

   (d) $h_{oe} = \dfrac{I_c}{V_c} = \dfrac{10 \text{ mA}}{3 \text{ V}} = \mathbf{3.33 \text{ mS}}$

4. $\beta_{ac} = h_{fe} = \mathbf{147}$

   $\alpha_{ac} = \dfrac{\beta_{ac}}{\beta_{ac}+1} = \dfrac{146.67}{147.67} = \mathbf{0.993}$

   $r'_e = \dfrac{h_{re}}{h_{oe}} = \dfrac{0.0001}{3.33 \text{ mS}} = \mathbf{30 \text{ m}\Omega}$

   $r'_b = h_{ie} - \dfrac{h_{re}}{h_{oe}}(1 + h_{fe}) = 134 \ \Omega - (0.03 \ \Omega)(147.67) = \mathbf{130 \ \Omega}$

   $r'_c = \dfrac{h_{re}+1}{h_{oe}} = \dfrac{1.0001}{3.33 \text{ mS}} = \mathbf{300 \ \Omega}$

5. $I_C = \beta_{DC} I_B = 130(10 \ \mu\text{A}) = \mathbf{1.3 \text{ mA}}$

   $I_E = \dfrac{I_C}{\alpha_{DC}} = \dfrac{1.3 \text{ mA}}{0.99} = \mathbf{1.31 \text{ mA}}$

   $r'_e \cong \dfrac{25 \text{ mV}}{I_E} = \dfrac{25 \text{ mV}}{1.31 \text{ mA}} = \mathbf{19 \ \Omega}$

Chapter 6

6. $\beta_{DC} = \dfrac{I_C}{I_B} = \dfrac{2\text{ mA}}{15\text{ μA}} = \mathbf{133}$

$\beta_{ac} = \dfrac{\Delta I_c}{\Delta I_B} = \dfrac{0.35\text{ mA}}{3\text{ μA}} = \mathbf{117}$

Section 6-3 Common-Emitter Amplifiers

7. See Figure 6-1.

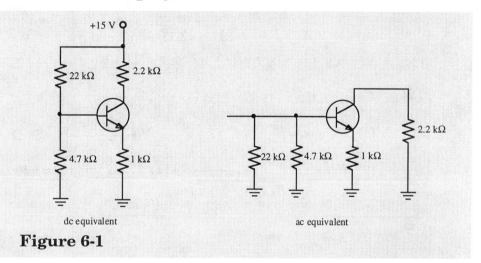

Figure 6-1

8. (a) $V_B = \left(\dfrac{4.7\text{ kΩ}}{4.7\text{ kΩ} + 22\text{ kΩ}}\right)15\text{ V} = 2.64\text{ V}$

$V_E = 2.64\text{ V} - 0.7\text{ V} = 1.94\text{ V}$

$I_E = \dfrac{1.94\text{ V}}{1\text{ kΩ}} = 1.94\text{ mA}$

$r'_e \cong \dfrac{25\text{ mV}}{I_E} = \dfrac{25\text{ mV}}{1.94\text{ mA}} = 12.9\text{ Ω}$

$R_{in(base)} = \beta_{ac}(r'_e + R_E) = 100(1012.9\text{ Ω}) \cong \mathbf{101\text{ kΩ}}$

(b) $R_{in} = R_{in(base)} \parallel R_1 \parallel R_2 = 101\text{ kΩ} \parallel 22\text{ kΩ} \parallel 4.7\text{ kΩ} = \mathbf{3.73\text{ kΩ}}$

(c) $A_v = \dfrac{R_C}{R_E + r'_e} = \dfrac{2.2\text{ kΩ}}{12.02\text{ Ω}} = \mathbf{2.17}$

9. (a) $R_{in(base)} = \beta_{ac}r'_c = 100(12.9\text{ Ω}) = \mathbf{1.29\text{ kΩ}}$

(b) $R_{in} = 1.29\text{ kΩ} \parallel 22\text{ kΩ} \parallel 4.7\text{ kΩ} = \mathbf{968\text{ Ω}}$

(c) $A_v = \dfrac{R_C}{r'_e} = \dfrac{2.2\text{ kΩ}}{12.9\text{ Ω}} = \mathbf{171}$

10. (a) $R_{in(base)} = \beta_{ac}r'_c = 100(12.9\text{ Ω}) = \mathbf{1.29\text{ kΩ}}$

(b) $R_{in} = 1.29\text{ kΩ} \parallel 22\text{ kΩ} \parallel 4.7\text{ kΩ} = \mathbf{968\text{ Ω}}$

(c) $A_v = \dfrac{R_c}{r'_e} = \dfrac{R_c \parallel R_L}{r'_e} = \dfrac{2.2\text{ kΩ} \parallel 10\text{ kΩ}}{12.9\text{ Ω}} = \mathbf{140}$

Chapter 6

11. (a) $V_B = \left(\dfrac{R_2 \| \beta_{DC}R_E}{R_1 + R_2 \| \beta_{DC}R_E}\right)V_{CC} = \left(\dfrac{12\ k\Omega \| 75(1\ k\Omega)}{47\ k\Omega + 12\ k\Omega \| 75(1\ k\Omega)}\right)18\ V = \mathbf{3.25\ V}$

(b) $V_E = V_B - 0.7\ V = \mathbf{2.55\ V}$

(c) $I_E = \dfrac{V_E}{R_E} = \dfrac{2.55\ V}{1\ k\Omega} = \mathbf{2.55\ mA}$

(d) $I_C \cong I_E = \mathbf{2.55\ mA}$

(e) $V_C = V_{CC} - I_C R_C = 18\ V - (2.55\ mA)(3.3\ k\Omega) = \mathbf{9.59\ V}$

(f) $V_{CE} = V_C - V_E = 9.59\ V - 2.55\ V = \mathbf{7.04\ V}$

12. From Problem 11, $I_E = 2.55\ mA$

(a) $R_{in(base)} = \beta_{ac}r'_e \cong \beta_{ac}\left(\dfrac{25\ mV}{I_E}\right) = 70\left(\dfrac{25\ mV}{2.55\ mA}\right) = \mathbf{686\ \Omega}$

(b) $R_{in} = R_1 \| R_2 \| R_{in(base)} = 47\ k\Omega \| 12\ k\Omega \| 686\ \Omega = \mathbf{640\ \Omega}$

(c) $A_v = \dfrac{R_C \| R_L}{r'_e} = \dfrac{3.3\ k\Omega \| 10\ k\Omega}{9.8\ \Omega} = \mathbf{253}$

(d) $A_i = \beta_{ac} = \mathbf{70}$

(e) $A_p = A_v A_i = (253)(70) = \mathbf{17{,}710}$

13. $V_b = \left(\dfrac{R_{in}}{R_{in} + R_s}\right)V_{in} = \left(\dfrac{640\ \Omega}{640\ \Omega + 600\ \Omega}\right)12\ \mu V$

Attenuation of the input network is

$\left(\dfrac{R_{in}}{R_{in} + R_s}\right) = \left(\dfrac{640\ \Omega}{640\ \Omega + 600\ \Omega}\right) = 0.516$

$A'_v = 0.516 A_v = 0.516(253) = \mathbf{131}$

$\theta = \mathbf{180°}$

14. $V_B = \left(\dfrac{R_2 \| \beta_{DC}R_E}{R_1 + R_2 \| \beta_{DC}R_E}\right)V_{CC} = \left(\dfrac{3.3\ k\Omega \| 150(100\ \Omega)}{12\ k\Omega + 3.3\ k\Omega \| 150(100\ \Omega)}\right)8\ V = \mathbf{1.47\ V}$

$I_E = \dfrac{V_B - 0.7\ V}{R_E} = \dfrac{1.47\ V - 0.7\ V}{100\ \Omega} = 7.7\ mA$

$r'_e = \dfrac{25\ mV}{I_E} = \dfrac{25\ mV}{7.7\ mA} = 3.25\ \Omega$

$A_{v(min)} = \dfrac{R_C}{R_E + r'_e} = \dfrac{330\ \Omega}{100\ \Omega + 3.25\ \Omega} = \mathbf{3.2}$

$A_{v(max)} = \dfrac{R_C}{r'_e} = \dfrac{330\ \Omega}{3.25\ \Omega} = \mathbf{102}$

Chapter 6

15. Maximim gain is at $R_e = 0\ \Omega$.

$R_{IN(base)} = \beta_{DC}R_E = 150(100\ \Omega) = 15\ k\Omega$

$V_B = \left(\dfrac{R_2 \| R_{IN(base)}}{R_1 + R_2 \| R_{IN(base)}}\right)V_{CC} = \left(\dfrac{3.3\ k\Omega \| 15\ k\Omega}{12\ k\Omega + 3.3\ k\Omega \| 15\ k\Omega}\right)8\ V = 1.47\ V$

$I_E = \dfrac{V_B - V_{BE}}{R_E} = \dfrac{1.47\ V - 0.7\ V}{100\ \Omega} = 7.7\ mA$

$r'_e \cong \dfrac{25\ mV}{7.7\ mA} = 3.25\ \Omega$

$A_{v(max)} = \dfrac{R_C \| R_L}{r'_e} = \dfrac{330\ \Omega \| 600\ \Omega}{3.25\ \Omega} = \mathbf{65.5}$

Minimum gain is at $R_e = 100\ \Omega$.

$A_{v(min)} = \dfrac{R_C \| R_L}{R_E + r'_e} = \dfrac{212.9\ \Omega}{103.25\ \Omega} = \mathbf{2.06}$

16. $R_{in} = R_1 \| R_2 \| \beta_{ac}r'_e = 3.3\ k\Omega \| 12\ k\Omega \| 150(3.25\ \Omega) = 410\ \Omega$

Attenuation of the input network is

$\dfrac{R_{in}}{R_{in} + R_s} = \dfrac{410\ \Omega}{410\ \Omega + 300\ \Omega} = 0.5777$

$A_v = \dfrac{R_c}{r'_e} = \dfrac{330\ \Omega \| 1\ k\Omega}{3.25\ \Omega} = 76.3$

$A'_v = 0.5777 A_v = 0.5777(76.3) = \mathbf{44}$

17. See Figure 6-2.

$r'_e \cong \dfrac{25\ mV}{2.55\ mA} = 9.8\ \Omega$

$R_e \geq 10 r'_e$

Set $R_e = 100\ \Omega$

The gain is reduced to

$A_v = \dfrac{R_C}{R_e + r'_e} = \dfrac{3.3\ k\Omega}{109.8\ \Omega} = \mathbf{30.1}$

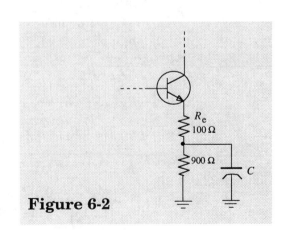

Figure 6-2

Chapter 6

Section 6-4 Common-Collector Amplifiers

18.
$$V_B = \left(\frac{R_2}{R_1 + R_2}\right)V_{CC} = \left(\frac{4.7 \text{ k}\Omega}{14.7 \text{ k}\Omega}\right)5.5 \text{ V} = 1.76 \text{ V}$$

$$I_E = \frac{V_B - 0.7 \text{ V}}{R_E} = \frac{1.76 \text{ V} - 0.7 \text{ V}}{1 \text{ k}\Omega} = 1.06 \text{ mA}$$

$$r'_e \cong \frac{25 \text{ mV}}{1.06 \text{ mA}} = 23.6 \text{ }\Omega$$

$$A_v = \frac{R_E}{R_E + r'_e} = \frac{1 \text{ k}\Omega}{1 \text{ k}\Omega + 23.6 \text{ }\Omega} = \textbf{0.977}$$

19.
$$R_{in} = R_1 \parallel R_2 \parallel \beta_{ac}(r'_e + R_E) \cong R_1 \parallel R_2 \parallel \beta_{ac}R_E = 10 \text{ k}\Omega \parallel 4.7 \text{ k}\Omega \parallel 100 \text{ k}\Omega = \textbf{3.1 k}\Omega$$

$$V_{OUT} = V_B - 0.7 \text{ V} = \left(\frac{R_2}{R_1 + R_2}\right)V_{CC} - 0.7 \text{ V} = \left(\frac{4.7 \text{ k}\Omega}{14.7 \text{ k}\Omega}\right)5.5 \text{ V} - 0.7 \text{ V} = \textbf{1.06 V}$$

20. The voltage gain is **reduced** because $A_v = \dfrac{R_e}{R_e + r'_e}$.

21.
$$V_B = \left(\frac{R_2}{R_1 + R_2}\right)V_{CC} = \left(\frac{4.7 \text{ k}\Omega}{14.7 \text{ k}\Omega}\right)5.5 \text{ V} = 1.76 \text{ V}$$

$$I_E = \frac{V_B - V_{BE}}{R_E} = \frac{1.76 \text{ V} - 0.7 \text{ V}}{1 \text{ k}\Omega} = 1.06 \text{ mA}$$

$$r'_e \cong \frac{25 \text{ mV}}{I_E} = \frac{25 \text{ mV}}{1.06 \text{ mA}} = 23.6 \text{ }\Omega$$

$$A_v = \frac{R_E \parallel R_L}{r'_e + R_E \parallel R_L}$$

$$A_v(r'_e + R_E \parallel R_L) = R_E \parallel R_L$$

$$R_E \parallel R_L - A_v(R_E \parallel R_L) = A_v r'_e$$

$$(R_E \parallel R_L)(1 - A_v) = A_v r'_e$$

$$(R_E \parallel R_L) = \frac{A_v r'_e}{(1 - A_v)} = \frac{0.9(23.6 \text{ }\Omega)}{1 - 0.9} = 212.4 \text{ }\Omega$$

$$R_L R_E = 212.4 R_L + 212.4 R_E$$

$$R_L R_E - 212.4 R_L = 212.4 R_E$$

$$R_L = \frac{212.4 R_E}{R_E - 212.4} = \frac{(212.4 \text{ }\Omega)(1000 \text{ }\Omega)}{1000 \text{ }\Omega - 212.4 \text{ }\Omega} = \textbf{270 }\Omega$$

Chapter 6

22. (a) $V_{C1} = \mathbf{10\ V}$

$$V_{B1} = \left(\frac{R_2}{R_1 + R_2}\right)V_{CC} = \left(\frac{22\ k\Omega}{55\ k\Omega}\right)10\ V = \mathbf{4\ V}$$

$V_{E1} = V_{B1} - 0.7\ V = 4\ V - 0.7\ V = \mathbf{3.3\ V}$
$V_{C2} = \mathbf{10\ V}$
$V_{B2} = V_{E1} = \mathbf{3.3\ V}$
$V_{E2} = V_{B2} - 0.7\ V = 3.3\ V - 0.7\ V = \mathbf{2.6\ V}$

(b) $\beta'_{DC} = \beta_{DC1}\beta_{DC2} = (150)(100) = \mathbf{15{,}000}$

(c) $I_{E1} = \dfrac{V_{E1}}{\beta_{DC2}R_E} = \dfrac{3.3\ V}{(100)(1.5\ k\Omega)} = \mathbf{22\ \mu A}$

$r'_{e1} \cong \dfrac{25\ mV}{I_{E1}} = \dfrac{25\ mV}{22\ \mu A} = \mathbf{1.14\ k\Omega}$

$I_{E2} = \dfrac{V_{E2}}{R_E} = \dfrac{2.6\ V}{1.5\ k\Omega} = 1.73\ mA$

$r'_{e2} \cong \dfrac{25\ mV}{I_{E2}} = \dfrac{25\ mV}{1.73\ mA} = \mathbf{14.5\ \Omega}$

(d) $R_{in} = R_1\ ||\ R_2\ ||\ R_{in(base\ 1)}$
$R_{in(base\ 1)} = \beta_{ac1}\beta_{ac2}R_E = (150)(100)(1.5\ k\Omega) = 22.5\ M\Omega$
$R_{in} = 33\ k\Omega\ ||\ 22\ k\Omega\ ||\ 22.5\ M\Omega = \mathbf{13.2\ k\Omega}$

23. $R_{in(base)} = \beta_{ac1}\beta_{ac2}R_E = (150)(100)(1.5\ k\Omega) = 22.5\ M\Omega$
$R_{in} = R_2\ ||\ R_1\ ||\ R_{in(base)} = 22\ k\Omega\ ||\ 33\ k\Omega\ ||\ 22.5\ M\Omega = 13.2\ k\Omega$

$I_{in} = \dfrac{V_{in}}{R_{in}} = \dfrac{1\ V}{13.2\ k\Omega} = 75.8\ \mu A$

$I_{in(base\ 1)} = \dfrac{V_{in}}{R_{in(base\ 1)}} = \dfrac{1\ V}{22.5\ M\Omega} = 44.4\ nA$

$I_e \cong \beta_{ac1}\beta_{ac2}I_{in(base\ 1)} = (150)(100)(44.4\ nA) = 667\ \mu A$

$A'_i = \dfrac{I_e}{I_{in}} = \dfrac{667\ \mu A}{75.8\ \mu A} = \mathbf{8.8}$

Section 6-5 Common-Base Amplifiers

24. The main disadvantages of a common-base amplifier is **low input impedance** and **unity current gain**.

Chapter 6

25. $V_E = \left(\dfrac{R_2}{R_1 + R_2}\right)V_{CC} - V_{BE} = \left(\dfrac{10 \text{ k}\Omega}{32 \text{ k}\Omega}\right)24 \text{ V} - 0.7 \text{ V} = 6.8 \text{ V}$

$I_E = \dfrac{6.8 \text{ V}}{620 \text{ }\Omega} = 10.97 \text{ mA}$

$R_{in(emitter)} = r'_e \cong \dfrac{25 \text{ mV}}{I_E} = \dfrac{25 \text{ mV}}{10.97 \text{ mA}} = \mathbf{2.28 \text{ }\Omega}$

$A_v = \dfrac{R_C}{r'_e} = \dfrac{1.2 \text{ k}\Omega}{2.28 \text{ }\Omega} = \mathbf{526}$

$A_i \cong \mathbf{1}$

$A_p = A_i A_v \cong \mathbf{526}$

26. (a) Common-base (b) Common-emitter (c) Common-collector

Section 6-6 Multistage Amplifiers

27. $A'_v = A_{v1}A_{v2} = (20)(20) = \mathbf{400}$

28. $A'_{v(dB)} = 10 \text{ dB} + 10 \text{ dB} + 10 \text{ dB} = \mathbf{30 \text{ dB}}$

$20\log A'_v = 30 \text{ dB}$

$\log A'_v = \dfrac{30}{20} = 1.5$

$A'_v = \mathbf{31.6}$

29. (a) $V_E = \left(\dfrac{R_2}{R_1 + R_2}\right)V_{CC} - V_{BE} = \left(\dfrac{8.2 \text{ k}\Omega}{33 \text{ k}\Omega + 8.2 \text{ k}\Omega}\right)15 \text{ V} - 0.7 \text{ V} = 2.29 \text{ V}$

$I_E = \dfrac{V_E}{R_E} = \dfrac{2.29 \text{ V}}{1 \text{ k}\Omega} = 2.29 \text{ mA}$

$r'_e \cong \dfrac{25 \text{ mV}}{I_E} = \dfrac{25 \text{ mV}}{2.29 \text{ mA}} = 10.9 \text{ }\Omega$

$R_{in(2)} = R_5 \| R_4 \| \beta_{ac}r'_e = 8.2 \text{ k}\Omega \| 33 \text{ k}\Omega \| 175(10.9 \text{ }\Omega) = 1.48 \text{ k}\Omega$

$A_{v1} = \dfrac{R_C \| R_{in(2)}}{r'_e} = \dfrac{33 \text{ k}\Omega \| 1.48 \text{ k}\Omega}{10.9 \text{ }\Omega} = \mathbf{93.6}$

$A_{v2} = \dfrac{R_C}{r'_e} = \dfrac{33 \text{ k}\Omega}{10.9 \text{ }\Omega} = \mathbf{302}$

(b) $A'_v = A_{v1}A_{v2} = (93.6)(302) = \mathbf{28{,}267}$

(c) $A_{v1(dB)} = 20\log(93.6) = \mathbf{39.4 \text{ dB}}$

$A_{v2(dB)} = 20\log(302) = \mathbf{49.6 \text{ dB}}$

$A'_{v(dB)} = 20\log(28{,}267) = \mathbf{89.0 \text{ dB}}$

Chapter 6

30. (a) $A_{v1} = \dfrac{R_C \| R_{in(2)}}{r'_e} = \dfrac{3.3 \text{ k}\Omega \| 1.48 \text{ k}\Omega}{10.92 \text{ }\Omega} = \mathbf{93.6}$

$A_{v2} = \dfrac{R_C \| R_L}{r'_e} = \dfrac{3.3 \text{ k}\Omega \| 18 \text{ k}\Omega}{10.92 \text{ }\Omega} = \mathbf{255}$

(b) $R_{in(1)} = R_1 \| R_2 \| r'_e = 33 \text{ k}\Omega \| 8.2 \text{ k}\Omega \| 175(10.92 \text{ }\Omega) = 1.48 \text{ k}\Omega$

Attenuation of the input network is

$\dfrac{R_{in(1)}}{R_{in(1)} + R_s} = \dfrac{1.48 \text{ k}\Omega}{1.48 \text{ k}\Omega + 75 \text{ }\Omega} = 0.95$

$A'_v = (0.95) A_{v1} A_{v2} = (0.95)(93.57)(255) = \mathbf{22{,}667}$

(c) $A_{v1(dB)} = 20\log(93.6) = \mathbf{39.4 \text{ dB}}$

$A_{v2(dB)} = 20\log(255) = \mathbf{48.1 \text{ dB}}$

$A'_{v(dB)} = 20\log(22{,}667) = \mathbf{87.1 \text{ dB}}$

31. $V_{B1} = \left(\dfrac{R_2}{R_1 + R_2}\right) V_{CC} = \left(\dfrac{22 \text{ k}\Omega}{122 \text{ k}\Omega}\right) 12 \text{ V} = \mathbf{2.16 \text{ V}}$

$V_{E1} = V_{B1} - 0.7 \text{ V} = \mathbf{1.46 \text{ V}}$

$I_{C1} \cong I_{E1} = \dfrac{V_{E1}}{R_4} = \dfrac{1.46 \text{ V}}{4.7 \text{ k}\Omega} = 0.311 \text{ mA}$

$V_{C1} = V_{CC} - I_{C1} R_3 = 12 \text{ V} - (0.311 \text{ mA})(22 \text{ k}\Omega) = \mathbf{5.16 \text{ V}}$

$V_{B2} = V_{C1} = \mathbf{5.16 \text{ V}}$

$V_{E2} = V_{B2} - 0.7 \text{ V} = 5.16 \text{ V} - 0.7 \text{ V} = \mathbf{4.46 \text{ V}}$

$I_{C2} \cong I_{E2} = \dfrac{V_{E2}}{R_6} = \dfrac{4.46 \text{ V}}{10 \text{ k}\Omega} = 0.446 \text{ mA}$

$V_{C2} = V_{CC} - I_{C2} R_5 = 12 \text{ V} - (0.446 \text{ mA})(10 \text{ k}\Omega) = \mathbf{7.54 \text{ V}}$

$r'_{e2} \cong \dfrac{25 \text{ mV}}{I_{E2}} = \dfrac{25 \text{ mV}}{0.446 \text{ mA}} = 56 \text{ }\Omega$

$R_{in(2)} = \beta_{ac} r'_{e2} = (125)(56 \text{ }\Omega) = 7 \text{ k}\Omega$

$r'_{e1} \cong \dfrac{25 \text{ mV}}{I_{E1}} = \dfrac{25 \text{ mV}}{0.311 \text{ mA}} = 80.4 \text{ }\Omega$

$A_{v1} = \dfrac{R_3 \| R_{in(2)}}{r'_{e1}} = \dfrac{22 \text{ k}\Omega \| 7 \text{ k}\Omega}{80.4 \text{ }\Omega} = \mathbf{66}$

$A_{v2} = \dfrac{R_5}{r'_{e2}} = \dfrac{10 \text{ k}\Omega}{56 \text{ }\Omega} = \mathbf{179}$

$A'_v = A_{v1} A_{v2} = (66)(179) = \mathbf{11{,}814}$

Chapter 6

32.
(a) 20log (12) = **21.6 dB**
(b) 20log (50) = **34.0 dB**
(c) 20log (100) = **40.0 dB**
(d) 20log (2500) = **68.0 dB**

33.
(a) $20\log\left(\dfrac{V_2}{V_1}\right) = 3$ dB
$\log\left(\dfrac{V_2}{V_1}\right) = \dfrac{3}{20} = 0.15$
$\dfrac{V_2}{V_1} = \mathbf{1.41}$

(b) $20\log\left(\dfrac{V_2}{V_1}\right) = 6$ dB
$\log\left(\dfrac{V_2}{V_1}\right) = \dfrac{6}{20} = 0.3$
$\dfrac{V_2}{V_1} = \mathbf{2}$

(c) $20\log\left(\dfrac{V_2}{V_1}\right) = 10$ dB
$\log\left(\dfrac{V_2}{V_1}\right) = \dfrac{10}{20} = 0.5$
$\dfrac{V_2}{V_1} = \mathbf{3.16}$

(d) $20\log\left(\dfrac{V_2}{V_1}\right) = 20$ dB
$\log\left(\dfrac{V_2}{V_1}\right) = \dfrac{20}{20} = 1$
$\dfrac{V_2}{V_1} = \mathbf{10}$

(e) $20\log\left(\dfrac{V_2}{V_1}\right) = 40$ dB
$\log\left(\dfrac{V_2}{V_1}\right) = \dfrac{40}{20} = 2$
$\dfrac{V_2}{V_1} = \mathbf{100}$

Section 6-7 Troubleshooting

34.
$V_E = \left(\dfrac{R_2}{R_1 + R_2}\right)10\text{ V} - 0.7\text{ V} = \left(\dfrac{10\text{ k}\Omega}{57\text{ k}\Omega}\right)10\text{ V} - 0.7\text{ V} = 1.05\text{ V}$

$I_E = \dfrac{V_E}{R_4} = \dfrac{1.05\text{ V}}{1\text{ k}\Omega} = 1.05\text{ mA}$

$V_C = 10\text{ V} - (1.05\text{ mA})(4.7\text{ k}\Omega) = 5.07\text{ V}$

$V_{CE} = 5.07\text{ V} - 1.05\text{ V} = 4.02\text{ V}$

$r'_{CE} \cong \dfrac{V_{CE}}{I_E} = \dfrac{4.02\text{ V}}{1.05\text{ mA}} = 3.83\text{ k}\Omega$

With C_2 shorted:
$R_{IN(2)} = R_6 \parallel \beta_{DC}R_8 = 10\text{ k}\Omega \parallel 125(1\text{ k}\Omega) = 9.26\text{ k}\Omega$

Looking from the collector of Q_1:

$\left(r'_{CE} + R_4\right) \parallel R_{IN(2)} = (3.83\text{ k}\Omega + 1\text{ k}\Omega) \parallel 9.26\text{ k}\Omega = 3.17\text{ k}\Omega$

$V_{C1} = \left(\dfrac{3.17\text{ k}\Omega}{3.17\text{ k}\Omega + 4.7\text{ k}\Omega}\right)10\text{ V} = \mathbf{4.03\text{ V}}$

Chapter 6

35. Q_1 is in **cutoff**. $I_C = 0$ A, so $V_{C2} = \mathbf{10\ V}$

36. (a) Reduced gain.
(b) No output signal.
(c) Reduced gain.
(d) Bias levels of first stage will change. I_C will increase and Q_1 will go into saturation.
(e) No signal at the Q_1 collector.
(f) Signal at the Q_2 base. No output signal.

37. $r'_e = 10.9\ \Omega$ $R_{in} = 1.48\ k\Omega$
$A_{v1} = 93.6$ $A_{v2} = 302$

Test Point	DC Volts	AC Volts (rms)
Input	0 V	25 µV
Q_1 base	2.99 V	20.8 µV
Q_1 emitter	2.29 V	0 V
Q_1 collector	7.44 V	1.95 mV
Q_2 base	2.99 V	1.95 mV
Q_2 emitter	2.29 V	0 V
Q_2 collector	7.44 V	589 mV
Output	0 V	589 mV

Section 6-8 System Application

38. For the block diagram of Figure 6–45 with no output from the power amplifier or preamplifier and only one faulty block, the power amplifier must be ok because the fault must be one that affects the preamplifier's output prior to the power amplifier. Check the input to the preamplifier.

Chapter 6

39. For the circuit of Figure 6–59, the dc and ac operating parameters are:

$V_{B1} = \left(\dfrac{15 \text{ k}\Omega}{83 \text{ k}\Omega}\right) 9 \text{ V} = (0.181)9 \text{ V} + 1.63 \text{ V}$

$V_E = 1.63 \text{ V} - 0.7 \text{ V} = 0.93 \text{ V}$

$I_{E1} = 927 \text{ }\mu A$

$r'_e = \dfrac{25 \text{ mV}}{927 \text{ }\mu A} = 27 \text{ }\Omega$

$A_{v(1)} = \dfrac{2.2 \text{ k}\Omega}{27 \text{ }\Omega} = 81.5 \text{ unloaded}$

$V_{B2} = \left(\dfrac{22 \text{ k}\Omega \parallel (200)(1.22 \text{ k}\Omega)}{100 \text{ k}\Omega + 22 \text{ k}\Omega \parallel (200)(1.22 \text{ k}\Omega)}\right) 9 \text{ V} = 0.81 \text{ V}$

$I_{E2} = \dfrac{0.81 \text{ V}}{1.22 \text{ k}} = 665 \text{ }\mu A$

$r'_e = \dfrac{25 \text{ mV}}{665 \text{ }\mu A} = 37.6 \text{ }\Omega$

$A_{v(2)} = \dfrac{4.7 \text{ k}\Omega}{220 \text{ }\Omega + 37.6 \text{ }\Omega} = 18.3 \text{ unloaded}$

$Z_{in(2)} = 100 \text{ k}\Omega \parallel 22 \text{ k}\Omega \parallel (200)(288 \text{ }\Omega) = 13.7 \text{ k}\Omega$

So, the loaded gain of Q_1 is equal to

$\dfrac{13.7 \text{ k}\Omega}{13.7 \text{ k}\Omega + 2.2 \text{ k}\Omega} = 0.862$ of the unloaded gain

(a) With C_1 open, the input circuit is developed in Figure 6–3.
From this,

$A_v = \dfrac{R_C}{R_4 \parallel \left(r'_e + (R_1 \parallel R_2)/\beta_{ac}\right)}$

$= \dfrac{2.2 \text{ k}\Omega}{1 \text{ k}\Omega \parallel \left(27 \text{ }\Omega + (68 \text{ k}\Omega \parallel 15 \text{ k}\Omega)/200\right)} = 27.1 \text{ unloaded}$

The loading factor is unchanged and stage 2 is unaffected so the overall ac gain is

$A'_v = (0.862)(27.1)(18.2) = 425$

$V_{out(2)} = 2 \text{ mV}(425) = \textbf{850 mV rms}$

$V_{C(2)} = 9 \text{ V} - (4.7 \text{ k}\Omega)(665 \text{ }\mu A) = \textbf{5.87 V dc}$

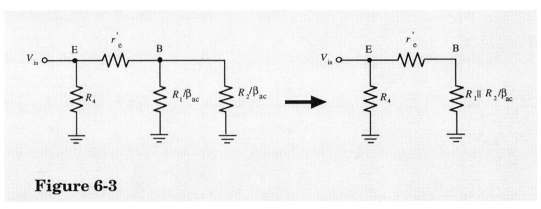

Figure 6-3

Chapter 6

(b) If C_2 is open, no input is applied so
$V_{out(2)} = \mathbf{0\ V}$
$V_{C(2)} = \mathbf{5.87\ V}$

(c) If C_3 is open, no is coupled to Q_2
$V_{out(2)} = \mathbf{0\ V}$
$V_{C(2)} = \mathbf{5.87\ V}$

(d) If C_4 is open, the gain of stage 2 changes to
$A_v = \dfrac{R_7}{r'_{e(2)} + R_8 + R_9} = \dfrac{4.7\ \text{k}\Omega}{37.6\ \Omega + 220\ \Omega + 1\ \text{k}\Omega} = 3.74$
$V_{out(2)} = (2\ \text{mV})(27.1)(3.74) = \mathbf{203\ mV\ rms}$
$V_{C(2)} = \mathbf{5.87\ V}$

(e) If the Q_1 collector is internally open, no signal reaches the base of Q_2
$V_{out} = \mathbf{0\ V}$
$V_{C(2)} = \mathbf{5.87\ V}$

(f) If the Q_2 emitter is shorted to ground, the transistor saturates.
$V_{out} = \mathbf{0\ V}$
$V_{C(2)} = \mathbf{0\ V}$

40. $V_{B2} = \left(\dfrac{220\ \text{k}\Omega\ \|\ (200)(1.22\ \text{k}\Omega)}{100\ \text{k}\Omega + 220\ \text{k}\Omega\ \|\ (200)(1.22\ \text{k}\Omega)}\right)9\ \text{V} = 4.83\ \text{V}$

$V_E = 4.83\ \text{V} - 0.7\ \text{V} = 4.13\ \text{V}$
$I_E = \dfrac{4.13\ \text{V}}{1.22\ \text{k}\Omega} = 3.38\ \text{mA}$
$r'_e = \dfrac{25\ \text{mV}}{3.38\ \text{mA}} = 7.39\ \Omega$
$V_{C(2)} = 9\ \text{V} - (4.7\ \text{k}\Omega)(3.38\ \text{mA}) = -6.9\ \text{V}$
The transistor is saturated, so $V_{out} = \mathbf{0\ V}$
$V_{C(2)} = \left(\dfrac{1.22\ \text{k}\Omega}{5.92\ \text{k}\Omega}\right)9\ \text{V} = \mathbf{1.85\ V}$

41. (a) $Q_1 = $ is in **cutoff**
(b) $V_{C1} = \mathbf{9\ V}$
(c) V_{C2} is unchanged and at **5.87 V**

Data Sheet Problems

42. From the partial data sheet in Figure 6–8:
(a) For a 2N3904, $\beta_{ac(min)} = \mathbf{100}$
(b) For a 2N3904, $r'_{e(min)} = \dfrac{h_{re}}{h_{oe}} = \dfrac{0.5\times10^{-4}}{40\ \mu\text{S}} = \mathbf{1.25\ \Omega}$
(c) For a 2N3904, $r'_{c(min)} = \dfrac{h_{re}+1}{h_{oe}} = \dfrac{1+0.5\times10^{-4}}{40\ \mu\text{S}} = \mathbf{25\ k\Omega}$

Chapter 6

43. From the partial data sheet in Figure 6–8:
(a) For a 2N3904, $\beta_{ac(max)} = \mathbf{400}$
(b) For a 2N3904, $r'_{e(max)} = \dfrac{h_{re}}{h_{oe}} = \dfrac{8 \times 10^{-4}}{1\,\mu S} = \mathbf{800\,\Omega}$
(c) For a 2N3904, $r'_{c(max)} = \dfrac{h_{re}+1}{h_{oe}} = \dfrac{1+8\times 10^{-4}}{1\,\mu S} = \mathbf{1\,M\Omega}$

44. For maximum current gain, a **2N3904** should be used.

45. In the circuit of Figure 6–59, a leaky coupling capacitor would affect the biasing of the transistors, attenuate the ac signal, and decrease the frequency response

46. See Figure 6–4.

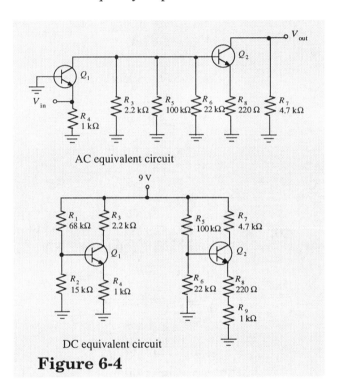

Figure 6-4

47. See Figure 6–5.

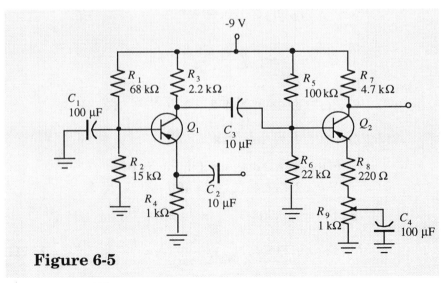

Figure 6-5

Chapter 6

48. $R_C > (100)(330\ \Omega) = 33\ \text{k}\Omega$

To prevent cutoff, V_C must be no greater than

$12\ \text{V} - (100)(1.414)(25\ \text{mV}) = 8.46\ \text{V}$

In addition, V_C must fall no lower than $8.46\ \text{V} - 3.54\ \text{V} = 4.93\ \text{V}$ to prevent saturation.

$R_C = 100(R_E + r'_e)$

$r'_e = \dfrac{25\ \text{mV}}{I_E}$

$12\ \text{V} - I_C R_C = 8.46\ \text{V}$

$I_C R_C = 3.54\ \text{V}$

$I_C\left(100(R_E + r'_e)\right) = 3.54\ \text{V}$

$I_C\left(100\left(330\ \Omega + \dfrac{25\ \text{mV}}{I_C}\right)\right) \cong 3.54\ \text{V}$

$(33\ \text{k}\Omega)I_C + 2.5\ \text{V} = 3.54\ \text{V}$

$I_C = 31.4\ \mu\text{A}$

$r'_e \cong \dfrac{25\ \text{mV}}{31.4\ \mu\text{A}} = 797\ \Omega$

$R_C = 100(330\ \Omega + 797\ \Omega) = 113\ \text{k}\Omega$

Let $R_C = 120\ \text{k}\Omega$

$V_C = 12\ \text{V} - (31.4\ \mu\text{A})120\ \text{k}\Omega) = 8.23\ \text{V}$

$V_{C(\text{sat})} = 8.23\ \text{V} - 3.54\ \text{V} = 4.69\ \text{V}$

$\dfrac{R_{E(tot)}}{R_C} = \dfrac{4.69\ \text{V}}{7.31\ \text{V}}$

$R_{E(tot)} = (0.642)(120\ \text{k}\Omega) = 77\ \text{k}\Omega$. Let $R_E = 68\ \text{k}\Omega$

$V_E = (31.4\ \mu\text{A})(68\ \text{k}\Omega) = 2.14\ \text{V}$

$V_B = 2.14\ \text{V} + 0.7\ \text{V} = 2.84\ \text{V}$

$\dfrac{R_2}{R_1} = \dfrac{2.84\ \text{V}}{9.16\ \text{V}} = 0.310$

$R_2 = 0.310 R_1$. If $R_1 = 20\ \text{k}\Omega$, $R_2 = 6.2\ \text{k}\Omega$

The amplifier circuit is shown in Figure 6–6.

Chapter 6

From the design

$V_B = \left(\dfrac{6.2 \text{ k}\Omega}{26.2 \text{ k}\Omega}\right) 12 \text{ V} = 2.84 \text{ V}$

$V_E = 2.14 \text{ V}$

$I_C \cong I_E = \dfrac{2.14 \text{ V}}{68.3 \text{ k}\Omega} = 31.3 \text{ }\mu\text{A}$

$r'_e = \dfrac{25 \text{ mV}}{31.3 \text{ }\mu\text{A}} = 798 \text{ }\Omega$

$A_v = \dfrac{120 \text{ k}\Omega}{795 \text{ }\Omega + 330 \text{ }\Omega} = 106 \text{ or } 40.5 \text{ dB}$

$V_C = 12 \text{ V} - (31.3 \text{ }\mu\text{A})(120 \text{ k}\Omega) = 8.24 \text{ V}$

The design is a close fit.

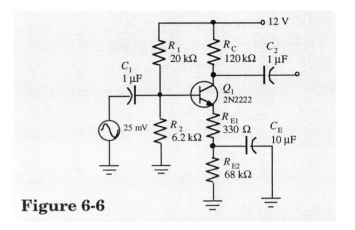

Figure 6-6

49. See Figure 6–7.

$R_{in} = 120 \text{ k}\Omega \parallel 120 \text{ k}\Omega \parallel (100)(5.1 \text{ k}\Omega) = 53.6 \text{ k}\Omega \text{ minimum}$

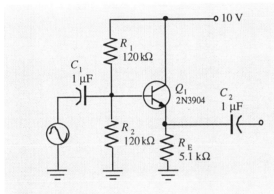

Figure 6-7

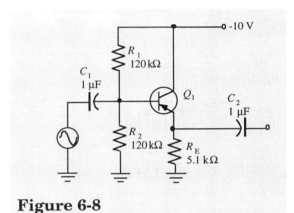

Figure 6-8

50. See Figure 6–8.

51. See Figure 6–9.

$I_C = \dfrac{6 \text{ V} - 0.7 \text{ V}}{510 \text{ }\Omega + 2 \text{ k}\Omega/100} = 10 \text{ mA}$

$r'_e = \dfrac{25 \text{ mV}}{10 \text{ mA}} = 2.5 \text{ }\Omega$

$A_v = \dfrac{180 \text{ }\Omega}{2.5 \text{ }\Omega} = 72.4$

This is reasonably close ($\approx 3.3\%$ off) and can be made closer
by putting a 7.5 Ω resistor in series with the 180 Ω collector resistor.

Chapter 6

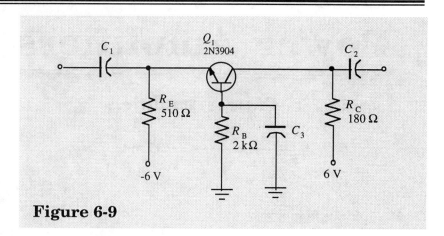

Figure 6-9

52. The cutoff frequency of C_3 is

$$\frac{1}{2\pi(10\ \mu F)(22\ k\Omega + (100\ k\Omega \parallel 22\ k\Omega \parallel (200)(220\ \Omega + 33\ \Omega)))} = 0.45\ Hz$$

The cutoff frequency of C_2 is

$$\frac{1}{2\pi(10\ \mu F)(1\ k\Omega \parallel 27\ \Omega)} = 606\ Hz$$

C_2 must be increased to

$$\frac{1}{2\pi(10\ Hz)(1\ k\Omega \parallel 27\ \Omega)} = \mathbf{606\ \mu F} \quad \text{(nearest standard value is 680 }\mu F\text{)}$$

Chapter 7
Power Amplifiers

Section 7-1 Class A Amplifiers

1. $$I_{C(sat)} = \frac{V_{CC}}{R_C + R_E} = \frac{12 \text{ V}}{5.7 \text{ k}\Omega} = \mathbf{2.11 \text{ mA}}$$
   $$V_{CE(cutoff)} = \mathbf{12 \text{ V}}$$

2. See Figure 7-1.
   $$I_{c(sat)} = I_{CQ} + \frac{V_{CEQ}}{R_c}$$
   $$R_c = R_C \parallel R_L = 4.7 \text{ k}\Omega \parallel 4.7 \text{ k}\Omega = 2.35 \text{ k}\Omega$$
   $$V_B = \left(\frac{R_2}{R_1 + R_2}\right)V_{CC} = \left(\frac{10 \text{ k}\Omega}{57 \text{ k}\Omega}\right)12 \text{ V} = 2.1 \text{ V}$$
   $$I_{CQ} \cong I_E = \frac{V_E}{R_E} = \frac{2.1 \text{ V} - 0.7 \text{ V}}{1 \text{ k}\Omega} = 1.4 \text{ mA}$$
   $$V_C = V_{CC} - I_{CQ}R_C = 12 \text{ V} - (1.4 \text{ mA})(4.7 \text{ k}\Omega) = 5.42 \text{ V}$$
   $$V_{CEQ} = V_C - V_E = 5.42 \text{ V} - 1.4 \text{ V} = 4.02 \text{ V}$$
   $$I_{c(sat)} = 1.4 \text{ mA} + \frac{4.02 \text{ V}}{2.35 \text{ k}\Omega} = \mathbf{1.71 \text{ mA}}$$

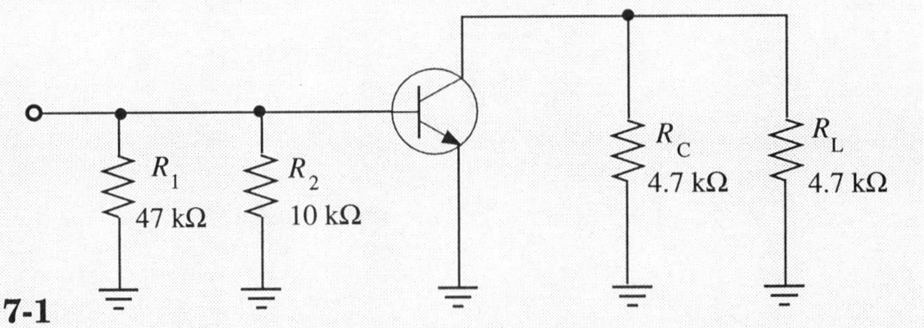

Figure 7-1

3. $$V_E = \left(\frac{R_2}{R_1 + R_2}\right)V_{CC} - V_{BE} = \left(\frac{10 \text{ k}\Omega}{57 \text{ k}\Omega}\right)12 \text{ V} - 0.7 \text{ V} = 1.41 \text{ V}$$
   $$I_E = \frac{V_E}{R_E} = \frac{1.41 \text{ V}}{1 \text{ k}\Omega} = 1.41 \text{ mA}$$
   $$I_{CQ} \cong 1.41 \text{ mA}$$
   $$V_C = V_{CC} - I_{CQ}R_C = 12 \text{ V} - (1.41 \text{ mA})(4.7 \text{ k}\Omega) = 5.37 \text{ V}$$
   $$V_{CEQ} = V_C - V_E = 5.37 \text{ V} - 1.41 \text{ V} = 3.96 \text{ V}$$
   $$V_{ce(cutoff)} = V_{CEQ} + I_{CQ}R_c = 3.96 \text{ V} + (1.41 \text{ mA})(4.7 \text{ k}\Omega \parallel 4.7 \text{ k}\Omega) = 3.96 \text{ V} + 3.31 \text{ V} = \mathbf{7.27 \text{ V}}$$

Chapter 7

4. (a) $R_{IN(base)} = \beta_{DC}(R_{E1} + R_{E2}) = (100)(49\ \Omega) = 4.9\ k\Omega$
   A 50 % increase in β_{DC} will have little effect on the dc bias values
   because $R_{IN(base)} \gg R_2$ already (4.9 k$\Omega \gg$ 330 Ω). $V_{out(max)}$ is not significantly affected.

   (b) $R_{IN(base)} = \beta_{DC}(R_{E1} + R_{E2}) = (75)(17\ \Omega) = 1275\ \Omega$
   Since $R_{IN(base)}$ is not ten times R_2, a 50 % increase in β_{DC} will result
   in a reduction in V_B which, in turn, causes an increase in I_E and
   I_C and an increase in V_C from its 5.55 V level. The maximum allowable V_{out} increases.

5. (a) $R_{IN(base)} = \beta_{DC}(R_{E1} + R_{E2}) = (125)(79.7\ \Omega) = 9.96\ k\Omega$
   Since $R_{IN(base)} > 10R_2$, it can be neglected.
   $$V_B = \left[\frac{R_2}{R_1 + R_2}\right]V_{CC} = \left(\frac{510\ \Omega}{680\ \Omega + 510\ \Omega}\right)12\ V = \left(\frac{510\ \Omega}{1190\ \Omega}\right)12\ V = 5.14\ V$$
   $V_E = V_B - 0.7\ V = 5.14\ V - 0.7\ V = 4.44\ V$
   $$I_{CQ} \cong I_E = \frac{V_E}{R_E} = \frac{4.44\ V}{79.7\ \Omega} = 55.7\ mA$$
   $V_{CQ} = V_{CC} - I_{CQ}R_C = 12\ V - (55.7\ mA)(100\ \Omega) = 6.43\ V$
   $V_{CEQ} = V_C - V_E = 6.43\ V - 4.44\ V = 1.99\ V$
   $R_c = R_C \parallel R_L = 100\ \Omega \parallel 100\ \Omega = 50\ \Omega$
   $V_{ce(cutoff)} = V_{CEQ} + I_{CQ}R_c = 1.99\ V + 55.7\ mA(50\ \Omega) = 4.78\ V$
   Since V_{CEQ} is closer to saturation, I_c is limited to
   $$I_{c(p)} = \frac{V_{CEQ}}{R_c} = \frac{1.99\ V}{50\ \Omega} = \mathbf{39.8\ mA}$$
   V_{out} is limited to
   $V_{out(p)} = V_{CEQ} = \mathbf{1.99\ V}$

   (b) $R_{IN(base)} = \beta_{DC}(R_{E1} + R_{E2}) = (120)(142\ \Omega) = 17\ k\Omega$
   Since $R_{IN(base)} < 10R_2$, it is taken into account.
   $$V_B = \left[\frac{R_2 \parallel R_{IN(base)}}{R_1 + R_2 \parallel R_{IN(base)}}\right]V_{CC} = \left(\frac{4.7\ k\Omega \parallel 17\ k\Omega}{12\ k\Omega + 4.7\ k\Omega \parallel 17\ k\Omega}\right)12\ V = \left(\frac{3.68\ k\Omega}{15.68\ k\Omega}\right)12\ V = 2.82\ V$$
   $V_E = V_B - 0.7\ V = 2.82\ V - 0.7\ V = 2.12\ V$
   $I_{CQ} \cong I_E = V_E/R_E = 2.12\ V / 142\ \Omega = 14.9\ mA$
   $V_{CQ} = V_{CC} - I_{CQ}R_C = 12\ V - (14.9\ mA)(470\ \Omega) = 5.0\ V$
   $V_{CEQ} = V_{CQ} - V_E = 5.0\ V - 2.12\ V = 2.88\ V$
   $R_c = R_C \parallel R_L = 470\ \Omega \parallel 470\ \Omega = 235\ \Omega$
   $V_{ce(cutoff)} = V_{CEQ} + I_{CQ}R_c = 2.88\ V + 14.9\ mA(235\ \Omega) = 6.38\ V$
   Since V_{CEQ} is closer to saturation, I_c is limited to
   $$I_{c(p)} = \frac{V_{CEQ}}{R_c} = \frac{2.88\ V}{235\ \Omega} = \mathbf{12.3\ mA}$$
   V_{out} is limited to $V_{out(p)} = V_{CEQ} = \mathbf{2.88\ V}$

Chapter 7

6.

(a) $A_v \cong \dfrac{R_c}{R_{E1}} = \dfrac{R_C \| R_L}{R_{E1}} = \dfrac{100\,\Omega \| 100\,\Omega}{4.7\,\Omega} = \dfrac{50\,\Omega}{4.7\,\Omega} = \mathbf{10.6}$

(b) $A_v \cong \dfrac{R_c}{R_{E1}} = \dfrac{R_C \| R_L}{R_{E1}} = \dfrac{470\,\Omega \| 470\,\Omega}{22\,\Omega} = \dfrac{235\,\Omega}{22\,\Omega} = \mathbf{10.7}$

7.

(a) $V_{rms(in)} = \dfrac{0.707 V_{out(p)}}{A_v} = \dfrac{(0.707)(1.99\,\text{V})}{10.6} = \mathbf{133\,mV\ rms}$

(b) $V_{rms(in)} = \dfrac{0.707 V_{out(p)}}{A_v} = \dfrac{(0.707)(2.88\,\text{V})}{10.7} = \mathbf{190\,mV\ rms}$

8.

(a) $R_{IN(base)} = \beta_{DC} R_E = 90(130\,\Omega) = 11.7\,\text{k}\Omega$

$R_2 \| R_{IN(base)} = 1\,\text{k}\Omega \| 11.7\,\text{k}\Omega = 921\,\Omega$

$V_B = \left(\dfrac{R_2 \| R_{IN(base)}}{R_1 + R_2 \| R_{IN(base)}}\right) V_{CC} = \left(\dfrac{921\,\Omega}{5.62\,\text{k}\Omega}\right) 24\,\text{V} = 3.93\,\text{V}$

$V_E = V_B - 0.7\,\text{V} = 3.93\,\text{V} - 0.7\,\text{V} = 3.23\,\text{V}$

$I_{CQ} \cong I_E = \dfrac{V_E}{R_E} = \dfrac{3.23\,\text{V}}{130\,\Omega} = 24.8\,\text{mA}$

$V_C = V_{CC} - I_{CQ} R_C = 24\,\text{V} - (24.8\,\text{mA})(560\,\Omega) = 13.9\,\text{V}$

$V_{CEQ} = V_C - V_E = 13.9\,\text{V} - 3.23\,\text{V} = 10.7\,\text{V}$

$P_{D(min)} = P_{DQ} = I_{CQ} V_{CEQ} = (24.8\,\text{mA})(10.7\,\text{V}) = \mathbf{265\,mW}$

Chapter 7

9. (a) From Problem 8: $I_{CQ} = 24.8$ mA and $V_{CEQ} = 10.7$ V

$V_{ce(cutoff)} = V_{CEQ} + I_{CQ}R_c = 10.7$ V $+ (24.8$ mA$)264\,\Omega = 17.2$ V

The Q point is closer to cutoff than to saturation.

$P_{out} = 0.5I_{CQ}^2 R_c = 0.5(24.8$ mA$)^2 264\,\Omega = \mathbf{81.2}$ **mW**

$eff = \dfrac{P_{out}}{P_{DC}} = \dfrac{P_{out}}{V_{CC}I_{CC}} = \dfrac{P_{out}}{V_{CC}I_{CQ}} = \dfrac{81.2 \text{ mW}}{(24 \text{ V})(24.8 \text{ mA})} = \mathbf{0.136}$

Section 7-2 Class B and Class AB Push-Pull Amplifiers

10. Assuming Q_1 and Q_2 are biased right at cutoff:

$I_T = \dfrac{V_{CC}}{R_1 + R_2 + R_3 + R_4} = \dfrac{30 \text{ V}}{17.2 \text{ k}\Omega} = 1.75$ mA

$V_1 = V_{CC} - I_T R_1 = 30$ V $- (1.75$ mA$)(8.2$ k$\Omega) = \mathbf{15.7}$ **V**

$V_2 = I_T R_4 = (1.75$ mA$)(8.2$ k$\Omega) = \mathbf{14.5}$ **V**

$V_3 = V_1 - 0.7$ V $= 15.65$ V $- 0.7$ V $= \mathbf{15.0}$ **V**

$V_4 = \mathbf{0}$ **V**

11. Bias current:

$I_T = \dfrac{V_{CC} - 1.4 \text{ V}}{R_1 + R_2} = \dfrac{20 \text{ V} - 1.4 \text{ V}}{780\,\Omega} = 23.9$ mA

$V_{B1} = V_{CC} - I_T R_1 = 20$ V $- (23.9$ mA$)(390\,\Omega) = \mathbf{10.7}$ **V**

$V_{E1} = V_{B1} - 0.7$ V $= 10.7$ V $- 0.7$ V $= \mathbf{10}$ **V**

$V_{B2} = V_{B1} - 1.4$ V $= 10.7$ V $- 1.4$ V $= \mathbf{9.3}$ **V**

$V_{E2} = V_{B2} + 0.7$ V $= 9.3$ V $+ 0.7$ V $= \mathbf{10}$ **V**

$V_{CEQ1} = V_{C1} - V_{E1} = 20$ V $- 10$ V $= \mathbf{10}$ **V**

$V_{CEQ2} = V_{E2} - V_{C2} = 10$ V $- 0$ V $= \mathbf{10}$ **V**

12. $V_{out(p)} = V_{CEQ} = \dfrac{V_{CC}}{2} = \dfrac{20 \text{ V}}{2} = \mathbf{10}$ **V**

$I_{L(p)} = I_{c(sat)} = \dfrac{V_{CEQ}}{R_e} = \dfrac{10 \text{ V}}{16\,\Omega} = \mathbf{625}$ **mA**

Chapter 7

13. $I_{c(sat)} = \dfrac{V_{CEQ}}{R_e} = \dfrac{10 \text{ V}}{16 \text{ }\Omega} = 625 \text{ mA}$

$P_{out} = 0.5 V_{CEQ} I_{c(sat)} = (0.5)(10 \text{ V})(625 \text{ mA}) = \mathbf{3.13 \text{ W}}$

$P_{DC} = V_{CC} I_{CC} = V_{CC}\left(\dfrac{I_{c(sat)}}{\pi}\right) = 20 \text{ V}\left(\dfrac{625 \text{ mA}}{\pi}\right) = \mathbf{3.98 \text{ W}}$

14. $\eta = \dfrac{P_{out}}{P_{DC}}$

$P_{out} = \eta P_{DC} = (0.71)(16.4 \text{ W}) = \mathbf{11.6 \text{ W}}$

15. $I_{CC} = \dfrac{I_{c(sat)}}{\pi} = \dfrac{V_{CEQ}/R_e}{\pi} = \dfrac{12 \text{ V}/8\Omega}{\pi} = \mathbf{478 \text{ mA}}$

$P_{DC} = V_{CC} I_{CC} = 2V_{CEQ} I_{CC} = (24 \text{ V})(478 \text{ mA}) = \mathbf{11.5 \text{ W}}$

$I_{c(sat)} = \pi I_{CC} = \pi(478 \text{ mA}) = 1.5 \text{ A}$

$P_{out} = 0.5 V_{CEQ} I_{c(sat)} = (0.5)(12 \text{ V})(1.5 \text{ A}) = \mathbf{9 \text{ W}}$

$V_{CC} = 2V_{CEQ} = \mathbf{24 \text{ V}}$

16. $V_{out(p)} = V_{CEQ} = \dfrac{V_{CC}}{2} = \dfrac{24 \text{ V}}{2} = 12 \text{ V}$

$V_{in(p)} = V_{out(p)}$ when $A_v = 1$

$V_{in} = (0.707)(12 \text{ V}) = \mathbf{8.48 \text{ V rms}}$

Section 7-3 Class C Amplifiers

17. $P_{D(avg)} = \left(\dfrac{t_{on}}{T}\right) V_{CE(sat)} I_{C(sat)} = (0.1)(0.18 \text{ V})(25 \text{ mA}) = \mathbf{450 \text{ }\mu W}$

18. $f_r = \dfrac{1}{2\pi\sqrt{LC}} = \dfrac{1}{2\pi\sqrt{(10 \text{ mH})(0.001 \text{ }\mu F)}} = \mathbf{50.3 \text{ kHz}}$

19. $V_{out(pp)} = 2V_{CC} = 2(12 \text{ V}) = \mathbf{24 \text{ V}}$

20. $P_{out} = \dfrac{0.5 V_{CC}^2}{R_c} = \dfrac{0.5(15 \text{ V})^2}{50 \text{ }\Omega} = 2.25 \text{ W}$

$P_{D(avg)} = \left(\dfrac{t_{on}}{T}\right) V_{CE(sat)} I_{C(sat)} = (0.1)(0.18 \text{ V})(25 \text{ mA}) = 0.45 \text{ mW}$

$\eta = \dfrac{P_{out}}{P_{out} + P_{D(avg)}} = \dfrac{2.25 \text{ W}}{2.25 \text{ W} + 0.45 \text{ mW}} = \mathbf{0.9998}$

Section 7-4 Troubleshooting

21. With C_1 open, only the negative half of the input signal appears across R_L.

Chapter 7

22. One of the transistors is open between the collector and emitter or a coupling capacitor is open.

23. (a) No dc supply voltage
(b) Diode D_1 or D_2 open
(c) Circuit is OK
(d) Q_1 shorted from collector to emitter

Section 7-5 System Application

24. For the block diagram of Figure 7–41 with no signal from the power amplifier or preamplifier, but with the microphone working, the problem is in the power amplifier or preamplifier. Check for an output from the preamp. If one is present, the preamp is not at fault.

25. For the circuit of Figure 7–42 with the base–emitter junction of the 2N6043 open the dc output will be approximately 6 V with a signal output having the positive alternations of the input signal.

26. For the circuit of Figure 7–42 with the base–emitter junction of the 2N6040 open the dc output will be 0 V with no signal output

27. On the circuit board of Figure 7–56, the input coupling capacior C_1 has bee installed backwards. The positive lead should connect into the circuit.

Data Sheet Problems

28. *From the 2N6040 data sheet of Figure 7–43*
(a) $\beta_{DC(min)} = \mathbf{100}$ @ $I_C = 8.0$ A, $V_{CE} = 4$ V
$\beta_{DC(min)} = \mathbf{1000}$ @ $I_C = 4.0$ A, $V_{CE} = 4$ V
(b) For a 2N6041, $V_{CE(max)} = \mathbf{80\ V}$
(c) $P_{D(max)} = \mathbf{75\ W}$ @ $T_C = 25°C$
(d) $I_{C(max)} = 8.0$ A continuous or 16.0 A peak

29. $P_D = 75\ \text{W} - (65°C - 25°C)(0.6\ \text{W/°C}) = 75\ \text{W} - 24\ \text{W} = \mathbf{51\ W}$

30. $P_D = 2.2\ \text{W} - (80°C - 25°C)(0.0175\ \text{W/°C}) = 2.2\ \text{W} - 963\ \text{mW} = \mathbf{1.24\ W}$

31. As the frequency increases the small–signal current gain **decreases**

32. $h_{fe} \cong \mathbf{2800}$ @ $f = 2$ kHz
$h_{fe} \cong \mathbf{700}$ @ $f = 100$ kHz

Advanced Problems

33. T_C is much closer to the actual junction temperature than T_A. In a given operating environment, T_A is always less than T_C.

Chapter 7

34. $I_{C(sat)} = \dfrac{24\text{ V}}{330\text{ }\Omega + 100\text{ }\Omega} = \dfrac{24\text{ V}}{430\text{ }\Omega} = \mathbf{55.8\text{ mA}}$

$V_{CE(cutoff)} = \mathbf{24\text{ V}}$

$V_{BQ} = \left(\dfrac{1\text{ k}\Omega}{1\text{ k}\Omega + 4.7\text{ k}\Omega}\right)24\text{ V} = 4.21\text{ V}$

$V_{EQ} = 4.21\text{ V} - 0.7\text{ V} = 3.51\text{ V}$

$I_{EQ} \cong I_{CQ} = \dfrac{3.51\text{ V}}{100\text{ }\Omega} = 35.1\text{ mA}$

$R_c = 330\text{ }\Omega \parallel 330\text{ }\Omega = 165\text{ }\Omega$

$V_{CQ} = 24\text{ V} - (35.1\text{ mA})(165\text{ }\Omega) = 12.4\text{ V}$

$V_{CEQ} = 12.4\text{ V} - 3.51\text{ V} = 8.90\text{ V}$

$I_{c(sat)} = 35.1\text{ }mA + \dfrac{8.90\text{ V}}{165\text{ }\Omega} = \mathbf{89.1\text{ mA}}$

$V_{ce(cutoff)} = 8.90\text{ V} - (35.1\text{ mA})(165\text{ }\Omega) = \mathbf{14.7\text{ V}}$

See Figure 7–2.

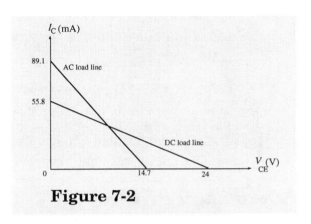

Figure 7-2

35. See Figure 7–3.

$I_{R1} \cong I_{R2} = \dfrac{15\text{ V}}{86\text{ }\Omega} = 174\text{ mA}$

$V_B \cong \left(\dfrac{18\text{ }\Omega}{86\text{ }\Omega}\right)15\text{ V} = 3.14\text{ V}$

$V_E = 3.14\text{ V} - 0.7\text{ V} = 2.44\text{ V}$

$I_E \cong I_C = \dfrac{2.44\text{ V}}{4.85\text{ }\Omega} = 503\text{ mA}$

$V_C = 15\text{ V} - (10\text{ }\Omega)(503\text{ mA}) = 9.97\text{ V}$

$V_{CE} = 7.53\text{ V}$

$r'_e = \dfrac{25\text{ mV}}{503\text{ mA}} = 0.05\text{ }\Omega$

The ac resistance affecting the load line is

$R_c + R_e + r'_e = 10\text{ }\Omega$

$\beta_{ac} = \beta_{DC} \geq 100$

$I_{c(sat)} = 503\text{ mA} + \dfrac{7.53\text{ V}}{10.2\text{ }\Omega} = 1.24\text{ A}$

$V_{ce(cutoff)} = 7.53\text{ V} + (503\text{ mA})(10.2\text{ }\Omega) = 12.7\text{ V}$

The Q point is closer to cutoff so

$P_{out} = (0.5)(503\text{ mA})^2(10.2\text{ }\Omega) = 1.29\text{ W}$

As loading occurs, the Q point will still be closer to cutoff. The circuit will have $P_{out} \geq 1$ W for $R_L \geq 37.7\text{ }\Omega$ (39 Ω standard)

Chapter 7

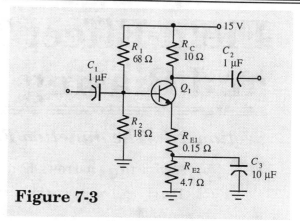

Figure 7-3

36. To modify the circuit of Figure 7–46 to operate on dc power for 8 hours continuously, remove the rectifier connections (with a switch possibly) and connect the power terminals of the preamp and amplifier boards to a 12 V battery (possibly with the same switch as that which disconnects the power supply). Because the preamp operates on 9 V, a zener or other regulator must be used to set the proper voltage on this board.

Chapter 8
Field-Effect Transistors and Biasing

Section 8-1 The Junction Field-Effect Transistor (JFET)

1. (a) A greater V_{GS} **narrows** the depletion region
   (b) The channel resistance **increases** with increased V_{GS}.

2. The gate-to-source voltage of an n-channel JFET must be zero or negative in order to maintain the required reverse-bias condition.

3. See Figure 8-1.

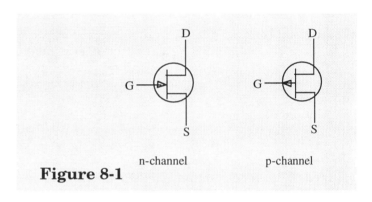

Figure 8-1

n-channel   p-channel

4. See Figure 8-2.

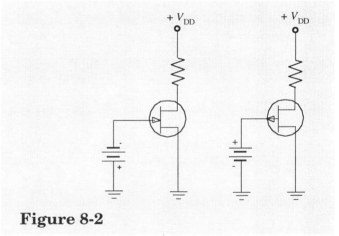

Figure 8-2

Section 8-2 JFET Characteristics and Parameters

5. $V_{DS} = V_P = 5$ V at point where I_D becomes constant.

6. $V_{GS(off)} = -V_P = -6$ V
   The device is **on**, because $V_{GS} = -2$ V.

Chapter 8

7. By definition, $I_D = I_{DSS}$ when $V_{GS} = 0$ V for values of $V_{DS} > V_P$.
Therefore, $I_D =$ **10 mA**.

8. Since $V_{GS} > V_{GS(off)}$, the JFET is off and $I_D =$ **0 A**.

9. $V_P = -V_{GS(off)} = -(-4V) = 4$ V
The voltmeter reads V_{DS}. As V_{DD} is increased, V_{DS} also increases. The point at which I_D reaches a constant value is $V_{DS} = V_P =$ **4 V**

10.
$$I_D = I_{DSS}\left(1 - \frac{V_{GS}}{V_{GS(off)}}\right)^2$$

$$I_D = 5 \text{ mA}\left(1 - \frac{0 \text{ V}}{-8 \text{ V}}\right)^2 = 5 \text{ mA}$$

$$I_D = 5 \text{ mA}\left(1 - \frac{-1 \text{ V}}{-8 \text{ V}}\right)^2 = 3.83 \text{ mA}$$

$$I_D = 5 \text{ mA}\left(1 - \frac{-2 \text{ V}}{-8 \text{ V}}\right)^2 = 2.81 \text{ mA}$$

$$I_D = 5 \text{ mA}\left(1 - \frac{-3 \text{ V}}{-8 \text{ V}}\right)^2 = 1.95 \text{ mA}$$

$$I_D = 5 \text{ mA}\left(1 - \frac{-4 \text{ V}}{-8 \text{ V}}\right)^2 = 1.25 \text{ mA}$$

$$I_D = 5 \text{ mA}\left(1 - \frac{-5 \text{ V}}{-8 \text{ V}}\right)^2 = 0.703 \text{ mA}$$

$$I_D = 5 \text{ mA}\left(1 - \frac{-6 \text{ V}}{-8 \text{ V}}\right)^2 = 0.313 \text{ mA}$$

$$I_D = 5 \text{ mA}\left(1 - \frac{-7 \text{ V}}{-8 \text{ V}}\right)^2 = 0.078 \text{ mA}$$

$$I_D = 5 \text{ mA}\left(1 - \frac{-8 \text{ V}}{-8 \text{ V}}\right)^2 = 0 \text{ mA}$$

See Figure 8-3.

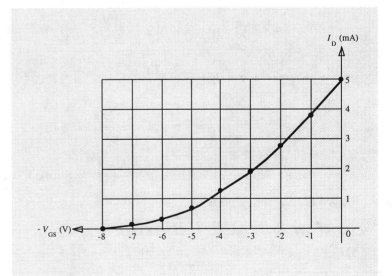

Figure 8-3

Chapter 7

11.
$$I_D = I_{DSS}\left(1 - \frac{V_{GS}}{V_{GS(off)}}\right)^2$$

$$1 - \frac{V_{GS}}{V_{GS(off)}} = \sqrt{\frac{I_D}{I_{DSS}}}$$

$$\frac{V_{GS}}{V_{GS(off)}} = 1 - \sqrt{\frac{I_D}{I_{DSS}}}$$

$$V_{GS} = V_{GS(off)}\left(1 - \sqrt{\frac{I_D}{I_{DSS}}}\right)$$

$$V_{GS} = -8\,V\left(1 - \sqrt{\frac{2.25\,mA}{5\,mA}}\right) = -8\,V(0.329) = \mathbf{-2.63\,V}$$

12. $g_m = g_{m0}\left(1 - \frac{V_{GS}}{V_{GS(off)}}\right) = 3200\,\mu S\left(1 - \frac{-4V}{-8\,V}\right) = \mathbf{1600\,\mu S}$

13. $g_m = g_{m0}\left(1 - \frac{V_{GS}}{V_{GS(off)}}\right) = 2000\,\mu S\left(1 - \frac{-2V}{-7\,V}\right) = \mathbf{1429\,\mu S}$

$y_{fs} = g_m = \mathbf{1429\,\mu S}$

14. $R_{IN} = \frac{V_{GS}}{I_{GSS}} = \frac{10\,V}{5\,nA} = \mathbf{2000\,M\Omega}$

15. $V_{GS} = 0\,V$: $I_D = I_{DSS}\left(1 - \frac{V_{GS}}{V_{GS(off)}}\right)^2 = 8\,mA(1-0)^2 = \mathbf{8\,mA}$

$V_{GS} = -1\,V$: $I_D = 8\,mA\left(1 - \frac{-1\,V}{-5\,V}\right)^2 = 8\,mA(1-0.2)^2 = 8\,mA(0.8)^2 = \mathbf{5.12\,mA}$

$V_{GS} = -2\,V$: $I_D = 8\,mA\left(1 - \frac{-2\,V}{-5\,V}\right)^2 = 8\,mA(1-0.4)^2 = 8\,mA(0.6)^2 = \mathbf{2.88\,mA}$

$V_{GS} = -3\,V$: $I_D = 8\,mA\left(1 - \frac{-3\,V}{-5\,V}\right)^2 = 8\,mA(1-0.6)^2 = 8\,mA(0.4)^2 = \mathbf{1.28\,mA}$

$V_{GS} = -4\,V$: $I_D = 8\,mA\left(1 - \frac{-4\,V}{-5\,V}\right)^2 = 8\,mA(1-0.8)^2 = 8\,mA(0.2)^2 = \mathbf{0.320\,mA}$

$V_{GS} = -5V$: $I_D = 8\,mA\left(1 - \frac{-5\,V}{-5\,V}\right)^2 = 8\,mA(1-1)^2 = 8\,mA(0)^2 = \mathbf{0\,mA}$

Section 8-3 JFET Biasing

16. $V_{GS} = -I_D R_S = -(12\,mA)(100\,\Omega) = \mathbf{-1.2\,V}$

17. $R_S = \left|\frac{V_{GS}}{I_D}\right| = \left|\frac{-4\,V}{5\,mA}\right| = \mathbf{800\,\Omega}$

18. $R_S = \left|\frac{V_{GS}}{I_D}\right| = \left|\frac{-3\,V}{2.5\,mA}\right| = \mathbf{1.2\,k\Omega}$

Chapter 8

19. (a) $I_D = I_{DSS} = $ **20 mA**
(b) $I_D = $ **0 A**
(c) I_D **increases**

20. (a) $V_S = (1\text{ mA})(1\text{ k}\Omega) = 1\text{ V}$
$V_D = 12\text{ V} - (1\text{ mA})(4.7\text{ k}\Omega) = 7.3\text{ V}$
$V_G = 0\text{ V}$
$V_{GS} = V_G - V_S = 0\text{ V} - 1\text{ V} = $ **- 1 V**
$V_{DS} = 7.3\text{ V} - 1\text{ V} = $ **6.3 V**

(b) $V_S = (5\text{ mA})(100\text{ }\Omega) = 0.5\text{ V}$
$V_D = 9\text{ V} - (5\text{ mA})(470\text{ }\Omega) = 6.65\text{ V}$
$V_G = 0\text{ V}$
$V_{GS} = V_G - V_S = 0\text{ V} - 0.5\text{ V} = $ **- 0.5 V**
$V_{DS} = 6.65\text{ V} - 0.5\text{ V} = $ **6.15 V**

(c) $V_S = (-3\text{ mA})(470\text{ }\Omega) = -1.41\text{ V}$
$V_D = -15\text{ V} + (3\text{ mA})(2.2\text{ k}\Omega) = -8.4\text{ V}$
$V_G = 0\text{ V}$
$V_{GS} = V_G - V_S = 0\text{ V} - (-1.41\text{ V}) = $ **1.41 V**
$V_{DS} = -8.4\text{ V} - (-1.41\text{ V}) = $ **- 6.99 V**

21. From the graph, $V_{GS} \cong -2\text{ V}$ at $I_D = 9.5\text{ mA}$

$$R_S = \left|\frac{V_{GS}}{I_D}\right| = \left|\frac{-2\text{ V}}{9.5\text{ mA}}\right| = \textbf{211 }\Omega$$

22. $I_D = \dfrac{I_{DSS}}{2} = \dfrac{14\text{ mA}}{2} = \textbf{7 mA}$

$V_{GS} = \dfrac{V_{GS(off)}}{3.414} = \dfrac{-10\text{ V}}{3.414} = \textbf{- 2.93 V}$

Since $V_G = 0\text{ V}$, $V_S = V_G$

$R_S = \left|\dfrac{V_{GS}}{I_D}\right| = \dfrac{2.93\text{ V}}{7\text{ mA}} = \textbf{419 }\Omega$ (The nearest standard value is 430 Ω)

$R_D = \dfrac{V_{DD} - V_D}{I_D} = \dfrac{24\text{V} - 12\text{ V}}{7\text{ mA}} = \textbf{1.7 k}\Omega$ (The nearest standard value is 1.8 kΩ)

Select $R_G = 1\text{ M}\Omega$. See Figure 8-4.

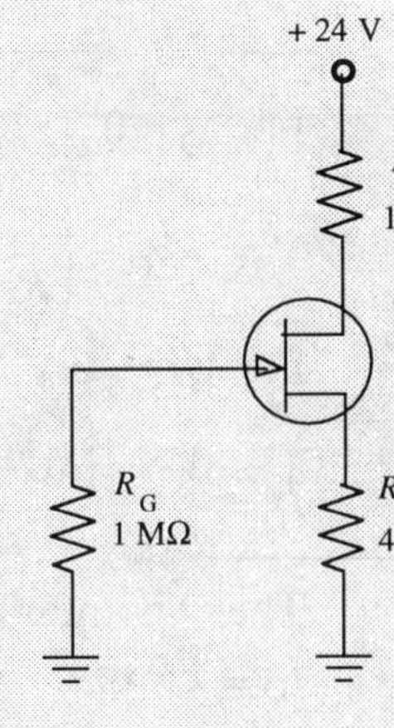

Figure 8-4

73

Chapter 8

23. $R_{IN(total)} = R_G \| R_{IN}$

$R_{IN} = \left|\dfrac{V_{GS}}{I_{GSS}}\right| = \left|\dfrac{-10\text{ V}}{20\text{ nA}}\right| = 500\text{ M}\Omega$

$R_{IN(total)} = 10\text{ M}\Omega \| 500\text{ M}\Omega = \mathbf{9.8\text{ M}\Omega}$

24. For $I_D = 0$
$V_{GS} = -I_D R_S = (0)(330\ \Omega) = 0\text{ V}$
For $I_D = I_{DSS} = 5\text{ mA}$
$V_{GS} = -I_D R_S = -(5\text{ mA})(330\ \Omega) = -1.65\text{ V}$
From the graph in Figure 8-61, the Q point is
$V_{GS} \cong \mathbf{-0.95\text{ V}}$ and $I_D \cong \mathbf{2.9\text{ mA}}$

25. For $I_D = 0$
$V_{GS} = 0\text{ V}$
For $I_D = I_{DSS} = 10\text{ mA}$
$V_{GS} = -I_D R_S = (10\text{ mA})(390\ \Omega) = 3.9\text{ V}$
From the graph in Figure 8-62, the Q point is
$V_{GS} \cong \mathbf{2.1\text{ V}}$ and $I_D \cong \mathbf{5.3\text{ mA}}$

26. Since $V_{R_D} = 9\text{ V} - 5\text{ V} = 4\text{ V}$

$I_D = \dfrac{V_{R_D}}{R_D} = \dfrac{4\text{ V}}{4.7\text{ k}\Omega} = 0.85\text{ mA}$

$V_S = I_D R_S = (0.85\text{ mA})(3.3\text{ k}\Omega) = 2.81\text{ V}$

$V_G = \left(\dfrac{R_2}{R_1 + R_2}\right)V_{DD} = \left(\dfrac{2.2\text{ M}\Omega}{12.2\text{ M}\Omega}\right)9\text{ V} = 1.62\text{ V}$

$V_{GS} = V_G - V_S = 1.62\text{ V} - 2.81\text{ V} = -1.19\text{ V}$

Q point: $I_D = \mathbf{0.85\text{ mA}}$, $V_{GS} = \mathbf{-1.19\text{ V}}$

27. For $I_D = 0$

$V_{GS} = V_G = \left(\dfrac{R_2}{R_1 + R_2}\right)V_{DD} = \left(\dfrac{2.2\text{ M}\Omega}{5.5\text{ M}\Omega}\right)12\text{ V} = 4.8\text{ V}$

For $V_{GS} = 0\text{ V}$, $V_S = 4.8\text{ V}$

$I_D = \dfrac{V_S}{R_S} = \dfrac{|V_G - V_{GS}|}{R_S} = \dfrac{4.8\text{ V}}{3.3\text{ k}\Omega} = 1.45\text{ mA}$

The Q point is taken from the graph in Figure 8–64.
$I_D \cong \mathbf{1.9\text{ mA}}$, $V_{GS} = \mathbf{-1.5\text{ V}}$

Chapter 8

Section 8-4 The Metal Oxide Semiconductor FET (MOSFET)

28. See Figure 8-5.

Figure 8-5

29. An *n*–channel D–MOSFET wi a positive V_{GS} is operating in the **enhancement mode**.

30. An E-MOSFET has no physical channel or depletion mode. A D-MOSFET has a physical channel and can be operated in either depletion or enhancement modes.

31. MOSFETs have a very high input resistance because the gate is insulated from the channel by an SiO_2 layer.

Section 8-5 MOSFET Characteristics and Parameters

32. (a) n-channel

(b) $I_D = I_{DSS}\left(1 - \dfrac{V_{GS}}{V_{GS(off)}}\right)^2$ $I_D = 8\text{ mA}\left(1 - \dfrac{-5\text{ V}}{-5\text{ V}}\right)^2 = \mathbf{0\text{ A}}$

$I_D = 8\text{ mA}\left(1 - \dfrac{-4\text{ V}}{-5\text{ V}}\right)^2 = \mathbf{0.32\text{ A}}$ $I_D = 8\text{ mA}\left(1 - \dfrac{-3\text{ V}}{-5\text{ V}}\right)^2 = \mathbf{1.28\text{ A}}$

$I_D = 8\text{ mA}\left(1 - \dfrac{-2\text{ V}}{-5\text{ V}}\right)^2 = \mathbf{2.88\text{ A}}$ $I_D = 8\text{ mA}\left(1 - \dfrac{-1\text{ V}}{-5\text{ V}}\right)^2 = \mathbf{5.12\text{ A}}$

$I_D = 8\text{ mA}\left(1 - \dfrac{0\text{ V}}{-5\text{ V}}\right)^2 = \mathbf{8\text{ A}}$ $I_D = 8\text{ mA}\left(1 - \dfrac{1\text{ V}}{-5\text{ V}}\right)^2 = \mathbf{11.5\text{ A}}$

$I_D = 8\text{ mA}\left(1 - \dfrac{2\text{ V}}{-5\text{ V}}\right)^2 = \mathbf{15.7\text{ A}}$ $I_D = 8\text{ mA}\left(1 - \dfrac{3\text{ V}}{-5\text{ V}}\right)^2 = \mathbf{20.5\text{ A}}$

$I_D = 8\text{ mA}\left(1 - \dfrac{4\text{ V}}{-5\text{ V}}\right)^2 = \mathbf{25.9\text{ A}}$ $I_D = 8\text{ mA}\left(1 - \dfrac{5\text{ V}}{-5\text{ V}}\right)^2 = \mathbf{32\text{ A}}$

(c) See Figure 8-6.

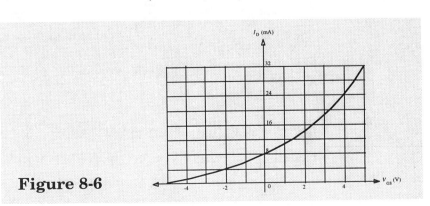

Figure 8-6

75

Chapter 8

33.
$$I_D = I_{DSS}\left(1 - \frac{V_{GS}}{V_{GS(off)}}\right)^2$$

$$I_{DSS} = \frac{I_D}{\left(1 - \frac{V_{GS}}{V_{GS(off)}}\right)^2} = \frac{3\text{ mA}}{\left(1 - \frac{-2\text{ V}}{-10\text{ V}}\right)^2} = \textbf{4.69 mA}$$

34.
$$K = \frac{I_{D(on)}}{\left(V_{GS} - V_{GS(th)}\right)^2} = \frac{10\text{ mA}}{(-12\text{ V} + 3\text{ V})^2} = 0.12\text{ mA/V}^2$$

$$I_D = K\left(V_{GS} - V_{GS(off)}\right)^2 = (0.12\text{ mA/V}^2)(-6\text{ V} + 3\text{ V})^2 = \textbf{1.08 mA}$$

Section 8-6 MOSFET Biasing

35. (a) Depletion
 (b) Enhancement
 (c) Zero bias
 (d) Depletion

36. (a) $V_{GS} = \left(\dfrac{10\text{ M}\Omega}{14.7\text{ M}\Omega}\right)10\text{ V} = \textbf{6.8 V}$ This MOSFET is **on**.

 (b) $V_{GS} = \left(\dfrac{1\text{ M}\Omega}{11\text{ M}\Omega}\right)(-25\text{ V}) = \textbf{-2.27 V}$ This MOSFET is **off**.

37. Since $V_{GS} = 0$ V for each circuit, $I_D = I_{DSS} = 8$ mA.
 (a) $V_{DS} = V_{DD} - I_D R_D = 12\text{ V} - (8\text{ mA})(1\text{ k}\Omega) = \textbf{4 V}$
 (b) $V_{DS} = V_{DD} - I_D R_D = 15\text{ V} - (8\text{ mA})(1.2\text{ k}\Omega) = \textbf{5.4 V}$
 (c) $V_{DS} = V_{DD} - I_D R_D = -9\text{ V} - (-8\text{ mA})(560\text{ }\Omega) = \textbf{-4.52 V}$

38. (a) $I_{D(on)} = 3$ mA @ 4 V, $V_{GS(th)} = 2$ V

$$V_{GS} = \left(\frac{R_2}{R_1 + R_2}\right)V_{DD} = \left(\frac{4.7\text{ M}\Omega}{14.7\text{ M}\Omega}\right)10\text{ V} = \textbf{3.2 V}$$

$$K = \frac{I_{D(on)}}{\left(V_{GS} - V_{GS(th)}\right)^2} = \frac{3\text{ mA}}{(4\text{ V} - 2\text{ V})^2} = \frac{3\text{ mA}}{(2\text{ V})^2} = 0.75\text{ mA/V}^2$$

$$I_D = K\left(V_{GS} - V_{GS(th)}\right)^2 = (0.75\text{ mA/V}^2)(3.2\text{ V} - 2\text{ V})^2 = 1.08\text{ mA}$$

$$V_{DS} = V_{DD} - I_D R_D = 10\text{ V} - (1.08\text{ mA})(1\text{ k}\Omega) = 10\text{ V} - 1.08\text{ V} = \textbf{8.92 V}$$

Chapter 8

(b) $I_{D(on)} = 2$ mA @ 4 V, $V_{GS(th)} = 1.5$ V

$$V_{GS} = \left(\frac{R_2}{R_1 + R_2}\right)V_{DD} = \left(\frac{10 \text{ M}\Omega}{20 \text{ M}\Omega}\right)5 \text{ V} = \mathbf{2.5 \text{ V}}$$

$$K = \frac{I_{D(on)}}{\left(V_{GS} - V_{GS(th)}\right)^2} = \frac{2 \text{ mA}}{(3 \text{ V} - 1.5 \text{ V})^2} = \frac{2 \text{ mA}}{(1.5 \text{ V})^2} = 0.89 \text{ mA/V}^2$$

$$I_D = K\left(V_{GS} - V_{GS(th)}\right)^2 = \left(0.89 \text{ mA/V}^2\right)(2.5 \text{ V} - 1.5 \text{ V})^2 = \mathbf{0.89 \text{ mA}}$$

$$V_{DS} = V_{DD} - I_D R_D = 5 \text{ V} - (0.89 \text{ mA})(1.5 \text{ k}\Omega) = 5 \text{V} - 1.34 \text{ V} = \mathbf{3.66 \text{ V}}$$

39. (a) $V_{DS} = V_{GS} = \mathbf{5 \text{ V}}$

$$I_D = \frac{V_{DD} - V_{DS}}{R_D} = \frac{12 \text{ V} - 5 \text{ V}}{2.2 \text{ k}\Omega} = \mathbf{3.18 \text{ mA}}$$

(b) $V_{DS} = V_{GS} = \mathbf{3.2 \text{ V}}$

$$I_D = \frac{V_{DD} - V_{DS}}{R_D} = \frac{8 \text{ V} - 3.2 \text{ V}}{4.7 \text{ k}\Omega} = \mathbf{1.02 \text{ mA}}$$

40. $V_{DS} = V_{DD} - I_D R_D = 15 \text{ V} - (1 \text{ mA})(8.2 \text{ k}\Omega) = 6.8 \text{ V}$

$V_{GS} = V_{DS} - I_G R_G = 6.8 \text{ V} - (50 \text{ pA})(22 \text{ M}\Omega) = \mathbf{6.799 \text{ V}}$

Section 8-7 Troubleshooting

41. When I_D goes to zero, the possible faults are:

R_D or R_S open, JFET drain to source open, no supply voltage, or ground connection open

42. If I_D goes to 16 mA, the possible faults are:

The JFET is shorted from drain to source or V_{DD} has increased.

43. If V_{DD} is changed to -20 V, I_D will change very little or none because the device is operating in the constant current region of the characteristic curve.

44. The device is off. The gate bias voltage must be less than $V_{GS(th)}$. The gate could be shorted or partially shorted to ground.

45. The device is saturated, so there is very little voltage from drain to source. This indicates that V_{GS} is too high. The 1 MΩ bias resistor is probably **open**.

Chapter 8

Section 8-8 System Application

46. With the 100 µF capacitor open, power supply noise or ripple *could* affect the sensor outputs, producing false readings and alarms.

47. From the graph in Figure 8–53:
For pH = 5, V_{OUT} = **300 mV**
For pH = 9, V_{OUT} = **–400 mV**

48. A possible problem is that the voltmeter has an input resistance of 1 MΩ instead of 10 MΩ and is loading the sensor ouput.

49. $V_{OUT} \cong 15\text{ V} - (2.9\text{ mA})(1\text{ k}\Omega)$ 15 V – 2.9 V = **12.1 V**

Data Sheet Problems

50. The 2N5457 is an *n*–channel JFET.

51. From the data sheet in Figure 8–14:
(a) For a 2N5457, $V_{GS(off)}$ = **–0.5 V** minimum
(b) For a 2N5457, $V_{DS(max)}$ = **25 V**
(c) For a 2N5458 @ 25°C, $P_{D(max)}$ = **310 mW**
(d) For a 2N5459, $V_{GS(rev)}$ = **–25 V** maximum

52. $P_{D(max)}$ = 310 mW – (2.82 mW/°C)(65°C – 25°C) = 310 mW –113 mW = **197 mW**

53. $g_{mo(min)} = y_{fs} =$ **2000 µS**

54. Typical $I_D = I_{DSS}$ = **9 mA**

55. From the data sheet in Figure 8–41:
Minimum $V_{GS(th)}$ = **1 V**

56. For a 2N7008 with V_{GS} = 10 V, I_D = **500 mA**

57. From the data sheet graph in Figure 8–52:
At V_{GS} = +3 V, $I_D \cong$ **13 mA**
At V_{GS} = –2 V, $I_D \cong$ **0.4 mA**

58. y_{fs} = 1500 µS at f = 1 kHz and at f = 1 MHz for both the 2N3796 and 2N3797.
There is **no change** in y_{fs} over the frequency range.

59. For a 2N3796, $V_{GS(off)}$ = **–3.0 V** typical

Chapter 8

Advanced Problems

60. For the circuit of Figure 8–71:

$$I_D = I_{DSS}\left(1 - \frac{V_{GS}}{V_{GS(OFF)}}\right)^2 \text{ Where } V_{GS} = I_D R_S$$

From the 2N5457 data sheet:

$I_{DSS(min)} = 1.0$ mA and $V_{GS(off)} = -0.5$ V minimum
$I_D = 66.3$ μA
$V_{GS} = -(66.3$ μA$)(5.6$ kΩ$) = \mathbf{-0.371}$ **V**
$V_{DS} = 12$ V $- (66.3$ μA$)(10$ kΩ $+ 5.6$ kΩ$) = \mathbf{11.0}$ **V**

61. For the circuit of Figure 8–72:

$$V_G = \left(\frac{3.3 \text{ k}\Omega}{13.3 \text{ k}\Omega}\right)9 \text{ V} = (0.248)(9 \text{ V}) = 2.23 \text{ V}$$

From the equation,

$$I_D = I_{DSS}\left(1 - \frac{V_{GS}}{V_{GS(OFF)}}\right)^2 \text{ Where } V_{GS} = V_G - I_D R_S$$

I_D is maximum for $I_{DSS(max)}$ and $V_{GS(off)}$ max, so that
$I_{DSS} = 16$ mA and $V_{GS(off)} = -8.0$ V
$I_D = \mathbf{3.58}$ **mA**
$V_{GS} = 2.23$ V $- (3.58$ mA$)(1.8$ kΩ$) = 2.23$ V $- 6.45$ V $= \mathbf{-4.21}$ **V**

62. From the 2N5457 data sheet:

$I_{DSS(min)} = 1.$ mA and $V_{GS(off)} = -0.5$ V minimum
$I_{D(min)} = \mathbf{66.3}$ **μA**
$V_{DS(max)} = 12$ V $- (66.3$ μA$)(15.6$ kΩ$) = \mathbf{11.0}$ **V**

and

$I_{DSS(max)} = 5.$ mA and $V_{GS(off)} = -6.0$ V maximum
$I_{D(max)} = \mathbf{677}$ **μA**
$V_{DS(min)} = 12$ V $- (677$ μA$)(15.6$ kΩ$) = \mathbf{1.4}$ **V**

63. $V_{pH} = +300$ mV
$I_D = (2.9$ mA$)(1 + 0.3$ V$/5.0$ V$)^2 = (2.9$ mA$)(1.06)^2 = 3.26$ mA
$V_{DS} = 15$ V $- (3.26$ mA$)(2.76$ kΩ$) = 15$ V $- 8.99$ V $= \mathbf{+6.01}$ **V**

Chapter 8

64. $1 \text{ mA} = I_{DSS}\left(1 - \frac{(1 \text{ mA})R_S}{V_{GS(off)}}\right)^2$

$1 \text{ mA} = 2.9 \text{ mA}\left(1 - \frac{(1 \text{ mA})R_S}{-0.5 \text{ V}}\right)^2$

$0.345 = \left(1 - \frac{(1 \text{ mA})R_S}{-0.5 \text{ V}}\right)^2$

$0.587 = 1 - \frac{(1 \text{ mA})R_S}{-0.5 \text{ V}}$

$0.413 = \frac{(1 \text{ mA})R_S}{-0.5 \text{ V}}$

$R_S = 2.06 \text{ k}\Omega$

Use $R_S = \mathbf{2.2 \text{ k}\Omega}$

Then $I_D = 963 \text{ }\mu\text{A}$

$V_{GS} = V_S = (963 \text{ }\mu\text{A})(2.2 \text{ k}\Omega) = 2.19 \text{ V}$

So, $V_D = 2.19 \text{ V} + 4.5 \text{ V} = 6.62 \text{ V}$

$R_D = \frac{9 \text{ V} - 6.62 \text{ V}}{963 \text{ }\mu\text{A}} = 2.47 \text{ k}\Omega$

Use $R_D = \mathbf{2.4 \text{ k}\Omega}$

So, $V_{DS} = 9 \text{ V} - (963 \text{ }\mu\text{A})(4.6 \text{ k}\Omega) = 4.57 \text{ V}$

65. Let $I_D = 20 \text{ mA}$

$R_D = \frac{4 \text{ V}}{20 \text{ mA}} = \mathbf{200 \text{ }\Omega}$

Let $V_S = 2 \text{ V}$

$R_S = \frac{2 \text{ V}}{20 \text{ mA}} = \mathbf{100 \text{ }\Omega}$

For the 2N7008

$K = \frac{I_{D(on)}}{\left(V_{GS(on)} - V_{GS(th)}\right)^2} = \frac{500 \text{ mA}}{(10 \text{ V} - 1 \text{ V})^2} = 6.17 \text{ mA}/\text{V}^2$

Let $I_D = 20 \text{ mA}$

$\left(V_{GS} - 1 \text{ V}\right)^2 = \frac{20 \text{ V}}{6.17 \text{ mA}/\text{V}^2} = 3.24$

$V_{GS} - 1 \text{ V} = 1.8 \text{ V}$

$V_{GS} = 2.8 \text{ V}$

$V_G = V_S + 2.8 \text{ V} = 4.8 \text{ V}$

For the voltage divider:

$\frac{R_1}{R_2} = \frac{7.2 \text{ V}}{4.8 \text{ V}} = 1.5$

Let $R_2 = \mathbf{10 \text{ k}\Omega}$

$R_1 = (1.5)(10 \text{ k}\Omega) = \mathbf{15 \text{ k}\Omega}$

Chapter 9
Small Signal FET Amplifiers

Section 9-1 Small-Signal Amplifier Operation

1. (a) N-channel D-MOSFET with zero-bias.
   $V_{GS} = 0$ V.
   (b) P-channel JFET with self-bias.
   $V_{GS} = -I_D R_S = (-3 \text{ mA})(330 \text{ }\Omega) = -0.99$ V
   N-channel E-MOSFET with voltage-divider bias.
   (c) $V_{GS} = \left(\dfrac{R_2}{R_1 + R_2}\right) V_{DD} = \left(\dfrac{4.7 \text{ k}\Omega}{14.7 \text{ k}\Omega}\right) 12 \text{ V} = 3.84$ V

2. (a) $V_G = 0$ V, $V_S = 0$ V
   $V_D = V_{DD} - I_D R_D = 15 \text{ V} - (8 \text{ mA})(1 \text{ k}\Omega) = 7$ V
   (b) $V_G = 0$ V
   $V_S = -I_D R_D = -(3 \text{ mA})(330 \text{ }\Omega) = -0.99$ V
   $V_D = V_{DD} - I_D R_D = -10 \text{ V} - (-3 \text{ mA})(1.5 \text{ k}\Omega) = -5.5$ V
   (c) $V_G = \left(\dfrac{R_2}{R_1 + R_2}\right) V_{DD} = \left(\dfrac{4.7 \text{ k}\Omega}{14.7 \text{ k}\Omega}\right) 12 \text{ V} = 3.84$ V
   $V_S = 0$ V
   $V_D = V_{DD} - I_D R_D = 12 \text{ V} - (6 \text{ mA})(1 \text{ k}\Omega) = 6$ V

3. (a) n-channel D-MOSFET
   (b) n-channel JFET
   (c) p-channel E-MOSFET

4. From the curve in Figure 9-7(a) in the text:
   $I_{d(pp)} \cong 3.9 \text{ mA} - 1.3 \text{ mA} = 2.6$ mA

5. From the curve in Figure 9-7(b) in the text:
   $I_{d(pp)} \cong 6 \text{ mA} - 2 \text{ mA} = 4$ mA
   From the curve in Figure 9-7(c) in the text:
   $I_{d(pp)} \cong 4.5 \text{ mA} - 1.3 \text{ mA} = 3.2$ mA

Chapter 9

Section 8-2 FET Amplification

6.
    (a) $I_D = g_m V_{gs} = (6000\ \mu S)(10\ mV) = \mathbf{60\ \mu A}$
    (b) $I_D = g_m V_{gs} = (6000\ \mu S)(150\ mV) = \mathbf{900\ \mu A}$
    (c) $I_D = g_m V_{gs} = (6000\ \mu S)(0.6\ V) = \mathbf{3.6\ mA}$
    (d) $I_D = g_m V_{gs} = (6000\ \mu S)(1\ V) = \mathbf{6\ mA}$

7. $A_v = g_m R_d$

$$R_d = \frac{A_v}{g_m} = \frac{20}{3500\ \mu S} = \mathbf{5.71\ k\Omega}$$

8. $A_v = \left(\dfrac{R_D r_{ds}}{R_D + r_{ds}}\right) g_m = \left(\dfrac{(4.7\ k\Omega)(12\ k\Omega)}{16.7\ k\Omega}\right) 4.2\ mS = \mathbf{14.2}$

9. $R_d = R_D \parallel r_{ds} = 4.7\ k\Omega \parallel 12\ k\Omega = 3.38\ k\Omega$

$$A_v = \frac{g_m R_d}{1 + g_m R_s} = \frac{(4.2\ mS)(3.38\ k\Omega)}{1 + (4.2\ mS)(1\ k\Omega)} = \mathbf{2.73}$$

Section 9-3 Common-Source Amplifiers

10. $V_D = V_{DD} - I_D R_D = 12\ V - (2.83\ mA)(1.5\ k\Omega) = \mathbf{7.76\ V}$
$V_S = I_D R_S = (2.83\ mA)(1\ k\Omega) = \mathbf{2.83\ V}$
$V_{DS} = V_D - V_S = 7.76\ V - 2.83\ V = \mathbf{4.93\ V}$
$V_{GS} = V_G - V_S = 0\ V - 2.83\ V = \mathbf{-2.83\ V}$

11. $A_v = g_m R_d = g_m(R_D \parallel R_L) = 5000\ \mu S(1.5\ k\Omega \parallel 10\ k\Omega) = 6.52$
$V_{pp(out)} = (2.828)(50\ mV)(6.52) = \mathbf{920\ mV}$

12. $A_v = g_m R_d$
$R_d = 1.5\ k\Omega \parallel 1.5\ k\Omega = 750\ \Omega$
$A_v = (5000\ \mu S)(750\ \Omega) = 3.75$
$V_{out} = A_v V_{in} = (3.75)(50\ mV) = \mathbf{188\ mV}$ rms

13.
    (a) $A_v = g_m R_d = g_m(R_D \parallel R_L) = 3.8\ mS(1.2\ k\Omega \parallel 22\ k\Omega) = 3.8\ mS(1138\ \Omega) = \mathbf{4.32}$
    (b) $A_v = g_m R_d = g_m(R_D \parallel R_L) = 5.5\ mS(2.2\ k\Omega \parallel 10\ k\Omega) = 5.5\ mS(1.8\ k\Omega) = \mathbf{9.92}$

Chapter 9

14. See Figure 9-1.

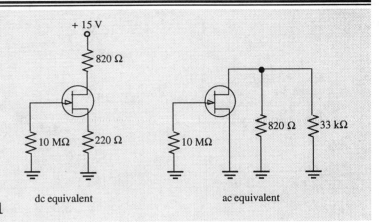

Figure 9-1

15. $I_D = \dfrac{I_{DSS}}{2} = \dfrac{15 \text{ mA}}{2} = \textbf{7.5 mA}$

16. $V_{GS} = (7.5 \text{ mA})(220 \text{ }\Omega) = 1.65 \text{ V}$

$g_{m0} = \dfrac{2I_{DSS}}{|V_{GS(off)}|} = \dfrac{2(15 \text{ mA})}{4 \text{ V}} = 7.5 \text{ mS}$

$g_m = (7.5 \text{ mS})(1 - 1.65 \text{ V}/4 \text{ V}) = 4.41 \text{ mS}$

$A_v = \dfrac{g_m R_d}{1 + g_m R_s} = \dfrac{(4.41 \text{ mS})(820 \text{ }\Omega \parallel 33 \text{ k}\Omega)}{1 + (4.41 \text{ mS})(220 \text{ }\Omega)} = \dfrac{(4.41 \text{ mS})(800 \text{ }\Omega)}{1 + 0.97} = \textbf{1.79}$

17. $A_v = g_m R_d = (4.41 \text{ mS})(820 \text{ }\Omega \parallel 33 \text{ k}\Omega \parallel 4.7 \text{ k}\Omega) = (4.41 \text{ mS})(684 \text{ }\Omega) = \textbf{3.02}$

18. $I_D = \dfrac{I_{DSS}}{2} = \dfrac{9 \text{ mA}}{2} = \textbf{4.5 mA}$

$V_{GS} = -I_D R_S = -(4.5 \text{ mA})(330 \text{ }\Omega) = \textbf{-1.49 V}$

$V_{DS} = V_{DD} - I_D(R_D + R_S) = 9 \text{ V} - (4.5 \text{ mA})(1.33 \text{ k}\Omega) = \textbf{3 V}$

19. $A_v = g_m R_d = g_m(R_D \parallel R_L) = 3700 \text{ }\mu\text{S}(1 \text{ k}\Omega \parallel 10 \text{ k}\Omega) = 3700 \text{ }\mu\text{S}(909 \text{ }\Omega) = 3.36$

$V_{out} = A_v V_{in} = (3.36)(10 \text{ mV}) = \textbf{33.6 mV rms}$

20. $V_{GS} = \left(\dfrac{R_2}{R_1 + R_2}\right)V_{DD} = \left(\dfrac{6.8 \text{ k}\Omega}{24.8 \text{ k}\Omega}\right)20 \text{ V} = \textbf{5.48 V}$

$K = \dfrac{I_{D(on)}}{\left(V_{GS} - V_{GS(th)}\right)^2} = \dfrac{18 \text{ mA}}{\left(10 \text{ V} - 2.5 \text{ V}\right)^2} = 0.32 \text{ mA/V}^2$

$I_D = K\left(V_{GS} - V_{GS(th)}\right)^2 = 0.32 \text{ mA/V}^2(5.48 \text{ V} - 2.5 \text{ V})^2 = \textbf{2.84 mA}$

$V_{DS} = V_{DD} - I_D R_D = 20 \text{ V} - (2.84 \text{ mA})(1 \text{ k}\Omega) = \textbf{17.2 V}$

21. $R_{IN} = \left|\dfrac{V_{GS}}{I_{GSS}}\right| = \left|\dfrac{-15 \text{ V}}{25 \text{ nA}}\right| = 600 \text{ M}\Omega$

$R_{in} = 10 \text{ M}\Omega \parallel 600 \text{ M}\Omega = \textbf{9.84 M}\boldsymbol{\Omega}$

Chapter 9

22. $A_v = g_m R_d = 4.8\text{ mS}(1\text{ k}\Omega \parallel 10\text{ M}\Omega) \cong 4.8$

$V_{out} = A_v V_{in} = 4.8(10\text{ mV}) = \mathbf{48\text{ mV rms}}$

$I_D = I_{DSS} = 15\text{ mA}$

$V_D = 24\text{ V} - (15\text{ mA})(1\text{ k}\Omega) = \mathbf{9\text{ V}}$

See Figure 9-2.

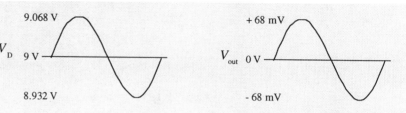

Figure 9-2

23. $V_{GS} = \left(\dfrac{R_2}{R_1+R_2}\right)V_{DD} = \left(\dfrac{47\text{ k}\Omega}{94\text{ k}\Omega}\right)18\text{ V} = \mathbf{9\text{ V}}$

$K = \dfrac{I_{D(on)}}{\left(V_{GS}-V_{GS(th)}\right)^2} = \dfrac{8\text{ mA}}{(12\text{ V}-4\text{ V})^2} = 0.125\text{ mA/V}^2$

$I_{D(on)} = K\left(V_{GS}-V_{GS(th)}\right)^2 = 0.125\text{ mA/V}^2(9\text{ V}-4\text{ V})^2 = \mathbf{3.13\text{ mA}}$

$V_{DS} = V_{DD} - I_D R_D = 18\text{ V} - (3.125\text{ mA})(1.5\text{ k}\Omega) = \mathbf{13.3\text{ V}}$

$A_v = g_m R_D = 4500\text{ μS}(1.5\text{ k}\Omega) = 6.75$

$V_{ds} = A_v V_{in} = 6.75(100\text{ mV}) = \mathbf{675\text{ mV rms}}$

Section 9-4 Common-Drain Amplifiers

24. $R_s = 1.2\text{ k}\Omega \parallel 10\text{ M}\Omega \cong 1.2\text{ k}\Omega$

$A_v = \dfrac{g_m R_s}{1+g_m R_s} = \dfrac{(5500\text{ μS})(1.2\text{ k}\Omega)}{1+(5500\text{ μS})(1.2\text{ k}\Omega)} = \mathbf{0.868}$

$R_{IN} = \left|\dfrac{V_{GS}}{I_{BSS}}\right| = \left|\dfrac{-15\text{ V}}{50\text{ pA}}\right| = 3\times 10^{11}\text{ Ω}$

$R_{in} = 10\text{ M}\Omega \parallel 3\times 10^{11}\text{ Ω} \cong \mathbf{10\text{ M}\Omega}$

25. $R_s = 1.2\text{ k}\Omega \parallel 10\text{M}\Omega \cong 10\text{ M}\Omega$

$A_v = \dfrac{g_m R_s}{1+g_m R_s} = \dfrac{(3000\text{ μS})(10\text{ M}\Omega)}{1+(3000\text{ μS})(10\text{ M}\Omega)} = \mathbf{0.783}$

$R_{IN} = \left|\dfrac{V_{GS}}{I_{GSS}}\right| = \left|\dfrac{-15\text{ V}}{50\text{ pA}}\right| = 3\times 10^{11}\text{ Ω}$

$R_{in} = 10\text{M}\Omega \parallel 3\times 10^{11}\text{ Ω} \cong \mathbf{10\text{ M}\Omega}$

Chapter 9

26. (a) $R_s = 4.7 \text{ k}\Omega \parallel 47 \text{ k}\Omega = 4.27 \text{ k}\Omega$

$$A_v = \frac{g_m R_s}{1 + g_m R_s} = \frac{(3000 \text{ μS})(4.27 \text{ k}\Omega)}{1 + (3000 \text{ μS})(4.27 \text{ k}\Omega)} = \mathbf{0.928}$$

(b) $R_s = 1 \text{ k}\Omega \parallel 100 \text{ }\Omega = 90.9 \text{ k}\Omega$

$$A_v = \frac{g_m R_s}{1 + g_m R_s} = \frac{(4300 \text{ μS})(90.9 \text{ }\Omega)}{1 + (4300 \text{ μS})(90.9 \text{ k}\Omega)} = \mathbf{0.281}$$

27. (a) $R_s = 4.7 \text{ k}\Omega \parallel 10 \text{ k}\Omega = 3.2 \text{ k}\Omega$

$$A_v = \frac{g_m R_s}{1 + g_m R_s} = \frac{(3000 \text{ μS})(3.2 \text{ k}\Omega)}{1 + (3000 \text{ μS})(3.2 \text{ k}\Omega)} = \mathbf{0.906}$$

(b) $R_s = 100 \text{ }\Omega \parallel 10 \text{ k}\Omega = 99 \text{ }\Omega$

$$A_v = \frac{g_m R_s}{1 + g_m R_s} = \frac{(4300 \text{ μS})(99 \text{ }\Omega)}{1 + (4300 \text{ μS})(99 \text{ }\Omega)} = \mathbf{0.299}$$

Section 9-5 Common-Gate Amplifiers

28. $A_v = g_m R_d = 4000 \text{ μS}(1.5 \text{ k}\Omega) = \mathbf{6.0}$

29. $R_{in(source)} = \dfrac{1}{g_m} = \dfrac{1}{4000 \text{ μS}} = \mathbf{250 \text{ }\Omega}$

30. $A_v = g_m R_d = 3500 \text{ μS}(10 \text{ k}\Omega) = \mathbf{35}$

$R_{in} = R_S \parallel \left(\dfrac{1}{g_m}\right) = 2.2 \text{ k}\Omega \parallel \left(\dfrac{1}{3500 \text{ μS}}\right) = \mathbf{253 \text{ }\Omega}$

Section 9-6 Troubleshooting

31. (a) $V_{D1} = V_{DD}$; No signal at Q_1 drain; No output signal
(b) $V_{D1} \cong 0$ V (floating); No signal at Q_1 drain; No output signal
(c) $V_{GS1} = 0$ V; $V_S = 0$ V; V_{D1} less than normal; Clipped output signal
(d) Correct signal at Q_1 drain; No signal at Q_2 gate; No output signal
(e) $V_{D2} = V_{DD}$; Correct signal at Q_2 gate; No Q_2 drain signal or output signal

Chapter 9

32. (a) $V_{out} = 0$ V if C_1 is open.

(b) $A_{v1} = g_m R_d = 5000 \, \mu S(1.5 \, k\Omega) = 7.5$

$A_{v2} = \dfrac{g_m R_d}{1 + g_m R_s} = \dfrac{7.5}{1 + (5000 \, \mu S)(470 \, \Omega)} = 2.24$

$A_v = A_{v1} A_{v2} = (7.5)(2.24) = 16.8$

$V_{out} = A_v V_{in} = (16.8)(10 \, mV) = 168 \, mV$

(c) No effect on V_{out} unless V_D is so low that clipping occurs.

(d) No V_{out} because there is no signal at the Q_2 gate.

Section 9-7 System Application

33. The 10 µF capacitor between the drain of Q_1 and the gate of Q_2 is open.

34. At test point 2: 250 mV is correct

At test point 3: 800 mV is approximately correct

At test point 4: 530 mV is too low

At test point 5: 2.12 V is too low but consistent with TP4

Most likely, the coupling capacitor between stage 1 and stage 2 is leaky. Replace

35. $V_{D2} = 12 \, V - (5.10 \, mA)(1.5 \, k\Omega) = \mathbf{4.35 \, V}$

$V_{d1} = (100 \, mV)(2200 \, \mu S)(1.5 \, k\Omega) = 330 \, mV$

$V_{d2} = (330 \, mV)(2600 \, \mu S)(1.5 \, k\Omega) = \mathbf{1.29 \, V \, rms}$

Data Sheet Problems

36. The 2N3796 FET is an **n–channel D–MOSFET**.

37. (a) For a 2N3797, the typical $V_{GS(off)} = \mathbf{-3.0 \, V}$
(b) For a 2N3797, $V_{DS(max)} = \mathbf{20 \, V}$
(c) At $T_A = 25°C$, $P_{D(max)} = \mathbf{200 \, mW}$
(d) For a 2N3797, $V_{GS(max)} = \mathbf{\pm 10 \, V}$

38. $P_D = 200 \, mW - (1.14 \, mW/°C)(55°C - 25°C) = \mathbf{166 \, mW}$

39. For a 2N3796 with $f = 1$ kHz, $g_{m0} = \mathbf{900 \, \mu S}$ minimum

40. At $V_{GS} = 3.5$ V and $V_{DS} = 10$ V,

$I_{D(min)} = \mathbf{9.0 \, mA}$, $I_{D(typ)} = \mathbf{14 \, mA}$, $I_{D(max)} = \mathbf{18 \, mA}$

41. For a zero–biased 2N3796, $I_{D(typ)} = \mathbf{1.5 \, mA}$

42. $A_{v(max)} = (1800 \, \mu S)(2.2 \, k\Omega) = \mathbf{3.96}$

Chapter 9

Advanced Problems

43. $R_{d(min)} = 1 \text{ k}\Omega \parallel 4 \text{ k}\Omega = 800 \text{ }\Omega$
$A_{v(min)} = (2.5 \text{ mS})(800 \text{ }\Omega) = \mathbf{2.0}$
$R_{d(max)} = 1 \text{ k}\Omega \parallel 10 \text{ k}\Omega = 909 \text{ }\Omega$
$A_{v(min)} = (7.5 \text{ mS})(909 \text{ }\Omega) = \mathbf{6.82}$

44. $I_{DSS(typ)} = 2.9 \text{ mA}$
$R_D + R_S = \dfrac{12 \text{ V}}{2.9 \text{ mA}} = 4.14 \text{ k}\Omega$
$\dfrac{1}{g_m} = \dfrac{1}{2300 \text{ }\mu S} = 435 \text{ }\Omega$
If $R_S = 0 \text{ }\Omega$, then $R_D \cong 4 \text{ k}\Omega$ (3.9 kΩ standard)
$A_v = (2300 \text{ }\mu S)(3.9 \text{ k}\Omega) = \mathbf{8.97}$
$V_{DS} = 24 \text{ V} - (2.9 \text{ mA})(3.9 \text{ k}\Omega) = 24 \text{ V} - 11.3 \text{ V} = \mathbf{12.7 \text{ V}}$
The circuit is a common–source zero–biased amplifier
with a drain resistor of 3.9 kΩ

45. To maintain $V_{DS} = 12$ V for the range of I_{DSS} values:
For $I_{DSS(min)} = 2$ mA
$R_D = \dfrac{12 \text{ V}}{2 \text{ mA}} = 6 \text{ k}\Omega$
For $I_{DSS(max)} = 6$ mA
$R_D = \dfrac{12 \text{ V}}{6 \text{ mA}} = 2 \text{ k}\Omega$
To maintain $A_v = 9$ for the range of g_m (y_{fs}) values:
For $g_{m(min)} = 1500 \text{ }\mu S$
$R_D = \dfrac{9}{1500 \text{ }\mu S} = 6 \text{ k}\Omega$
For $g_{m(max)} = 3000 \text{ }\mu S$
$R_D = \dfrac{9}{3000 \text{ }\mu S} = 3 \text{ k}\Omega$
A drain resistance consisting of a 2.2 kΩ fixed resistor in
series with a 5 kΩ variable resistor will provide more than sufficient
range to maintain a gain of 9 over the specified range of g_m values.
The dc voltage at the drain will vary with adjustment and depends on I_{DSS}.
The circuit cannot be modified to maintain both $V_{DS} = 12$ V and $A_v = 9$
over the full range of transistor parmeter values.

Chapter 10
Amplifier Frequency Response

Section 10-1 General Concepts

1. If $C_1 = C_2$, the critical frequencies are equal and they will both cause the gain to decrease at 40 dB/decade below f_c.

2. At sufficiently high frequencies, the reactances of the coupling capacitors become very small and the capacitors appear effectively as shorts, thus negligible signal voltage is dropped across them.

3. Bipolar: C_{be}, C_{bc}, and C_{ce}
   FET: C_{gs}, C_{gd}, and C_{ds}

Section 10-2 The Decibel

4. $$A_p = \frac{P_{out}}{P_{in}} = \frac{5 \text{ W}}{0.5 \text{ W}} = 10$$

   $$A_p(\text{dB}) = 10\log\left(\frac{P_{out}}{P_{in}}\right) = 10\log 10 = \mathbf{10 \text{ dB}}$$

5. $$V_{in} = \frac{V_{out}}{A_v} = \frac{1.2 \text{ V}}{50} = \mathbf{24 \text{ mV rms}}$$

   $$A_v(\text{dB}) = 20\log(A_v) = 20\log 50 = \mathbf{34.0 \text{ dB}}$$

6. The gain reduction is $20\log\left(\frac{25}{65}\right) = \mathbf{-8.3 \text{ dB}}$

7. (a) $10\log\left(\frac{2 \text{ mW}}{1 \text{ mW}}\right) = \mathbf{3 \text{ dBm}}$

   (b) $10\log\left(\frac{1 \text{ mW}}{1 \text{ mW}}\right) = \mathbf{0 \text{ dBm}}$

   (c) $10\log\left(\frac{4 \text{ mW}}{1 \text{ mW}}\right) = \mathbf{6 \text{ dBm}}$

   (d) $10\log\left(\frac{0.25 \text{ mW}}{1 \text{ mW}}\right) = \mathbf{-6.02 \text{ dBm}}$

Chapter 10

8. $V_B = \left(\dfrac{4.7 \text{ k}\Omega}{37.7 \text{ k}\Omega}\right) 20 \text{ V} = 1.79 \text{ V}$

$I_E = \dfrac{1.79 \text{ V}}{560 \text{ }\Omega} = 3.20 \text{ mA}$

$r'_e = \dfrac{25 \text{ mV}}{3.2 \text{ mA}} = 7.81 \text{ }\Omega$

$A_v = \dfrac{5.6 \text{ k}\Omega \parallel 2.2 \text{ k}\Omega}{7.81 \text{ }\Omega} = 202$

$A_{v(dB)} = 20\log(202) = \mathbf{46.1 \text{ dB}}$

At the critical frequencies,

$A_{v(dB)} = 46.1 \text{ dB} - 3 \text{ dB} = \mathbf{43.1 \text{ dB}}$

Section 10-3 Low-Frequency Amplifier Response

9. (a) $f_c = \dfrac{1}{2\pi RC} = \dfrac{1}{2\pi(100 \text{ }\Omega)(5 \text{ µF})} = \mathbf{318 \text{ Hz}}$

(b) $f_c = \dfrac{1}{2\pi RC} = \dfrac{1}{2\pi(1 \text{ k}\Omega)(0.1 \text{ µF})} = \mathbf{1.59 \text{ kHz}}$

10. $R_{\text{IN(base)}} = \beta_{DC} R_E = 12.5 \text{ k}\Omega$

$V_E = \left(\dfrac{R_2 \parallel R_{\text{IN(base)}}}{R_1 + R_2 \parallel R_{\text{IN(base)}}}\right) 9 \text{ V} - 0.7 \text{ V} = \left(\dfrac{4.7 \text{ k}\Omega \parallel 12.5 \text{ k}\Omega}{12 \text{ k}\Omega + 4.7 \text{ k}\Omega \parallel 12.5 \text{ k}\Omega}\right) 9 \text{ V} - 0.7 \text{ V} = 1.3 \text{ V}$

$I_E = \dfrac{V_E}{R_E} = \dfrac{1.3 \text{ V}}{100 \text{ }\Omega} = 13 \text{ mA}$

$r'_e = \dfrac{25 \text{ mV}}{13 \text{ mA}} = 1.92 \text{ }\Omega$

$R_{in(base)} = \beta_{ac} r'_e = (125)(1.92 \text{ }\Omega) = 240 \text{ }\Omega$

$R_{in} = 50 \text{ }\Omega + R_{in(base)} \parallel R_1 \parallel R_2 = 50 \text{ }\Omega + 240 \text{ }\Omega \parallel 12 \text{ k}\Omega \parallel 4.7 \text{ k}\Omega = 274 \text{ }\Omega$

For the input network:

$f_c = \dfrac{1}{2\pi R_{in} C_1} = \dfrac{1}{2\pi(274 \text{ }\Omega)(1 \text{ µF})} = \mathbf{578 \text{ Hz}}$

For the output network:

$f_c = \dfrac{1}{2\pi(R_c + R_L) C_2} = \dfrac{1}{2\pi(900 \text{ }\Omega)(1 \text{ µF})} = \mathbf{177 \text{ Hz}}$

For the bypass network:

$R_{TH} = R_1 \parallel R_2 \parallel R_s = 12 \text{ k}\Omega \parallel 4.7 \text{ k}\Omega \parallel 50 \text{ }\Omega \cong 49.3 \text{ }\Omega$

$f_c = \dfrac{1}{2\pi(r'_e + R_{TH}/\beta_{DC} \parallel R_E) C_3} = \dfrac{1}{2\pi(2.31 \text{ }\Omega)(10 \text{ µF})} = \mathbf{6.89 \text{ kHz}}$

$A_v = \dfrac{R_C \parallel R_L}{r'_e} = \dfrac{220 \text{ }\Omega \parallel 680 \text{ }\Omega}{1.92 \text{ }\Omega} = 86.6$

$A_v(\text{dB}) = 20\log(86.6) = 38.8 \text{ dB}$

The **bypass network** produces the dominant low critical frequency. See Figure 10-1.

Chapter 10

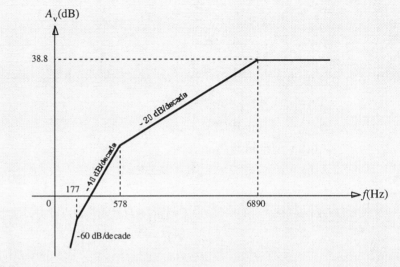

Figure 10-1

11. From Problem 10:
$A_{v(mid)} = 86.6$
$A_{v(mid)}(dB) = 38.7$ dB
For the input RC network: $f_c = 578$ Hz
For the output RC network: $f_c = 177$ Hz
For the bypass RC network: $f_c = 6.89$ kHz
The f_c of the bypass network is the dominant low critical frequency.
At $f = f_c = 6.89$ kHz
$A_v = A_{v(mid)} - 3$ dB $= 38.7$ dB $- 3$ dB $= \mathbf{35.7\ dB}$
At $f = 0.1 f_c$
$A_v = 38.75$ dB $- 20$ dB $= \mathbf{18.7\ dB}$
At $10 f_c$ (neglecting any high frequency effects)
$A_v = A_{v(mid)} = \mathbf{38.7\ dB}$

12. At $f = f_c$, $X_C = R$
$\theta = \tan^{-1}\left(\dfrac{X_C}{R}\right) = \tan^{-1}(1) = \mathbf{45°}$
At $f = 0.1 f_c$, $X_C = 10R$
$\theta = \tan^{-1}(10) = \mathbf{84.3°}$
At $f = 10 f_c$, $X_C = 0.1R$
$\theta = \tan^{-1}(0.1) = \mathbf{5.7°}$

Section 10-4 Miller Capacitance

13. Low frequency response: C_1, C_2, and C_3
High frequency response: C_{bc}, C_{be}, and C_{ce}

Chapter 10

14.
$$V_E \cong \left(\frac{R_2}{R_1+R_2}\right)V_{CC} - 0.7\text{ V} = \left(\frac{4.7\text{ k}\Omega}{37.7\text{ k}\Omega}\right)20\text{ V} - 0.7\text{ V} = 1.79\text{ V}$$

$$I_E = \frac{V_E}{R_E} = \frac{1.79\text{ V}}{560\text{ }\Omega} = 3.2\text{ mA}$$

$$r'_e = \frac{25\text{ mV}}{3.2\text{ mA}} = 7.8\text{ }\Omega$$

$$A_v = \frac{R_c}{r'_e} = \frac{2.2\text{ k}\Omega\text{ }\|\text{ }5.6\text{ k}\Omega}{7.8\text{ }\Omega} = 202$$

$$C_{in(miller)} = C_{bc}(A_v + 1) = 4\text{ pF}(202 + 1) = \mathbf{812\text{ pF}}$$

15.
$$C_{out(miller)} = C_{bc}\left(\frac{A_v+1}{A_v}\right) = 4\text{ pF}\left(\frac{203}{202}\right) = \mathbf{4\text{ pF}}$$

16.
$$V_B = \left(\frac{22\text{ k}\Omega}{22\text{ k}\Omega + 47\text{ k}\Omega}\right)12\text{ V} = 3.83\text{ V}$$

$$V_E = V_B - 0.7\text{ V} = 3.83\text{ V} - 0.7\text{ V} = 3.13\text{ V}$$

$$I_E = \frac{V_E}{R_E} = \frac{3.13\text{ V}}{270\text{ }\Omega} = 11.6\text{ mA}$$

$$r'_e = \frac{25\text{ mV}}{I_E} = \frac{25\text{ mV}}{11.6\text{ mA}} = 2.16\text{ }\Omega$$

$$A_v = \frac{R_c}{r'_e} = \frac{560\text{ }\Omega\text{ }\|\text{ }10\text{ k}\Omega}{2.16\text{ }\Omega} = 246$$

$$C_{in(miller)} = C_{bc}(A_v + 1) = 2\text{ pF}(247\text{ pF}) = \mathbf{494\text{ pF}}$$

$$C_{out(miller)} = C_{bc}\left(\frac{A_v+1}{A_v}\right) = 2\text{ pF}\left(\frac{247}{246}\right) \cong \mathbf{2\text{ pF}}$$

17. See Figure 10-2.

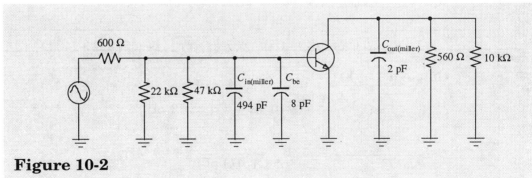

Figure 10-2

Chapter 10

18. $I_D = 3.36$ mA using program
$V_{GS} = -(3.36\text{ mA})(1\text{ k}\Omega) = -3.36$ V

$g_{m0} = \dfrac{2(10\text{ mA})}{8\text{ V}} = 2.5$ mS

$g_m = (2.5\text{ mS})\left(1 - \dfrac{3.36\text{ V}}{8\text{ V}}\right) = 1.45$ mS

$A_v = g_m R_d = (1.45\text{ mS})(1\text{ k}\Omega \parallel 10\text{ k}\Omega) = 1.32$

$C_{gd} = C_{rss} = 3$ pF

$C_{in(miller)} = C_{gd}(A_v + 1) = 3\text{ pF}(2.32) = \mathbf{6.95\text{ pF}}$

$C_{out(miller)} = C_{gd}\left(\dfrac{A_v + 1}{A_v}\right) = 3\text{ pF}\left(\dfrac{2.32}{1.32}\right) = \mathbf{5.28\text{ pF}}$

$C_{gs} = C_{iss} - C_{rss} = 10\text{ pF} - 3\text{ pF} = 7$ pF

See Figure 10-3.

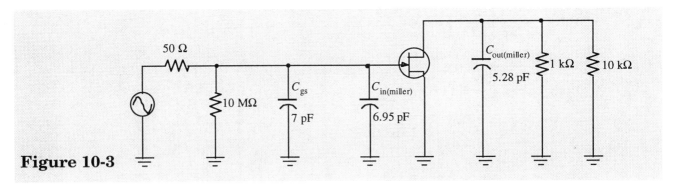

Figure 10-3

Section 10-5   High-Frequency Amplifier Response

19. From Problems 10 and 11:

$r_e' = 1.92\ \Omega$ and $A_{v(mid)} = 86.6$

Input network:

$C_{in(miller)} = C_{bc}(A_v + 1) = 10\text{ pF}(86.6) = 876$ pF

$C_T = C_{be} \parallel C_{in(miller)} = 25\text{ pF} + 876\text{ pF} = 901$ pF

$f_c = \dfrac{1}{2\pi(R_s \parallel R_1 \parallel R_2 \parallel \beta_{ac}r_e)C_T} = \dfrac{1}{2\pi(50\ \Omega \parallel 12\text{ k}\Omega \parallel 4.7\text{ k}\Omega \parallel 240\ \Omega)901\text{ pF}} = \mathbf{4.32\text{ MHz}}$

Output network:

$C_{out(miller)} = C_{bc}\left(\dfrac{A_v + 1}{A_v}\right) = 10\text{ pF}\left(\dfrac{87.6}{86.6}\right) = 10.1$ pF

$f_c = \dfrac{1}{2\pi R_c C_{out(miller)}} = \dfrac{1}{2\pi(166\ \Omega)(10.1\text{ pF})} = \mathbf{94.9\text{ MHz}}$

Therefore, the dominant high critical frequency is determined by the input network: $f_c = 4.32$ MHz. See Figure 10-4.

Chapter 10

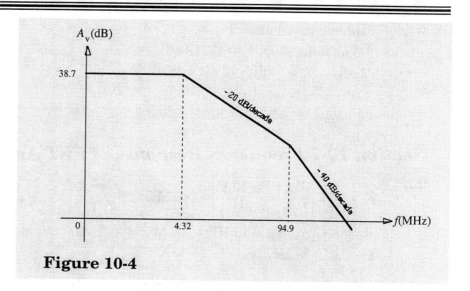

Figure 10-4

20. At $f = 0.1f_c = 458$ kHz:
$A_v = A_{v(mid)} = $ **38.7 dB**
At $f = f_c = 4.58$ MHz:
$A_v = A_{v(mid)} - 3$ dB $= 38.75$ dB $- 3$ dB $=$ **35.7 dB**
At $f = 10f_c = 45.8$ MHz:
$A_v = A_{v(mid)} - 20$ dB $= 38.75$ dB $- 20$ dB $=$ **18.7 dB**
At $f = 100f_c = 458$ MHz:
The rolloff rate changes to -40 dB/decade at $f = 94.6$ MHz. So, for frequencies from 45.8 MHz to 94.6 MHz, the rolloff rate is -20 dB/decade and above 94.6 MHz it is -40 dB/decade.
The change in frequency from 45.8 MHz to 94.63 MHz represents
$\dfrac{94.6 \text{ MHz} - 45.8 \text{ MHz}}{458 \text{ MHz} - 45.8 \text{ MHz}} \times 100\% = 11.8\%$
So, for 11.8 % of the decade from 45.8 MHz to 458 MHz, the rolloff rate is -20 dB/decade and for the remaining 88.2 % of the decade, the rolloff rate is -40 dB/decade.
$A_v = 18.7$ dB $- (0.118)(20$ dB$) - (0.882)(40$ dB$) = 18.7$ dB $- 2.36$ dB $- 35.3$ dB $=$ **- 19 dB**

Section 10-6 Total Amplifier Frequency Response

21. $f_{cl} =$ **136 Hz**
$f_{cu} =$ **8 kHz**

22. From Problems 10 and 19:
$f_{cu} = 4.32$ MHz and $f_{cl} = 6.89$ kHz
$BW = f_{cu} - f_{cl} = 4.32$ MHz $- 6.89$ kHz $=$ **4.313 MHz**

23. $f_T = (BW)A_{v(mid)}$
$BW = \dfrac{f_T}{A_{v(mid)}} = \dfrac{200 \text{ MHz}}{38} =$ **5.26 MHz**
Therefore, $f_{cu} \cong BW =$ **5.26 MHz**

Chapter 10

24. 6 dB/octave rolloff:

At $2f_{cu}$: $A_v = 50$ dB - 6 dB = **44 dB**

At $4f_{cu}$: $A_v = 50$ dB - 12 dB = **38 dB**

20 dB/decade rolloff:

At $10f_{cu}$: $A_v = 50$ dB - 20 dB = **30 dB**

Section 10-7 Frequency Response of FET Amplifiers

25.
$$R_{in(gate)} = \left|\frac{V_{GS}}{I_{GSS}}\right| = \left|\frac{-10 \text{ V}}{50 \text{ nA}}\right| = 200 \text{ M}\Omega$$

$R_{in} = R_G \parallel R_{in(gate)} = 10 \text{ M}\Omega \parallel 200 \text{ M}\Omega = 9.52 \text{ M}\Omega$

For the input network:
$$f_c = \frac{1}{2\pi R_{in} C_1} = \frac{1}{2\pi(9.52 \text{ M}\Omega)(0.005 \text{ µF})} = \textbf{3.34 Hz}$$

For the output network:
$$f_c = \frac{1}{2\pi(R_D + R_L)C_2} = \frac{1}{2\pi(560 \text{ }\Omega + 10 \text{ k}\Omega)(0.005 \text{ µF})} = \textbf{3.01 kHz}$$

The **output network is dominant**. See Figure 10-5.

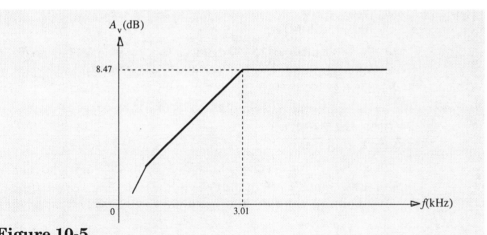

Figure 10-5

26. (a) $g_m = g_{m0} = \dfrac{2(15 \text{ mA})}{6 \text{ V}} = 5 \text{ mS}$

$A_{v(mid)} = g_m(R_D \parallel R_L) = 5 \text{ mS}(560 \text{ }\Omega \parallel 10 \text{ k}\Omega) = 2.65$

$A_{v(mid)}(\text{dB}) = 8.47$ dB

At f_c:

$A_v = 8.47$ dB - 3 dB = **5.47 dB**

At $0.1f_c$:

$A_v = 8.47$ dB - 20 dB = **-11.5 dB**

At $10f_c$:

$A_v = A_{v(mid)} =$ **8.47 dB** (if $10f_c$ is still in midrange)

Chapter 10

(b) At $f = f_c$, $X_C = R$

$$\theta = \tan^{-1}\left(\frac{X_C}{R}\right) = \tan^{-1}(1) = \mathbf{45°}$$

At $f = 0.1f_c$, $X_C = 10R$

$$\theta = \tan^{-1}\left(\frac{X_C}{R}\right) = \tan^{-1}(10) = \mathbf{84.3°}$$

At $f = 10f_c$, $X_C = 0.1R$

$$\theta = \tan^{-1}\left(\frac{X_C}{R}\right) = \tan^{-1}(0.1) = \mathbf{5.7°}$$

27. $C_{gd} = C_{rss} = 4$ pF
$C_{gs} = C_{iss} - C_{rss} = 10$ pF $- 4$ pF $= 6$ pF

Input network:

$C_{in(miller)} = C_{gd}(A_v + 1) = 4$ pF$(2.65 + 1) = 14.6$ pF

$C_T = C_{gs} \| C_{in(miller)} = 6$ pF $+ 14.6$ pF $= 20.6$ pF

$$f_c = \frac{1}{2\pi R_s C_T} = \frac{1}{2\pi(600\ \Omega)(20.6\ \text{pF})} = \mathbf{12.9\ MHz}$$

Output network:

$$C_{out(miller)} = C_{gd}\left(\frac{A_v + 1}{A_v}\right) = 4\ \text{pF}\left(\frac{2.65 + 1}{2.65}\right) = 5.51\ \text{pF}$$

$$f_c = \frac{1}{2\pi R_d C_{out(miller)}} = \frac{1}{2\pi(530\ \Omega)(5.51\ \text{pF})} = \mathbf{54.5\ MHz}$$

The input network is dominant.

28. From Problem 27: For the input network, $f_c = 12.9$ MHz and for the outp;ut network, $f_c = 54.5$ MHz
The dominant critical frequency is 12.9 MHz.
At $f = 0.1f_c = 1.29$ MHz: $A_v = A_{v(mid)} = \mathbf{8.47\ dB}$, $\theta = \mathbf{0°}$

At $f = f_c = 12.9$ MHz: $A_v = A_{v(mid)} - 3$ dB $= 8.47$ dB $- 3$ dB $= \mathbf{5.47\ dB}$, $\theta = \tan^{-1}(1) = \mathbf{45°}$
At $f = 10f_c = 129$ MHz:
From 12.9 MHz to 54.5 MHz the rolloff is -20 dB/decade. From 54.5 MHz to 129 MHz the rolloff is -40 dB/decade.
The change in frequency from 12.9 MHz to 54.5 MHz represents
$$\frac{54.5\ \text{MHz} - 12.9\ \text{MHz}}{129\ \text{MHz} - 12.9\ \text{MHz}} \times 100\ \% = 35.8\ \%$$
So, for 35.8 % of the decade, the rolloff rate is -20 dB/decade and for 64.2 % of the decade, the rate is -40 dB/decade.
$A_v = 5.47$ dB $- (0.358)(20$ dB$) - (0.642)(40$ dB$) = \mathbf{-13.1\ dB}$
At $f = 100f_c = 1290$ MHz: $A_v = -13.1$ dB $- 40$ dB $= \mathbf{-53.1\ dB}$

Chapter 10

Section 10-8 Frequency Response of Multistage Amplifiers

29. Dominant f'_{cl} = **230 Hz**

Dominant f'_{cu} = **1.2 MHz**

30. $BW = 1.2 \text{ MHz} - 230 \text{ Hz} \cong \mathbf{1.2 \text{ MHz}}$

31. $f'_{cl} = \dfrac{400 \text{ Hz}}{\sqrt{2^{1/2} - 1}} = \dfrac{400 \text{ Hz}}{0.643} = 622 \text{ Hz}$

$f'_{cu} = (800 \text{ kHz})\sqrt{2^{1/2} - 1} = 0.643(800 \text{ kHz}) = 515 \text{ kHz}$

$BW = 515 \text{ kHz} - 622 \text{ Hz} \cong \mathbf{514 \text{ kHz}}$

32. $f'_{cl} = \dfrac{50 \text{ Hz}}{\sqrt{2^{1/3} - 1}} = \dfrac{50 \text{ Hz}}{0.510} = \mathbf{98.1 \text{ Hz}}$

33. $f'_{cl} = \dfrac{125 \text{ Hz}}{\sqrt{2^{1/2} - 1}} = \dfrac{125 \text{ Hz}}{0.643} = 194 \text{ Hz}$

$f'_{cu} = 2.5 \text{ MHz}$

$BW = 2.5 \text{ MHz} - 194 \text{ Hz} \cong \mathbf{2.5 \text{ MHz}}$

Section 10-9 Frequency Response Measurement

34. $f_{cl} = \dfrac{0.35}{t_f} = \dfrac{0.35}{1 \text{ ms}} = \mathbf{350 \text{ Hz}}$

$f_{ch} = \dfrac{0.35}{t_r} = \dfrac{0.35}{20 \text{ ns}} = \mathbf{17.5 \text{ MHz}}$

35. Increase the frequency until the output voltage drops to 3.54 V (3 dB below the midrange output voltage). This is the upper critical frequency.

36. $t_r \cong 3 \text{ DIV} \times 5 \text{ μs/DIV} = 15 \text{ μs}$

$t_f \cong 6 \text{ DIV} \times 0.1 \text{ ms/DIV} = 600 \text{ μs}$

$f_{cl} = \dfrac{0.35}{t_f} = \dfrac{0.35}{600 \text{ μs}} = 583 \text{ Hz}$

$f_{ch} = \dfrac{0.35}{t_r} = \dfrac{0.35}{15 \text{ μs}} = 23.3 \text{ kHz}$

$BW = 23.3 \text{ kHz} - 583 \text{ Hz} = \mathbf{22.7 \text{ kHz}}$

Chapter 10

Section 10-10 System Application

37.
$$V_B = \left(\frac{13\ k\Omega}{113\ k\Omega}\right)12\ V = 1.38\ V,\ V_E = 0.68\ V$$

$I_E = 2.13\ mA,\ r'_e = 11.7\ \Omega$

$R_{in} = 22\ k\Omega\ \|\ 100\ k\Omega\ \|\ (112\ \Omega)(100) = 6.9\ k\Omega$ (*both stages*)

First stage:

$$f_{cl(in)} = \frac{1}{2\pi(6.9\ k\Omega)(1\ \mu F)} = \mathbf{23.1\ Hz}$$

$R_{out} = 4.7\ k\Omega + 6.9\ k\Omega = 11.6\ k\Omega$

$$f_{cl(out)} = \frac{1}{2\pi(11.6\ k\Omega)(1\ \mu F)} = \mathbf{13.7\ Hz}$$

$R_{bypass} = 220\ \Omega\ \|\ (112\ \Omega + 22\ k\Omega\ \|\ 100\ k\Omega\ /\ 100) = 125\ \Omega$

$$f_{cl(bypass)} = \frac{1}{2\pi(125\ \Omega)(100\ \mu F)} = \mathbf{12.7\ Hz}$$

Second stage:

$f_{cl(in)} = \mathbf{13.7\ Hz}$ (same as $f_{cl(out)}$ of first stage)

$R_{out} = 4.7\ k\Omega + 10\ k\Omega = 14.7\ k\Omega$

$$f_{cl(out)} = \frac{1}{2\pi(14.7\ k\Omega)(1\ \mu F)} = \mathbf{10.8\ Hz}$$

$R_{bypass} = 220\ \Omega\ \|\ (112\ \Omega + 22\ k\Omega\ \|\ 100\ k\Omega\ \|\ 4.7\ k\Omega/\ 100) = 88.8\ \Omega$

$$f_{cl(bypass)} = \frac{1}{2\pi(88.8\ \Omega)(100\ \mu F)} = \mathbf{17.9\ Hz}$$

$f_{cl(in)}$ of first stage is the dominant lower critical frequency.

38. Changing to 1 μF coupling capacitors does not significantly affect the overall bandwidth because the upper critical frequency is much greater than the dominant lower critcal frequency.

39. Increasing the load resistance on the output of the second stage has no affect on the dominant lower critical frequency because the critical frequency of the output circuit will decrease and the critical frequency of the first stage input circuit will remain dominant.

Chapter 10

40.
$$V_B = \left(\frac{13\ k\Omega}{113\ k\Omega}\right) 12\ V = 1.38\ V,\ V_E = 0.68\ V$$

$I_E = 2.13\ mA,\ r'_e = 11.7\ \Omega$

$R_{in} = 22\ k\Omega\ \|\ 100\ k\Omega\ \|\ (112\ \Omega)(100) = 6.9\ k\Omega$ (*both stages*)

First stage:

$$f_{cl(in)} = \frac{1}{2\pi(6.9\ k\Omega)(10\ \mu F)} = \mathbf{2.31\ Hz}$$

$R_{out} = 4.7\ k\Omega + 6.9\ k\Omega = 11.6\ k\Omega$

$$f_{cl(out)} = \frac{1}{2\pi(11.6\ k\Omega)(10\ \mu F)} = \mathbf{1.37\ Hz}$$

$R_{bypass} = 220\ \Omega\ \|\ (112\ \Omega + 22\ k\Omega\ \|\ 100\ k\Omega\ /\ 100) = 125\ \Omega$

$$f_{cl(bypass)} = \frac{1}{2\pi(125\ \Omega)(100\ \mu F)} = \mathbf{12.7\ Hz}$$

Second stage:

$f_{cl(in)} = \mathbf{1.37\ Hz}$ (same as $f_{cl(out)}$ of first stage)

$R_{out} = 4.7\ k\Omega + 10\ k\Omega = 14.7\ k\Omega$

$$f_{cl(out)} = \frac{1}{2\pi(14.7\ k\Omega)(10\ \mu F)} = \mathbf{1.08\ Hz}$$

$R_{bypass} = 220\ \Omega\ \|\ (112\ \Omega + 22\ k\Omega\ \|\ 100\ k\Omega\ \|\ 4.7\ k\Omega/\ 100) = 88.8\ \Omega$

$$f_{cl(bypass)} = \frac{1}{2\pi(88.8\ \Omega)(100\ \mu F)} = \mathbf{17.9\ Hz}$$

First stage:
$R_c = 4.7\ k\Omega\ \|\ 100\ k\Omega\ \|\ 22\ k\Omega\ \|\ (100)(100\ \Omega + 11.7\ \Omega) = 2.8\ k\Omega$

$$A_{v1} = \frac{2.8\ k\Omega}{112\ \Omega} = 25$$

$C_{in(Miller)} = (25 + 1)4\ pF = 112\ pF$

$C_{in(Tot)} = 112\ pF + 8\ p\ 120\ pF$

$$C_{out(Miller)} = \left(\frac{25 + 1}{25}\right) 4\ pF = 4.16\ pF$$

$$f_{cu(in)} = \frac{1}{2\pi(6.9\ k\Omega)(120\ pF)} = \mathbf{192\ kHz}$$

$$f_{cu(out)} = \frac{1}{2\pi(2.8\ k\Omega)(4.16\ \mu F)} = \mathbf{13.7\ MHz}$$

Continued

Chapter 10

Second stage:
$R_c = 4.7 \text{ k}\Omega \parallel 10 \text{ k}\Omega = 3.2 \text{ k}\Omega$

$A_{v1} = \dfrac{3.2 \text{ k}\Omega}{112 \text{ }\Omega} = 28.6$

$C_{in(Miller)} = (28.6 + 1)4 \text{ pF} = 119 \text{ pF}$

$C_{in(Tot)} = 119 \text{ pF} + 8 \text{ pF} = 127 \text{ pF}$

$C_{out(Miller)} = \left(\dfrac{28.6 + 1}{28.6}\right)4 \text{ pF} = 4.14 \text{ pF}$

$f_{cu(in)} = \dfrac{1}{2\pi(2.8 \text{ k}\Omega)(127 \text{ pF})} = \mathbf{448 \text{ kHz}}$

$f_{cu(out)} = \dfrac{1}{2\pi(3.2 \text{ k}\Omega)(4.14 \text{ pF})} = \mathbf{12.0 \text{ MHz}}$

$t_f = \dfrac{0.35}{17.9 \text{ Hz}} = \mathbf{19.5 \text{ ms}}$

$t_f = \dfrac{0.35}{192 \text{ kHz}} = \mathbf{1.82 \text{ }\mu\text{s}}$

Data Sheet Problems

41. $C_{in(Tot)} = (25 + 1)4 \text{ pF} + 8 \text{ pF} = \mathbf{112 \text{ pF}}$

42. $BW_{min} = \dfrac{f_T}{A_{v(mid)}} = \dfrac{300 \text{ MHz}}{50} = \mathbf{6 \text{ MHz}}$

43. $C_{gd} = C_{rss} = \mathbf{1.3 \text{ pF}}$
$C_{gs} = C_{iss} - C_{rss} = 5 \text{ pF} - 1.3 \text{ pF} = \mathbf{3.7 \text{ pF}}$
$C_{ds} = C_d - C_{rss} = 5 \text{ pF} - 1.3 \text{ pF} = \mathbf{3.7 \text{ pF}}$

Advanced Problems

44. From Problem 8: $r'_e = 7.81 \text{ }\Omega$ and $I_E = 3.2 \text{ mA}$

$V_C \cong 20 \text{ V} - (3.2 \text{ mA})(2.2 \text{ k}\Omega) = 13 \text{ V dc}$

The maximum peak output signal can be approximately 6 V

The maximum allowable gain for the two stages is

$A_{v(max)} = \dfrac{6 \text{ V}}{1.414(10 \text{ mV})} = 424$

For stage 1:
$R_c = 2.2 \text{ k}\Omega \parallel 33 \text{ k}\Omega \parallel 4.7 \text{ k}\Omega \parallel (150)(7.81 \text{ }\Omega) = 645 \text{ }\Omega$

$A_{v1} = \dfrac{645 \text{ }\Omega}{7.81 \text{ }\Omega} = 82.6$

For stage 2:
$R_c = 2.2 \text{ k}\Omega \parallel 5.6 \text{ k}\Omega = 1.58 \text{ k}\Omega$

$A_{v1} = \dfrac{1.58 \text{ k}\Omega}{7.81 \text{ }\Omega} = 202$

$A_{v(Tot)} = (82.6)(202) = 16{,}685$

Chapter 10

The amplifier will **not operate linearly** with a 10 mV rms input signal.

The gains of both stages can be reduced or the gain of the second stage only can be reduced.

One approach is leave the gain of the first stage as is and bypass a portion of the emitter resistance in the second stage to achieve a gain of 424/82.6 = 5.13.

$$A_v = \frac{R_c}{R_e + r'_e} = 5.13$$

$$R_e = \frac{R_c - 5.13 r'_e}{5.13} = \frac{1.58 \text{ k}\Omega - 40.1 \text{ }\Omega}{5.13} = 300 \text{ }\Omega$$

Modification: Replace the 560 Ω emitter resistor in the second stage with an unbypassed 300 Ω resistor and a bypassed 260 Ω resistor(closest standard value is 270 Ω).

45. From Problems 25, 26, and 27:
$C_T = C_{gs} \parallel C_{in(miller)} = 20.6$ pF

$$C_{out(miller)} = 4 \text{ pF}\left(\frac{2.65 + 1}{2.65}\right) = 5.51 \text{ pF}$$

Stage 1:

$$f_{cl(in)} = \frac{1}{2\pi R_{in} C_1} = \frac{1}{2\pi (9.52 \text{ M}\Omega)(0.005 \text{ }\mu\text{F})} = 3.34 \text{ Hz}$$

$$f_{cl(out)} = \frac{1}{2\pi (9.52 \text{ M}\Omega)(0.005 \text{ }\mu\text{F})} = 3.34 \text{ Hz since } R_{in(2)} \gg 560 \text{ }\Omega$$

$$f_{cu(in)} = \frac{1}{2\pi (600 \text{ }\Omega)(20.6 \text{ pF})} = 12.9 \text{ MHz}$$

$$f_{cu(out)} = \frac{1}{2\pi (560 \text{ }\Omega)(20.6 \text{ pF} + 5.51 \text{ pF})} = 10.5 \text{ MHz}$$

Stage 2:

$$f_{cl(in)} = \frac{1}{2\pi R_{in} C_1} = \frac{1}{2\pi (9.52 \text{ M}\Omega)(0.005 \text{ }\mu\text{F})} = 3.34 \text{ Hz}$$

$$f_{cl(out)} = \frac{1}{2\pi (10.6 \text{ k}\Omega)(0.005 \text{ }\mu\text{F})} = 3.01 \text{ kHz}$$

$$f_{cu(in)} = \frac{1}{2\pi (560 \text{ }\Omega)(20.6 \text{ pF} + 5.51 \text{ pF})} = 10.5 \text{ MHz}$$

$$f_{cu(out)} = \frac{1}{2\pi (560 \text{ }\Omega \parallel 10 \text{ k}\Omega)(5.51 \text{ pF})} = 54.5 \text{ MHz}$$

Overall:
$f_{cl(out)} = 3.01$ kHz and $f_{cu(in)} = 10.5$ MHz
$BW \cong$ **10.5 MHz**

Chapter 10

46. $R_{in(1)} = 22\text{ k}\Omega \parallel (100)(320\text{ }\Omega) = 13\text{ k}\Omega$

$V_{B(1)} = \left(\dfrac{13\text{ k}\Omega}{113\text{ k}\Omega}\right)12\text{ V} = 1.38, \quad V_{E(1)} = 0.684\text{ V}$

$I_{E(1)} = \dfrac{0.684\text{ V}}{320\text{ }\Omega} = 2.14\text{ mA}, \quad r'_e = 11.7\text{ }\Omega$

$R_{c(1)} = 4.7\text{ k}\Omega \parallel 33\text{ k}\Omega \parallel 22\text{ k}\Omega \parallel (100)(100\text{ }\Omega) = 2.57\text{ k}\Omega$

$A_{v(1)} = \dfrac{2.57\text{ k}\Omega}{112\text{ }\Omega} = 23$

$R_{in(2)} = 22\text{ k}\Omega \parallel (100)(1010\text{ }\Omega) = 18\text{ k}\Omega$

$V_{B(2)} = \left(\dfrac{18\text{ k}\Omega}{51\text{ k}\Omega}\right)12\text{ V} = 4.42, \quad V_{E(1)} = 3.54\text{ V}$

$I_{E(2)} = \dfrac{3.54\text{ V}}{1.01\text{ k}\Omega} = 3.51\text{ mA}, \quad r'_e = 7.13\text{ }\Omega$

$R_{c(2)} = 3\text{ k}\Omega \parallel 10\text{ k}\Omega = 2.31\text{ k}\Omega$

$A_{v(2)} = \dfrac{2.31\text{ k}\Omega}{107.13\text{ }\Omega} = 24\text{ maximum}$

$A_{v(2)} = \dfrac{2.31\text{ k}\Omega}{1.01\text{ k}\Omega + 7.13\text{ }\Omega} = 2.27\text{ minimum}$

$A_{v(Tot)} = (23)(24) = 554\text{ maximum.}$

$A_{v(Tot)} = (23)(2.27) = 52.3\text{ minimum.}$

This is a bit high, so adjust $R_{c(1)}$ to 3 kΩ, then

$A_{v(1)} = \dfrac{3\text{ k}\Omega \parallel 22\text{ k}\Omega \parallel 33\text{ k}\Omega \parallel 101\text{ k}\Omega}{112\text{ }\Omega} = 21.4$

Now,

$A_{v(Tot)} = (21.3)(24) = \mathbf{513}\text{ maximum.}$

$A_{v(Tot)} = (21.3)(2.27) = \mathbf{48.5}\text{ minimum.}$

Thus, A_v is within 3% of the desired specifications.

Frequency response for stage 1:

$R_{in} = 22\text{ k}\Omega \parallel 100\text{ k}\Omega \parallel 32\text{ k}\Omega = 11.5\text{ k}\Omega$

$f_{cl(in)} = \dfrac{1}{2\pi(11.5\text{ k}\Omega)(10\text{ }\mu\text{F})} = 1.38\text{ Hz}$

$R_{emitter} = 220\text{ }\Omega \parallel (100\text{ }\Omega + 11.7\text{ }\Omega + (22\text{ k}\Omega \parallel 100\text{ k}\Omega)100) = 125\text{ }\Omega$

$f_{cl(bypass)} = \dfrac{1}{2\pi(125\text{ }\Omega)(100\text{ }\mu\text{F})} = 12.7\text{ Hz}$

$R_{out} = 3\text{ k}\Omega + (33\text{ k}\Omega \parallel 22\text{ k}\Omega \parallel (100)(107\text{ }\Omega) = 8.91\text{ k}\Omega$

$f_{cl(out)} = \dfrac{1}{2\pi(8.91\text{ k}\Omega)(10\text{ }\mu\text{F})} = 1.79\text{ Hz}$

Chapter 10

Frequency response for stage 2:
$f_{cl(in)} = 1.79$ Hz (same as $f_{cl(out)}$ for stage 1)
$R_{out} = 3$ kΩ + 10 kΩ = 13 kΩ
$$f_{cl(out)} = \frac{1}{2\pi(13 \text{ k}\Omega)(10 \text{ }\mu\text{F})} = 1.22 \text{ Hz}$$
This means that $C_{E(2)}$ is the frequency limiting capacitance.
$R_{emitter} = 910 \text{ }\Omega \parallel (100 \text{ }\Omega + 7 \text{ }\Omega + (22 \text{ k}\Omega \parallel 33 \text{ k}\Omega \parallel 3 \text{ k}\Omega)/100) = 115 \text{ }\Omega$
For $f'_{cl} = 1$ kHz:
$$C_{E(2)} = \frac{1}{2\pi(115 \text{ }\Omega)(1 \text{ kHz})} = 1.38 \text{ }\mu\text{F}$$
1.5 µF is the closest standard value and gives
$$f_{cl(bypass)} = \frac{1}{2\pi(115 \text{ }\Omega)(1.5 \text{ }\mu\text{F})} = \textbf{922 Hz}$$
This value can be moved closer to 1 kHz by using additional parallel bypass capacitors in stage 2.to fine tune the response.

Chapter 11
Thyristor and Other Devices

Section 11-1 The Shockley Diode

1. $$I_A = I_K = \frac{I_{CBO1} + I_{CBO2}}{1 - (\alpha_{dc1} + \alpha_{dc2})} = \frac{75 \text{ nA} + 80 \text{ nA}}{1 - (0.38 + 0.38)} = \mathbf{646 \text{ nA}}$$

2. (a) Because I_A in the forward blocking region is very small as determined in Problem 1, the drop across R_S can be neglected and $V_{AK} = 25$ V. The forward blocking resistance is
$$R_{AK} = \frac{V_{AK}}{I_A} = \frac{25 \text{ V}}{645.83 \text{ nA}} = \mathbf{38.7 \text{ M}\Omega}$$
   (b) From 25 V to 50 V for an increase of **25 V**.

Section 11-2 The Silicon-Controlled Rectifier (SCR)

3. See Section 11-2 in the text.

4. Neglecting the SCR voltage drop,
$$R_{max} = \frac{30 \text{ V}}{10 \text{ mA}} = \mathbf{3 \text{ k}\Omega}$$

Section 11-3 SCR Applications

5. Add a transistor to provide inversion of the negative half-cycle in order to obtain a positive gate trigger.

6. D_1 and D_2 are full-wave rectifier diodes.

7. See Figure 11-1.

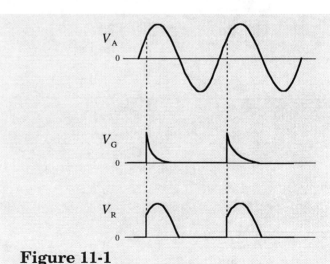

Figure 11-1

Chapter 11

Section 11-4 The Silicon-Controlled Switch (SCS)

8.   See Section 11-4 in the text..

9.   Anode, cathode, anode gate, and cathode gate.

Section 11-5 The Diac and Triac

10. $V_{in(p)} = 1.414 V_{in(rms)} = 1.414(25 \text{ V}) = 35.4 \text{ V}$

$I_p = V_{in(p)} = \dfrac{35.35 \text{ V}}{1 \text{ k}\Omega} = 35.4 \text{ mA}$

Current at breakover $= \dfrac{20 \text{ V}}{1 \text{ k}\Omega} = 20 \text{ mA}$

See Figure 11-2 .

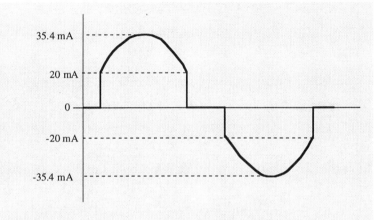

Figure 11-2

11. $I_p = \dfrac{15 \text{ V}}{4.7 \text{ k}\Omega} = 3.19 \text{ mA}$

See Figure 11-3.

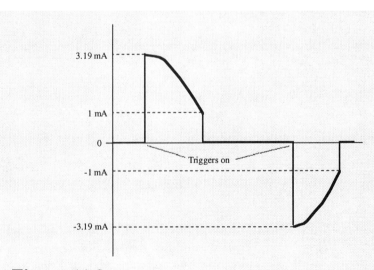

Figure 11-3

Chapter 11

Section 11-6 The Unijunction Transistor (UJT)

12. $\eta = \dfrac{r'_{B1}}{r'_{B1} + r'_{B2}} = \dfrac{2.5 \text{ k}\Omega}{2.5 \text{ k}\Omega + 4 \text{ k}\Omega} = \mathbf{0.385}$

13. $V_p = \eta V_{BB} + V_{pn} = 0.385(15 \text{ V}) + 0.7 \text{ V} = \mathbf{6.48 \text{ V}}$

14. $\dfrac{V_{BB} - V_v}{I_v} < R_1 < \dfrac{V_{BB} - V_P}{I_p}$

$\dfrac{12 \text{ V} - 0.8 \text{ V}}{15 \text{ mA}} < R_1 < \dfrac{12 \text{ V} - 10 \text{ V}}{10 \text{ }\mu\text{A}}$

$\mathbf{747 \text{ }\Omega < R_1 < 200 \text{ k}\Omega}$

Section 11-7 The Programmable UJT (PUT)

15. (a) $V_A = \left(\dfrac{R_3}{R_2 + R_3}\right)V_B + 0.7 \text{ V} = \left(\dfrac{10 \text{ k}\Omega}{22 \text{ k}\Omega}\right)20 \text{ V} + 0.7 \text{ V} = \mathbf{9.79 \text{ V}}$

(b) $V_A = \left(\dfrac{R_3}{R_2 + R_3}\right)V_B + 0.7 \text{ V} = \left(\dfrac{47 \text{ k}\Omega}{94 \text{ k}\Omega}\right)9 \text{ V} + 0.7 \text{ V} = \mathbf{5.2 \text{ V}}$

16. (a) From Problem 15(a), $V_A = 9.79$ V at turn on.

$I = \dfrac{9.79 \text{ V}}{470 \text{ }\Omega} = 20.8 \text{ mA}$ at turn on

$I_p = \dfrac{10 \text{ V}}{470 \text{ }\Omega} = 21.3 \text{ mA}$

See Figure 11-4.

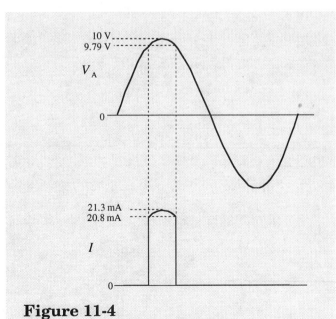

Figure 11-4

Chapter 11

(b) From Problem 15(b), $V_A = 5.2$ V at turn on.

$$I = \frac{5.2 \text{ V}}{330 \text{ }\Omega} = 15.8 \text{ mA at turn on}$$

$$I_p = \frac{10 \text{ V}}{330 \text{ }\Omega} = 30.3 \text{ mA}$$

See Figure 11-5.

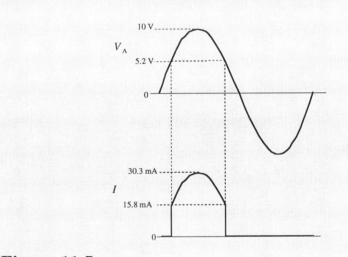

Figure 11-5

17. $V_A = \left(\dfrac{R_3}{R_2 + R_3}\right) 6 \text{ V} + 0.7 \text{ V} = \left(\dfrac{10 \text{ k}\Omega}{20 \text{ k}\Omega}\right) 6 \text{ V} + 0.7 \text{ V} = 3.7 \text{ V at turn on}$

$V_{R1} \cong V_A = 3.7$ V at turn on.

See Figure 11-6.

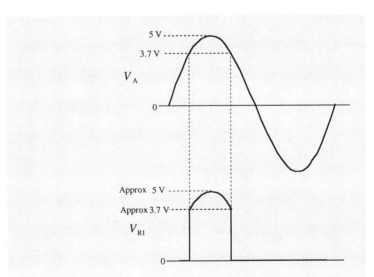

Figure 11-6

Chapter 11

Section 11-8 The Phototransistor

18. $I_C = \beta_{DC} I_\lambda = (200)(100\ \mu A) = \mathbf{20\ mA}$

19. (a) $V_{OUT} = \mathbf{12\ V}$
    (b) $V_{OUT} = \mathbf{0\ V}$

20. $I_{\lambda 1} = (50\ lm/m^2)(1\ \mu A/lm/m^2) = 50\ \mu A$
    $I_E = \beta_{DC1}\beta_{DC2}I_{\lambda 1} = (100)(150)(50\ \mu A) = \mathbf{750\ mA}$

Section 11-9 The Light Activiated SCR (LASCR)

21. When the switch is closed, the battery V2 causes illumination of the lamp. The light energy causes the LASCR to conduct and thus energize the relay. When the relay is energized, the contacts close and 115 V ac are applied to the motor.

22. See Figure 11-7.

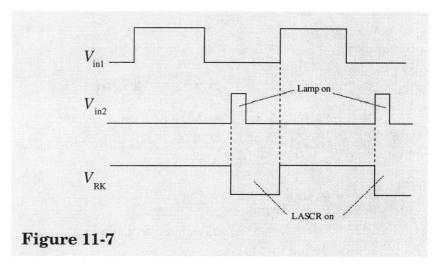

Figure 11-7

Section 11-10 Optical Couplers

23. $I_{out} = (0.30)(100\ mA) = \mathbf{30\ mA}$

24. $\dfrac{I_{OUT}}{I_{IN}} = 0.6$

    $I_{IN} = \dfrac{I_{OUT}}{0.6} = \dfrac{10\ mA}{0.6} = \mathbf{16.7\ mA}$

Section 11-11 System Application

25. The motor runs fastest at **0 V** for the motor speed control circuit.

26. If the rheostat resistance increases, the SCR turns on **later** in the ac cycle.

27. As the PUT gate voltage increases in the circuit, the PUT triggers later in the ac cycle causing the SCR to fire later in the cycle, conduct for a shorter time, and decrease the power to the motor.

Chapter 11

Advanced Problems

28. D_1: 15 V zener (1N4744)

R_1: 100 Ω, 1 W

R_2: 100 Ω, 1 W

Q_1: Any SCR with a 1 A minimum rating (1.5 A would be better)

R_3: 150 Ω, 1 W

29. See Figure 11–8.

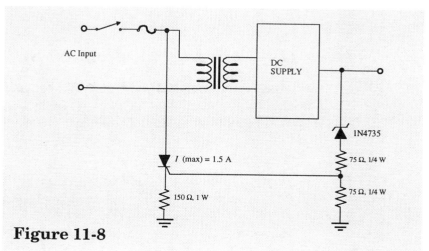

Figure 11-8

30. $V_p = \eta V_{BB} + V_{pn} = (0.75)(12\text{ V}) + 0.7\text{ V} = 9.7\text{ V}$

$I_v = 10$ mA and $I_p = 20$ μA

$R_1 < \dfrac{12\text{ V} - 9.7\text{ V}}{20\text{ μA}} = 115\text{ kΩ}$

$R_1 > \dfrac{12\text{ V} - 1\text{ V}}{10\text{ mA}} = 1.1\text{ kΩ}$

Select $R_1 = 51$ kΩ as an intermediate value.

During the charging cycle:

$V(t) = V_F - (V_F - V_0)e^{-t_1/R_1 C}$

$9.7\text{ V} = 12\text{ V} - (12\text{ V} - 1\text{ V})e^{-t_1/R_1 C}$

$-\dfrac{t_1}{R_1 C} = \ln\left(\dfrac{2.3\text{ V}}{11\text{ V}}\right)$

$t_1 = -R_1 C \ln\left(\dfrac{2.3\text{ V}}{11\text{ V}}\right) = 1.56 R_1 C = 79.8 \times 10^3 C$

Chapter 11

During the discharging cycle (assuming $R_2 \gg R_{B1}$):

$V(t) = V_F - (V_F - V_0)e^{-t_2/R_2C}$

$1\text{ V} = 0\text{ V} - (0\text{ V} - 9.3\text{ V})e^{-t_2/R_2C}$

$-\dfrac{t_2}{R_2C} = \ln\left(\dfrac{1\text{ V}}{9.3\text{ V}}\right)$

$t_2 = -R_2C \ln\left(\dfrac{1\text{ V}}{9.3\text{ V}}\right) = 2.23 R_2 C$

Let $R_2 = 100\text{ k}\Omega$, so $t_2 = 223 \times 10^3 C$

Since $f = 2.5\text{ kHz}$, $T = 400\text{ }\mu\text{s}$

$T = t_1 + t_2 = 79.8 \times 10^3 + 223 \times 10^3 C = 303 \times 10^3 C = 400\text{ }\mu\text{s}$

$C = \dfrac{400\text{ }\mu\text{s}}{303 \times 10^3} = 0.0013\text{ }\mu\text{F}$

See Figure 11–9.

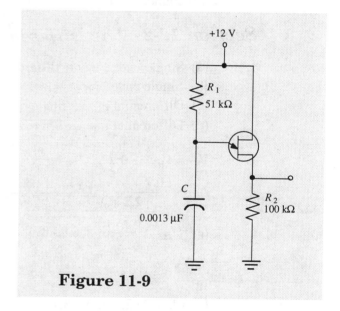

Figure 11-9

Chapter 12
Operational Amplifiers

Section 12-1 Introduction to Operational Amplifiers

1. *Practical op-amp*: High open-loop gain, high input impedance, low output impedance, and high CMRR.
   Ideal op-amp: Infinite open-loop gain, infinite input impedance, zero output impedance, and infinite CMRR.

2. Op amp 2 is more desirable because it has a higher input impedance, a lower output impedance, and a higher open-loop gain.

Section 12-2 The Differential Amplifier

3. (a) Single-ended input; differntial ouput
   (b) Single-ended input; single-ended output
   (c) Differential input; single-ended output
   (d) Differential input; differential output

4. $V_{E1} = V_{E2} = -0.7$ V

   $I_{RE} = \dfrac{-0.7 \text{ V} - (-15 \text{ V})}{2.2 \text{ k}\Omega} = \dfrac{14.3 \text{ V}}{2.2 \text{ k}\Omega} = 6.5$ mA

   $I_{E1} = I_{E2} = \dfrac{6.5 \text{ mA}}{2} = 3.25$ mA

   $\dfrac{I_{C1}}{I_{E1}} = \alpha = 0.98$

   $I_{C1} = 0.98(3.25 \text{ mA}) = 3.19$ mA
   $I_{C2} = 0.975(3.25 \text{ mA}) = 3.17$ mA
   $V_{C1} = 15 \text{ V} - (3.19 \text{ mA})(3.3 \text{ k}\Omega) = 4.49$ V
   $V_{C2} = 15 \text{ V} - (3.169 \text{ mA})(3.3 \text{ k}\Omega) = 4.54$ V
   $V_{OUT} = V_{C2} - V_{C1} = 4.54 \text{ V} - 4.49 \text{ V} = \mathbf{53.6 \text{ mV}}$

5. V_1: Differential output voltage
   V_2: Noninverting-input voltage
   V_3: Single-ended output voltage
   V_4: Differential input voltage
   I_1: Bias current

6. $V_{OUT(diff)} = (I_{C1} - I_{C2})R_C = (1.35 \text{ mA} - 1.29 \text{ mA})5.1 \text{ k}\Omega = \mathbf{306 \text{ mV}}$

Chapter 12

Section 12-3 Op-Amp Parameters

7. $I_{BIAS} = \dfrac{8.3\ \mu A - 7.9\ \mu A}{2} = \textbf{8.1}\ \mu\textbf{A}$

8. Input bias current is the average of the two input currents. Input offset current is the difference between the two input currents.

$I_{OS} = |8.3\ \mu A - 7.9\ \mu A| = \textbf{400 nA}$

9. CMRR(dB) = 20log (250,000) = **108 dB**

10. CMRR(dB) = $20\log\left(\dfrac{A_{ol}}{A_{cm}}\right) = 20\log\left(\dfrac{175,000}{0.18}\right) = \textbf{120 dB}$

11. CMRR = $\dfrac{A_{ol}}{A_{cm}}$

$A_{cm} = \dfrac{A_{ol}}{\text{CMRR}} = \dfrac{90,000}{300,000} = \textbf{0.3}$

12. Slew rate = $\dfrac{24\ V}{15\ \mu s} = \textbf{1.6 V/}\mu\textbf{s}$

13. $\Delta t = \dfrac{\Delta V_{out}}{\text{slew rate}} = \dfrac{20\ V}{0.5\ V/\mu s} = \textbf{40}\ \mu\textbf{s}$

Section 12-5 Op-Amp Configurations with Negative Feedback

14. (a) Voltage follower
(b) Noninverting
(c) Inverting

15. $B = \dfrac{R_i}{R_i + R_f} = \dfrac{1\ k\Omega}{101\ k\Omega} = 9.90 \times 10^{-3}$

$V_f = BV_{out} = (9.90 \times 10^{-3})5\ V = 0.0495\ V = \textbf{49.5 mV}$

16. (a) $A_{cl(NI)} = \dfrac{1}{B} = \dfrac{1}{1.5\ k\Omega / 561.5\ k\Omega} = \textbf{374}$

(b) $V_{out} = A_{cl(NI)}V_{in} = (374)(10\ mV) = \textbf{3.74 V rms}$

(c) $V_f = \left(\dfrac{1.5\ k\Omega}{561.5\ k\Omega}\right)3.74\ V = \textbf{9.99 mV rms}$

Chapter 12

17.
(a) $A_{cl(NI)} = \dfrac{1}{B} = \dfrac{1}{4.7\ \text{k}\Omega/51.7\ \text{k}\Omega} = \mathbf{11}$

(b) $A_{cl(NI)} = \dfrac{1}{B} = \dfrac{1}{10\ \text{k}\Omega/1.01\ \text{M}\Omega} = \mathbf{101}$

(c) $A_{cl(NI)} = \dfrac{1}{B} = \dfrac{1}{4.7\ \text{k}\Omega/224.7\ \text{k}\Omega} = \mathbf{47.8}$

(d) $A_{cl(NI)} = \dfrac{1}{B} = \dfrac{1}{1\ \text{k}\Omega/23\ \text{k}\Omega} = \mathbf{23}$

18.
(a) $1 + \dfrac{R_f}{R_i} = A_{cl(NI)}$

$R_f = R_i\left(A_{cl(NI)} - 1\right) = 1\ \text{k}\Omega(50 - 1) = \mathbf{49\ k\Omega}$

(b) $\dfrac{R_f}{R_i} = A_{cl(I)}$

$R_f = -R_i\left(A_{cl(I)}\right) = -10\ \text{k}\Omega(-300) = \mathbf{3\ M\Omega}$

(c) $R_f = R_i\left(A_{cl(NI)} - 1\right) = 12\ \text{k}\Omega(7) = \mathbf{84\ k\Omega}$

(d) $R_f = -R_i\left(A_{cl(I)}\right) = -2.2\ \text{k}\Omega(-75) = \mathbf{165\ k\Omega}$

19.
(a) $A_{cl(VF)} = \mathbf{1}$

(b) $A_{cl(I)} = -\left(\dfrac{R_f}{R_i}\right) = -\left(\dfrac{100\ \text{k}\Omega}{100\ \text{k}\Omega}\right) = \mathbf{-1}$

(c) $A_{cl(NI)} = \dfrac{1}{\left(\dfrac{R_i}{R_i + R_f}\right)} = \dfrac{1}{\left(\dfrac{47\ \text{k}\Omega}{47\ \text{k}\Omega + 1\ \text{M}\Omega}\right)} = \mathbf{22}$

(d) $A_{cl(I)} = -\left(\dfrac{R_f}{R_i}\right) = -\left(\dfrac{330\ \text{k}\Omega}{33\ \text{k}\Omega}\right) = \mathbf{-10}$

20.
(a) $V_{out} \cong V_{in} = \mathbf{10\ mV,\ in\ phase}$

(b) $V_{out} = A_{cl}V_{in} = -\left(\dfrac{R_f}{R_i}\right)V_{in} = -(1)(10\ \text{mV}) = \mathbf{-10\ mV,\ 180°\ out\ of\ phase}$

(c) $V_{out} = \left(\dfrac{1}{\left(\dfrac{R_i}{R_i + R_f}\right)}\right)V_{in} = \left(\dfrac{1}{\left(\dfrac{47\ \text{k}\Omega}{1047\ \text{k}\Omega}\right)}\right)10\ \text{mV} = \mathbf{223\ mV,\ in\ phase}$

(d) $V_{out} = -\left(\dfrac{R_f}{R_i}\right)V_{in} = -\left(\dfrac{330\ \text{k}\Omega}{33\ \text{k}\Omega}\right)10\ \text{mV} = \mathbf{-100\ mV,\ 180°\ out\ of\ phase}$

Chapter 12

21. (a) $I_{in} = \dfrac{V_{in}}{R_{in}} = \dfrac{1\text{ V}}{2.2\text{ k}\Omega} = \mathbf{455\ \mu A}$

(b) $I_f \cong I_{in} = \mathbf{455\ \mu A}$

(c) $V_{out} = -I_f R_f = -(455\ \mu A)(22\text{ k}\Omega) = \mathbf{-10\text{ V}}$

(d) $A_{cl(I)} = -\left(\dfrac{R_f}{R_i}\right) = -\left(\dfrac{22\text{ k}\Omega}{2.2\text{ k}\Omega}\right) = \mathbf{-10}$

Section 12-6 Effects of Negative Feedback on Op-Amp Impedances

22. (a) $B = \dfrac{2.5\text{ k}\Omega}{562.5\text{ k}\Omega} = 0.00444$

$Z_{in(NI)} = (1 + A_{ol})Z_{in} = [1 + (175{,}000)(0.00444)]10\text{ M}\Omega = \mathbf{7.79\text{ G}\Omega}$

$Z_{out(NI)} = \dfrac{Z_{out}}{1 + A_{ol}B} = \dfrac{75\ \Omega}{1 + (175{,}000)(0.00444)} = \mathbf{96.3\text{ m}\Omega}$

(b) $B = \dfrac{1.5\text{ k}\Omega}{48.5\text{ k}\Omega} = 0.031$

$Z_{in(NI)} = (1 + A_{ol})Z_{in} = [1 + (200{,}000)(0.031)]1\text{ M}\Omega = \mathbf{6.20\text{ G}\Omega}$

$Z_{out(NI)} = \dfrac{Z_{out}}{1 + A_{ol}B} = \dfrac{25\ \Omega}{1 + (200{,}000)(0.031)} = \mathbf{4.04\text{ m}\Omega}$

(c) $B = \dfrac{56\text{ k}\Omega}{1.056\text{ M}\Omega} = 0.053$

$Z_{in(NI)} = (1 + A_{ol})Z_{in} = [1 + (50{,}000)(0.053)]1\text{ M}\Omega = \mathbf{5.30\text{ G}\Omega}$

$Z_{out(NI)} = \dfrac{Z_{out}}{1 + A_{ol}B} = \dfrac{50\ \Omega}{1 + (50{,}000)(0.053)} = \mathbf{19.0\text{ m}\Omega}$

23. (a) $Z_{in(VF)} = (1 + A_{ol})Z_{in} = (1 + 220{,}000)6\text{ M}\Omega = 1.32\times10^{12}\ \Omega = \mathbf{1.32\text{ T}\Omega}$

$Z_{out(VF)} = \dfrac{Z_{out}}{1 + A_{ol}} = \dfrac{100\ \Omega}{1 + 220{,}000} = \mathbf{455\ \mu\Omega}$

(b) $Z_{in(VF)} = (1 + A_{ol})Z_{in} = (1 + 100{,}000)5\text{ M}\Omega = 5\times10^{11}\ \Omega = \mathbf{500\text{ G}\Omega}$

$Z_{out(VF)} = \dfrac{Z_{out}}{1 + A_{ol}} = \dfrac{60\ \Omega}{1 + 100{,}000} = \mathbf{600\ \mu\Omega}$

(c) $Z_{in(VF)} = (1 + A_{ol})Z_{in} = (1 + 50{,}000)800\text{ k}\Omega = \mathbf{40\text{ G}\Omega}$

$Z_{out(VF)} = \dfrac{Z_{out}}{1 + A_{ol}} = \dfrac{75\ \Omega}{1 + 500{,}000} = \mathbf{1.5\text{ m}\Omega}$

Chapter 12

24. (a) $Z_{in(I)} \cong R_i = 10 \text{ k}\Omega$
$Z_{out(I)} = Z_{out} = 40 \text{ }\Omega$

(b) $Z_{in(I)} \cong R_i = 100 \text{ k}\Omega$
$Z_{out(I)} = Z_{out} = 50 \text{ }\Omega$

(c) $Z_{in(I)} \cong R_i = 470 \text{ }\Omega$
$Z_{out(I)} = Z_{out} = 70 \text{ }\Omega$

Section 12-7 Bias Current and Offset Voltage Compensation

25. (a) $R_{comp} = R_{in} = 75 \text{ }\Omega$ placed in the feedback path.
$I_{OS} = |42 \text{ }\mu\text{A} - 40 \text{ }\mu\text{A}| = 2 \text{ }\mu\text{A}$

(b) $V_{OUT(error)} = A_v I_{OS} R_{in} = (1)(2 \text{ }\mu\text{A})(75 \text{ }\Omega) = \mathbf{150 \text{ }\mu\text{V}}$

26. (a) $R_c = R_i \parallel R_f = 2.5 \text{ k}\Omega \parallel 560 \text{ k}\Omega = \mathbf{2.49 \text{ k}\Omega}$

(b) $R_c = R_i \parallel R_f = 1.5 \text{ k}\Omega \parallel 47 \text{ k}\Omega = \mathbf{1.45 \text{ k}\Omega}$

(c) $R_c = R_i \parallel R_f = 56 \text{ k}\Omega \parallel 1 \text{ M}\Omega = \mathbf{53 \text{ k}\Omega}$
See Figure 12-1.

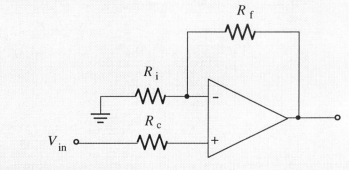

Figure 12-1

27. $V_{OUT(error)} = A_v V_{IO} = (1)(2 \text{ nV}) = \mathbf{2 \text{ nV}}$

28. $V_{OUT(error)} = (1 + A_{ol})V_{IO}$

$V_{IO} = \dfrac{V_{OUT(error)}}{A_{ol}} = \dfrac{35 \text{ mV}}{200{,}000} = \mathbf{175 \text{ nV}}$

Section 12-8 Troubleshooting

29. (a) Faulty op-amp or open R_1

(b) R_2 open, forcing open-loop operation

(c) Nonzero output offset voltge. R_4 faulty or needs adjustment

Chapter 12

30. (a) R_f is probably open or the wrong value (too large). Input signal may be too large

(b) If $V_{in} = V_{out}$, R_i is probably open.

(c) The null adjustment potentiometer is probably open or misadjusted.

31. The closed loop voltage gain will increase to and remain fixed at

$$\frac{100 \text{ k}\Omega}{1 \text{ k}\Omega} = 100$$

because the feedback resistance becomes the maximum potentiometer resistance (100 kΩ).

32. If pin 1 of the op amp opens, the offset null is ineffective; clipping on one peak of the output will most likely result.

Data Sheet Problems

33. From the data sheet of Figure 12–62

$B = \dfrac{470 \text{ }\Omega}{47 \text{ k}\Omega + 470 \text{ }\Omega} = 0.0099$

$A_{ol} = 2000,000$ (typical)

$Z_{in} = 2.)0 \text{ M}\Omega$ (typical)

$Z_{out} = 25 \text{ }\Omega$ (typical)

$Z_{in(NI)} = (1 + (0.0099)(200,000))(2 \text{ M}\Omega) = (1 + 1980)2 \text{ M}\Omega = \mathbf{3.96 \text{ G}\Omega}$

$Z_{out(NI)} = \dfrac{75 \text{ }\Omega}{1981} = \mathbf{37.9 \text{ m}\Omega}$

34. From the data sheet in Figure 12–62:

$Z_{in(I)} = R_i = \dfrac{R_f}{A_{cl}} = \dfrac{100 \text{ k}\Omega}{100} = \mathbf{1 \text{ k}\Omega}$

$Z_{out(I)} = r_o = \mathbf{75 \text{ }\Omega}$

35. $A_{ol} = 50 \text{ V/mV} = \dfrac{50 \text{ V}}{1 \text{ mV}} = \dfrac{50,000 \text{ V}}{1 \text{ V}} = \mathbf{50,000}$

36. *Slew rate* $= 0.5 \text{ V/}\mu\text{s}$

$\Delta V = 8 \text{ V} - (-8 \text{ V}) = 16 \text{ V}$

$\Delta t = \dfrac{16 \text{ V}}{0.5 \text{ V/}\mu\text{s}} = \mathbf{32 \text{ }\mu\text{s}}$

Chapter 12

Advanced Problems

37. Using available standard values of $R_f = 150$ kΩ and $R_i = 1$ kΩ

$A_v = 1 + \dfrac{150 \text{ k}\Omega}{1 \text{ k}\Omega} = 151$

$B = \dfrac{1 \text{ k}\Omega}{151 \text{ k}\Omega} = 6.62 \times 10^{-3}$

$Z_{in(NI)} = (1 + (6.62 \times 10^{-3})(50,000))300 \text{ k}\Omega = 99.6 \text{ M}\Omega$

$R_c = R_i \parallel R_f = 150 \text{ k}\Omega \parallel 1 \text{ k}\Omega = 993 \text{ }\Omega$

Exact single 5% resistor values for $A_v = 150$ are not available.

R_f can be set to 149 kΩ using a 100 kΩ, 39 kΩ, and 10 kΩ in series.

Then

$A_v = 150$

$B = 6.67 \times 10^{-3}$

$Z_{in(NI)} > 100 \text{ M}\Omega$

See Figure 12–2

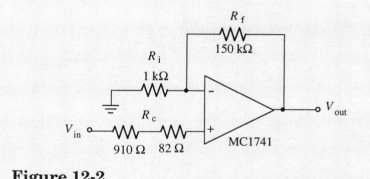

Figure 12-2

38. See Figure 12–3. 2% tolerance resistors are used to achieve a 5% gain tolerance.

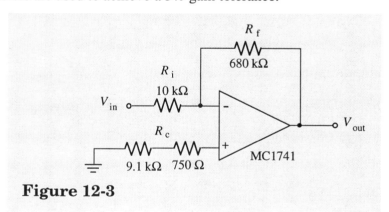

Figure 12-3

39. $CMRR = 90 \text{ dB} = 31,623$

$A_{cm(typical)} = \dfrac{200,000}{31,623} = \mathbf{6.32}$

116

Chapter 13
Op-Amp Frequency Response, Stability, and Compensation

Section 13-1 Basic Concepts

1. $A_{cl} = 120$ dB $- 50$ dB $= \mathbf{70}$ **dB**

2. The gain is ideally **175,000** at 200 Hz. The midrange dB gain is
    $20\log(175,000) = 105$ dB
    The actual gain at 200 Hz is
    $A_v(\text{dB}) = 105$ dB $- 3$ dB $= 102$ dB

    $A_v = \log^{-1}\left(\dfrac{102}{20}\right) = \mathbf{125{,}892}$

    $BW_{ol} = \mathbf{200}$ **Hz**

3. $\dfrac{f_c}{f} = \dfrac{X_C}{R}$

    $X_C = \dfrac{Rf_c}{f} = \dfrac{(1\text{ k}\Omega)(5\text{ kHz})}{3\text{ kHz}} = \mathbf{1.67\ k\Omega}$

4. (a) $\dfrac{V_{out}}{V_{in}} = \dfrac{1}{\sqrt{1+\left(\dfrac{f}{f_c}\right)^2}} = \dfrac{1}{\sqrt{1+\left(\dfrac{1\text{ kHz}}{12\text{ kHz}}\right)^2}} = \mathbf{0.997}$

    (b) $\dfrac{V_{out}}{V_{in}} = \dfrac{1}{\sqrt{1+\left(\dfrac{f}{f_c}\right)^2}} = \dfrac{1}{\sqrt{1+\left(\dfrac{5\text{ kHz}}{12\text{ kHz}}\right)^2}} = \mathbf{0.923}$

    (c) $\dfrac{V_{out}}{V_{in}} = \dfrac{1}{\sqrt{1+\left(\dfrac{f}{f_c}\right)^2}} = \dfrac{1}{\sqrt{1+\left(\dfrac{12\text{ kHz}}{12\text{ kHz}}\right)^2}} = \mathbf{0.707}$

    (d) $\dfrac{V_{out}}{V_{in}} = \dfrac{1}{\sqrt{1+\left(\dfrac{f}{f_c}\right)^2}} = \dfrac{1}{\sqrt{1+\left(\dfrac{20\text{ kHz}}{12\text{ kHz}}\right)^2}} = \mathbf{0.515}$

    (e) $\dfrac{V_{out}}{V_{in}} = \dfrac{1}{\sqrt{1+\left(\dfrac{f}{f_c}\right)^2}} = \dfrac{1}{\sqrt{1+\left(\dfrac{100\text{ kHz}}{12\text{ kHz}}\right)^2}} = \mathbf{0.119}$

Chapter 13

5. (a) $A_{ol} = \dfrac{A_{ol(mid)}}{\sqrt{1+\left(\dfrac{f}{f_{c(ol)}}\right)^2}} = \dfrac{80{,}000}{\sqrt{1+\left(\dfrac{100\text{ Hz}}{1\text{ kHz}}\right)^2}} = \mathbf{79{,}603}$

(b) $A_{ol} = \dfrac{A_{ol(mid)}}{\sqrt{1+\left(\dfrac{f}{f_{c(ol)}}\right)^2}} = \dfrac{80{,}000}{\sqrt{1+\left(\dfrac{1\text{ kHz}}{1\text{ kHz}}\right)^2}} = \mathbf{56{,}569}$

(c) $A_{ol} = \dfrac{A_{ol(mid)}}{\sqrt{1+\left(\dfrac{f}{f_{c(ol)}}\right)^2}} = \dfrac{80{,}000}{\sqrt{1+\left(\dfrac{10\text{ kHz}}{1\text{ kHz}}\right)^2}} = \mathbf{7960}$

(d) $A_{ol} = \dfrac{A_{ol(mid)}}{\sqrt{1+\left(\dfrac{f}{f_{c(ol)}}\right)^2}} = \dfrac{80{,}000}{\sqrt{1+\left(\dfrac{1\text{ MHz}}{1\text{ kHz}}\right)^2}} = \mathbf{80}$

6. (a) $f_c = \dfrac{1}{2\pi RC} = \dfrac{1}{2\pi(10\text{ k}\Omega)(0.01\text{ }\mu\text{F})} = 1.59\text{ kHz}; \;\; \theta = \tan^{-1}\left(\dfrac{f}{f_c}\right) = \tan^{-1}\left(\dfrac{2\text{ kHz}}{1.59\text{ kHz}}\right) = \mathbf{-51.5°}$

(b) $f_c = \dfrac{1}{2\pi RC} = \dfrac{1}{2\pi(1\text{ k}\Omega)(0.01\text{ }\mu\text{F})} = 15.9\text{ kHz}; \;\; \theta = \tan^{-1}\left(\dfrac{f}{f_c}\right) = \tan^{-1}\left(\dfrac{2\text{ kHz}}{15.9\text{ kHz}}\right) = \mathbf{-7.17°}$

(c) $f_c = \dfrac{1}{2\pi RC} = \dfrac{1}{2\pi(100\text{ k}\Omega)(0.01\text{ }\mu\text{F})} = 159\text{ Hz}; \;\; \theta = \tan^{-1}\left(\dfrac{f}{f_c}\right) = \tan^{-1}\left(\dfrac{2\text{ kHz}}{159\text{ Hz}}\right) = \mathbf{-85.5°}$

7. (a) $\theta = \tan^{-1}\left(\dfrac{f}{f_c}\right) = \tan^{-1}\left(\dfrac{100\text{ Hz}}{8.5\text{ kHz}}\right) = \mathbf{-0.674°}$

(b) $\theta = \tan^{-1}\left(\dfrac{f}{f_c}\right) = \tan^{-1}\left(\dfrac{400\text{ Hz}}{8.5\text{ kHz}}\right) = \mathbf{-2.69°}$

(c) $\theta = \tan^{-1}\left(\dfrac{f}{f_c}\right) = \tan^{-1}\left(\dfrac{850\text{ Hz}}{8.5\text{ kHz}}\right) = \mathbf{-5.71°}$

(d) $\theta = \tan^{-1}\left(\dfrac{f}{f_c}\right) = \tan^{-1}\left(\dfrac{8.5\text{ kHz}}{8.5\text{ kHz}}\right) = \mathbf{-45.0°}$

(e) $\theta = \tan^{-1}\left(\dfrac{f}{f_c}\right) = \tan^{-1}\left(\dfrac{25\text{ kHz}}{8.5\text{ kHz}}\right) = \mathbf{-71.2°}$

(f) $\theta = \tan^{-1}\left(\dfrac{f}{f_c}\right) = \tan^{-1}\left(\dfrac{85\text{ kHz}}{8.5\text{ kHz}}\right) = \mathbf{-84.3°}$

See Figure 13-1.

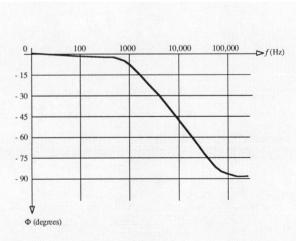

Figure 13-1

Chapter 13

Section 13-2 Open-Loop Response

8. (a) $A_{ol(mid)} = 30 \text{ dB} + 40 \text{ dB} + 20 \text{ dB} = \mathbf{90 \text{ dB}}$

(b) $\theta_1 = -\tan^{-1}\left(\dfrac{f}{f_c}\right) = -\tan^{-1}\left(\dfrac{10 \text{ kHz}}{600 \text{ Hz}}\right) = -86.6°$

$\theta_2 = -\tan^{-1}\left(\dfrac{f}{f_c}\right) = -\tan^{-1}\left(\dfrac{10 \text{ kHz}}{50 \text{ kHz}}\right) = -11.3°$

$\theta_3 = -\tan^{-1}\left(\dfrac{f}{f_c}\right) = -\tan^{-1}\left(\dfrac{10 \text{ kHz}}{200 \text{ kHz}}\right) = -2.86°$

$\theta_{tot} = -86.6° - 11.3° - 2.86° - 180° = \mathbf{-281°}$

9. (a) 0 dB/decade
(b) -20 dB/decade
(c) -40 dB/decade
(d) -60 dB/decade

Section 13-3 Closed-Loop Response

10. (a) $A_{cl(I)} = -\left(\dfrac{R_f}{R_i}\right) = -\left(\dfrac{68 \text{ k}\Omega}{2.2 \text{ k}\Omega}\right) = -30.9$; $A_{cl(I)}(\text{dB}) = 20\log(30.9) = \mathbf{29.8 \text{ dB}}$

(b) $A_{cl(NI)} = \dfrac{1}{B} = \dfrac{1}{15 \text{ k}\Omega/235 \text{ k}\Omega} = 15.7$; $A_{cl(NI)}(\text{dB}) = 20\log(15.7) = \mathbf{23.9 \text{ dB}}$

(c) $A_{cl(VF)} = 1$; $A_{cl(VF)}(\text{dB}) = 20\log(1) = \mathbf{0 \text{ dB}}$

These are all closed-loop gains.

11. $BW_{cl} = BW_{ol}(1 + BA_{ol(mid)}) = 1500 \text{ Hz}[1 + (0.015)(180{,}000)] = \mathbf{4.05 \text{ MHz}}$

12. $A_{ol}(\text{dB}) = 89 \text{ dB}$

$A_{ol} = 28{,}184$

$A_{cl}f_{c(cl)} = A_{ol}f_{c(ol)}$

$A_{cl} = \dfrac{A_{ol}f_{c(ol)}}{f_{c(cl)}} = \dfrac{(28{,}184)(750 \text{ Hz})}{5.5 \text{ kHz}} = 3843$

$A_{cl}(\text{dB}) = 20\log(3843) = \mathbf{71.7 \text{ dB}}$

13. $A_{cl} = \dfrac{A_{ol}f_{c(ol)}}{f_{c(cl)}} = \dfrac{(28{,}184)(750 \text{ Hz})}{5.5 \text{ kHz}} = 3843$

Unity-gain bandwidth $= A_{cl}f_{c(cl)} = (3843)(5.5 \text{ kHz}) = \mathbf{21.1 \text{ MHz}}$

Chapter 13

14. (a) $A_{cl(VF)} = 1$

$$BW = f_{c(cl)} = \frac{\text{Unity-gain } BW}{A_{cl}} = \frac{2.8 \text{ MHz}}{1} = \textbf{2.8 MHz}$$

(b) $A_{cl(I)} = -\dfrac{100 \text{ k}\Omega}{2.2 \text{ k}\Omega} = -45.5$

$$BW = \frac{2.8 \text{ MHz}}{45.5} = \textbf{61.6 kHz}$$

(c) $A_{cl(NI)} = 1 + \dfrac{12 \text{ k}\Omega}{1 \text{ k}\Omega} = 13$

$$BW = \frac{2.8 \text{ MHz}}{13} = \textbf{215 kHz}$$

(d) $A_{cl(I)} = -\dfrac{1 \text{ M}\Omega}{5.6 \text{ k}\Omega} = -179$

$$BW = \frac{2.8 \text{ MHz}}{179} = \textbf{15.7 kHz}$$

15. (a) $A_{cl} = \dfrac{150 \text{ k}\Omega}{22 \text{ k}\Omega} = 6.8$

$$f_{c(cl)} = \frac{A_{ol} f_{c(ol)}}{A_{cl}} = \frac{(120{,}000)(150 \text{ Hz})}{6.8} = 2.65 \text{ MHz}$$

$BW = f_{c(cl)} = \textbf{2.65 MHz}$

(b) $A_{cl} = \dfrac{1 \text{ M}\Omega}{10 \text{ k}\Omega} = 100$

$$f_{c(cl)} = \frac{A_{ol} f_{c(ol)}}{A_{cl}} = \frac{(195{,}000)(50 \text{ Hz})}{100} = 97.5 \text{ kHz}$$

$BW = f_{c(cl)} = \textbf{97.5 kHz}$

Section 13-4 Positive Feedback and Stability

16. $A_{cl} = \dfrac{10 \text{ M}\Omega}{2.7 \text{ k}\Omega} = 3704$

$A_{cl}(\text{dB}) = 71.37 \text{ dB}$

At 50 kHz, the midrange gain has dropped from 100 dB at a -20 dB/decade rate to

$$A_{ol} = \frac{A_{ol(mid)}}{\sqrt{1 + \left(\dfrac{f}{f_{c(ol)}}\right)^2}} = \frac{100}{\sqrt{1 + \left(\dfrac{50 \text{ kHz}}{1.2 \text{ kHz}}\right)^2}} = 2399$$

$A_{ol}(\text{dB}) = 20\log(2399) = 67.6 \text{ dB}$

Since $A_{cl} > A_{ol}$ (71.37 dB > 67.6 dB), the closed-loop gain intersects the open-loop gain on the -20 dB/decade slope. Therefore, the amplifier is **stable**.

Chapter 13

17. (a) $\theta_{pm} = 180° - \theta_{tot} = 180° - 30° = \mathbf{150°}$
 (b) $\theta_{pm} = 180° - \theta_{tot} = 180° - 60° = \mathbf{120°}$
 (c) $\theta_{pm} = 180° - \theta_{tot} = 180° - 120° = \mathbf{60°}$
 (d) $\theta_{pm} = 180° - \theta_{tot} = 180° - 180° = \mathbf{0°}$
 (e) $\theta_{pm} = 180° - \theta_{tot} = 180° - 210° = \mathbf{-30°}$

18. $\theta_1 = -\tan^{-1}\left(\dfrac{f}{f_c}\right) = -\tan^{-1}\left(\dfrac{50\text{ kHz}}{125\text{ kHz}}\right) = -89.9°$

$\theta_2 = -\tan^{-1}\left(\dfrac{f}{f_c}\right) = -\tan^{-1}\left(\dfrac{50\text{ kHz}}{25\text{ kHz}}\right) = -63.4°$

$\theta_3 = -\tan^{-1}\left(\dfrac{f}{f_c}\right) = -\tan^{-1}\left(\dfrac{50\text{ kHz}}{180\text{ kHz}}\right) = -15.5°$

$\theta_{tot} = -89.86° - 63.43° - 15.52° = \mathbf{-169°}$

19. (a) Unstable
 (b) Stable
 (c) Marginally stable

Section 13-5 Compensation

20. (a) The -20 dB/decade slope extends down to 60 dB. The total response must be lowered so that it extends down to 30 dB with a -20 dB/decade slope. This represents a 1.5 decade decrease in critical frequency from 100 Hz to 5 Hz.

 (b) See Figure 13-2.

 (c) See Figure 13-3.

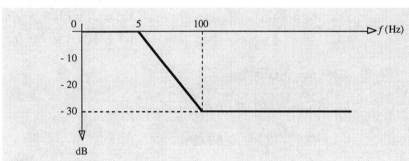

Figure 13-2

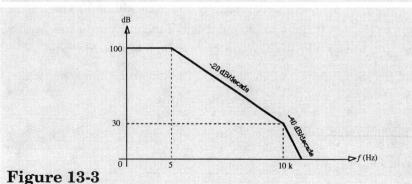

Figure 13-3

Chapter 13

21. The open-loop gain must be decreased so that the -20 dB/decade rolloff extends down to slightly less than 40 dB rather than to 60 dB. To do this, the midrange gain must be made to rolloff a decade sooner. Therefore, the critical frequency of the compensating network must be **25 Hz**.

22. The open-loop gain must be decreased so that the -20 dB/decade rolloff extends down to slightly less than 20 dB rather than to 60 dB. To do this, the midrange gain must be made to rolloff two decades sooner. Therefore, the critical frequency of the compensating network must be **2.5 Hz**.

Section 13-6 System Application

23. The push–pull stage will operate nonlinearly if D_1 or D_2 are shorted, Q_1 or Q_2 is faulty, the op amp stage has excessive gain, or if R_6 is open or shorted.

24. If a 2.2 MΩ resistor is used for R_3, the gain of the op amp will be ten times too high, probably causing a clipped output waveform.

25. If D_1 opens, the emitter current of Q_1 is diverted to the base of Q_2 producing saturation. Q_3 will also saturate. The result is a signal voltage of **0 V** on the output

Data Sheet Problems

26. From the data sheet in Figure 13–37:
(a) Highest dc voltages for an LM201A are **±22 V**.
(b) Maximum power for an LM201A in a plastic DIP at 65° is
625 mW – (65°C – 25°C)(5.0 mW/°C) = **425 mW**
(c) Maximum peak output for an LM101A with ±15 V supplies and a 10 kΩ load is **±14 V**
(d) Minimum open–loop gain for an LM101A is 25 V/mV = **25,000**

27. CMRR = 96 dB typical
$$CMRR = 20\log\left(\frac{V_2}{V_1}\right) = 96 \text{ dB}$$
$$\frac{V_2}{V_1} = \log^{-1}\left(\frac{96 \text{ dB}}{20}\right) = \mathbf{63{,}096}$$

28. (a) Maximum open–loop voltage gain is **100 dB**
(b) The approximate –3 dB bandwidth is **10 Hz**
(c) The approximate value of the unity gain bandwidth is **4 MHz**
(d) The open loop roll–off rate is **–20dB/decade**

Chapter 13

Advanced Problems

29. From Figure 13–38:
$f_c = 10$ kHz at $A_v = 40$ dB $= 100$
In this circuit
$A_v = 1 + \dfrac{33\ k\Omega}{333\ \Omega} = 100.1 \cong 100$
The compensating resistor is
$R_c = 33\ k\Omega \parallel 333\ \Omega = 330\ \Omega$
See Figure 13–4.

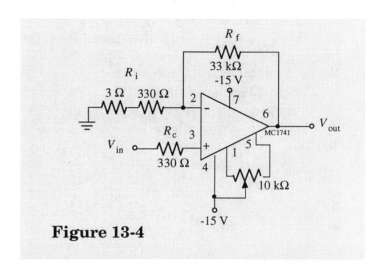

Figure 13-4

30. From Figure 13–39:
For a ±10 V output swing minimum, the load must be 600 Ω for +10 V and ≈ 620 Ω for –10 V. So, the minimum load is **620 Ω**

31. For the amplifier
$A_v = -\dfrac{100\ k\Omega}{2\ k\Omega} = -50$
The compensating resistor is
$R_c = 100\ k\Omega \parallel 2\ k\Omega = 1.96\ k\Omega \cong 2\ k\Omega$
See Figure 13–5.

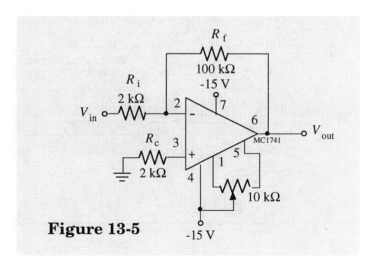

Figure 13-5

32. From Figure 3–38, the maximum 741 closed loop gian with BW = 5 kHz is approximately
60 dB – (20 dB)(log(5 kHz/1 kHz)) = 60 dB – (20 dB)(0.7) = **46 dB**
$A_{v(dB)}\ 20\log A_v$
$A_v = \log_?^{-1}\left(\dfrac{A_{v(dB)}}{20}\right) = \log_?^{-1}\left(\dfrac{46}{20}\right) = \mathbf{200}$

Chapter 14
Basic Op-Amp Circuits

Section 14-1 Comparators

1. $V_{out(p)} = A_{ol}V_{in} = (80{,}000)(0.15 \text{ mV})(1.414) = 16.9 \text{ V}$
   Since 12 V is the peak limit, the op-amp saturates.
   $V_{out(pp)} = \mathbf{24 \text{ V}}$ **with distortion due to clipping.**

2. (a) Maximum negative
   (b) Maximum positive
   (c) Maximum negative

3. $V_{UTP} = \left(\dfrac{R_2}{R_1 + R_2}\right)(+10 \text{ V}) = \left(\dfrac{18 \text{ k}\Omega}{65 \text{ k}\Omega}\right)10 \text{ V} = \mathbf{2.77 \text{ V}}$

   $V_{LTP} = \left(\dfrac{R_2}{R_1 + R_2}\right)(-10 \text{ V}) = \left(\dfrac{18 \text{ k}\Omega}{65 \text{ k}\Omega}\right)(-10 \text{ V}) = \mathbf{-2.77 \text{ V}}$

4. $V_{HYS} = V_{UTP} - V_{LTP} = 2.77 \text{ V} - (-2.77 \text{ V}) = \mathbf{5.54 \text{ V}}$

5. See Figure 14-1.

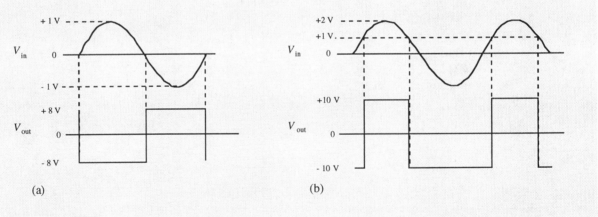

Figure 14-1

Chapter 14

6. $V_{UTP} = \left(\dfrac{R_2}{R_1 + R_2}\right)(+V_{out(max)}) = \left(\dfrac{18\ k\Omega}{51\ k\Omega}\right)11\ V = 3.88\ V$

$V_{LTP} = -3.88\ V$

$V_{HYS} = V_{UTP} - V_{LTP} = 3.88\ V - (-3.88\ V) = \mathbf{7.76\ V}$

$V_{UTP} = \left(\dfrac{R_2}{R_1 + R_2}\right)(+V_{out(max)}) = \left(\dfrac{68\ k\Omega}{218\ k\Omega}\right)11\ V = 3.43\ V$

$V_{LTP} = -3.43\ V$

$V_{HYS} = V_{UTP} - V_{LTP} = 3.43\ V - (-3.43\ V) = \mathbf{6.86\ V}$

7. When the zener is forward biased:

$V_{out} = \left(\dfrac{18\ k\Omega}{18\ k\Omega + 47\ k\Omega}\right)V_{out} - 0.7\ V$

$V_{out} = (0.277)V_{out} - 0.7\ V$

$V_{out}(1 - 0.277) = -0.7\ V$

$V_{out} = \dfrac{-0.7\ V}{1 - 0.277} = \mathbf{-0.968\ V}$

When the zener is reverse biased:

$V_{out} = \left(\dfrac{18\ k\Omega}{18\ k\Omega + 47\ k\Omega}\right)V_{out} + 6.2\ V$

$V_{out} = (0.277)V_{out} + 6.2\ V$

$V_{out}(1 - 0.277) = +6.2\ V$

$V_{out} = \dfrac{+6.2\ V}{1 - 0.277} = \mathbf{+8.57\ V}$

8. $V_{out} = \left(\dfrac{10\ k\Omega}{10\ k\Omega + 47\ k\Omega}\right)V_{out} \pm (4.7\ V + 0.7\ V)$

$V_{out} = (0.175)V_{out} \pm 5.4\ V$

$V_{out} = \dfrac{\pm 5.4\ V}{1 - 0.175} = \pm 6.55\ V$

$V_{UTP} = (0.175)(+6.55\ V) = +1.15\ V$

$V_{LTP} = (0.175)(-6.55\ V) = -1.15\ V$

See Figure 14-2.

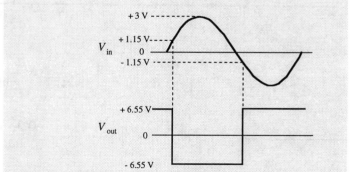

Figure 14-2

Chapter 14

Section 14-2 Summing Amplifiers

9.

(a) $V_{OUT} = -\dfrac{R_f}{R_i}(+1\text{ V} + 1.5\text{ V}) = -1(1\text{ V} + 1.5\text{ V}) = \mathbf{-2.5\text{ V}}$

(b) $V_{OUT} = -\dfrac{R_f}{R_i}(0.1\text{ V} + 1\text{ V} + 0.5\text{ V}) = -\dfrac{22\text{ k}\Omega}{10\text{ k}\Omega}(1.6\text{ V}) = \mathbf{-3.52\text{ V}}$

10.

(a) $V_{R1} = \mathbf{1\text{ V}}$
$V_{R2} = \mathbf{1.8\text{ V}}$

(b) $I_{R1} = \dfrac{1\text{ V}}{22\text{ k}\Omega} = 45.5\text{ }\mu\text{A}$

$I_{R2} = \dfrac{1.8\text{ V}}{22\text{ k}\Omega} = 81.8\text{ }\mu\text{A}$

$I_f = I_{R1} + I_{R2} = 45.5\text{ }\mu\text{A} + 81.8\text{ }\mu\text{A} = \mathbf{127\text{ }\mu\text{A}}$

(c) $V_{OUT} = -I_f R_f = -(127.27\text{ }\mu\text{A})(22\text{ k}\Omega) = \mathbf{-2.8\text{ V}}$

11.

$5V_{in} = \left(\dfrac{R_f}{R}\right)V_{in}$

$\dfrac{R_f}{R} = 5$

$R_f = 5R = 5(22\text{ k}\Omega) = \mathbf{110\text{ k}\Omega}$

12. See Figure 14-3.

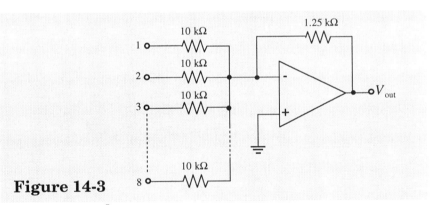

Figure 14-3

13.

$V_{OUT} = -\left[\left(\dfrac{R_f}{R_1}\right)V_1 + \left(\dfrac{R_f}{R_2}\right)V_2 + \left(\dfrac{R_f}{R_3}\right)V_3 + \left(\dfrac{R_f}{R_4}\right)V_4\right]$

$= -\left[\left(\dfrac{10\text{ k}\Omega}{10\text{ k}\Omega}\right)2\text{ V} + \left(\dfrac{10\text{ k}\Omega}{33\text{ k}\Omega}\right)3\text{ V} + \left(\dfrac{10\text{ k}\Omega}{91\text{ k}\Omega}\right)3\text{ V} + \left(\dfrac{10\text{ k}\Omega}{180\text{ k}\Omega}\right)6\text{ V}\right]$

$= -\left(2\text{ V} + 0.91\text{ V} + 0.33\text{ V} + 0.33\text{ V}\right) = \mathbf{-3.57\text{ V}}$

$I_f = \dfrac{V_{OUT}}{R_f} = \dfrac{3.57\text{ V}}{10\text{ k}\Omega} = \mathbf{357\text{ }\mu\text{A}}$

Chapter 14

14. $R_f = 100$ kΩ

Input resistors: $R_1 = 100$ kΩ, $R_2 = 50$ kΩ, $R_3 = 25$ kΩ, $R_4 = 12.5$ kΩ, $R_5 = 6.25$ kΩ, $R_3 = 3.125$ kΩ,

Section 14-3 The Integrator and Differentiator

15. $\dfrac{dV_{out}}{dt} = -\dfrac{V_{IN}}{RC} = -\dfrac{5 \text{ V}}{(56 \text{ k}\Omega)(0.02 \text{ }\mu\text{F})} = -4.46 \text{ mV/}\mu\text{s}$

16. See Figure 14-4.

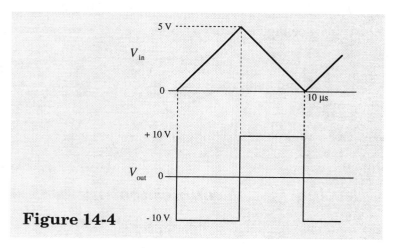

Figure 14-4

17. $I = \dfrac{CV_{pp}}{T/2} = \dfrac{(0.001 \text{ }\mu\text{F})(5 \text{ V})}{10 \text{ }\mu\text{s}/2} = 1 \text{ mA}$

18. $V_{out} = \pm RC\left(\dfrac{V_{pp}}{T/2}\right) = \pm (15 \text{ k}\Omega)(0.05 \text{ }\mu\text{F})\left(\dfrac{2 \text{ V}}{0.5 \text{ ms}}\right) = \pm 3 \text{ V}$

See Figure 14-5.

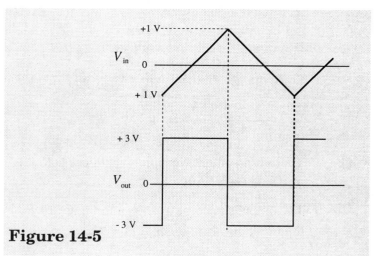

Figure 14-5

Chapter 14

19. For the 10 ms interval when the switch is in position 2:

$$\frac{\Delta V_{out}}{\Delta t} = -\frac{V_{IN}}{RC} = -\frac{5\text{ V}}{(10\text{ k}\Omega)(10\text{ }\mu\text{F})} = -\frac{5\text{ V}}{0.1\text{ s}} = -50\text{ V/s} = -50\text{ mV/ms}$$

$$\Delta V_{out} = (-50\text{ mV/ms})(10\text{ ms}) = -500\text{ mV} = -0.5\text{ V}$$

For the 10 ms interval when the switch is in position 1:

$$\frac{\Delta V_{out}}{\Delta t} = -\frac{V_{IN}}{RC} = -\frac{-5\text{ V}}{(10\text{ k}\Omega)(10\text{ }\mu\text{F})} = -\frac{-5\text{ V}}{0.1\text{ s}} = +50\text{ V/s} = +50\text{ mV/ms}$$

$$\Delta V_{out} = (+50\text{ mV/ms})(10\text{ ms}) = +500\text{ mV} = +0.5\text{ V}$$

See Figure 14-6.

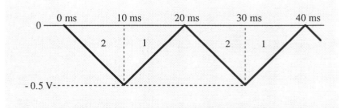

Figure 14-6

Section 14-4 Troubleshooting

20.
$$V_B = \left(\frac{R_2}{R_1 + R_2}\right)V_{out} \pm (V_Z + 0.7\text{ V})$$

$$V_B = \frac{\pm (V_Z + 0.7\text{ V})}{1 - \left(\frac{R_2}{R_1 + R_2}\right)}$$

Normally, V_B should be

$$V_B = \frac{\pm (4.3\text{ V} + 0.7\text{ V})}{1 - 0.5} = \pm 10\text{ V}$$

Since the negative portion of V_B is only -1.4 V, zener **D_2 must be shorted**:

$$V_B = \frac{-(0\text{ V} + 0.7\text{ V})}{1 - 0.5} = -1.4\text{ V}$$

21. There is no output when the input goes below +2 V. This indicates that either **op-amp 2 or diode D_2 is faulty**.

22. The output should be as shown in Figure 14-8. V_2 has no effect on the output. This indicates that R_2 **is open**.

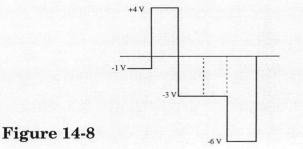

Figure 14-8

Chapter 14

23. $A_v = \dfrac{2.5 \text{ k}\Omega}{10 \text{ k}\Omega} = 0.25$

The output should be as shown in Figure 14-9. An **open R_2** $\left(V_2 \text{ is missing}\right)$ will produce the observed output, which is incorrect.

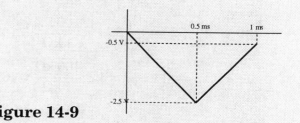

Figure 14-9

Section 14-5 System Application

24. The D_2 input is missing (acts as a constant 0). This indicates an **open 50 kΩ resistor**.

25. The first thing that you should always do is visually inspect the circuit for bad contacts or loose connections, shorts from solder splashes or wire clippings, incorrect components, and incorrectly installed components. In this case, after careful inspection, you will find that the **middle op-amp IC is installed incorrectly** (notice where pin 1 is as indicated by the dot).

26. An open integrator capacitor will cause the output of IC2 to saturate positively.

27. If a 1 kΩ resistor is used for R_1, the output of IC2 will be ten times larger for the sample–and–hold operation most likely causing the integrator to ramp into saturation.

Advanced Problems

28. For a 741S op amp with a 12 V/µs slew rate and 500 kHz sample pulse rate, the ramp up and ramp down must take

$\tau = \dfrac{1}{500 \text{ kHz}} = 2 \text{ µs}$

With a fixed interval of 1 µs for ramp up, this leaves a 1 µs ramp down interval.
If $-V_{REF} = -8$ V as in the system application, with a -8 V/µs ramp down rate, the ramp down can accomodate an 8 V ramp–up peak corresponding to +8 V input. However, if full slew rate is utilized and a -12 V reference voltge dis used, a +12 V input can be accomodated.

29. A maximum of + 0.5 V can be used.

30. 100 mV/µs = 5 V/R_iC

$R_iC = \dfrac{5 \text{ V}}{100 \text{ mV/µs}} = 50 \text{ µs}$

For $C = 3300$ pF

$R_i = \dfrac{50 \text{ µs}}{3300 \text{ pF}} = 15.15 \text{ k}\Omega = 15 \text{ k}\Omega + 150 \text{ }\Omega$

For a 5 V peak–peak triangle waveform:

$t_{ramp\,up} = t_{ramp\,down} = \dfrac{5 \text{ V}}{100 \text{ mV/µs}} = 50 \text{ µs}$

$\tau = 2(50 \text{ µs}) = 100 \text{ µs}$

$f_{in} = 1/100 \text{ µs} = \textbf{100 kHz}$

See Figure 14–10.

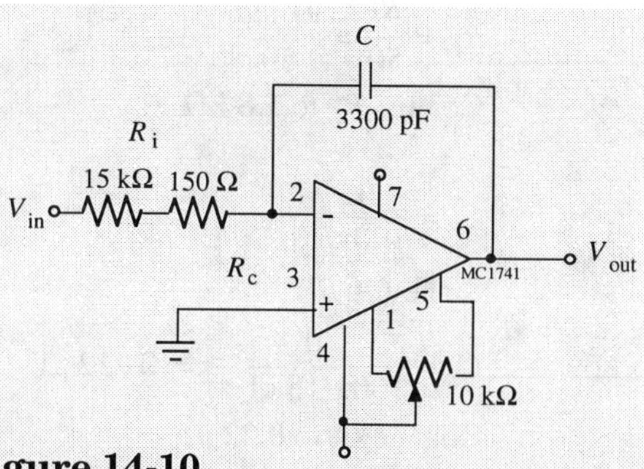

Figure 14-10

Chapter 15
More Op-Amp Circuits

Section 15-1 Instrumentation Amplifiers

1.
$$A_{v(1)} = 1 + \frac{R_1}{R_G} = 1 + \frac{100 \text{ k}\Omega}{1 \text{ k}\Omega} = \mathbf{101}$$

$$A_{v(2)} = 1 + \frac{R_2}{R_G} = 1 + \frac{100 \text{ k}\Omega}{1 \text{ k}\Omega} = \mathbf{101}$$

2.
$$A_{cl} = 1 + \frac{2R}{R_G} = 1 + \frac{200 \text{ k}\Omega}{1 \text{ k}\Omega} = \mathbf{201}$$

3.
$$V_{out} = A_{cl}\left(V_{in(1)} - V_{in(2)}\right) = 202(10 \text{ mV} - 5 \text{ mV}) = \mathbf{1.005 \text{ V}}$$

4.
$$A_v = 1 + \frac{2R}{R_G}$$

$$\frac{2R}{R_G} = A_v - 1$$

$$R_G = \frac{2R}{A_v - 1} = \frac{2(100 \text{ k}\Omega)}{1000 - 1} = \frac{200 \text{ k}\Omega}{999} = 200.2 \text{ }\Omega \cong \mathbf{200 \text{ }\Omega}$$

5.
$$A_v = \frac{R_S}{R_G} = \frac{91 \text{ k}\Omega}{10 \text{ k}\Omega} = \mathbf{9.1}$$

6.
$$C_x = \frac{1}{100\pi f_c}$$

$$f_c = \frac{1}{100\pi C_x} = \frac{1}{100\pi(0.022 \text{ }\mu\text{F})} = 145 \text{ kHz}$$

$$BW \cong f_c = \mathbf{145 \text{ kHz}}$$

7.
$$A_v = \frac{R_S}{R_G} = 50$$

$$R_G = \frac{R_S}{50} = \frac{91 \text{ k}\Omega}{50} = 1820 \text{ }\Omega$$

Change R_G to **1.8 kΩ**

8.
$$C_x = \frac{1}{100\pi f_c}$$

Since $f_c \cong BW$,

$$C_x = \frac{1}{100\pi(15 \text{ kHz})} = 0.212 \text{ }\mu\text{F}$$

Change C_x to **0.22 μF**

Chapter 15

Section 15-2 Isolation Amplifiers

9. $A_{v(total)} = (30)(0.75)(10) = \mathbf{225}$

10. (a) $A_{v(input)} = 1 + \dfrac{R_F}{R_1} = 1 + \dfrac{18 \text{ k}\Omega}{8.2 \text{ k}\Omega} = 3.2$

$A_{v(output)} = \dfrac{75 \text{ k}\Omega + R_{ext}}{30 \text{ k}\Omega} = \dfrac{75 \text{ k}\Omega + 150 \text{ k}\Omega}{30 \text{ k}\Omega} = 7.5$

$A_v = 0.4 A_{v(input)} A_{v(output)} = 0.4(3.2)(7.5) = \mathbf{9.59}$

(b) $A_{v(input)} = 1 + \dfrac{R_F}{R_1} = 1 + \dfrac{330 \text{ k}\Omega}{1 \text{ k}\Omega} = 331$

$A_{v(output)} = \dfrac{75 \text{ k}\Omega}{30 \text{ k}\Omega} = \dfrac{75 \text{ k}\Omega + 150 \text{ k}\Omega}{30 \text{ k}\Omega} = 2.5$

$A_v = 0.4 A_{v(input)} A_{v(output)} = 0.4(331)(2.5) = \mathbf{331}$

11. $A_v = 0.4 A_{v(input)} A_{v(output)} = 100$

$A_{v(input)} = \dfrac{100}{0.4 A_{v(output)}} = \dfrac{100}{(0.4)(7.5)} = 33.3$

$A_{v(input)} = 1 + \dfrac{R_F}{R_1}$

$\dfrac{R_F}{R_1} = A_{v(input)} - 1$

$R_F = R_1 \left(A_{v(input)} - 1 \right) = 8.2 \text{ k}\Omega (32.3) = 265 \text{ k}\Omega$

Change R_F to **270 kΩ**.

12. $A_v = 0.4 A_{v(input)} A_{v(output)} = 100$

$A_{v(output)} = \dfrac{100}{0.4 A_{v(input)}} = \dfrac{100}{(0.4)(331)} = 0.76$

The minimum gain possible for the output section is

$A_{v(output)} = \dfrac{75 \text{ k}\Omega}{30 \text{ k}\Omega} = 2.5$

Therefore, it is **not possible** to achieve an overall gain of 100 by changing only the gain of the output section.

Chapter 15

13. To acheive unity gain in an AD295, connect pin 23 directly to pin 22 to produce a gain for the output section of

$$A_{v(output)} = \frac{75 \text{ k}\Omega}{30 \text{ k}\Omega} = 2.5$$

Connect pin 38 directly to pin 40 to produce a gain for the input section of

$$A_{v(input)} = 1 + \frac{R_F}{R_i} = 1 + \frac{0}{R_i} = 1$$

The overall gain is

$$A_{v(total)} = 0.4 A_{v(input)} A_{v(output)} = 0.4(1)(2.5) = 1$$

Section 15-3 Operational Transconductance Amplifiers (OTAs)

14.
$$g_m = \frac{I_{out}}{V_{in}} = \frac{10 \text{ μA}}{10 \text{ mV}} = \mathbf{1 \text{ mS}}$$

15. $I_{out} = g_m V_{in} = (5000 \text{ μS})(100 \text{ mV}) = \mathbf{500 \text{ μA}}$
$V_{out} = I_{out} R_L = (500 \text{ μA})(10 \text{ k}\Omega) = \mathbf{5 \text{ V}}$

16. $g_m = \dfrac{I_{out}}{V_{in}}$

$I_{out} = g_m V_{in} = (4000 \text{ μS})(100 \text{ mV}) = 400 \text{ μA}$

$$R_L = \frac{V_{out}}{I_{out}} = \frac{3.5 \text{ V}}{400 \text{ μA}} = \mathbf{8.75 \text{ k}\Omega}$$

17.
$$I_{BIAS} = \frac{+12 \text{ V} - (-12 \text{ V}) - 0.7 \text{ V}}{R_{BIAS}} = \frac{+12 \text{ V} - (-12 \text{ V}) - 0.7 \text{ V}}{220 \text{ k}\Omega} = \frac{23.3 \text{ V}}{220 \text{ k}\Omega} = 106 \text{ μA}$$

From the graph in Figure 15-46:
$g_m = K I_{BIAS} \cong (16)(106 \text{ μA}) = 1.70 \text{ mS}$

$$A_v = \frac{V_{out}}{V_{in}} = \frac{I_{out} R_L}{V_{in}} = g_m R_L = (1.70 \text{ mS})(6.8 \text{ k}\Omega) = \mathbf{11.6}$$

18. The maximum voltage gain occurs when the 10 kΩ potentiometer is set to 0 Ω and was determined in Problem 17.

$A_{v(max)} = \mathbf{11.6}$

The minimum voltage gain occurs when the 10 kΩ potentiometer is set to 10 kΩ:

$$I_{BIAS} = \frac{+12 \text{ V} - (-12 \text{ V}) - 0.7 \text{ V}}{220 \text{ k}\Omega + 10 \text{ k}\Omega} = \frac{23.3 \text{ V}}{230 \text{ k}\Omega} = 101 \text{ μA}$$

$g_m \cong (16)(101 \text{ μS}) = 1.62 \text{ mS}$

$A_{v(min)} = g_m R_L = (1.62 \text{ mS})(6.8 \text{ k}\Omega) = \mathbf{11.0}$

Chapter 15

19. The V_{MOD} waveform is applied to the bias input.
The gain and output voltage for each value of V_{MOD} is determined as follows using $K = 16$. The output waveform is shown in Figure 15-1

For $V_{MOD} = +8$ V:

$$I_{BIAS} = \frac{+8 \text{ V} - (-9 \text{ V}) - 0.7 \text{ V}}{39 \text{ k}\Omega} = \frac{16.3 \text{ V}}{39 \text{ k}\Omega} = 418 \text{ }\mu\text{A}$$

$$g_m = KI_{BIAS} \cong 16(418 \text{ }\mu\text{A}) = 6.69 \text{ mS}$$

$$A_v = \frac{V_{out}}{V_{in}} = \frac{I_{out}R_L}{V_{in}} = g_mR_L = (6.69 \text{ mS})(10 \text{ k}\Omega) = 66.9$$

$$V_{out} = A_vV_{in} = (66.9)(100 \text{ mV}) = \mathbf{6.69 \text{ V}}$$

For $V_{MOD} = +6$ V:

$$I_{BIAS} = \frac{+6 \text{ V} - (-9 \text{ V}) - 0.7 \text{ V}}{39 \text{ k}\Omega} = \frac{14.3 \text{ V}}{39 \text{ k}\Omega} = 367 \text{ }\mu\text{A}$$

$$g_m = KI_{BIAS} \cong 16(367 \text{ }\mu\text{A}) = 5.87 \text{ mS}$$

$$A_v = \frac{V_{out}}{V_{in}} = \frac{I_{out}R_L}{V_{in}} = g_mR_L = (5.87 \text{ mS})(10 \text{ k}\Omega) = 58.7$$

$$V_{out} = A_vV_{in} = (58.7)(100 \text{ mV}) = \mathbf{5.87 \text{ V}}$$

For $V_{MOD} = +4$ V:

$$I_{BIAS} = \frac{+4 \text{ V} - (-9 \text{ V}) - 0.7 \text{ V}}{39 \text{ k}\Omega} = \frac{12.3 \text{ V}}{39 \text{ k}\Omega} = 315 \text{ }\mu\text{A}$$

$$g_m = KI_{BIAS} \cong 16(315 \text{ }\mu\text{A}) = 5.04 \text{ mS}$$

$$A_v = \frac{V_{out}}{V_{in}} = \frac{I_{out}R_L}{V_{in}} = g_mR_L = (5.04 \text{ mS})(10 \text{ k}\Omega) = 50.4$$

$$V_{out} = A_vV_{in} = (50.4)(100 \text{ mV}) = \mathbf{5.04 \text{ V}}$$

For $V_{MOD} = +2$ V:

$$I_{BIAS} = \frac{+2 \text{ V} - (-9 \text{ V}) - 0.7 \text{ V}}{39 \text{ k}\Omega} = \frac{10.3 \text{ V}}{39 \text{ k}\Omega} = 264 \text{ }\mu\text{A}$$

$$g_m = KI_{BIAS} \cong 16(264 \text{ }\mu\text{A}) = 4.22 \text{ mS}$$

$$A_v = \frac{V_{out}}{V_{in}} = \frac{I_{out}R_L}{V_{in}} = g_mR_L = (4.22 \text{ mS})(10 \text{ k}\Omega) = 42.2$$

$$V_{out} = A_vV_{in} = (42.2)(100 \text{ mV}) = \mathbf{4.22 \text{ V}}$$

For $V_{MOD} = +1$ V:

$$I_{BIAS} = \frac{+1 \text{ V} - (-9 \text{ V}) - 0.7 \text{ V}}{39 \text{ k}\Omega} = \frac{9.3 \text{ V}}{39 \text{ k}\Omega} = 238 \text{ }\mu\text{A}$$

$$g_m = KI_{BIAS} \cong 16(238 \text{ }\mu\text{A}) = 3.81 \text{ mS}$$

$$A_v = \frac{V_{out}}{V_{in}} = \frac{I_{out}R_L}{V_{in}} = g_mR_L = (3.81 \text{ mS})(10 \text{ k}\Omega) = 38.1$$

$$V_{out} = A_vV_{in} = (38.1)(100 \text{ mV}) = \mathbf{3.81 \text{ V}}$$

Chapter 15

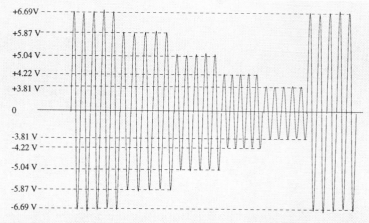

Figure 15-1

20. $I_{BIAS} = \dfrac{+9 \text{ V} - (-9 \text{ V}) - 0.7 \text{ V}}{39 \text{ k}\Omega} = \dfrac{17.3 \text{ V}}{39. \text{k}\Omega} = 444 \text{ μA}$

$V_{TRIG(+)} = I_{BIAS}R_1 = (444 \text{ μA})(10 \text{ k}\Omega) = \textbf{+4.44 V}$

$V_{TRIG(-)} = -I_{BIAS}R_1 = (-444 \text{ μA})(10 \text{ k}\Omega) = \textbf{-4.44 V}$

21. See Figure 15-2.

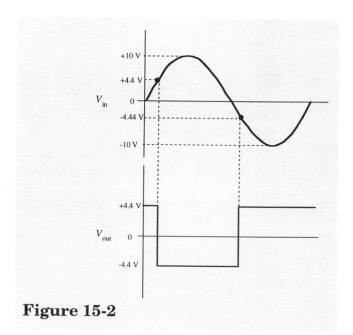

Figure 15-2

Section 15-4 Log and Antilog Amplifiers

22. (a) $\ln(0.5) = \textbf{-0.693}$
   (b) $\ln(2) = \textbf{0.693}$
   (c) $\ln(50) = \textbf{3.91}$
   (d) $\ln(130) = \textbf{4.87}$

Chapter 15

23. (a) $\log_{10}(0.5) = \mathbf{-0.301}$
(b) $\log_{10}(2) = \mathbf{0.301}$
(c) $\log_{10}(50) = \mathbf{1.70}$
(d) $\log_{10}(130) = \mathbf{2.11}$

24. Antilog $x = 10^x$ or e^x, depending on the base used.
INV ln $= e^{1.6} = \mathbf{4.95}$
INV Log $= 10^{1.6} = \mathbf{39.8}$

25. The output of a log amplifier is limited to **0.7 V** because the output voltage is limited to the barrier potential of the transistor's pn junction.

26. $V_{out} \cong -(0.025 \text{ V}) \ln\left(\dfrac{V_{in}}{I_s R_{in}}\right)$

$= -(0.025 \text{ V}) \ln\left(\dfrac{3 \text{ V}}{(100 \text{ nA})(82 \text{ k}\Omega)}\right) = -(0.025 \text{ V}) \ln(365.9) = \mathbf{-148 \text{ mV}}$

27. $V_{out} \cong -(0.025 \text{ V}) \ln\left(\dfrac{V_{in}}{I_{EBO} R_{in}}\right)$

$= -(0.025 \text{ V}) \ln\left(\dfrac{1.5 \text{ V}}{(60 \text{ nA})(47 \text{ k}\Omega)}\right) = -(0.025 \text{ V}) \ln(531.9) = \mathbf{-157 \text{ mV}}$

28. $V_{out} = -R_F I_{EBO} \text{antilog}\left(\dfrac{V_{in}}{25 \text{ mV}}\right) = -R_F I_{EBO} e^{\left(\frac{V_{in}}{25 \text{ mV}}\right)}$

$V_{out} = -(10 \text{ k}\Omega)(60 \text{ nA}) e^{\left(\frac{0.225 \text{ V}}{25 \text{ mV}}\right)} = -(10 \text{ k}\Omega)(60 \text{ nA}) e^9 = -(10 \text{ k}\Omega)(60 \text{ nA})(8103) = \mathbf{-4.86 \text{ V}}$

29. $V_{out(max)} \cong -(0.025 \text{ V}) \ln\left(\dfrac{V_{in}}{I_{EBO} R_{in}}\right) = -(0.025 \text{ V}) \ln\left(\dfrac{1 \text{ V}}{(60 \text{ nA})(47 \text{ k}\Omega)}\right)$

$= -(0.025 \text{ V}) \ln(354.6) = \mathbf{-147 \text{ mV}}$

$V_{out(min)} \cong -(0.025 \text{ V}) \ln\left(\dfrac{V_{in}}{I_{EBO} R_{in}}\right) = -(0.025 \text{ V}) \ln\left(\dfrac{100 \text{ mV}}{(60 \text{ nA})(47 \text{ k}\Omega)}\right)$

$= -(0.025 \text{ V}) \ln(35.5) = \mathbf{-89.2 \text{ mV}}$

The signal compression allows larger signals to be reduced without causing smaller amplitudes to be lost (in this case, the 1 V paeak is reduced 85 % but the 100 mV peak is reduced only 10%.)

Chapter 15

Section 15-5 Converters and Other Op-Amp Circuits

30. (a) $V_{IN} = V_Z = 4.7$ V

$$I_L = \frac{V_{IN}}{R_i} = \frac{4.7 \text{ V}}{1 \text{ k}\Omega} = \textbf{4.7 mA}$$

(b) $V_{IN} = \left(\dfrac{10 \text{ k}\Omega}{20 \text{ k}\Omega}\right) 12 \text{ V} = 6 \text{ V}$

$R_i = 10 \text{ k}\Omega \parallel 10 \text{ k}\Omega + 100 \text{ }\Omega = 5.1 \text{ k}\Omega$

$$I_L = \frac{V_{IN}}{R_i} = \frac{6 \text{ V}}{5.1 \text{ k}\Omega} = \textbf{1.18 mA}$$

31. See Figure 15-3.

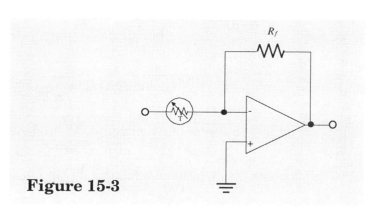

Figure 15-3

Chapter 15

Section 15-6 System Application

32. The circuit on this board is represented by the schematic in Figure 15-40. For the isolation amplifier IC_1:

$$A_{v(input)} = 1 + \frac{R_3}{R_2} = 1 + \frac{100 \text{ k}\Omega}{10 \text{ k}\Omega} = 1 + 10 = 11$$

$$A_{v(output)} = \frac{75 \text{ k}\Omega}{30 \text{ k}\Omega} = 2.5$$

$$A_{v(total)} = 0.4(11)(2.5) = 11$$

For the IC_2 filter:

$$A_{v(mid)} = 1 + \frac{R_9}{R_{10}} = 1 + \frac{3.3 \text{ k}\Omega}{5.6 \text{ k}\Omega} = 1 + 0.59 = 1.59$$

$$f_c = \frac{1}{2\pi RC} = \frac{1}{2\pi(100 \text{ k}\Omega)(0.015 \text{ }\mu\text{F})} = 106 \text{ Hz, so the 50 Hz input is in the midrange.}$$

For IC_3:

$$A_v = \frac{R_{16} + R_{17}}{R_{11}} = \frac{125 \text{ k}\Omega}{1 \text{ k}\Omega} = 125, \text{ assuming } R_{17} \text{ is set at 25 k}\Omega.$$

TP 1 is at the output of IC_2:

$V_{TP1} = (1.59)(11 \text{ mV}) = $ **17.5 mV @ 50 Hz**

TP 2 is at pin2 of IC_2:

$$V_{TP2} = \left(\frac{5.6 \text{ k}\Omega}{8.9 \text{ k}\Omega}\right) V_{TP1} = \textbf{11 mV @ 50 Hz}$$

TP 3 is at the output of IC_1:

$V_{TP3} = A_{v(total)} V_{in} = (11)(1 \text{ mV}) = $ **11 mV @ 50 Hz**

TP 4 is at the supply voltage of **+12 V DC.**

TP 5 is at the output of IC_3:

$V_{TP5} = A_v V_{TP1} = (125)(17.9 \text{ mV}) = $ **2.19 V @ 50 Hz**

33. The IC_2 filter was found in Problem 32 to have a critical frequency of 106 Hz. Therefore the 1kHz input signal is outside of the bandwidth.

$V_{TP1} \cong \textbf{0 V}$

$V_{TP2} \cong \textbf{0 V}$

The voltage gain of IC_1 was found in Problem 32 to be 11.

$V_{TP3} = (11)(2 \text{ mV}) = $ **22 mV @ 1 kHz**

$V_{TP4} = $ **+ 12 V DC**

$V_{TP5} \cong \textbf{0 V}$

Chapter 16
Active Filters

Section 16-1 Basic Filter Responses

1. (a) Band-pass
   (b) High-pass
   (c) Low-pass
   (d) Band-stop

2. $BW = f_c = \textbf{800 Hz}$

3. $f_c = \dfrac{1}{2\pi RC} = \dfrac{1}{2\pi(2.2\ k\Omega)(0.0015\ \mu F)} = \textbf{48.2 kHz}$

   No, the upper response rolloff due to internal device capacitances is unknown.

4. The rolloff is **20 dB/decade** because this is a single-pole filter.

5. $BW = f_{ch} - f_{cl} = 3.9\ kHz - 3.2\ kHz = 0.7\ kHz = \textbf{700 Hz}$

   $f_0 = \sqrt{f_{cl}f_{ch}} = \sqrt{(3.2\ kHz)(3.9\ kHz)} = 3.53\ kHz$

   $Q = \dfrac{f_0}{BW} = \dfrac{3.53\ kHz}{700\ Hz} = \textbf{5.04}$

6. $Q = \dfrac{f_0}{BW}$

   $f_0 = Q(BW) = 15(1\ kHz) = \textbf{15 kHz}$

Section 16-2 Filter Response Characteristics

7. (a) 2nd order, 1 stage

   $DF = 2 - \dfrac{R_3}{R_4} = 2 - \dfrac{1.2\ k\Omega}{1.2\ k\Omega} = 2 - 1 = \textbf{1}$ **Not Butterworth.**

   (b) 2nd order, 1 stage

   $DF = 2 - \dfrac{R_3}{R_4} = 2 - \dfrac{560\ \Omega}{1\ k\Omega} = 2 - 0.56 = \textbf{1.44}$ **Approximately Butterworth.**

   (c) 3rd order, 2 stages 1st stage (2 poles):

   $DF = 2 - \dfrac{R_3}{R_4} = 2 - \dfrac{330\ \Omega}{1\ k\Omega} = \textbf{1.67}$

   2nd stage (1 pole):

   $DF = 2 - \dfrac{R_6}{R_7} = \textbf{1.67}$ **Not Butterworth**

Chapter 16

8. (a) From Table 16-1, the damping factor must be 1.414 therefore

$$\frac{R_3}{R_4} = 0.586$$

$R_3 = 0.586 R_4 = 0.586(1.2 \text{ k}\Omega) = \mathbf{703\ \Omega}$

Nearest standard value: **720 Ω**

(b) $\dfrac{R_3}{R_4} = 0.56$

This is an approximate Butterworth response
(as close as you can get using standard 5% resistors)

(c) From Table 16-1, the damping factor of both stages must be 1, therefore

$\dfrac{R_3}{R_4} = 1$

$R_5 = R_4 = R_6 = R_7 = \mathbf{1\ k\Omega}$ (for both stages)

9. (a) Chebyshev
(b) Butterworth
(c) Bessel
(d) Butterworth

Section 16-3 Active Low-Pass Filters

10. **High Pass**
1st stage:

$$DF = 2 - \frac{R_3}{R_4} = 2 - \frac{1 \text{ k}\Omega}{6.8 \text{ k}\Omega} = 1.85$$

2nd stage:

$$DF = 2 - \frac{R_7}{R_8} = 2 - \frac{6.8 \text{ k}\Omega}{5.6 \text{ k}\Omega} = 0.786$$

From Table 16-1:
1st stage $DF = 1.848$ and 2nd stage $DF = 0.765$
Therefore, this filter is **approximately Butterworth**.
Rolloff rate = **80 dB/decade**

11. $f_c = \dfrac{1}{2\pi\sqrt{R_1 R_2 C_1 C_2}} = \dfrac{1}{2\pi\sqrt{R_5 R_6 C_3 C_4}} = \dfrac{1}{2\pi\sqrt{(4.7 \text{ k}\Omega)(6.8 \text{ k}\Omega)(0.22\ \mu\text{F})(0.1\ \mu\text{F})}} = \mathbf{190\ Hz}$

12. $R = R_1 = R_2 = R_5 = R_6$ and $C = C_1 = C_2 = C_3 = C_4$
Let $C = \mathbf{0.22\ \mu F}$ (for both stages)

$$f_c = \frac{1}{2\pi\sqrt{R^2 C^2}} = \frac{1}{2\pi RC}$$

$$R = \frac{1}{2\pi f_c C} = \frac{1}{2\pi(189.8 \text{ Hz})(0.22\ \mu\text{F})} = 3.81 \text{ k}\Omega$$

Choose $R = \mathbf{3.9\ k\Omega}$ (for both stages)

Chapter 16

13. See Figure 16-1.

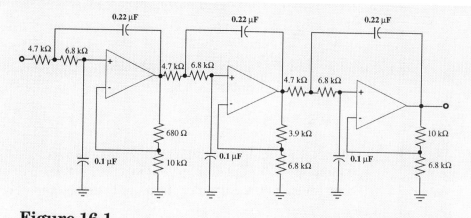

Figure 16-1

14. See Figure 16-2.

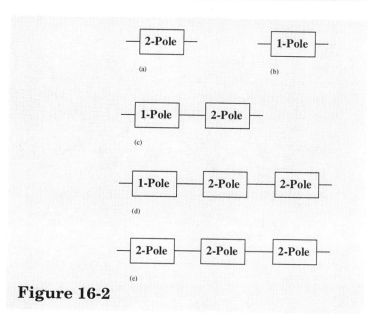

Figure 16-2

Section 16-4 Active High-Pass Filters

15. Exchange the positions of the resistors and the capacitors. See Figure 16-3.

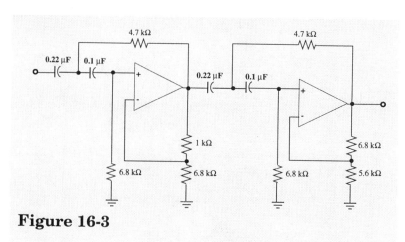

Figure 16-3

Chapter 16

16. $f_c = \dfrac{1}{2\pi RC}$

$f_0 = \dfrac{189.8 \text{ Hz}}{2} = 94.9 \text{ Hz}$

$R = \dfrac{1}{2\pi f_c R} = \dfrac{1}{2\pi(94.9 \text{ Hz})(0.22 \text{ μF})} = 7623 \text{ Ω}$

Let $R = 7.5 \text{ kΩ}$ Change all resistors to **7.5 kΩ**

17. (a) Decrease R_1 and R_2 or C_1 and C_2.

 (b) Increase R_3 or decrease R_4.

Section 16-5 Active Band-Pass Filters

18. (a) Cascaded high-pass/low-pass filters
  (b) Multiple feedback
  (c) State variable

19. (a) 1st stage:

$f_{c1} = \dfrac{1}{2\pi RC} = \dfrac{1}{2\pi(1 \text{ kΩ})(0.047 \text{ μF})} = 3.39 \text{ kHz}$

2nd stage:

$f_{c2} = \dfrac{1}{2\pi RC} = \dfrac{1}{2\pi(1 \text{ kΩ})(0.022 \text{ μF})} = 7.23 \text{ kHz}$

$f_0 = \sqrt{f_{c1}f_{c2}} = \sqrt{(3.39 \text{ kHz})(7.23 \text{ kHz})} = \textbf{4.95 kHz}$

$BW = 7.23 \text{ kHz} - 3.39 \text{ Hz} = \textbf{3.84 kHz}$

(b) $f_0 = \dfrac{1}{2\pi C}\sqrt{\dfrac{R_1+R_2}{R_1 R_2 R_3}} = \dfrac{1}{2\pi(0.022 \text{ μF})}\sqrt{\dfrac{47 \text{ kΩ} + 1.8 \text{ kΩ}}{(47 \text{ kΩ})(1.8 \text{ kΩ})(150 \text{ kΩ})}} = \textbf{449 Hz}$

$Q = \pi f_0 C R_3 = \pi(448.6 \text{ Hz})(0.022 \text{ μF})(150 \text{ kΩ}) = 4.65$

$BW = \dfrac{f_0}{Q} = \dfrac{448.6 \text{ Hz}}{4.65} = \textbf{96.5 Hz}$

(c) For each integrator:

$f_c = \dfrac{1}{2\pi RC} = \dfrac{1}{2\pi(10 \text{ kΩ})(0.001 \text{ μF})} = 1.59 \text{ kHz}$

$f_0 = f_c = \textbf{15.9 kHz}$

$Q = \dfrac{1}{3}\left(\dfrac{R_6}{R_4}+1\right) = \dfrac{1}{3}\left(\dfrac{560 \text{ kΩ}}{10 \text{ kΩ}}+1\right) = \dfrac{1}{3}(56+1) = 19$

$BW = \dfrac{f_0}{Q} = \dfrac{15.9 \text{ kHz}}{19} = \textbf{838 Hz}$

Chapter 16

20. $Q = \dfrac{1}{3}\left(\dfrac{R_6}{R_7} + 1\right)$

Select $R_7 = $ **1 kΩ**

$Q = \dfrac{R_6}{3R_7} + \dfrac{1}{3} = \dfrac{R_6 + R_7}{3R_7}$

$3R_7Q = R_6 + R_7$

$R_6 = 3R_7Q - R_7 = 3(1\text{ k}\Omega)(50) - 10\text{ k}\Omega = 150\text{ k}\Omega - 10\text{ k}\Omega = $ **140 kΩ**

$f_0 = \dfrac{1}{2\pi(12\text{ k}\Omega)(0.01\text{ μF})} = 1.33\text{ kHz}$

$BW = \dfrac{f_0}{Q} = \dfrac{1.33\text{ kHz}}{50} = $ **26.6 Hz**

Section 16-6 Active Band-Stop Filters

21. See Figure 16-4.

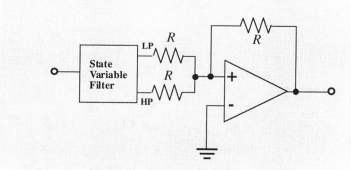

Figure 16-4

22. $f_0 = f_c = \dfrac{1}{2\pi RC}$

Let C remain 0.01 μF

$R = \dfrac{1}{2\pi f_0 C} = \dfrac{1}{2\pi(120\text{ Hz})(0.01\text{ μF})} = $ **133 kΩ**

Change R in the integrators from 12 kΩ to 133 kΩ.

Chapter 17
Oscillators and the Phase-Locked Loop

Section 17-1 The Oscillator

1. An oscillator requires no input other than the dc supply voltage.

2. Amplifier and positive feedback circuit

Section 17-2 Oscillator Principles

3. Unity gain around the closed loop is required for sustained oscillation.
$$A_{cl} = A_v B = 1$$
$$B = \frac{1}{A_v} = \frac{1}{75} = 0.0133$$

4. To insure startup:
$$A_{cl} > 1$$
Since $A_v = 75$, B must be greater than $1/75$ in order to produce the condition $A_v B > 1$.
For example, if $B = 1/50$,
$$A_v B = 75\left(\frac{1}{50}\right) = 1.5$$

Section 17-3 Oscillators with RC Feedback Circuits

5. $$\frac{V_{out}}{V_{in}} = \frac{1}{3}$$
$$V_{out} = \left(\frac{1}{3}\right) V_{in} = \frac{2.2 \text{ V}}{3} = 733 \text{ mV}$$

6. $$f_r = \frac{1}{2\pi RC} = \frac{1}{2\pi(6.2 \text{ k}\Omega)(0.02 \text{ }\mu\text{F})} = 1.28 \text{ kHz}$$

7. $R_1 = 2R_2$
$$R_2 = \frac{R_1}{2} = \frac{100 \text{ k}\Omega}{2} = 50 \text{ k}\Omega$$

8. When dc power is first applied, both zener diodes appear as opens because there is insufficient output voltage. This places R_3 in series with R_1, thus increasing the closed-loop gain to a value greater than unity to assure that oscillation will begin.

Chapter 17

9. The gain changes when
$$V_{out} = V_{Z(D1)} + V_{F(D2)} = 6.8 \text{ V} + 0.7 \text{ V} = \mathbf{7.5 \text{ V}}$$
At this value the zener path bypasses R_3 taking it out of the circuit.
$$A_{cl} = \frac{R_1 + R_2 + R_3}{R_2} = \frac{50 \text{ k}\Omega + 100 \text{ k}\Omega + 47 \text{ k}\Omega}{50 \text{ k}\Omega} = \mathbf{3.94}$$

10. $f_r = \dfrac{1}{2\pi(1 \text{ k}\Omega)(0.015 \text{ }\mu\text{F})} = \mathbf{10.6 \text{ kHz}}$

11. $B = \dfrac{1}{29}$

$A_{cl} = \dfrac{1}{B} = 29$

$A_{cl} = \dfrac{R_f}{R_i}$

$R_f = A_{cl}R_i = 29(4.7 \text{ k}\Omega) = \mathbf{136 \text{ k}\Omega}$

$f_r = \dfrac{1}{2\pi\sqrt{6}\left((4.7 \text{ k}\Omega)(0.02 \text{ }\mu\text{F})\right)} = \mathbf{691 \text{ Hz}}$

Section 17-4 Oscillators with LC Feedback Circuits

12. (a) *Colpitts:*. C_1 and C_3 are the feedback capacitors.

$$f_r = \frac{1}{2\pi\sqrt{L_1 C_T}}$$

$$C_T = \frac{C_1 C_3}{C_1 + C_3} = \frac{(100 \text{ }\mu\text{F})(1000 \text{ pF})}{1100 \text{ pF}} = 90.9 \text{ pF}$$

$$f_r = \frac{1}{2\pi\sqrt{(5 \text{ mH})(90.9 \text{ pF})}} = \mathbf{236 \text{ kHz}}$$

(b) *Hartley*:

$$f_r = \frac{1}{2\pi\sqrt{L_T C_2}}$$

$L_T = L_1 + L_2 = 1.5 \text{ mH} + 10 \text{ mH} = 11.5 \text{ mH}$

$$f_r = \frac{1}{2\pi\sqrt{(11.5 \text{ mH})(470 \text{ pF})}} = \mathbf{68.5 \text{ kHz}}$$

13. $B = \dfrac{50 \text{ pF}}{470 \text{ pF}} = 0.106$

The condition for sustained oscillation is

$A_v = \dfrac{1}{B} = \dfrac{1}{0.106} = \mathbf{9.4}$

Chapter 17

Section 17-5 Nonsinusoidal Oscillators

14. Triangular waveform.

$$f = \frac{1}{4R_1C}\left(\frac{R_2}{R_3}\right) = \frac{1}{4(22\text{ k}\Omega)(0.022\text{ μF})}\left(\frac{56\text{ k}\Omega}{18\text{ k}\Omega}\right) = \mathbf{1.61\text{ kHz}}$$

15. Change f to 10 kHz by changing R_1:

$$f = \frac{1}{4R_1C}\left(\frac{R_2}{R_3}\right)$$

$$R_1 = \frac{1}{4fC}\left(\frac{R_2}{R_3}\right) = \frac{1}{4(10\text{ kHz})(0.022\text{ μF})}\left(\frac{56\text{ k}\Omega}{18\text{ k}\Omega}\right) = \mathbf{3.54\text{ k}\Omega}$$

16.

$$T = \frac{V_p - V_F}{\left(\frac{|V_{IN}|}{RC}\right)}$$

$$V_p = \left(\frac{R_5}{R_4 + R_5}\right)12\text{ V} = \left(\frac{47\text{ k}\Omega}{147\text{ k}\Omega}\right)12\text{ V} = 3.84\text{ V}$$

PUT triggers at about $+3.84\text{ V} + 0.7\text{ V} = 4.54\text{ V}$
Amplitude $= +4.54\text{ V} - 1\text{ V} = \mathbf{3.54\text{ V}}$

$$V_{IN} = \left(\frac{R_2}{R_1 + R_2}\right)(-12\text{ V}) = \left(\frac{22\text{ k}\Omega}{122\text{ k}\Omega}\right)(-12\text{ V}) = -2.16\text{ V}$$

$$T = \frac{4.54\text{ V} - 1\text{ V}}{\left(\frac{2.16\text{ V}}{(100\text{ k}\Omega)(0.002\text{ μF})}\right)} = 328\text{ μs}$$

$$f = \frac{1}{T} = \frac{1}{328\text{ μs}} = \mathbf{3.05\text{ kHz}}$$

See Figure 17-1.

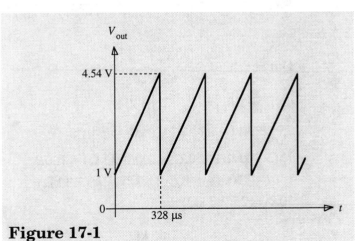

Figure 17-1

Chapter 17

17. $V_G = 5$ V. Assume $V_{AK} = 1$ V.

$$V_G = \left(\frac{R_5}{R_4 + R_5}\right) 12 \text{ V}$$

Change R_4 to get $V_G = 5$ V

$$5 \text{ V}(R_4 + 47 \text{ k}\Omega) = (47 \text{ k}\Omega) 12 \text{ V}$$

$$R_4(5 \text{ V}) = (47 \text{ k}\Omega) 12 \text{ V} - (47 \text{ k}\Omega) 5 \text{ V}$$

$$R_4 = \frac{(12 \text{ V} - 5 \text{ V}) 47 \text{ k}\Omega}{5 \text{V}} = \mathbf{65.8 \text{ k}\Omega}$$

18. $T = \dfrac{V_p - V_F}{\left(\dfrac{V_{IN}}{RC}\right)}$

$$V_p = \left(\frac{V_{IN}}{RC}\right) T + V_F = \left(\frac{3 \text{ V}}{(4.7 \text{ k}\Omega)(0.001 \text{ μF})}\right) 10 \text{ μs} + 1.2 \text{ V} = 7.58 \text{ V}$$

$$V_{pp(out)} = V_p - V_F = 7.58 \text{ V} - 1.2 \text{ V} = \mathbf{6.38 \text{ V}}$$

Section 17-6 The 555 Timer As An Oscillator

19. $\dfrac{1}{3} V_{CC} = \dfrac{1}{3}(10 \text{ V}) = \mathbf{3.33 \text{ V}}$

$\dfrac{2}{3} V_{CC} = \dfrac{2}{3}(10 \text{ V}) = \mathbf{6.67 \text{ V}}$

20. $f = \dfrac{1.44}{(R_1 + 2R_2) C_{ext}} = \dfrac{1.44}{(1 \text{ k}\Omega + 6.6 \text{ k}\Omega)(0.047 \text{ μF})} = \mathbf{4.03 \text{ kHz}}$

21. $f = \dfrac{1.44}{(R_1 + 2R_2) C_{ext}}$

$$C_{ext} = \dfrac{1.44}{(R_1 + 2R_2) f} = \dfrac{1.44}{(1 \text{ k}\Omega + 6.6 \text{ k}\Omega)(25 \text{ kHz})} = \mathbf{0.0076 \text{ μF}}$$

22. Duty cycle (dc) $= \dfrac{R_1 + R_2}{R_1 + 2R_2} \times 100\%$

$$dc(R_1 + 2R_2) = (R_1 + R_2) 100$$

$$75(3.3 \text{ k}\Omega + 2R_2) = (3.3 \text{ k}\Omega + R_2) 100$$

$$75(3.3 \text{ k}\Omega) + 150 R_2 = 100(3.3 \text{ k}\Omega) + 100 R_2$$

$$150 R_2 - 100 R_2 = 100(3.3 \text{ k}\Omega) - 75(3.3 \text{ k}\Omega)$$

$$50 R_2 = 25(3.3 \text{ k}\Omega)$$

$$R_2 = \dfrac{25(3.3 \text{ k}\Omega)}{50} = \mathbf{1.65 \text{ k}\Omega}$$

Chapter 17

Section 17-7 The Phase-Locked Loop

23. $f_{min} = f_0 - 0.15f_0 = 50$ kHz $- 75$ kHz $= \mathbf{42.5}$ **kHz**
$f_{max} = f_0 + 0.15f_0 = 50$ kHz $+ 75$ kHz $= \mathbf{57.5}$ **kHz**

24. $f_{sum} = f_0 + f_i = 15$ kHz $+ 7.5$ kHz $= \mathbf{22.5}$ **kHz**
$f_{diff} = f_0 - f_i = 15$ kHz $- 7.5$ kHz $= \mathbf{7.5}$ **kHz**

25. For a 50 mV, 25 kHz sine wave applied to a PLL, when the PLL is in lock the VCO output frequency is
$f_{VCO} = \mathbf{25}$ **kHz**

Chapter 18
Voltage Regulators

Section 18-1 Voltage Regulation

1. $$\text{Percent line regulation} = \left(\frac{\Delta V_{OUT}}{\Delta V_{IN}}\right)100\% = \left(\frac{2\text{ mV}}{6\text{ V}}\right)100\% = \mathbf{0.0333\%}$$

2. $$\text{Percent line regulation} = \left(\frac{\Delta V_{OUT}/V_{OUT}}{\Delta V_{IN}}\right)100\% = \left(\frac{2\text{ mV}/8\text{ V}}{6\text{ V}}\right)100\% = \mathbf{0.00417\ \%/V}$$

3. $$\text{Percent load regulation} = \left(\frac{V_{NL} - V_{FL}}{V_{FL}}\right)100\% = \left(\frac{10\text{ V} - 9.90\text{ V}}{9.90\text{ V}}\right)100\% = \mathbf{1.01\ \%}$$

4. From Problem 3, the percent load regulation is 1.01 %. For a full load current of 250 mA, this can be expressed as
$$\frac{1.01\ \%}{250\text{ mA}} = \mathbf{0.00404\ \%/mA}$$

Section 18-2 Basic Series Regulators

5. See Figure 18-1.

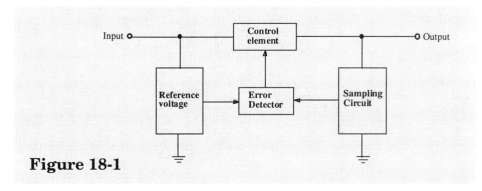

Figure 18-1

6. $$V_{OUT} = \left(1 + \frac{R_2}{R_3}\right)V_{REF} = \left(1 + \frac{33\text{ k}\Omega}{10\text{ k}\Omega}\right)2.4\text{ V} = \mathbf{10.3\text{ V}}$$

7. $$V_{OUT} = \left(1 + \frac{R_2}{R_3}\right)V_{REF} = \left(1 + \frac{5.6\text{ k}\Omega}{2.2\text{ k}\Omega}\right)2.4\text{ V} = \mathbf{8.51\text{ V}}$$

Chapter 18

8. For $R_3 = 2.2 \text{ k}\Omega$:

$$V_{OUT} = \left(1 + \frac{R_2}{R_3}\right)V_{REF} = \left(1 + \frac{5.6 \text{ k}\Omega}{2.2 \text{ k}\Omega}\right)2.4 \text{ V} = 8.5 \text{ V}$$

For $R_3 = 4.7 \text{ k}\Omega$:

$$V_{OUT} = \left(1 + \frac{R_2}{R_3}\right)V_{REF} = \left(1 + \frac{5.6 \text{ k}\Omega}{4.7 \text{ k}\Omega}\right)2.4 \text{ V} = 5.23 \text{ V}$$

The output voltage **decreases by 3.27 V** when R_3 is changed from 2.2 kΩ to 4.7 kΩ.

9. $V_{OUT} = \left(1 + \frac{R_2}{R_3}\right)V_{REF} = \left(1 + \frac{5.6 \text{ k}\Omega}{2.2 \text{ k}\Omega}\right)2.7 \text{ V} = \textbf{9.57 V}$

10. $I_{L(max)} = \frac{0.7 \text{ V}}{R_4}$

$R_4 = \frac{0.7 \text{ V}}{I_{L(max)}} = \frac{0.7 \text{ V}}{250 \text{ mA}} = \textbf{2.8 }\Omega$

$P = I_{L(max)}^2 R_4 = (250 \text{ mA})^2 2.8 \text{ }\Omega = \textbf{0.175 W}$, Use a 0.25 W

11. $R_4 = \frac{2.8 \text{ }\Omega}{2} = 1.4 \text{ }\Omega$

$I_{L(max)} = \frac{0.7 \text{ V}}{R_4} = \frac{0.7 \text{ V}}{1.4 \text{ }\Omega} = \textbf{500 mA}$

Section 18-3 Basic Shunt Regulators

12. Q_1 conducts more when the load current increases, assuming that the output voltage attempts to increases. When the output voltage tries to increase due to a change in load current, the attempted increase is sensed by R_3 and R_4 and a proportional voltage is applied to the op-amp's noninverting input. The resulting difference voltage increases the op-amp output, driving Q_1 more and thus increasing its collector current.

13. $\Delta I_C = \frac{\Delta V_{R1}}{R_1} = \frac{1 \text{ V}}{100 \text{ }\Omega} = \textbf{10 mA}$

14. $V_{OUT} = \left(1 + \frac{R_3}{R_4}\right)V_{REF} = \left(1 + \frac{8.2 \text{ k}\Omega}{3.9 \text{ k}\Omega}\right)5.1 \text{ V} = 15.8 \text{ V}$

$I_{L1} = \frac{V_{OUT}}{R_{L1}} = \frac{15.8 \text{ V}}{1 \text{ k}\Omega} = 15.8 \text{ mA}$

$I_{L2} = \frac{V_{OUT}}{R_{L2}} = \frac{15.8 \text{ V}}{1.2 \text{ k}\Omega} = 13.2 \text{ mA}$

$\Delta I_L = 13.2 \text{ mA} - 15.8 \text{ mA} = -2.60 \text{ mA}$

$\Delta I_S = -\Delta I_L = \textbf{2.60 mA}$

Chapter 18

15. $I_{L(max)} = \dfrac{V_{IN}}{R_1} = \dfrac{25\ V}{100\ \Omega} = \mathbf{250\ mA}$

$P_{R1} = I_{L(max)}^2 R_1 = (250\ mA)^2 100\ \Omega = \mathbf{6.25\ W}$

Section 18-4 Basic Switching Regulators

16. $V_{OUT} = \left(\dfrac{t_{on}}{T}\right) V_{IN}$

$t_{on} = T - t_{off}$

$T = \dfrac{1}{f} = \dfrac{1}{100\ Hz} = 0.01\ s = 10\ ms$

$V_{OUT} = \left(\dfrac{4\ ms}{10\ ms}\right) 12\ V = \mathbf{4.8\ V}$

17. $f = 100\ Hz,\ t_{off} = 6\ ms$

$T = \dfrac{1}{f} = \dfrac{1}{100\ Hz} = 10\ ms$

$t_{on} = T - t_{off} = 10\ ms - 6\ ms = 4\ ms$

duty cycle $= \dfrac{t_{on}}{T} = \dfrac{4\ ms}{10\ ms} = 0.4$

percent duty cycle $= 0.4 \times 100\ \% = \mathbf{40\ \%}$

18. percent duty cycle $= \left(\dfrac{t_{on}}{T}\right) 100\% = 40\%$

$\dfrac{t_{on}}{T} = 0.4$

$V_{OUT} = \left(\dfrac{T}{t_{on}}\right) V_{IN} = 2.5(20\ V) = \mathbf{50\ V}$

19. The output voltage **increases.**

Section 18-5 Integrated Circuit Voltage Regulators

20. (a) 7806: **+ 6 V**
(b) 7905.2: **- 5.2 V**
(c) 7818: **+ 18 V**
(d) 7924: **- 24 V**

21. $V_{OUT} = \left(1 + \dfrac{R_2}{R_1}\right) V_{REF} + I_{ADJ} R_2 = \left(1 + \dfrac{10\ k\Omega}{1\ k\Omega}\right) 1.25\ V + (50\ \mu A)(10\ k\Omega)$

$= 13.7\ V + 0.5\ V = \mathbf{14.3\ V}$

Chapter 18

22.
$$V_{OUT(min)} = -\left[\left(1 + \frac{R_{2(min)}}{R_1}\right)V_{REF} + I_{ADJ}R_{2(min)}\right]$$

$R_{2(min)} = 0 \ \Omega$

$V_{OUT(min)} = -\left(1.25 \ V(1 + 0) + 0\right) = \mathbf{-1.25 \ V}$

$$V_{OUT(max)} = -\left[\left(1 + \frac{R_{2(max)}}{R_1}\right)V_{REF} + I_{ADJ}R_{2(max)}\right] = -\left[1.25 \ V\left(1 + \frac{10 \ k\Omega}{470 \ \Omega}\right) + (50 \ \mu A)(10 \ k\Omega)\right]$$

$$= -\left(1.25 \ V(22.28) + 0.5 \ V\right) = \mathbf{-28.4 \ V}$$

23. The regulator current equals the current through $R_1 + R_2$:

$$I_{REG} \cong \frac{V_{OUT}}{R_1 + R_2} = \frac{14.3 \ V}{11 \ k\Omega} = \mathbf{1.3 \ mA}$$

24. $V_{IN} = 18 \ V$, $V_{OUT} = 12 \ V$

$I_{REG(max)} = 2 \ mA$, $V_{REF} = 1.25 \ V$

$$R_1 = \frac{V_{REF}}{I_{REG}} = \frac{1.25 \ V}{2 \ mA} = \mathbf{625 \ \Omega}$$

Neglecting I_{ADJ}:

$V_{R2} = 12 \ V - 1.25 \ V = 10.8 \ V$

$$R_2 = \frac{V_{R2}}{I_{REG}} = \frac{10.8 \ V}{2 \ mA} = \mathbf{5.4 \ k\Omega}$$

For R_1 use **620 Ω** and for R_2 use either **5600 Ω** or a 10 kΩ potentiometer for precise adjustment to 12 V.

Section 18-6 Applications of IC Voltage Regulators

25. $V_{Rext(min)} = 0.7 \ V$

$$R_{ext} = \frac{0.7 \ V}{I_{max}} = \frac{0.7 \ V}{250 \ mA} = \mathbf{2.8 \ \Omega}$$

26. $V_{OUT} = +12 \ V$

$$I_L = \frac{12 \ V}{10 \ \Omega} = 1200 \ mA = 1.2 \ A$$

$I_{ext} = I_L - I_{max} = 1.2 \ A - 0.5 \ A = 0.7 \ A$

$P_{ext} = I_{ext}(V_{IN} - V_{OUT}) = 0.7 \ A(15 \ V - 12 \ V) = 0.7 \ A(3 \ V) = \mathbf{2.1 \ W}$

27. $V_{Rlim(min)} = 0.7 \ V$

$$R_{lim(min)} = \frac{0.7 \ V}{I_{ext}} = \frac{0.7 \ V}{2 \ A} = \mathbf{0.35 \ \Omega}$$

See Figure 18-2.

Chapter 18

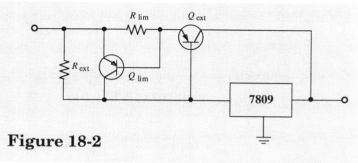

Figure 18-2

28. $R = \dfrac{1.25 \text{ V}}{500 \text{ mA}} = 2.5 \text{ }\Omega$

See Figure 18-3.

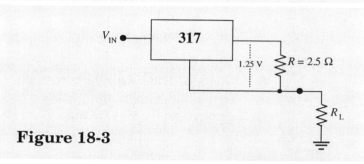

Figure 18-3

29. $R = \dfrac{9 \text{ V}}{500 \text{ mA}} = 18 \text{ }\Omega$

See Figure 18-4.

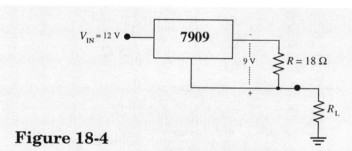

Figure 18-4

30. $V_{REF} = 1.25 \text{ V}$

The voltage divider must reduce the output voltage (12 V) down to the reference voltage (1.25 V). See Figure 18-37 in the text.

$V_{REF} = \left(\dfrac{R_1}{R_1 + R_2}\right) V_{OUT}$

$\dfrac{R_1}{R_1 + R_2} = \dfrac{V_{REF}}{V_{OUT}}$

$R_1 = R_1\left(V_{REF}/V_{OUT}\right) + R_2\left(V_{REF}/V_{OUT}\right)$

$R_2 = \dfrac{R_1 - R_1\left(V_{REF}/V_{OUT}\right)}{\left(V_{REF}/V_{OUT}\right)} = \dfrac{R_1\left(1 + V_{REF}/V_{OUT}\right)}{\left(V_{REF}/V_{OUT}\right)}$

Let $R_1 = \mathbf{10 \text{ k}\Omega}$

$R_2 = \dfrac{10 \text{ k}\Omega\left(1 - 1.25 \text{ V}/12 \text{ V}\right)}{\left(1.25 \text{ V}/12 \text{ V}\right)} = \mathbf{86 \text{ k}\Omega}$

Selected Results for System Applications

Chapter 2
The Components
Transformer: 9 V rms
Diode: 1N5400, 1N4719, or MR500
Surge resistor: 1 Ω
Fuse: 250 mA slow-blow
Filter capacitor: 68,000 μF

Troubleshooting
Board 1: Fuse is open
Board 2: Diode open
Board 3: Third diode from top is open

Chapter 3
The Components
Regulator: 1N4733 5.1 V zener
Limiting resistor: 24 Ω
Series resistors: 36 Ω for LED, 330 kΩ for photodiode
Fuse: 250 mA slow-blow

Troubleshooting
Board 1: Photodiode defective
Board 2: Filter capacitor open
Board 3: Zener is open and not regulating

Chapter 4
The Components
Bias resistors: 1/4 W
Q6 collector resitor: 1 W max (depends on load of time delay circuit)
Relay: 12 V, 55 Ω, 0.15 A (relay A)
Diode: 1N4002

Troubleshooting
Board 1: CE junction of Q2 open
Board 2: CE junction of Q3 open
Board 3: R12 shorted

Chapter 5
Analysis of the Temperature-to-Voltage Conversion Circuit
At $T = 46°C$: $V_{OUT} = 4.78$ V
At $T = 50°C$: $V_{OUT} = 6.54$ V
At $T = 54°C$: $V_{OUT} = 7.06$ V

The transistor is operating linearly.

Chapter 5 (continued)
The Power Supply Circuit
Resistors: $R1 = 1\ \Omega$, $R2 = 6.8\ \Omega$, $R3 = 56\ \Omega$

Zener diodes: 1N4739, 9.1 V; 1N4733, 5.1 V. The 9.1 V zener should have a heat sink if there is no quaranteed minimum load.

Troubleshooting
Board 1: Most likely a 9.1 V zener instead of a 5.1 V has been inserted.

Board 2: Thermistor open

Board 3: CE junction of transistor open

Chapter 6
Analysis of the Preamplifier Circuit
Input resistance: $R_{in(1)} = 17\ \Omega$

Input power: $P = 362\ \mu W$

DC voltages:

$V_{B(1)} = 1.93$ V, $V_{E(1)} = 1.23$ V, $V_{C(1)} = 9.29$ V

$V_{B(2)} = 1.88$ V, $V_{E(2)} = 1.18$ V, $V_{C(2)} = 7.54$ V

Toltal voltage gain: Max $A_v = 733$, Min $A_v = 145$

DC current: 2.68 mA

Resistor power ratings: All 1/8 W

Lowest frequency: 935 Hz

The Power Supply Circuit
To adapt, change to a 12 V zener regulator such as a 1N4742.

Troubleshooting
Board 1: *R6 is open, causing Q2 to saturate.*

Board 2: Signal input, no signal output. No signal at collector of $Q1$, but dc voltage appears ok. Most likely fault is open $C1$.

Board 3: Gain of stage 2 is approximately 4, which is much too low. $C4$ is open.

Chapter 7
Analysis of the Power Amplifier Circuit
Input resistance: $R_{in(min)} = 8\ k\Omega$

voltage gain: 1360 (preamp and power amp combined)

Transistor power ratings: Not sufficient without the heat sink.

Troubleshooting
Board 1: The signal appears at the bases but not at the output. One of the darlington transistors is faulty.

Board 2: There is no signal at either base of the darlington transistors, but the dc voltages are ok indicating that the bias transistor junctions are not faulty. Since there is a signal through $C1$, there is no obvious fault other than an ac short to ground at both bases, which is unlikely. So, the scope measurements are faulty. Perhaps the probe is not making contact with test points 2 and 4 or something has happened to the scope between step 4 and step 5.

Chapter 8

The schematic for the circuit board is as follows:

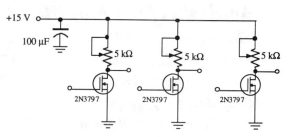

Analysis of the pH Sensor Circuits

Input resistance: $R_{in(min)} = 10 \times 10^{12}\ \Omega$

Rheostat: 4 kΩ maximum, 2.76 kΩ typical, 1.33 kΩ minimum

Output voltage range: 5.32 V to 8.52 V represent pH values from about 3.5 to about 9.5.

Troubleshooting

Board 1: $Q2$ is probably open although $R2$ could be shorted.

Board 2: V_{OUT} for sensor 2 to too high. The rheostat is probably miscalibrated or $Q2$ is faulty.

Chapter 9

Basic MOSFET Amplifier Design

Drain–to–source voltage: $V_{DS(min)} = 3$ V, $V_{DS(max)} = 9$ V

Voltage gain: $A_{v(min)} = 2.25$, $A_{v(max)} = 4.50$

Variation in I_{DSS} from one FET to another will affect the Q–point of the circuit. Use of voltage divider bias rather than zero–bias will lessen the dependency of the Q–point on I_{DSS}.

Since g_m varies from one device to another, the voltage gain will also vary. To minimize the influence of g_m, a swamping source resistor with a value much greater than $1/g_m$ can be used and the drain resistor adjusted accordingly.

Amplifier Performance on the Test Bench

Measurement 1: Variation in I_{DSS} for $Q1$ (larger for set 2)

Measurement 2: Variation in I_{DSS} for $Q2$ (larger for set 1)

Measurement 3: Variation in g_m for $Q1$ (larger for set 1)

Measurement 4: Variation in g_m for $Q2$ (larger for set 2)

Set 1 Q1: $I_{DSS} = 2.53$ mA, $g_m = 2070$ μS

Set 1 Q2: $I_{DSS} = 4.12$ mA, $g_m = 2270$ μS

Set 2 Q1: $I_{DSS} = 4.87$ mA, $g_m = 1700$ μS

Set 2 Q2: $I_{DSS} = 3.95$ mA, $g_m = 2780$ μS

Using FETs with maximum g_m and typical I_{DSS}, an FET amplifier with 118 stages is required to achieve the same maximum gain of the bipolar amplifier.

Recommendation

1. MOSFETs are not feasible replacements for the BJTs.
2. Device variation in parameters make mass production impossible because circuit must be "tweaked" to mathch the gains, unlike BJTs.
3. Retain the bipolar amplifier because 118 FET stages are required to match the gain of the two–stage bipolar amplifier.

Chapter 10
Analysis of the Amplifier Circuit

First stage: $f_{cl(in)} = 2.31$ Hz, $f_{cl(out)} = 1.37$ Hz, $f_{cl(bypass)} = 12.7$ Hz; $f_{cl(bypass)}$ *is dominant*
First stage: $f_{cu(in)} = 206$ kHz, $f_{cu(out)} = 13.7$ MHz, $f_{cu(in)}$ *is dominant*
Second stage: $f_{cl(in)} = 1.37$ Hz, $f_{cl(out)} = 1.08$ Hz, $f_{cl(bypass)} = 17.9$ Hz; $f_{cl(bypass)}$ *is dominant*
Second stage: $f_{cu(in)} = 450$ kHz, $f_{cu(out)} = 12$ MHz, $f_{cu(in)}$ *is dominant*
Overall lower critical frequency: 17.9 Hz
Overall upper critical frequency: 206 kHz
Overall bandwidth: approximately 206 kHz

Frequency Response on the Test Bench

Lower critical frequency: Calculated $f_{cl} = 17.9$ Hz, $T = 55.9$ ms;
55.9 ms/9 DIV = 6.2 ms/DIV. Closest setting is 5 ms/DIV. The actual frequency being measured is $f_{cl} = 1/(5$ ms/DIV$\times 9$ DIV$) = 22.2$ Hz

Upper critical frequency: Calculated $f_{cu} = 206$ kHz, $T = 4.85$ μs;
4.85 μs/0.8 DIV = 6 μs/DIV. Closest setting is 6 μs/DIV. The actual frequency being measured is $f_{cu} = 1/(6$ μs/DIV$\times 0.8$ DIV$) = 208$ kHz

Chapter 11
Analysis of the Motor Speed Control Circuit

PUT gate voltage of 0 V, assuming forward voltage of 0 V, and the potentiometer set at 25 kΩ:

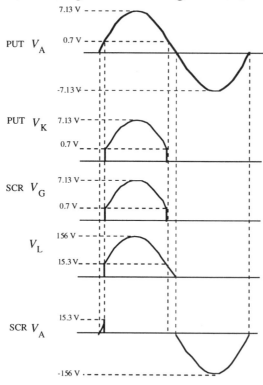

Chapter 11 (continued)

For the potentiometer set to 25 kΩ, V_A of the PUT is the same. With $V_G = 0$ V, 2 V, 4 V, 6 V, 8 V, and 10 V, the PUT conducts with $V_A = 0.7$ V, 2.7 V, 4.7 V, 6.7 V, 8.7 V, and 10.7 V respectively. Since $V_A = 7.13$ V maximum for $V_G = 8$ V and 10 V, the PUT never conducts and the SCR never fires and the load voltage is zero. The voltages across the load resistor are as follows:

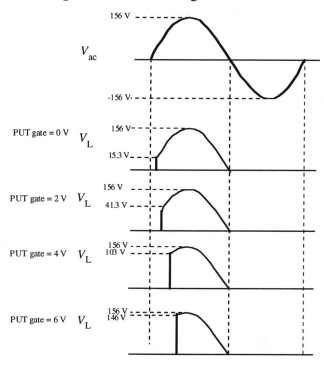

Troubleshooting

Board 1: The 50 kΩ resistor is open or the 1.2 kΩ resistor is shorted.
Board 2: The SCR is open.
Board 3: The SCR is shorted.
Board 4: The PUT is shorted.

Chapter 12
Analysis of the Photocell/Amplifier Circuit

$R_f = 10$ kΩ for a gain of 10.
$R_f = 18.6$ kΩ produces a gain of 18.6 for maximum linear output.

λ (nm)	V_{in} (mv)	≈V_{out} (mv)
400	1.5	28
450	50	930
500	120	2230
550	200	3720
600	290	5390
650	375	6800
700	430	8000

Chapter 12 (continued)

Troubleshooting

Board 1: The 1 kΩ resistor is open or the op–amp is faulty.
Board 2: The 100 kΩ pot is open or the 1 kΩ resistor is shorted.
Board 3: The 10 kΩ pot is open making the offset null ineffective.

Chapter 13
Analysis of the Audio Amplifier Circuit

Midrange voltage gain: $A_{v(mid)} = 46.8$
Lower critical frequency: $f_{cl} = 15.4$ Hz
Bandwidth: $BW \cong 15$ kHz
Maximum input: $V_{in(max)} = 470$ mV peak–to–peak
Speaker power: $P_{out(max)} = 3.78$ W

Troubleshooting

Board 1: The op–amp is faulty, improper connection at pins 3 or 6, or supply not on.
Board 2: R_5 is open or BE junction of $Q1$ is open.
Board 3: R_3 is open.

Chapter 14
Analysis of the ADC Circuit

Summing amplifier gain: $A_v = -1$
Slope of integrator ramp +2 V input: $\Delta V_{out}/\Delta t = 2$ V/μs
Slope of integrator ramp –8 V input: $\Delta V_{out}/\Delta t = -8$ V/μs
Dual slope output: Positive ramp from 0 V to +3 V in 1 μs followed by negative ramp back to 0 V in 0.375 μs
Sampling rate: 571 kHz

Troubleshooting

Board 1: IC3 output stuck high.
Board 2: R_1 or R_2 is open
Board 3: C_2 is shorted making IC2 a voltage follower.

Chapter 15
The Circuits

Isolation amplifier gain: $A_v = 11$
Filter bandwidth: ≈106 Hz
Filter gain: $A_v = 1.59$
Post amplifier gain: $A_{v(min)} = -100$, $A_{v(max)} = -150$
Amplifier gain: $A_{v(min)} = -1750$, $A_{v(max)} = -2620$
Voltage range at position pot wiper: $V_{min} = -59.7$ mV, $V_{max} = +59.7$ mV

Chapter 15 (continued)
Troubleshooting
Board 1: Several faults can produce no ouput including R_{11} open or IC3 output faulty or open.

Board 2: R_7 or R_8 open.

Board 3: R_{11} open.

Board 4: R_{16} or R_{17} open.

Chapter 16
The Filter Circuit
Sallen–Key critical frequencies: IC1 filter, 15.9 kHz; IC2 filter, 53 kHz; IC4 filter, 18.9 kHz; IC5 filter, 15.9 kHz

Multiple FB center frequency: 19 kHz

Bandwidths: approximately the same as the critical frequency for each filter.

Sallen–Key voltage gains: IC1 filter, 1.59; IC2 filter, 1.59; IC2 filter, 1.59; IC3 filter, 0.915; IC4 filter, 1.59; IC5 filter, 1.59;

Sallen–key response:. $R_1/R_2 = 0.589$ (approximately Butterworth)

Chapter 17
The Function Generator Circuit
Oscillator frequencies:

×1,: minimum $f = 0.73$ Hz, Maximum $f = 8.84$ Hz

×10,: minimum $f = 7.3$ Hz, Maximum $f = 88.4$ Hz

×100,: minimum $f = 73$ Hz, Maximum $f = 884$ Hz

×1 k,: minimum $f = 730$ Hz, Maximum $f = 8.84$ kHz

×10 k,: minimum $f = 7.3$ kHz, Maximum $f = 88.4$ kHz

Output voltages:

Sine wave: 25.4 V pp

Square wave: 30 V pp

Triangular wave: 12.6 V pp

Troubleshooting
Unit 1: Fault is in the IC1 wien–bridge oscillator block. IC1 output could be open or lead–lag feedback loop open.

Unit 2: Output of IC2 is open

Unit 3: Output of IC3 open or R_7 or R_{10} open.

Unit 4: Negative feedback path of IC3 is open causing it to saturate.

Chapter 18
The Power Supply Circuit

Bridge voltages at peak of input: Top corner: ≈17 V peak, bottom corner: ≈−17 V peak, left corner: −16.3 V peak, right corner: +16.3 V peak.

PIV: 33.2 V

Regulator input voltages: 7812: +16.3 V; 7912: −16.3 V

Regulator current: 250 mA from each regulator. Heat sinks are not necessary.

Troubleshooting

Board 1: Fuse may be blown. Transformer may have an open primary or secondary winding or a shorted primary winding.

Board 2: Input or output of IC1 may be open Pin 2 of IC1 may be open. *C*1 *or C*3 may be shorted.

Board 3: Input or output or pin 2 of IC2 may be open. *C*2 *or C*4 may be shorted.

Board 4: IC1 and IC2 may be swapped.

Tutorials and Exercise Results for Electronics Workbench/PSpice

Prepared by

Gary Snyder and Chuck Garbinski

Electronics Workbench (r) Tutorial
to accompany
Electronics Devices, 5th Ed. by Tom Floyd

Electronics Workbench (r) is a registered trademark of Interactive Image Technologies, Ltd.

Introduction

This tutorial is intended to help familiarize you with Electronics Workbench (referred to as EWB in this tutorial) so that they may complete the EWB circuit problems presented in *Electronics Devices*, 5th Ed. As you use this tutuorial, you should keep two major points in mind.

- This tutorial is NOT an exhaustive overview of the program, nor does it attempt to relate electronics theory to program operation beyond the scope of the textbook. Consequently, you should take all the explanations and examples with a "grain of salt", and not view this tutuorial as doctrine. All examples, whatever their nature, are intended to illustrate some specific part of a subject, rather than attempt to explain everything about the subject. As you learn more about electronics and gain more experience with EWB, you will be able to see where some details have been conveniently passed over for the sake of clarity.

- This tutorial is not meant to be recreational reading. You are not meant to read it without actually applying what is presented. You are expected to work with EWB as you proceed through the tutorial, rather than just read the tutorial without actually using the program. The tutorials are usually presented in the form of "step-by-step" instructions for using EWB. As you read through the tutorial, complete each step before proceeding to the next. In the first few sections, as you are learning about the mechanics of EWB, pay particular attention to what each of your actions actually does. It will make using the program on your own later much easier and more productive.

Because the Windows 95 version of EWB is meant to be used (although the circuit files will work with both the Windows 3.x and DOS versions of the program) you should already understand some of the basic Windows terminology (such as "drag", "pointer", "double-click", and so forth) and Windows 95 operation (such as copying files, opening files, saving files, and so on). As each new term is introduced the tutorial will provide a brief explanation, but you should already have a basic understanding of Windows 95 and general Windows operation. The tutorial also assumes that you will be using a mouse (or other pointing device), as using Windows 95 without a mouse is like eating dinner with only a knife. It can be done, but the process is awkward, tedious, and usually more effort than it's worth.

Section 1 - Introduction to EWB Basics

In this section you will learn how to build a basic circuit using EWB. For this tutorial, it is assumed that the Electronics Devices EWB folders and files were installed. If not, the instructions must be modified accordingly so that you are working with the correct drive and path.

- Start EWB from the Windows 95 desktop.

    There are a number of items shown in your display. Some of these are standard Windows 95 items, and some are specific to EWB. If you wish, you can look in the Electronics Workbench User's Guide for a description of each item. This tuturial will tell you specifically where to look and what to do to get something done, so you don't really need to know everything right now.

- In the Menu Bar at the top of your screen, **CLICK** on "File".

    "Click" means to position the pointer over the item to you wish to click, and to depress and release the left mouse button once. To click on File, position the pointer over the work File in the menu bar and depress and release the left mouse button once.

- In the File menu, click on "Open..."

    The "..." after "Open" means that Windows 95 will need you to provide more information for it to complete the operation. In this case, it needs you to tell it what file you want to open.

    If this is the first file you have opened this EWB session, EWB will show the contents of the default file folder, which is C:\WEWB41\SAMPLES (assuming that EWB has been installed to the C: drive). If you have already opened a file this session, EWB will show the folder containing the last file you opened.

- **NAVIGATE** to the Tutorial folder.

    "Navigate" means to work through the directory structure to the file or folder that you wish to work with. To navigate to the Tutorial folder
    1) Click on the down arrow to the right of the "Look in:" window.
    2) **DOUBLE-CLICK** on the icon of the hard drive containing your Electronics Devices files. "Double-click" means to position the pointer over the item you wish to double-click and to quickly depress and release the left mouse button twice. To double-click on the hard drive icon, position the pointer over the hard drive icon and quickly depress and release the left mouse button twice.
    3) Double-click the EWB folder in the folder contents window.
    4) Double-click the Tutorial folder in the folder contents window.

- Double-click the TUTOR_1.CA4 file in the folder contents window.

    This will open the TUTOR_1.CA4 circuit file and display the contents in the EWB workspace.

The TUTOR_1.CA4 circuit seems simple enough. At first glance it appears that it consists of only 2 items: a 12V battery and a 1 kohm resistor. In actuality, though, it consists of 7 items. These are:

    1) the 12V battery,
    2) the 1 kohm resistor,
    3) the battery ground,
    4) the resistor ground,

5) the wire segment between the battery and ground,
6) the wire segment between the resistor and ground, and
7) the wire segment between the battery and resistor.

This is mentioned because each of these items must be entered into the workspace when you build another copy of this circuit, which is what you are going to do next.

- Click on the Passive parts bin.

The parts bins are selected using the buttons on the second toolbar under the menu bar at the top of the screen. The Passive parts bin is selected by the button with the resistor symbol on it.

Note that when you select the Passive parts bin, two things happen. The first is that the selected parts bin button is highlighted. The second is that the contents of the parts bin is displayed in the window (which is parts bin) on the left side of the screen, with the name of the bin at the top of the window. Click on other parts bin buttons and see what happens. Before continuing to the next step, be sure that select the Passive parts bin again.

Now, build a second circuit below the first circuit, using the first circuit as a guide for placing the components.

- **DRAG** the battery from the parts bin to the workspace somewhere below the existng circuit.

"Drag" means to move the pointer while depressing the left mouse button at the same time. To drag the battery into the workspace, position the pointer over the battery symbol in the parts bin. As you do so, you will see the pointer change from an arrow to a hand, indicating that you can "grab" the part. Then, depress the left mouse button, move the pointer into the workspace while holding the left mouse button down, and release the left mouse button when you have positioned the battery where you want it. If you want to adjust the position of a part after you have released it, you can always use the mouse to drag it to where you want it at any time.

Note that after you release the left mouse button, the battery is highlighted. This is because it is the *active* component, which will mean more to you a little later.

- Drag the resistor from the parts bin to the workspace somewhere below the existing circuit.

Note that as soon as you click on the resistor in the parts bin, the battery is no longer highlighted. This is because the resistor has now become the active component.

- Drag a ground from the parts bin to the workspace somewhere below the battery.

As before, the ground becomes the active component.

- Drag another ground from the parts bin to the workspace somewhere below and to the right of the resistor.

This completes placing the components on the workspace. Of course, we still need to place the wires now to connect the parts together. If you check the passive parts bin, though, you won't find any wires. Don't bother checking the other parts bins, because they aren't in any of the parts bins. Where are they, then?

The answer is that wires are not really parts. Instead of placing wires, you draw them using the pointer and mouse. First, connect the cathode of the battery to ground.

- Position the pointer on the cathode terminal of the battery until you make a **CONNECTION**.

A connection is indicated by a small dot between the arrow pointer and the component you are trying to connect.

- Drag the wire to the ground terminal.

    As with the battery, you will see a connection appear when you touch the ground terminal with the pointer. Connect the wire to the ground terminal by releasing the mouse button.

You should now have a wire between the battery and ground terminal. Do not worry if the wire is not straight and has a "jog" in it. If you wish, you can drag the battery or ground to straighten it out. Now, continue to connect the components together.

- Connect the battery to the resistor.

- Connect the resistor to ground.

Congratulations! You have now entered your first circuit in EWB. Although it may not seem like much, every circuit comes down to putting components in the workspace (which you have done) and connecting them together (which you have also done). Of course, not every circuit is made up only of grounds, 12V batteries, and 1 kohm resistors, but these will be covered in future sections. The next section discusses how to work with components in more detail and how to save your work. For now, just exit EWB without saving the changes you've made.

- In the Menu Bar at the top of the screen, click on "File".

- In the File menu, click on "Exit".

    A dialogue box appears with the message "Save changes made to Circuit Tutor_1?" This is a precaution that EWB takes to make sure you don't lose any work you may have done since opening the file. In this case the changes aren't important, so you can lose them.

- Click on "No".

This completes Section 1 of the tutorial. In Section 2 you will learn more about working with circuit files and components in EWB.

Section 2 - More on EWB Basics

In the last section you learned how to open files, move components from parts bins into the workspace, and how to connect circuit components together. In this section you will build upon that knowledge and learn more about the basics of working with components and circuits in EWB.

- Start EWB from the Windows 95 desktop.

- Open the file TUTOR_2.CA4 in the EWB tutorial folder..

    As you can see, this circuit is very similar to the circuit of TUTOR_1.CA4 you worked with in Section 1. The obvious difference is that there are more components. More subtle differences are that these components have reference designators, or *labels,* and different values than before. There is one more, even subtler, difference that you will discover soon enough. For now, copy the circuit by placing corresponding components somewhere below the original circuit.

- Select the Passive parts bin from the toolbar.

- Drag a battery from the parts bin to the workspace somewhere below battery VS.

- Drag a resistor from the parts bin above and to the right of the battery you placed.

- Drag a second resistor from the parts bin to the right of the first resistor you placed.

    You've now uncovered the final subtle difference in the circuit you are copying. The resistors you've been draggng are oriented horizontally (side-to-side), but resistor R2 in the original circuit is oriented vertically (top-to-bottom). There is nothing wrong with having all the resistors aligned the same way, but it makes for neater schematics if you can orient components both horizontally and vertically. To make your resistor match R2, you will have to rotate it.

- On the Menu Bar at the top of the screen, click on "Circuit".

- In the Circuit menu, click on "Rotate".

    When you click on "Rotate", the resistor rotates 90 degrees and the Circuit menu closes. Note that *only* the highlighted resistor rotated. As with certain other commands that you will learn about, the Rotate command will only affect the active component. If the battery had been the active component, the Rotate command would rotate it instead.

    By now you may have noticed that some commands in the menus have text next to them. If you open the Circuit menu again, you will see that "Rotate" has "Ctrl+R". This means that if you wish, you can rotate the active component by holding down the "Ctrl" (control) key and pressing the "R" key rather than having to open the Circuit menu and clicking on "Rotate" each time. This is sometimes referred to as a "hot key" sequence. Each time you press the "R" key (it can be upper- or lower-case), the active component will rotate 90 degrees. This is faster and more convenient if, for some reason, you have to rotate a component 180 or 270 degrees. Try rotating the resistor a few times using the keyboard before proceeding to the next step. Remember to have the resistor vertically aligned before proceeeding.

- Drag a ground to the workspace below the battery you placed.

- Drag a ground to the workspace below the resistor you rotated.

- Wire the battery and resistors together in series, as shown in the original circuit.

Now that you have placed the components you need in the workspace, you need to assign proper values to them. To assign values, you will use the Value command in the Circuit menu.

- Click on the battery to select it.

- In the Menu Bar at the top of the screen, click on "Circuit".

- In the Circuit menu, click on "Value..." (Pop Quiz: What does the "..." after "Value" mean?)

    A dialog box will open with the title "Battery", indicating that the battery is the active component. It will also display the current value of the battery, namely 12V, in the text windows. In the text window to the right of "Voltage (V):", enter the value "5" (without the quotes). Leave the units as volts, indicated by the "V" in the units window.

- Click the "Accept" button.

    The battery will now have the value 5V instead of 12V.

Repeat the process to change the resistor values to those shown in the original circuit.

- Select the resistor nearest the battery.

- In the Menu Bar at the top of the screen, click on "Circuit".

- In the Circuit menu, click on "Value..."

    A dialog box will open with the title "Resistor", indicating that a resistor is the active component. In the text window to the right of "Resistance (R):", enter the value "2.2" (without the quotes). Leave the units as kilohms, indicated by the "kΩ" in the second window.

- Click the "Accept" button.

    The resistor will now have the value 2.2 kΩ instead of 1 kΩ.

There is an even quicker way to change a component value. If you double-click on a passive component, you will automatically bring up the box to edit the component value. Try this method to change the value of the second resistor.

- Double-click on the resistor furthest the battery.

    The dialog box to change the resistor value again opens. In the text window to the right of "Resistance (R):", enter the value "100". Because the resistance is 100 Ω, rather than 100 kΩ, you must change the units in the second text window. Clicking the up arrow to the right of the units window will increase the units by 1000 times (e.g., kΩ would become MΩ). Clicking the down arrow arrow will decrease the units by 1000 times (e.g., Ω would become mΩ.) Click once on the down arrow to the right of the units windows to change the units from kΩ to Ω.

- Click the "Accept" button.

    The resistor will now have the value 100 Ω instead of 1 kΩ.

You're almost done! Now all that remains is to add labels to the components. You will do this with the Label command in the Circuit menu. As with the Rotate command, Label will affect only the active component, so you must select each component before you give it a label.

- Click on the battery to select it.

- In the Menu Bar at the top of the screen, click on "Circuit".

- In the Circuit menu, click on "Label..." Note that the keyboard equivalent is "Ctrl+L".

    A dialogue box will open with the title "Label of Battery". EWB knows you want to label the battery, because it is the active component.

- Type "VS" (without the quotes) in the text box.

    If you make a mistake, use the backspace key to correct the label name.

- Click the "OK" Button.

    The battery will now have the label "VS" next to it.

Now, add the labels R1 and R2 to the resistors in the same way. Rather than use the Circuit menu, however, use "Ctrl + L" hot key sequence rather than the Circuit menu to add the labels.

- Select the resistor nearest the battery so that it is the active component.

- Hold down the "Ctrl" key and press "L".

- Type "R1" (without the quotes) in the text box.

- Click the "OK" button.

- Select the middle resistor so that it is the active component.

- Hold down the "Ctrl" key and press "L".

- Type "R2" in the text box.

- Click the "OK" button.

And you're done! You now know the basics for entering schematics in EWB. Now, let's save our work and exit EWB. You actually will not be using this file again, but you should now have to save your work. Even the best-behaved systems can crash unexpectedly, so saving your work often is a good habit to develop. Saving a file in EWB is very similar to opening a file.

- Select "File" in the Menu Bar.

- Select "Save As..." in the File menu.

    You could have selected "Save", but you this will overwrite the original circuit file and you may wish to keep it should you or someone else want to go through the tutorial in the future. As it turns out, EWB will always warn you whenever you will be overwriting another file, so should you ever accidently select "Save" when you meant "Save As..." you can cancel the save operation and try again.

If this is the first file you have saved this EWB session, EWB will show the contents of the default file folder, which is C:\WEWB41\SAMPLES (assuming that EWB has been installed to the C: drive). If you have already saved a file this session, EWB will show the folder containing the last file you saved.

- Navigate to the folder in which you wish to save your file.

    This is similar to navigating when you opened TUTOR_1.CA4.
    1) Click on the down arrow to the right of the "Save in:" window.
        The default name "UNTITLED" is displayed in the file name text box. Do not change this until you get to the folder in which you wish to save the file.
    2) Double-click on the icon of the drive on which you wish to save your file.
    3) Double-click through the directory tree to the folder in in which you wish to save your file.
    4) Click on the "File name:" text box.
    5) Type in the filename under which you wish to save the file.
        You do not need to add the ".CA4" extension. This is added automatically added by EWB if you are saving the file as a 4.1 Circuit type..
    6) Click on the "OK" button.

You have now saved your file, so you are ready to exit. You can exit as you did in Section 1, or you can use the following standard Windows 95 shortcut instead.

- Click on the Title Bar exit button (the button with the "X") in the upper right hand corner of the screen to close and exit from EWB.

    Had you forgotten to save the file before exiting (as in Section 1), EWB would have warned you so that you could either

    1) save the file under the current name,
    2) exit without saving, or
    3) cancel the exit operation.

    Despite this safeguard, it's best to always save work you want to save *before* attempting to exit. It's easy to fall into the habit of quitting all programs without saving your work and very dangerous to expect all applications to have safeguards in place like EWB.

This completes Section 2 of the tutorial. In Section 3 you will learn some useful techniques for working with circuit files in EWB.

Section 3 - Copying and Deleting Components

In the previous sections, as you have built basic circuits, you have been primarily working with placing components on the workspace and wiring them together. In this section you will learn how to manipulate components already on the workspace.

- Start EWB from the Windows 95 desktop.

- Open the circuit file TUTOR_3.CA4 in the EWB tutorial folder.

This circuit is more complicated than the first two circuits, but you know all the commands needed to select the parts bins, place the components in the workspace, and specify the component values and labels for the entire circuit. You may notice, however, that the right half of the circuit is identical to part of the left half. Rather than build the entire circuit one component at a time, however, you can build the left half the circuit and then copy the necessary components to create the right half. First, build the left half of the circuit.

- Place battery, resistor, inductor, and capacitor on the workspace beneath the original circuit.

- Add the corresponding grounds to your circuit.

- Wire the components together to match the left half of the original circuit.

- Modify the component values in your circuit to match the components in the left half of the original circuit.

- Label the components in your circuit to match the components in the left half of the original circuit.

You are now ready to use the Copy command to create the right half of the circuit.

- Select the battery in your circuit.

- In the Menu Bar at the top of the screen, click on "Edit".

    Note that "Paste" is grayed out, meaning that it cannot be selected from the Edit menu. This is because EWB has nothing that it can paste into the workspace.

- In the Edit menu, click on "Copy".

    Although nothing has appeared to happen, EWB has captured the active component, in this case the resistor.

- Click on "Edit" in the Menu Bar again.

    Note that the "Paste" command is no longer grayed out. This is because EWB now has an image that it can paste into the workspace.

- Click on "Paste" in the Edit menu.

    A new battery appears near the middle of the workspace on your screen. Note that, unlike batteries from the Passive parts bin, this battery has both the label and value of the battery you are copying. Note also that the new copy, rather than the battery you selected to copy, is highlighted and is now the active component. This is so that you can move the copy to where you want it without affecting any of the original circuit that might be under the copy. Why this is so important will become clear in later sections when you learn how to work with several components at once and how to modify existing circuits.

- Drag the battery copy somewhere to the right of your circuit.

- Copy and position the remaining components in your circuit.

- Wire the components you copied to match your original circuit.

You now have two identical copies of the circuit you initially built from the parts bin in the workspace below below the original circuit. But clearly something is wrong. In the original circuit there is only one battery, not two. To make the circuit look like the original, you will have to delete the copy of the battery and its ground and modify some of the wires. Do so now.

- Select the battery.

- Click on "Edit" in the Menu Bar.

- Click on "Delete" in the Edit menu. (Note that the hot key sequence for this command is "Del", or the Delete key. Surprised?)

    A dialog box appears with the message "Delete selected components?" This is to confirm that you didn't click on the wrong item in the Edit menu. Since this wasn't a mistake, confirm that you do wish to delete the battery.

- Click on the "OK" button.

    The battery disappears. Note that the battery's ground is wired directly to the resistor since the intervening battery is gone. Now, delete the ground. This time, rather than using the Edit menu, use the hot key sequence.

- Select the ground connection.

- Press the "Delete" key.

    The ground disappears. Since there is nothing for the resistor wire to connect to anymore, it also disappears.

- Wire the resistor so that your circuit matches the original circuit.

- Add component labels to match those of the original circuit.

You're now done. Rather than having to enter all the parts from the parts bin for this circuit, you only entered in half the circuit and used the Copy command to construct the other half. But even without copying and deleting the battery and its ground (which was just to let you see how to delete components in EWB) you didn't really save all that much time. It's true that you didn't have to modify any component values, but you still had to create and position each copy and add labels to each component.

Fortunately EWB permits you to copy (and label, delete, move, and rotate) several components at once, which can save a great deal of time. You'll find out how in the next section. For now, exit EWB (you don't have to save your changes) and take a break.

Section 4 - Working with Several Components

In the previous sections you have always worked with one component at a time. This is because whenever you selected a component and made it active EWB would release the component that was previously active. In this section you will learn how to work with several components. The commands you have learned for moving, deleting, copying, and otherwise working with components are the same. It is just that you will now be able to apply them to several components at once, which will prove to be very useful and quite a time-saver in some circuits.

- Start EWB from the Windows 95 desktop.

- Open the file TUTOR_4.CA4 in the EWB tutorial folder.

You will now copy the original circuit in its entirety and paste it into the workspace below the original circuit. To do so, select each component of the original circuit in turn, but hold the down the Ctrl (control) key as you click. Before, when you selected a component, you made it the active component. By holding the Ctrl key down as you select a component, you add the component to the *active group*. Each component in the active group will be highlighted so that you can tell which components are selected and which are not.

- Select the battery VS by clicking on it.

  The battery is highlighted, as usual.

- Add R1 to the active group by holding down Ctrl and clicking on R1.

  Both VS and R1 will be highlighted.

  Note that if you accidently select a component you didn't mean to add to the active group, you can always deselect it by holding down the Ctrl and clicking on it again. This will be useful later.

- Add R2, R3, R4, R5, and the grounds to the active group in the same way.

  All the components are now highlighted. Now each command that you know will apply to all the components, since all the components are active. For now, you want to copy the circuit, so

- Click on "Edit" in the Menu Bar.

- Click on "Copy" in the Edit menu.

  The circuit has now been captured and is ready to paste into the workspace.

- Click on "Edit" in the Menu Bar.

- Click on "Paste" in the Edit menu.

A copy of the circuit now appears in the middle of the workspace. As before, the copies are highlighted so that you can move them without affecting the original circuit, should the copies overlap the original circuit. Moving the components is identical to moving a single component, except that all the components in the group will move.

- Drag any of the highlighted components to where you wish to place the circuit beneath the original circuit. Note: Be careful to be on a highlighted component when you attempt to drag the group. If you miss, the entire group will be de-selected and you will have to re-select them all manually.

    As you drag the component you chose, all the components will move. Note that only outlines of the components are displayed as you drag them. This speeds up the process, as EWB has less to redraw on the screen. Note that the group is still active when you release the left mouse button.

- Wire the components together as in the original circuit.

That was easy! A lot easier than if you had to do it one component at a time, at any rate. And you probably noticed that wires between copied components were also copied, saving you time rewiring the circuit. But suppose you had to work with a hundred components instead of just six? Selecting them all would be quite a chore. Fortunately, once again, there is an easy alternative. Rather than selecting the components, you can **WINDOW** the group you wish to work with.

    "Window" means to drag the pointer from one corner of an imaginary box containing the group you wish to work with to the diagonally opposite corner. In this case, you will window the circuit copy you just made and delete it.

- Position the pointer to a spot just above and to the left of the copy of VS.

- Drag the pointer to a spot just below and to the right of the copy of R5's ground.

    As you drag the pointer (holding the left mouse button down as you move the mouse) you will see a rectangle appear, showing the boundaries that will contain the group you select. Continue to drag the pointer down and to the right until all the components of the circuit copy are contained inside the rectangle.

- Release the left mouse button.

When you release the mouse, all the components in the rectangle will highlight and the rectangle will disappear. You can now proceed to work with the entire group, this time to delete it.

- Delete the group by pressing the Del (delete) key.

That was even easier, wasn't it? Why then would you ever want to select components one at a time like when you copied the circuit the first time?

The answer is that you must always window in the shape of rectangles, and not all circuits are laid out so that rectangles may not be able to capture all the components you want to move, copy, delete, or whatever without picking up components you don't want to affect. Recall, however, that you can always deselect any unwanted components you may inadvertently have caught in the window. Being able to select and deselect components individually is a very useful feature.

A question that naturally arises now is: If you can't select all the components you want with just one window, do you have to perform the command you wish more than once for every "piece" of the group? The answer is: No! You can perform all your selecting first using the Ctrl key, and then perform the command you want only once on the entire group. Recall that the Ctrl key adds items to the active group. You can use Ctrl to individually add components to an active group you have already selected by windowing. To demonstrate this, copy the circuit again using a variety of selection methods.

- Window VS, R1, R2, and their grounds.

This establishes the intial active group.

- Hold down the Ctrl key and select R3.

    You have just added R3 to the active group.

- Hold down the Ctrl key and select the remaining components..

    All the components are now selected.

- Copy (capture) the active group.

- Paste the copy in the workspace below the original circuit.

As you can see, it is very simple to select any or all of a circuit by windowing and individually selecting components. One limitation with EWB is that you cannot window more than one group - as soon as you attempt to window another group, even using the Ctrl key, the active group is lost. One workaround to this limitation is to window around as many of the components as you need and then to individually select and deselect the components as needed.

Now, try one last thing before exiting to determine what the Rotate command will do. Will the Rotate command rotate the entire group, or rotate the components in the group individually?

- Use the "Ctrl + R" hot key sequence.

    As you can see the components rotate individually, rather than as a group. If you ever need to rotate the entire group 90 degrees, you must move the components as well as rotate them.

- Exit EWB. Do not bother to save the changes you have made.

This completes this section of the tutorial. In the next section you will learn some basic techniques for modifying existing EWB circuits.

Section 5 - Modifying Existing Circuits

In most of the previous sections you have been building circuits from scratch using components from the parts bin, or copying sections of existing circuits. In many cases, however, you may have a circuit that is very similar to the circuit you wish to build. In these cases it is quicker to modify the existing circuit than it is to build a whole new circuit. Sometimes you only need to change component values and labels. Other times the modifications are more extensive. In this section you will learn some basic techniques for modifying a circuit. The modifications you will make are fairly simple, but the techniques can be applied to any circuit you may wish to change.

- Start EWB from the Windows 95 Desktop.

- Open the file TUTOR_5.CA4 in the EWB tutorial folder.

    Note that this file contains two circuits. The circuit on the left is the original circuit. The circuit on the right is the circuit after modifications that you will make have been put in.

- Copy the original circuit (on the left) to the workspace beneath.

- Wire the circuit to match the original circuit on the upper left.

For the first modification, rotate the diode D1.

- **DISCONNECT** the wire between D1 and C1.

    "Disconnect" means to drag the end of the wire from its connection on a component, exactly opposite to the way you would connect the end of a wire to a component. Move the pointer to where the wire connects to D1 so that the connection appears next to the pointer. Then, hold the left mouse button down and drag the end of the wire away so that the connection disappears (you don't have to move the pointer very far for this to happen). When you release the button, the wire disappears. This is the only way to delete a wire from a schematic without deleting components connected to them.

- Disconnect the wire between VS and D1.

    Do this the same way you disconnect the wire between D1 and C1.

- Rotate D1.

- Connect D1 back to VS and C1 to match the final circuit on the upper right.

A question you may be asking is: What if you had rotated D1 without disconnecting if from the circuit first? The answer is that the wires would have just twisted around: the anode of D1 would still have been connected to VS and the cathode to C1. You would still have had to disconnect D1 and rewire eventually, and doing it before rotating keeps the circuit neater.

Now, add R1 into the circuit. One way is to disconnect the wire between D1 and C1, put a resistor into the workspace, and then add the wires back in, but there is an even easier way. EWB allows you to insert certain components directly into a circuit without disconnecting and reconnecting wires. First, you must make room for the resistor, and then insert it into the circuit.

- Move C1 and its attached ground to the right.

- Drag a resistor from the Passive parts bin on the workspace above the wire between D1 and C1.

This is just so you can make sure that there is room for the resistor between D1 and C1. If there is not enough room, move C1 and its attached ground further to the right. When there is enough room, proceed.

- **DRAG AND DROP** the resistor onto the wire between D1 and C1.

    "Drag and drop" just means to drag an object and release the left mouse button when the object is at a specific point. In this case, you wish to release the resistor when its leads line up with the wire into which you are inserting it. If you have lined it up properly when you drop it, the wire will break and reattach to the ends of the resistor.

- Verify the resistor is attached to the circuit by moving the resistor slightly up or down.

    If the resistor has been inserted into the circuit, the wires will stretch to follow the resistor. If you can move the resistor without affecting the wires, the resistor has not been inserted into the circuit. Repeat the drag and drop process until you succeed.

- Insert a fuse into the circuit between VS and D1.

- Delete the ground on load resistor RL.

    Note that the wire on the bottom of RL disappears, as you expected.

- Delete the load resistor RL.

    Note that the wire originally between C1 and RL also disappears.

- Modify the component labels and values to match that of the original circuit on the upper right.

    Your circuit should now look like the circuit on the upper right. By disconnecting and reconnecting wires and copying, deleting, and inserting components you can modify any existing circuit to if you need to build another similar circuit. Sometimes it actually is quicker and simpler to build a circuit from scratch (especially after you are used to working with EWB) so you will have to personally decide whether building or modifying is more effective on a circuit-by-circuit basis.

- Exit EWB. As before, you do not need to save your changes.

This completes this section of the tutorial. In the next section, you will learn about meter components and actually learn how to simulate a circuit using EWB.

Section 6 - Using DC Meters

In previous sections you have been using EWB to draw schematics. In this section you will actually begin to see the real purpose of EWB, which is to allow you to simulate circuits. As its name indicates, Electronics Workbench is a tool for building virtual circuits on your computer and letting you see what happens without the problems of cutting and stripping wire, forming component leads, burning yourself with a soldering iron, burning out components, and running the risk of occasional electrocution. In this section you will use meters in your circuit to monitor the circuit voltage and current.

- Start EWB from the Windows 95 desktop.

- Open the file TUTOR_6.CA4 in the EWB tutorial folder.

    As you can see, this circuit is a simple voltage divider circuit.

- Select the Indicators parts bin by clicking on the button with the picture of what appears to be a glowing lamp on it. (If you can't tell from the pictures on the buttons, click on "Window" in the Menu Bar and then click on "Indicators" in the Window menu.)

    The Indicators part pin is displayed to the left of the workspace. The component at the top of the parts bin is a voltmeter, as indicated by the "V". The one just below it is an ammeter, as shown by the "A". Note that each has a black stripe on one side to indicate meter polarity and indicates which side of the meter connects to the negative side of the circuit. Unlike some real meters, you will not damage them by hooking them in backwards. All that will happen is that the reading will be negative.

- Insert an ammeter between VDC and R1. The marked end should connect to R1.

- Connect a voltmeters in parallel across R1 so that the marked end connects to the circuit between R1 and R2. You will probably want to rotate the meter first to make wiring it in to the circuit easier.

- Connect a voltmeter in parallel across R2.

You are now ready to power up the circuit. At the top right of your screen, just above the workspace, is a switch. Currently the switch has a "0" on it, indicating that the circuit is unpowered.

- Click on the power switch to apply power to the circuit.

    Note that the switch now has a "1", indicating that there is power to your circuit.

    As you should have expected, the ammeter now shows 6 mA of current flowing through the circuit, and the voltmeters show 6V each across R1 and R2. Now, see what happens if the value of one of the resistors changes.

- Change the value of R2 to 2 kΩ.

Note that the meters go blank and the power switch displays a "0" again. Anytime you change a circuit so that the the voltages and currents might be affected, EWB will remove power from the circuit. Manually clicking on the power switch will also shut power off. This is actually a good practice to develop for when you work with real circuits so that you will not injure yourself or others or damage the circuit.

- Click on the power switch again.

The ammeter now shows 4 mA of current, the voltmeter across R1 reads 4V and the voltmeter across R2 indicates 8V. Thus far the meter shows exactly what you should have expected from Ohm's Law. Now, let's try something a little more extreme.

- Change the value of R1 to 10 MΩ.

- Change the value or R2 to 20 MΩ.

- Click on the power switch.

    The ammeter now shows about 6.45 µA of current, 5.86 V across R1, and 6.14 V across R2.

That's certainly unexpected. The current should have been reduced to about 400 nA and the voltages across R1 and R2 should not have changed from your last reading. What is happening here?

The answer is that, unlike programs like PSPICE, you cannot probe a circuit without affecting it (just as in the real world). All meters have impedance, and can load a circuit. The voltmeters in EWB have a default impedance of 1 MΩ, which is much smaller than the 10 MΩ and 20 MΩ resistors in the voltage divider you are measuring. The two voltmeters are forming a voltage divider of their own, consisting of two 1 MΩ resistors in series. As a result, the voltages measured across each resistor are about equal. If you had a real voltmeter and tried to measure the voltages across high resistances, you would undoubtedly see voltmeter loading effects as well.

So, now that you know what is causing the problem, you can correct it by changing the meter impedances. To do so, just do the the same thing you did to change component values.

- Double-click on the voltmeter across R1.

    A dialog box will open showing that the meter resistance is 1 MΩ and that the meter is in DC mode.

- Change the value of meter resistance to 1000 MΩ.

    This value will prevent loading virtually any circuit.

- Click on the "Accept" button.

    The meter displays go blank and the power is again removed from the circuit.

- Change the resistance of the voltmeter across R2 to 1000 MΩ.

- Click on the power switch.

    The ammeter now shows 410 nA, with 4.03V across R1 and 7.97V across R2 which is much closer to the expected values. There is still some deviation, but these are due to very large and very small values causing a some loss of accuracy in EWB. In most practical circuits you will not have to worry about this.

- Exit EWB. You do not need to save your changes.

This completes this section of the tutorial. In the next section you will work with AC meters.

Section 7 - Using AC Meters

In the last section you finally got to power up your circuit and use DC meters to display current and voltage values. You also learned about some issues with using meters in the circuit, such as loading effects and accuracy issues. In this section you will work with AC meters and learn about some issues with them.

- Start EWB from the Windows 95 desktop.

- Open the file TUTOR_7.CA4.

    This circuit is similar to the circuit of TUTOR_6.CA4, except that a 12V AC source is connected to the circuit.

- Insert an ammeter into the circuit between VAC and R1.

- Place a voltmeter in parallel across R1.

- Place a voltmeter in parallel across R2.

- Click on the power switch to apply power to the circuit.

    The ammeter and voltmeters all read 0.

You may have expected the ammeter to read 4 mA and the voltmeters 6V each, since Ohm's Law applies to both DC and AC circuits. Instead, you are reading nothing. What is happening here?

The answer lies in the fact that, although you are working with an AC circuit, the meters from the parts bin default to DC mode (as you may have remembered from the last tutorial section). At the moment, EWB is telling you that the DC values in the circuit are all 0. Change the meters to AC mode.

- Double-click on the ammeter.

    The Mode window shows the meter is set for DC measurements.

- Click the down arrow to the right of the Mode window.

    A drop-down window appears showing two options: AC and DC.

- Click on "AC" in the drop-down window.

- Click on the "Accept" button.

    As expected, the meters go blank and EWB removes power from the circuit.

- Change the mode of the voltmeter across R1 to AC.

- Change the mode of the voltmeter across R2 to AC.

- Apply power to the circuit.

    The meters now show the expected current and voltage values.

As with DC meters, AC meters can also load the circuit. Also as with DC meters, you can change the meter resistance as needed to prevent extreme loading. There is one other thing to note about AC meters in EWB, as you will now find out.

- Delete the AC source from the circuit.

- Insert the clock (essentially a pulse generator) from the Passive parts bin between ground and R1.

    The clock, which in this case will be used as a square wave source, is the component just below the polarized capacitor in the Passive parts bin. This source has a default 50% duty cycle, 5V peak-to-peak amplitude, 0V DC offset, and 1 kHz frequency. For now, the amplitude is all that concerns you.

- Apply power to the circuit.

    The ammeter measures 1.25 mA of AC current and each voltmeter shows 1.25 VAC across each of the resistors. In other words, the AC meters are measuring the peak value of the square wave, which is also the RMS value of a true square wave.

What does this tell you? It tells you two things.

The first is that all AC values in EWB are RMS values. The 12V AC source you first used is 12Vrms, rather than 12V peak or 12V peak-to-peak. Similarly, all the AC values displayed on ammeters and voltmeters in EWB are RMS values. You will verify this when you learn about oscilloscopes.

The second thing is that the EWB AC meters, which measure the RMS value of the input, are actually true-RMS meters. Some real-world digital meters will measure the peak-to-peak value of the input and display 0.354 of this value as the RMS, or AC, value. This is fine if you are measuring a sinusoidal waveform (which these meters assume), but this method will give wrong answers if you are working with triangular or square waves. If you see a discrepancy between your real-world meters and EWB's meters, that may be the reason why.

- Exit EWB. Do not bother to save the changes you have made.

This completes this section of the tutorial. In the next section you will learn more about the AC voltage source in EWB.

Section 8 - More About the AC Voltage Source

In this section you will learn more about sources in EWB. Like components, sources have values that you can modify to suit your purposes. You have already used three sources: the battery (a DC source), the AC source, and the square wave source. In this section you will learn more about the AC voltage source, as (aside from the battery) this is the one that you will most likely use most frequently.

- Start EWB from the Windows 95 Desktop.

- Open the circuit TUTOR_8.CA4.

- Attach an AC voltmeter in parallel across R1.

- Apply power to the circuit.

    As you can see, virtually none of the voltage applied to the RC filter is reaching the resistor. The AC source has 3 parameters that can be modified: amplitude, frequency, and phase. The three values shown next to the AC source ("120V/60Hz/0Deg") indicate that the AC source amplitude is 120 V, the frequency is 60 Hz, and the phase is 0 degrees. For now, change the frequency to 100 kHz.

- Double-click on the AC voltage source.

- Change the value in the text box next to "Frequency:" to 100.

- Click the up arrow next to the frequency units box to change "Hz" to "kHz".

- Click the "Accept" button.

    The AC source value changes to "120V/100kHz/0Deg" to indicate the amplitude is 120 V, the frequency is 100 kHz, and the phase is 0 degrees.

- Apply power to the circuit.

    Now the voltmeter across R1 reads 119 V, indicating that almost all the voltage is across the resistor. This shouldn't be a surprise, since this is a high-pass filter circuit.

The AC source amplitude and phase are changed in the same way. The amplitude is straightforward enough, but how exactly does the phase work? Phase must be measured relative to something, and the voltage source is the only signal in the circuit.

It turns out that the phase parameter is relative to an EWB reference that you don't actually see. The output of every AC is relative to it, however, so that AC voltages with different phases can be put into the circuit. Try it now.

- Copy the AC source.

- Insert the copy of the AC source into the circuit between the original source and C1.

- Apply power to the circuit.

    The voltage across the resistor is now 240 V. This is because both AC sources have a phase of 0 degrees, and so are *in phase* with each other. Consequently their amplitudes add together.

- Change the phase of one of the AC sources to 90.

- Apply power to the circuit.

    The voltage across the resistor is 170 V. Now the AC sources are out of phase by 90 degrees so that the amplitudes must be added using phasors. Since the source phasors are 90 degrees out of phase, the amplitude of the resultant phasor is just the square root of the sum of the squares of the source voltage phasors.

- Modify the AC source you did not change last time so that the phase is 270 degress.

- Apply power to the circuit.

    Now because one source has a phase of 90 degrees and the other has a phase of 270 degrees, the two AC sources are 180 degrees out of phase with each other. The two voltage waveforms exactly cancel, resulting in an output of 0 volts.

One AC source parameter that cannot be directly modified is the DC offset. The AC sources from the parts bin will always be centered around 0 V. If you wish to have a DC offset, you must put a battery of the proper amplitude in series with the source, or use the function generator (which will be discussed in a later section).

- Exit EWB. You do not need to save any of your changes.

This completes this section of the tutorial. In the next section you will learn about using the multimeter.

Section 9 - Using Instruments: Multimeter

In addition to parts bins containing assorted circuit components, EWB offers a selection of test instruments like those technicians use to check out real circuits. Instruments are very much like components in that they can be connected into circuits to measure and display such circuit parameters as voltage, current, frequency response, and so forth. They do differ in some important ways, however, that will be discussed in the next few sections. In this section, you will learn about EWB's multimeter, which is very similar to actual multimeters and is used the same way.

- Start EWB from the Windows 95 desktop.

- Open the circuit TUTOR_9.CA4 in the tutorial folder.

    This is a voltage divider circuit similar to that used in Sections 6 and 7. In this case, however, the circuit contains both a DC and AC source.

- Drag the multimeter from the instrument shelf just below the Menu Bar into the workspace to the right of the resistors.

    The multimeter is the instrument on the far left of the instrument shelf. As with components, it is highlighted as the active device when you bring it into the workspace.

- Connect the multimeter across R1.

    Connecting the multimeter is done the same way as connecting a component. In this case, be sure to connect the positive multimeter lead to the top of R1 and the negative lead to the bottom of R1. If you do not so so the meter will still work, but the readings will be negative rather than positive.

- Double-click the multimeter to expand it.

    This is one of the major differences between instruments and components. Instruments have an enlarged view that allows you to see the instrument controls and measurements more clearly. You can move the enlarged view the same way you can move components in the workspace. Sometimes this is necessary to prevent parts of the circuit from being blocked.

    In the case of the multimeter the controls consist of

    1) meter type buttons for measuring voltage (V), current (A), resistance (Ω), and decibels (dB),
    2) buttons to select AC or DC measurements, and
    3) a settings button for modifying the meter specifications.

    First, set the meter to measure the DC voltage across R1.

- Click on the voltmeter button (the button marked with a "V").

- Click on the DC measurement button (the button with the straight horizontal line on it).

- Apply power to the circuit.

    The meter displays 5.000V, which is the DC component of the voltage across R1. Note that 4 digits of accuracy are shown. Note also that the measurement is shown on the enlarged multimeter view, rather than on the object you dragged from the instrument shelf.

Now, check the AC voltage.

- Click on the AC measurement button (the button with a sine wave on it).

  The meter reading changes to 2.500V, which is the AC component of the voltage across R1. Again, 4 digits of accuracy are shown. Note that EWB did not shut off power this time, so that the AC measurement was displayed on the multimeter immediately. The multimeter is not considered part of the circuit, so that changing the measurement type did not change the circuit. This is another difference between instruments and components.

- Disconnect the negative multimeter lead from the top of R1 and connect it to the bottom of R2.

  The meter reading changes to 5.000V, which is the AC component across both R1 and R2. Again, EWB did not shut power off so that the display changed immediately without your having to apply power to the circuit again..

Now, measure the DC and AC current in the circuit.

- Disconnect the wire between VDC and R1.

- Note that EWB shuts the power to the circuit off, because you have changed the circuit.

- Move the negative multimeter lead to the top of R1.

- Move the positive multimeter lead to the top of VDC.

  This puts the ammeter in series with the current path.

- Click on the ammeter button (the button marked with an "A").

- Apply power to the circuit.

  The ammeter shows that the AC component of the supply current is 2.501mA.

- Click on the DC measurement button.

  The ammeter shows that the DC component of the supply current is 5.000mA.

Finally, check out the settings that you can modify for the multimeter.

- Click on the "SETTINGS" button.

  A dialogue box appears showing the ammeter resistance, the voltmeer resistance, the ohmmeter current, and the decibel reference voltage for the multimeter. You probably will never have to change the default setting for the meter, but this is where they are located if you ever need to. For now, go back to the workspace without editing any of the settings.

- Click on the "Cancel" button.

You have now been introduced to the EWB multimeter. At this point you may be wondering what other differences (in addition to those discussed above) there are between it and the component meters you have used. In summary, the important differences to keep in mind are these:

1) You can use as many component meters as you like in your circuit to display voltages and currents. There is only one multimeter, so that you can only see one voltag or current at a time.

2) You cannot delete the multimeter, or any other instrument, from EWB. To remove one from the workspace, you must drag it back to the instrument shelf. If you have enlarged the instrument, the enlarged view of the instrument will automatically close.

3) The multimeter can be much closer to an ideal meter than can the component meters. Whereas you can set the voltmeter resistance range to MΩ and the ammeter resistance range to mΩ for component meters, you can set the multimeter voltmeter resistance range to TΩ and the ammeter resistance range to pΩ if you wish.

- Exit EWB. You do not have to save the changes you have made.

This ends this section of the tutorial. In the next section you will learn about the EWB oscilloscope.

Section 10 - Using Instruments: Oscilloscope

In the last section you learned some facts about using the test instruments in EWB, and about the multimeter in general. In this section you will learn about using the EWB oscilloscope. Oscilloscopes are used to measure and observe time-varying voltages, typically periodic and AC voltages. It is assumed that you know how to use a standard oscilloscope, so the basics of oscilloscope operation will not be covered in this tutorial. Instead, some of the features of the EWB oscilloscope will be discussed so that you will be able to use the oscilloscope to observe typical circuits.

- Start EWB from the Windows 95 desktop.

- Open the file TUTOR_10.CA4 in the EWB tutorial folder.

  The circuit is a standard inverting amplifier, with a theoretical gain of -10.

- Drag the oscilloscope from the instrument shelf to the workspace above the amplifier circuit.

  The oscilloscope is third instrument from the left, and looks pretty much like an oscilloscope.

  When you examine the oscillosope, you will see two connection points on the bottom and two connection points on the right-hand side. The connection points on the bottom are the two signal input channels to the scope, referred to as Channel A and Channel B. The two connection points on the right side of the oscilloscope are the reference (ground) connections for the channels and the external trigger input. Channel A's connection is the left signal input, and the ground connection is the top reference connection.

- Connect Channel A to the connection dot to the left of R1.

- Connect Channel B to the output of the amplifier.

- Connect the oscilloscope ground connections to ground.

  You can get a ground component out of the Passive parts bin and place it next to the oscilloscope if you wish to keep the wiring neater.

- Double-click on the oscilloscope to expand it.

  The enlarged view of the oscilloscope looks much like a standard two-channel oscilloscope. You can click on the up and down arrows to adjust the time base and volts/div scale for Channel A and Channel B. Set the oscilloscope controls as follows:

Time Base:	0.02 ms/div
	0.00 X position
	Y/T (amplitude vs. time) display
Trigger Section:	Positive-edge trigger
	0.00 V trigger level
	Auto
Channel A:	100 mV/div
	1.60 Y position
	DC coupling

    Channel B: 1 V/div
          -1.60 Y position
          DC coupling

- Apply power to the circuit.

    EWB will begin to simulate the circuit. The oscilloscope display will show the changing input and output waveforms as the simulation runs. After a brief time (depending on your computer) the circuit will reach steady-state and the oscilloscope display will stop changing.

The oscilloscope display clearly shows two sinusoidal waveforms 180 degrees out of phase with each other, just as you would expect for an inverting amplifier. You could determine the period and amplitude of each signal using the time base and volts/div settings and the division marks on the screeen, but there is a much easier way. You can enlarge the oscilloscope yet again to get a clearer and more accurate view of the waveforms.

- **ZOOM** the oscilloscope.

    "Zoom" means to zoom in on, or enlarge, the oscilloscope. To zoom the oscilloscope, click on the "Zoom" button at the top of the oscilloscope.

After zooming, the oscilloscope will show the same oscilloscope controls as on the reduced instrument view with a much larger display screen above. You can use the X and Y position controls to adjust the waveforms on the screen to measure the amplitude and frequency of each, but an even more convenient way is to use the built-in display cursors. These cursors are referred to as Curson 1 and Cursor 2, and are marked with an inverted triangle with the numbers 1 and 2 on them. Cursor 1 will initially be on the left side of the display, and Cursor 2 on the right side of the display.

- Drag Cursor 1 so that it lines up with a positive peak on Channel A.

    Note that you can only drag the cursors by the labeled triangles.

    As you drag the cursor, notice that the numbers in two of the windows below the display change. These numbers correspond to the time and amplitude measurements for the waveforms at the cursor position.

- Drag Cursor 2 so that it lines up with the first negative peak to the right of Cursor 1 on Channel A.

    Again, the numbers in two of the windows below the display will change, corresponding to time and amplitude measurements at the cursor position.

The left and middle windows contain raw measurement values for Cursor 1 and Cursor 2, respectively. T1 is the time mark that Cursor 1 is currently at, VA1 the voltage on Channel A at that time mark, and VB1 the voltage on Channel B at that time mark. T2, VA2, and VB2 are the corresponding measurements for Cursor 2. The right window contains differential time and voltage measurements between the two cursors. In this case "VA2 - VA1" is peak-to-peak voltage for Channel A (the input signal to the amplifier), and "VB2 - VB1" the peak-to-peak voltage for Channel B (the output voltage of the amplifier). "T2 - T1" is half the period of the waveforms, as can be seen from the cursor positions. As expected, the output amplitude is 10 times the magnitude of the input, and period of the waveforms 100 µs.

One unusual control on the zoomed oscilloscope is the "Reverse" button. If you wish, you can invert the display colors so that you have white waveforms on a black background or black waveforms on a white background.

- Click on the "Reverse" button.

    The display colors invert.

- Click on the "Reverse" button again.

    The display reverts to its original colors.

You are pretty much finished here, so you can return to the reduced oscilloscope display. Note that if you change any of the oscilloscope settings on the zoomed display, the settings will be changed in reduced display. They are, after all, only different views of the same oscilloscope. The only exception to this is the reversed oscilloscope display. The reduced display always has black waveforms against a white background.

- Click on the "Reduce" button.

    The reduced oscilloscope is displayed again.

- Exit EWB. You do not have to save your changes.

This completes this section of the tutorial. In the next section you will learn about the EWB function generator.

Section 11 - Using Instruments: Function Generator

When an AC or clock signal was required for circuits in previous tutorial sections, a source component from the Passive parts bin was used. In this section you will be introduced to the EWB function generator. Like the oscilloscope in the last secton, you will see that the EWB function generator is very similar to those used in the real world.

- Start EWB from the Windows 95 desktop.

- Open the file TUTOR_11.CA4 in the EWB tutorial folder.

  You should recognize this circuit as an RL high-pass filter. In this section we will be using it as a simple differentiator circuit.

- Drag the function generator from the instrument shelf to the workspace to the left of the circuit.

  The function generator is the instrument immediately to the right of the multimeter.

  You will see that the function generator has 3 connection points. The two marked "+" and "-" are the signal outputs and are relative to the middle connection, which is ground.

- Drag the oscilloscope from the instrument shelf to the workspace above the circuit.

- Connect the postive terminal of the function generator to Vin.

- Connect the function generator ground connection to ground.

- Connect Channel A of the oscilloscope to Vin.

- Connect Channel B of the oscilloscope to Vout.

- Connect the oscilloscope ground connection to ground.

- Enlarge the function generator by double-clicking on it.

  The controls for the function generator are fairly straightforward and consistent with other EWB instruments you have used. At the top are 3 buttons to select a sinusoidal, triangular, or rectangular output. Below are standard windows to set the frequency, amplitude, duty cycle, and DC offset of the generator output.

- Enlarge the oscilloscope by double-clicking on it.

  When you enlarge the oscilloscope, it may cover the function generator. If it does, simply drag it to the side to reveal the function generator again. If you reduce the oscilloscope and enlarge it again, it will enlarge to whatever new position you have moved it

You are now ready to simulate the circuit. Since you have already worked with sine and square waves, which are also available as components, this section will use a triangular waveform (sometimes referred to as a ramp or sawtooth waveform).

- Select a triangular waveform for the output.

- Set the generator output for a 100 kHz, 1V output with a 50% duty cycle and no DC offset.

- Apply power to the circuit.

- Adjust the oscilloscope controls so that both channel signals fit on the display and you can see 5 to 10 cycles on each channel. Be sure that both channels are DC-coupled.

As you can see, the input signal is being *differentiated*: the amplitude of the output voltage is proporational to how rapidly the input voltage is changing with time. As the input ramps up at a constant rate, the output shows a constant positive voltage. As the input ramps down at a constant rate, the output shows a constant negative voltage. The amplitude of the output voltage shows the relative rates that the input is ramping. In this case, since the input waveform is symmetric (the input ramps up and down at the same rate) the output amplitude is symmetric as well. To test this claim, you can use the duty cycle control on the function generator.

- Change the duty cycle to 25%.

  For rectangular waveforms on the function generator the duty cycle refers to the ratio of the pulse width to the period of the square wave. For the triangle wave the duty cycle refers to the ratio of the ramp up time to the period of the square wave. A 25% duty cycle means that waveform ramps up the first 25% of the cycle, and ramps down the other 75%. Since the ramp up time is 3 times faster than the ramp down time, you would expect that the postive peak of the output would be 3 times larger than the negative peak.

- Apply power to the circuit.

  As you can readily see, the magnitude of the positive peak is larger than that of the negative peak.

- Zoom the oscillosope.

- Use the cursors to measure the amplitude of the output waveform.
-
  You should see that the output ranges from about -2.67 V to about +8 V. As expected, the positive magnitude is 3 times that of the negative magnitude.

Note that the areas under the waveforms remain equal: although the positive peak is three times larger than the negative peak, it is also one-third the width. This is not affected by the DC offset, as the output of a differentiator depends solely on the rate of change of the input, rather than the absolute magnitude. You can verify this quite easily.

- Set the function generator DC offset to 2 V.

- Apply power to the circuit.

  The oscilloscope shows that, although the input voltage move upward on the oscilloscope display, the output voltage remains unchanged.

This completes this section of the tutorial. In the next section you will learn about the last EWB analog instrument, the Bode plotter.

Section 12 - Using Instruments: Bode Plotter

The Bode plotter is the last EWB analog instrument, and the last that will be discussed. As its name suggests, the Bode plotter is an instrument for generating Bode plots. Bode plots summarize the frequency response of a circuit, and present both amplitude and phase information.

- Start EWB from the Windows 95 desktop.

- Open the file TUTOR_12.CA4 in the EWB tutorial folder.

    You should recognize this circuit as an RC low-pass filter cascaded with an RC high-pass filter. Using the standard formula for an RC circuit, you should be able to verify that the corner frequency of the low-pass filter is 15.9 kHz and that the corner frequency for the high-pass filter is 0.159 Hz.

- Drag the Bode plotter from the instrument shelf to the workspace to the left of the circuit.

    The Bode plotter is the instrument immediately to the right of the oscilloscope.

    You will see that the Bode plotter has 4 connection points, arranged as one pair marked "IN" and a second pair marked "OUT". The Bode plotter essentially compares the signal across the "OUT" terminals to the signal across the "IN" terminal for a range of frequencies, and displays the results.

- Connect the "IN" connections of the Bode plotter across VS of the circuit.

    To do this, wire one of the "IN" connections between VS and R1 and the other "IN" connection to ground.

- Connect the "OUT" connections of the Bode plotter across R2 (the output of the circuit).

    To do this, wire one of the "OUT" connections between C2 and R2 and the other "OUT" connection to ground.

- Enlarge the Bode plotter by double-clicking on it.

    The controls for the Bode plotter are self-explanatory. At the top left are 2 buttons to select whether the circuit's amplitude or phase will be plotted. Below are controls to define the vertical and horizontal axes of the display. "LOG" means the plot will be displayed using a logarithmic scale, while "LIN" means that a linear scale will be used. "F" and "I" specify the final and initial (or maximum and minimum) values on the axes, respectively.

- For now, set the Bode plotter for a magnitude plot with the following axes:

    Vertical: Log scale
                 Final amplitude: 40 dB
                 Initial amplitude: -80 dB

    Horizontal: Log scale
                 Final frequency: 10 MHz
                 Initial frequency: 1 mHz

You are now ready to simulate the circuit. The settings you have made will sweep the circuit from 1 mHz to 10 MHz, and display the results as a log-log plot (which means to say that both the axes use a logarithmic scale) with a vertical range of -80 dB to 40 dB.

- Apply power to the circuit.

    The Bode plotter will show a classic bandpass Bode plot, with a flat midband and 20 dB/decade rolloffs at either side.

Unlike the oscilloscope, the Bode plotter cannot be zoomed for a better view of the display. There is, however, a cursor so that you can determine the amplitude for specific frequencies. Below the axes control sections are two buttons with arrows and two windows displaying dB amplitude and frequency values corresponding to the cursor position.. Initially the cursor is at the far left, with corresponding measurements of -44.0 dB at 1.00 mHz. You can move the cursors to the left and right using the corresonding arrow buttons.

- Position the pointer over the right arrow button and hold the left mouse button down on it.

    The cursor moves to the right. As it does so, the frequency and amplitude values in the windows change, corresponding to the plot under the cursor.

- Position the pointer over the left arrow button and hold the left mouse button down on it.

    The cursor moves to the left. Again, the frequency and amplitude values to reflect the plot values at the cursor position.

If clicking on the arrow buttons seems too slow to you, you can also drag the cursor left and right to where you wish to position it. How you choose to move the cursor is up to you. Typically the arrow buttons are used to "fine tune" the position, and dragging the cursor used for placing the cursor in a general area of the plot. Now, use the cursors to determine some useful information about the circuit.

- Move the cursor to the midband region of the plot.

    Again, how you move the cursor is up to you. You should get a midband amplitude of about -0.09 dB. This makes sense, as there is no amplification in the circuit and very little attentuation in the midband.

- Move the cursor to the lower breakpoint of the plot.

    This is also referred to as the the lower critical frequency, or lower half-power point. It is the lower frequency at which the amplitude is -3 dB relative to the midband amplitude. You should get a value of about 158 mHz when the amplitude is about -3 to -3.1dB.

- Move the cursor to the upper breakpoint of the plot.

    Again, this is when the amplitude is -3 dB relative to the midband amplitude. You should measure an upper critical frequency of about 15.8 kHz when the amplitude is about -3 to -3.1 dB.

As expected, the RC bandpass filter has a lower cutoff frequency of about 0.159 Hz and an upper cutoff frequency of about 15.9 kHz. At these frequencies the phase shift should be 45 degrees leading or lagging the midband phase shift, as the reactance and resistance are equal at these frequencies. You can use the phase plot on the Bode plotter to confirm this.

- Click on the "PHASE" button to select a phase plot.

    Note that the display changes to show the phase information. Note also that, although the horizontal axes values do not change and still refer to frequency, the vertical axis values now display degrees.

- Set the vertical axis for logarithmic scale with a range of -180 degrees to +180 degress.

  The display changes to reflect the new vertical axis settings.

- Move the cursor to midband.

  The phase angle is very close to 0 degress.

- Move the cursor to 158 mHz.

  The phase angles is very close to 45 degrees. The slight deviation is due mostly to the other pole in the circuit and the resolution of the plot.

- Move the cursor to 15.8 kHz.

  The phase angle is very close to -45 degrees. As before, the slight deviation is mostly due to the other pole in the circuit and the resolution in the plot.

As a final exercise, take look a linear amplitude display.

- Select the amplitude plot.

- Change the vertical axis to a linear scale, but leave the horizontal axis as a logarithmic scale.

  Now the vertical axis displays the actual ratio of the circuit output to circuit input, rather than the decibel equivalents.

- Set the vertical and horizontal axes controls so that the plot fills the display.

  You should have the vertical scale ranging from 0 to 1, and the horizontal scale ranging from 1 mHz to 10 MHz.

- Move the cursor to midband.

  The amplitude reads about 1, indicating that the input and output signals are about the same at midband.

- Move the cursor to 158 mHz.

  The amplitude reads about 0.71, or 71%. This indicates that the circuit attenuates the input signal to about 71% at 158 mHz. Ideally it should be about 70.7%, which is what the half-power, or -3 dB, point is.

- Move the cursor to 15.8 kHz.

  Again, the amplitude reads about 0.71.

- Exit EWB. You do not have to save your circuit changes.

This completes this section of the tutorial. In the next section you will look as some special components in EWB.

Section 13 - Special Components: Variable Value Devices and Switches

In all the previous sections the components you have used have had static, or fixed values. When you wished to see the effects of other component values on the circuit response, you have had to edit the component, and run another simulation. In this section you will learn about some special components that may be useful to you in working with circuit simulations. These component are variable value devices, as they can be dynamically adjusted, or varied, to different values. Specifically, this section will look at four of these components: switches, variable resistors, variable inductors, and variable capacitors.

Start EWB from the Windows 95 desktop.

- Open the file TUTOR_13.CA4 in the EWB tutorial folder.

This circuit is essentially a parallel RLC circuit with a switch to apply and disconnect and input (essentially an "on-off" switch). L1 and C1 are variable so that the tank circuit can be tuned to different frequencies. RW, representing the inductor winding resistance, can be adjusted as well to control the Q of the coil.

You will note that the switch and each of the variable value components has some extra information associated with it that you have not seen before. This extra information determines the range of values the component can assume and how these values are selected. For the switch only two values are permitted: open and closed, so that a range is not given. For now, determine the frequency response for the default settings.

- Drag the Bode plotter from the instrument shelf to the workspace above the circuit.

- Set the Bode plotter to display –200 dB to 0 dB from 1 Hz to 1 MHz.

- Connect the "IN" connections of the Bode plotter across VS of the circuit.

  To do this, wire one of the "IN" connections between VS and R1 and the other "IN" connection to ground.

- Connect the "OUT" connections of the Bode plotter across the tank circuit.

  To do this, wire one of the "OUT" connections between R1 and RW and the other "OUT" connection to ground.

- Enlarge the Bode plotter by double-clicking on it.

- Apply power to the circuit.

  The Bode plotter will show a classic parallel RLC peaking response with a center frequency of about 1.0 kHz.

- Stop the simulation.

For the simulation you just ran the default values of the variable components were used. This was 50% of the full-range value of the component, as indicated by the 50% shown in the information next to the resistor, inductor, and capacitor. The full range value of the each component is also shown. For the resistor the full-range value is 1 Ω, so that the value used in this simulation was 0.5 Ω. Similarly, the full-range values of the inductor and capacitor were 10 mH and 10 µF, respectively, so that the values used in the simulation were 5 mH and 5 µF. The nominal resonant frequency of a tank circuit with 5 mH and 5 µF in parallel is about 1.01 kHz, so the simulation appears to be correct.

This explains two of the three pieces of information associated with the variable components. The last piece is the information contained inside the square brackets ([Space] for the SW1, [R] for RW, [C] for C1, and [L] for L1. As you may have guessed, this indicates which key is used to vary the component value. For now, experiment with the keys to see what happens. Before proceeding, be sure that your CAPS LOCK key is OFF.

- Press the SPACE bar once.

  You should see SW1 open. Because the switch can only open and close, pressing the SPACE bar will toggle the state of the switch.

- Press SPACE bar again.

  SW1 closes.

- Press the R key once.

  You should see the 50% in the variable resistor information change to 45%.

- Press the R key again.

  You should see the 45% change to 40%. Unlike the switch, there are a number of values that RW can take, so pressing the R key more than once will simply continue to decrease the value of RW. This is also true for the values of C1 and L1 using the C and L keys.

- Press the L key twice.

  L1 should now show its value as being 40% of full-range.

- Press the C key three times.

  C1's value should now be 35% of full-range.

If you continue to press the control keys for R1, C1, and L1 you will eventually reach 0%, which is the minimum you can have. This is because the control keys are case-sensitive (that is, upper- and lower-case mean different things) and you are using lower-case, which decreases the component value. To increase component values, you must use upper-case.

- Press SHIFT + R to enter an upper-case (capital) R.

  This just means to press the R key while holding down the SHIFT key. You should see the RW value increase by 5%.

- Press SHIFT + L twice.

  You should see the L1 value increase by 10%.

- Press SHIFT + C three times.

  You should see the C1 value increase by 15%.

If you continue to enter upper-case characters, you will eventually reach 100% of the full-range value. Entering additional upper-case characters will have no effect. Now, adjust the circuit to an extreme case.

- Adjust C1 to 0% of full-range.

- Adjust L1 to 100% of full range.

- Adjust RW to 0% of full-range.

- Start the simulation.

    The Bode plotter shows classic high-pass response with a corner frequency of about 15.8 kHz. This is because with no capacitance or winding resistance the circuit has become a series RL circuit with the output taken across the inductor.

- Stop the simulation.

Now, take the other extreme case.

- Adjust C1 to 100% of full-range.

- Adjust L1 to 0 % of full-range.

- Adjust RW to 100% of full range.

- Set the Bode plotter to display –40 dB to –200 dB.

- Start the simulation.

    As you could have guessed, the response is now that of a low-pass filter with a corner frequency of about 15.8 kHz. In the passband the output is –60 dB because the output across the 1 Ω resistor is only about 1./1000th of the input signal.

Now that you know the basics of variable components, you may be wondering about some practical aspects of using them. Suppose, for example, you wished to have something other than 10 mH as the full-range inductance value? Even more critical, suppose you had multiple variable components of the same type in the same circuit? Pressing the components control key would change all of them at the same time!. This would be useful for "ganged" components, but not very practical for circuits with independent trimming components. To make full use of these components, you must edit them. Editing variable components is much like editing fixed-value components, but with some additional options. For simplicity only the resistor will be considered, but the techniques applies to variable capacitors and inductors as well.

- Double-click on RW.

    A window opens with options to set 4 separate parameters: Key, Resistance, Setting, and Increment. The Key parameter determines which key will adjust the resistance value, and has a default value of R for resistors. The Resistance parameter sets the full-scale value of the component and is identical to that for a fixed-value resistor, and has a program default value of 1 kΩ (although this was changed to 1 Ω for this tutorial section). The Setting parameter directly sets the full-range percentage of the component and has a default value of 50% (although it should now be 100% from the last simulation you ran). The Increment parameter determines how much the setting will change each time the control key is pressed, and has a default value of 5%.

- Change the Key value to L.

    It doesn't matter whether you enter an upper-case or lower-case L for this parameter, as EWB will automatically use upper-case to increase and lower-case to decrease the component value. All you need to do is say which key will be used. Note that this will give RW and L1 the same control key, causing them to be "ganged" components and increasing and decreasing at the same time. This makes sense, as the inductance and resistance of a component tend to be proportional to the number of windings. For independent control of variable components, you would enter a unique key value.

- Change the Setting to 0%.

    This will give RW the same full-range percentage as L1. Note that you cannot type a value for this parameter: you must use the arrow buttons to the right of the text box or the keyboard up-arrow and down-arrow keys to modify it. This is because EWB wants only integer values for percentages, and this enforces it. This is also true for the Increment value.

- Click the "Accept" button.

    The values for RW should now be "[L]/1Ω/0%".

- Press SHIFT + L.

    The values for both RW and L1 should increase to 5%.

- Press the L key to enter a lower-case L.

    Both RW and L1 should go back to 0%.

- Exit EWB. You do not have to save your circuit changes.

This completes this section of the tutorial. In the next section you will "put it all together" and use EWB to simulate a system application in *Electronic Devices*.

Section 14 - Putting It All Together

In this section you will use the EWB skills you have developed to build and simulate a system application circuit from *Electronics Devices*, 5th Ed. If you have any problems that you cannot resolve, your instructor will have a pre-built EWB circuit for this section called TUTOR_14.CA4 that you can use as a reference.

- Start EWB from the Windows 95 desktop.

- Construct the circuit shown in Fig. 6-46.

    Models for the 2N3904 transistor are found in the Active devices parts bin, located immediately to the right of the Passive devices parts bin, in the "2n" library.

This circuit is a common-base amplifier, followed by a common-emitter amplifier. You can use transistor amplifier analysis (asume a current gain of 204) to verify that the loaded gain of the first stage will be about 100, while the gain of the second stage will vary from about 4 to 19 (depending upon the how much of R9 is bypassed by C4) producing an overall gain of 400 to 1900. Once you have done this, use EWB to verify your calculations.

- Connect an AC voltage source to the input of the first stage.

- Edit the source to provide a 10 kHz 1mV signal.

- Connect a voltmeter from the Indicators parts bin to measure the AC signal on the collector of Q1.

    Remember to edit the voltmeter to set it for AC measurement and to minimize loading on the circuit.

- Connect a second voltmeter to measure the AC signal on the collector of Q2.

- Adjust R9 for minimum amplifier gain.

    This will be when R9 is unbypassed.

- Run the simulation.

    You should see about 95 mV on the output of the first stage and about 375 mV on the output of the second stage. This is in close agreement to the calculated values, which predicts about 100 mV and 395 mV.

- Stop the simulation.

Now, check for maximum gain.

- Adjust R9 for maximum gain.

    This will be when R9 is completely bypassed by C4.

- Run the simulation.

    You should see about 100 mV and 1.85 mV on the voltmeters. Again, this corresponds well to the calculated values of 100 mV and 1.95 V.

- Stop the simulation.

You have now simulated an systems application circuit using EWB. You can now, if you wish, run frequency analyses with the Bode plotter, view waveforms with the oscilloscope, and vary circuit values in this circuit using the techniques you have learned to do in previous sections of this tutorial.

- Exit EWB. You do not have to save your circuit changes.

This completes the EWB tutorial for *Electronic Devices*, 5th Ed.

Summary of Electronics Workbench Example Circuit Files Results for *Electronic Devices*, 5th Ed.

The following summarizes the specific values obtained for each EWB circuit in the specified text examples. Measured voltages within ±10% of of the calculated values are considered a close match.

Chapter 1:

No circuits.

Chapter 2:

Figure 2-6a: Calculated: 0 V to 4.3 V half-wave rectified waveform.
                        Measured: 0 V to 4.3 V half-wave rectified waveform.
                        Comments: Forward diode drop set to 0.7 V. Measured value matches calculated value. No problems.

Figure 2-6b: Calculated: 0 V to 99.3 V half-wave rectified waveform.
                        Measured: 0 V to 99.2 V half-wave rectified waveform.
                        Comments: Forward diode drop set to 0.7 V. Measured value closely matches calculated value. No problems.

Figure 2-10:   Calculated: 54.3 V half-wave rectified waveform.
                        Measured: 54.3 V half-wave rectified waveform.
                        Comments: Forward diode drop set to 0.7 V. Measured value matches calculated value. No problems.

Figure 2-18:   Calculated: 24.3 V peak full-wave rectified waveform across load.
                                          25.0 V peak sine wave across each half of the secondary.
                        Measured: 24.3 V peak full-wave rectified waveform across load.
                                          25.0 V peak sine wave across each half of the secondary.
                        Comments: Forward diode drop set to 0.7 V. Measured value matches calculated value. No problems.

Figure 2-30:   Calculated: $Vr = 1.13\ V_{PP}$
                                          $V_{DC} = 14.3\ V$
                        Measured: $Vr = 0.933\ V_{PP}$
                                          $V_{DC} = 14.4\ V$
                        Comments: The measured value of Vr is significantly less than the calculated value, as the calculated value is from a simplified form of the exact equation. Using the exact form of the equation given in Appendix B as

$$Vr_{(PP)} = V_p(\text{rect}) * (1 - e^{-(t/RC)})$$

where t is the discharge time, R the load resistance, and C the filter capacitance, gives Vr = 0.948 V. V_{DC} is within 10%

Figure 2-38:	Calculated:	-0.7 V to 9.09 V
	Measured:	-0.75 V to 9.09 V
	Comments:	Measured values closely match calculated values. No problems.
Figure 2-44:	Calculated:	-5.7 V to +7.7 V
	Measured:	-5.73 V to +7.71 V
	Comments:	Measured values closely match calculated values. No problems.
Figure 2-52:	Calculated:	+0.7 V to -47.3 V
	Measured:	+0.71 V to -45.6 V
	Comments:	Measured values closely match calculated values. No problems.

Chapter 3:

Figure 3-10:	Calculated:	V_{OUT} = 4.76 V for V_{IN} = 4.86 V
		V_{OUT} = 6.13 V for V_{IN} = 25.7 V
	Measured:	V_{OUT} = 4.65 V for V_{IN} = 4.86 V
		V_{OUT} = 5.38 V for V_{IN} = 25.7 V
	Comments:	Zener diodes for calculations were assumed to have a constant zener resistance of 7 Ω. EWB zener model does not have a constant zener resistance.
Fig. 3-13:	Calculated:	12 V for RL = 490 Ω
	Measured:	12 V for RL = 490 Ω
	Comments:	Zener test current set to 1 mA. Measured value shows circuit is still regulating for minimum load resistance. No problems.
Figure 3-17:	Calculated:	For 10V: +5.8 V to -4.0 V
		For 20V: +6.9 V to -15.7 V
	Measured:	For 10V: +5.62 V to -3.97 V
		For 20V: +6.96 V to -15.3 V
	Comments:	Zener test current set to 10 mA for both voltages. Measured values closely match calculated values. No problems.

Chapter 4:

Figure 4-8:	Calculated:	I_B = 430 μA
		I_C = 64.5 mA
		I_E = 64.9 mA
		V_{BE} = 0.7 V
		V_{CE} = 3.55 V
		V_{CB} = 2.85 V
	Measured:	I_B = 415 μA
		I_C = 62.5 mA
		I_E = 63.0 mA
		V_{BE} = 0.852 V
		V_{CE} = 3.75 V
		V_{CB} = 2.89 V
	Comments:	Measured value of $V_{BE} \neq 0.7$ V explains differences.

Figure 4-15:   Calculated: I_B = 230 µA
                            I_C = 9.8 mA
               Measured: I_B = 215 µA
                            I_C = 9.85 mA
                            V_{CE} = 154 mV (in saturation)
               Comments: Circuit value of $V_{BE} \neq 0.7$ V explains differences.

Figure 4-24:   Calculated: LED turns on and off.
               Measured: V_{CE} = 91.6 mV and I_C = 25.6 mA (LED ON)
                            V_{CE} = 8.46 V and I_C = 256 µA (LED OFF)
               Comments: The LED I_{ON} parameter set to 25 mA. Observed LED operation matches expected. No problems.

Chapter 5:

Figure 5-7:   Calculated: I_C = 39.6 mA
                            V_{CE} = 6.93 V
               Measured: I_C = 39.0 mA
                            V_{CE} = 7.13 V
               Comments: Measured values closely match calculated values. Circuit value of $V_{BE} \neq 0.7$ V explains differences.

Figure 5-10:   Calculated: For β = 100 I_C = 11.3 mA
                                           V_{CE} = 5.67 V
                            For β = 150 I_C = 17.0 mA
                                           V_{CE} = 2.48 V
               Measured: For β - 100 I_C = 11.2 mA
                                           V_{CE} = 5.73 V
                            For β = 150 I_C = 16.8 mA
                                           V_{CE} = 2.61 V
               Comments: Measured values closely match calculated values. Circuit value of $V_{BE} \neq 0.7$ V explains differences.

Figure 5-12:   Calculated: I_C = 1.80 mA
                            I_E = 1.80 mA
                            V_{CE} = 9.74 V
               Measured: I_C = 1.77 mA
                            I_E = 1.79 mA
                            V_{CE} = 9.82 V
               Comments: Measured values closely match calculated values. No problems.

Figure 5-16:   Calculated: V_E = 1.64 V
                            V_{CE} = -14.7 V
               Measured: V_E = 1.64 V
                            V_{CE} = -14.8 V
               Comments: Measured values closely match calculated values. No problems.

Figure 5-22:   Calculated: I_C = 5.16 mA (no base loading)
                             V_{CE} = 1.95 V (no base loading)
                             I_C = 4.77 mA (base loading)
                             V_{CE} = 2.56 V (base loading)
               Measured: I_C = 4.66 mA
                             V_{CE} = 2.70 V
               Comments: Measured values closely match calculated values when the loading effects on the base are considered.

Figure 5-26:   Calculated: I_C = 2.42 mA (no base loading)
                             V_{EC} = 2.26 V (no base loading)
                             I_C = 2.29 mA (base loading)
                             V_{EC} = 2.67 V (base loading)
               Measured: I_C = 2.24 mA
                             V_{EC} = 2.82 V
               Comments: Measured values closely match calculated values when the loading effects on the base are considered.

Figure 5-29:   Calculated: I_C = 845 µA
                             V_{CE} = 1.55 V
               Measured: I_C = 834 µA
                             V_{CE} = 1.58 V
               Comments: Measured values closely match calculated values.

Chapter 6:

Figure 6-24:   Calculated: V_C = 4.74 V_{DC} (no base loading)
                             Vout = 84.5 mV (no base loading)
                             V_C = 5.30 V_{DC} (base loading)
                             Vout = 79.9 mV (base loading)
               Measured: V_C = 5.28 V_{DC}
                             Vout = 79.5 mV
               Calculated: Measured values closes match calculated values when the loading effects on the base are considered.

Figure 6-31:   Calculated: Av = 0.989
               Measured: Av = 0.992
               Comments: Measured value closely matches calculated value. No problems.

Figure 6-35:   Calculated: Av = 76.3 (no base loading)
                             Av = 73.6 (base loading)
               Measured: Av = 69.7
               Comments: Measured value more closely matches calculated value when loading effects on the base are considered. Actual $V_{BE} \neq$ 0.7 V explains additional discrepancy.

Figure 6-37:	Calculated:	$A_V(1) = 68.5$ (no DC base loading)
		$A_V(2) = 197$ (no DC base loading)
		$A_V(\text{total}) = 13495$ (no DC base loading)
		$A_V(1) = 65.2$ (DC base loading)
		$A_V(2) = 181$ (DC base loading)
		$A_V(\text{total}) = 11801$ (DC base loading)
	Measured:	$A_V(1) = 65.1$
		$A_V(2) = 174.7$
		$A_V(\text{total}) = 11471$
	Comments:	Measured values closely match calculated values when the DC loading effects on the bases are considered. Actual $V_{BE} \neq 0.7$ V explains additional discrepancy.

Chapter 7:

Figure 7-10:	Calculated:	$I_c(\text{sat}) = 8.97$ mA
		$V_{ce}(\text{cutoff}) = 5.38$ V
	Measured:	$I_c(\text{sat}) = 9.49$ mA
		$V_{ce}(\text{cutoff}) = 5.67$ V
	Comments:	Measured value closely matches calculated value. No problems.
Figure 7-13:	Calculated:	$A_v = 120$
	Measured:	$A_v = 117.3$ for $V_{in} = 7$ mV.
	Comments:	Measured value closely matches calculated value. No problems.
Figure 7-16:	Calculated:	$I_{CQ} = 35$ mA (no base loading)
		$V_{CEQ} = 9.0$ V (no base loading)
		$I_{CQ} = 32.9$ mA (base loading)
		$V_{CEQ} = 9.84$ (base loading)
	Measured:	$I_{CQ} = 31.8$ mA
		$V_{CEQ} = 10.3$ V
	Comments:	Measured values more closely match calculated when loading effects on the base are considered. Actual $V_{BE} \neq 0.7$ V explains additional discrepancy.
Figure 7-27:	Calculated:	$V_{out}(\text{max}) = 20$ V_{PP}
	Measured:	$V_{out}(\text{max}) = 20$ V_{PP}
	Comments:	Measured value matches calculated value. No problems.

Chapter 8:

Figure 8-17:	Calculated:	$V_{GS} = -1.1$ V
		$I_D = 5.0$ mA
		$V_{DS} = -8.90$ V
	Measured:	$V_{GS} = -1.08$ V
		$I_D = 4.94$ mA
		$V_{DS} = -8.98$ V
	Comments:	Set $V_{TO} = -3.0$ V and $\beta = 0.001333$ A/V^2 to get $I_D = 4.94$ mA. Measured values closely match calculated values. No problems.

Figure 8-19:	Calculated:	$V_{GS} = -882$ mV
$I_D = 6.0$ mA
$V_D = 6.0$ V
	Measured:	$V_{GS} = -890$ mV
$I_D = 5.94$ mA
$V_D = 6.06$ V
	Comments:	Set $V_{TO} = -3.0$ V and $\beta = 0.0001333$ A/V^2 to get $I_D = 5.94$ mA.
Measured values closely match calculated values. No problems.
Figure 8-24:	Calculated:	$V_G = -1.54$ V
$V_S = 3.34$ V
$I_D = 1.52$ mA
$V_D = 7.0$ V
	Measured:	$V_G = -1.54$ V
$V_S = 3.45$ V
$I_D = 1.57$ mA
$V_D = 6.82$ V
	Comments:	Set $V_{TO} = -3$ V and $\beta = 0.001333$ A/V^2 to get target value of $I_D = 1.57$ mA. Measured values closely match calculated values. No problems.
Figure 8-26:	Calculated:	$V_{GS} = -1.8$ V
$I_D = 1.8$ mA
	Measured:	$V_{GS} = -1.83$ V
$I_D = 1.77$ mA
	Comments:	Set $V_{TO} = -3.0$ V and $\beta = 0.001333$ A/V^2 to get $I_D = 1.8$ mA.
Measured values closely match calculated values. No problems.
Figure 8-45:	Calculated:	$V_{GS} = 3.13$ V
$V_{DS} = 11.2$ V
	Measured:	$V_{GS} = 3.13$ V
$V_{DS} = 11.2$ V
	Comments:	Set $V_{TO} = 2$ V and $\beta = 0.05$ A/V^2 to get $V_{GS} = 3.13$ V.
Measured values match calculated values. No problems.

Chapter 9:

Figure 9-15:	Calculated:	$V_D = 5.53$ V
$V_{out} = 1.07$ V
	Measured:	$V_D = 5.51$ V
$V_{out} = 1.07$ V
	Comments:	Set $V_{TO} = -3$ V and $\beta = 0.001333$ A/V^2 to get $g_{m0} = 8$ mS and $g_m = 3.227$ mS.
Measured values closely match calculated values. No problems.
Figure 9-19:	Calculated:	$I_D = 200$ mA
$V_D = 8.4$ V
$V_{out} = 3.29$ V
	Measured:	$I_D = 212$ mA
$V_D = 7.99$ V
$V_{out} = 3.30$ V
	Comments:	Set $V_{TO} = -2.0$ V and $\beta = 0.05$ A/V^2 to get $g_{m0} = g_m = 200$ mS.
Actual $I_{DSS} = 212$ mA, rather than 200 mA, resulting in lower V_D than expected.

Figure 9-21:	Calculated:	V_{GS} = 2.23 V
		I_D = 2.65 mA
		V_{DS} = 6.26 V
		V_{out} = 1.73V
	Measured:	V_{GS} = 2.23 V
		I_D = 2.63 mA
		V_{DS} = 6.31 V
		V_{out} = 1.71 V
	Comments:	Set V_{TO} = 2.0 V and β = 0.05 A/V² to get I_D = 2.65 mA.
		Measured values closely match calculated values. No problems.
Figure 9-24:	Calculated:	Av = 0.909
	Measured:	Av = 0.868
	Comments:	Set V_{TO} = -0.75 V and β = 0.001778 A/V²
		Measured value closely matches calculated value. No problems.
Figure 9-27:	Calculated:	Av = 10 (V_{out} = 100 mV)
	Measured:	Av = 10.1 (V_{out} = 101 mV)
	Comments:	Measured value closely matches calculated value. No problems.

Chapter 10:

Figure 10-15:	Calculated:	f_C = 75.8 Hz
	Measured:	f_C = 71.1 Hz
	Comments:	Measured value within 5% of calculated value. No problems.
Figure 10-29:	Calculated:	$f_C(1)$ = 1.62 MHz
	Measured:	$f_C(1)$ = 1.72 Mhz
	Comments:	Measured value well within 10% of calculated value. No problems.
Figure 10-39:	Calculated:	f_C = 16.2 Hz
	Measured:	f_C = 16.1 Hz
	Comments:	An external Rin was needed to simulate the FET input impedance.
		Measured value closely matches calculated value. No problems.
Figure 10-41:	Calculated:	f_C = 17.3 Hz
	Measured:	f_C = 16.9 Hz (@ - 6dB point)
	Comments:	An external Rin was needed to simulate the FET input impedance.
		Measured value closely matches calculated value. No problems.

Chapter 11:

No circuits.

Chapter 12:

Figure 12-22:	Calculated:	Av = 22.3
	Measured:	Av = 22.3
	Comments:	Measured value matches calculated value. No problems.

Figure 12-26:   Calculated: $A_v = 100$ for $R_f = 220$ kΩ
                Measured: $A_v = 99.8$ for $R_f = 220$ kΩ
                Comments: Measured value closely matches calculated value. No problems.

Figure 12-29:   Calculated: $A_v = 23.0$
                Measured: $A_v = 23.0$
                Comments: Measured value matches calculated value. No problems..

Figure 12-32:   Calculated: $A_v = -100$
                Measured: $A_v = -100$
                Comments: Measured value matches calculated value. No problems.

Chapter 13:

Figure 13-9:   Calculated: a) BW = 44.3 kHz
                              b) BW = 63.8 kHz
                Measured: a) BW = 43.8 kHz
                              b) BW = 62.9 kHz
                Comments: Measured values closely match calculated values. No problems.

Chapter 14:

Figure 14-3:   Calculated: $V_{LTP} = 1.63$ V
                              $V_{UTP} = 1.63$ V
                Measured: $V_{LTP} = 1.689$ V
                              $V_{UTP} = 1.626$ V
                Comments: Measured values closely match calculated values. No problems.

Figure 14-9:   Calculated: $V_{LTP} = -2.5$ V
                              $V_{UTP} = +2.5$ V
                Measured: $V_{LTP} = -2.43$ V
                              $V_{UTP} = +2.47$ V
                Comments: Measured values closely match calculated values. No problems.

Figure 14-13:   Calculated: $V_{LTP} = -2.54$ V
                              $V_{UTP} = +2.54$ V
                Measured: $V_{LTP} = -2.214$ V
                              $V_{UTP} = +2.214$ V
                Comments: $V_Z \neq 4.7$ V at the diode current realized in the circuit simulation.

Figure 14-24:   Calculated: Vout = -12 V
                Measured: Vout = -12.0 V
                Comments: Measured value matches calculated value. No problems.

Figure 14-25:   Calculated: Vout = -7 V
                Measured: Vout = -7.000 V
                Comments: Measured value matches calculated value. No problems.

Figure 14-26:   Calculated: Vout = -2.5 V
                Measured: Vout = -2.500 V
                Comments: Measured value matches calculated value. No problems.

Figure 14-27:   Calculated: Vout = -8.84 V
                Measured: Vout = -8.838 V
                Comments: Measured value closely matches calculated value. No problems.

Figure 14-35:   Calculated: -50 mV/s ramp during input pulse high time.
                Measured: -48.5 mV/s ramp during input pulse high time.
                Comments: Analysis options must be set for transient analysis and pause after each
                              screen. Input voltage amplitude actually less than that assumed
                              explains lower ramp rate.

Chapter 15:

Figure 15-29:   Calculated: Vout = -150 mV
                Measured: Vout = -150 mV
                Comments: Set EWB zener parameter I_S = 50e-09 A to match I_R of problem.
                              Measured value matches calculated value. No problems.

Figure 15-32:   Calculated: Vout = -3.0 V
                Measured: Vout = -2.992 V
                Comments: Set EWB transistor I_S = 40e-09 A to match I_{EBO} of problem.
                              Measured value closely matches calculated value. No problems.

Chapter 16:

Figure 16-11:   Calculated: f_C = 7.96 kHz
                Measured: f_C = 7.87 kHz
                Comments: Measured value closely matches calculated value. No problems.

Figure 16-19:   Calculated: f_C = 736 Hz
                              BW = 177 Hz
                Measured: f_C = 736 Hz
                              BW = 177 Hz
                Comments: Measured values match calculated values. No problems.

Figure 16-22:   Calculated: f_C = 7.23 kHz
                              BW = 215 Hz
                Measured: f_C = 7.23 kHz
                              BW = 220 Hz
                Comments: Measured values matches calculated values. No problems.

Figure 16-25:   Calculated: f_C = 60 Hz
                Measured: f_C = 59.7 Hz
                Comments: Measured value closely matches calculated value. No problems.

Chapter 17:

Figure 17-12:   Calculated: f_{OSC} = 15.9 kHz
                Measured: f_{OSC} = 15.97 kHz
                Comments: The value of R1 was changed to 10.5 kΩ to compensate for the non-
                              ideal startup diodes providing too much gain in the circuit. Analysis
                              must run for some time to come to steady state.

Figure 17-14:   Calculated: 6.5 kHz with R_f = 290 kΩ
                Measured: 6.49 kHz with R_f = 290 kΩ
                Comments: Measured value closely matches calculated value. No problems.

Figure 17-30:   Calculated: f_{osc} = 8.25 kHz for R1 = 10 kΩ
                              f_{osc} = 20 kHz for R1 = 4.13 kΩ
                Measured: f_{osc} = 8.267 kHz for R1 = 10 kΩ
                              f_{osc} = 21.65 kHz for R1 = 4.13 kΩ
                Comments: Measured values well within 10% of calculated values. No problems.

Chapter 18:

Figure 18-6:   Calculated: Vout = 10.2 V
                Measured: Vout = 10.4 V
                Comments: Measured value closely matches calculated value. No problems.

Summary of Electronics Workbench Troubleshooting Circuit Files Results for *Electronic Devices*, 5th Ed.

Notes: All AC measurements are RMS unless otherwise noted.
Voltages less than 100 μV should be considered approximations and essentially zero.
The first circuit listed for each chapter indicates the design values measured with no fault.
For some circuits the values indicated are not steady-state measurements, as the circuit values had inordinately long settling times. All circuits were simulated using a 133-MHz Pentium system with at least 32 Mb of DRAM, so that analysis options and results may vary.

Chapter 1:

No circuits.

Chapter 2:

Figure 2-68: Measured: $V_{OUT} = 21.0$ VDC with about 1.3 V_{PP} of 120 Hz ripple
 Comments: No-fault circuit measurements.

Figure 2-68a: Measured: Vsec = 0 V
 Vout = 0 V
 Comments: No secondary voltage is indicative of a failed transformer or fuse. Visual inspection of an actual circuit would isolate the failure to the fuse.

Figure 2-68b: Measured: Same as Figure 2-68
 Comments: No fault.

Figure 2-68c: Measured: $V_{OUT} = 20.0$ VDC with about 2.70 V_{PP} of 60-Hz ripple.
 Comments: The large amount of 60-Hz ripple is indicative of an open diode in the bridge (in this case, D2).

Chapter 3:

Figure 3-48: Measured: Vout ≈ 15.3 V_{DC} with about 220 mV_{PP} of 120 Hz ripple
 Comments: No-fault circuit measurement.

Figure 3-48a: Measured: Vsec = 0 V
 Vout = 0 V
 Comments: No secondary voltage is indicative of a failed transformer or fuse. Visual inspection would isolate the failure to the transformer.

Figure 3-48b: Measured: Vsec = 24.3 V_{PP}
 $V_{OUT} = 0$ V
 Comments: No voltage across the output with secondary voltage present is indicative of R_{surge} open.

Figure 3-48c: Measured: Same as Figure 3-48
 Comments: No fault.

Figure 3-48d:	Measured:	$V_{OUT} \approx 23.1$ VDC with about 100 μV_{PP} of 120-Hz ripple.
	Comments:	Higher than normal DC voltage is indicative of loss of regulation due to D_Z open.

Chapter 4:

Figure 4-30:	Measured:	$V_B = 0.754$ VDC
		$V_C = 4.80$ VDC
	Comments:	No-fault circuit measurements.
Figure 4-30a:	Measured:	Same as Figure 4-30
	Comments:	No fault.
Figure 4-30b:	Measured:	$V_B = 0.658$ VDC
		$V_C = 5.64$ mVDC
	Comments:	Collector voltage about zero is indicative of R_C open.
Figure 4-30c:	Measured:	$V_B = 3.00$ VDC
		$V_C = 9.00$ VDC
	Comments:	Base and collector voltages equal to applied source voltages is indicative of a collector-emitter open in the transistor.

Chapter 5:

Figure 5-31:	Measured:	$V_B = 3.14$ VDC
		$V_E = 2.36$ VDC
		$V_C = 5.00$ VDC
	Comments:	No-fault circuit measurements.
Figure 5-31a:	Measured:	$V_B = 0.02$ μVDC
		$V_E = 0$ VDC
		$V_C = 10.0$ VDC
	Comments:	Base voltage about zero is indicative of R1 open or R2 shorted. Current or resistance checks in actual circuit would isolate failure to R1 open.
Figure 5-31b:	Measured:	$V_B = 3.20$ VDC
		$V_E = 0$ VDC
		$V_C = 10.0$ VDC
	Comments:	Transistor voltages are indicative of a base-emitter open in the transistor or an open emitter resistor. Resistance check of R_E would isolate the fault to the transistor.
Figure 5-31c:	Measured:	Same as Figure 5-31.
	Comments:	No fault.
Figure 5-31d:	Measured:	$V_B = 3.20$ VDC
		$V_E = 0$ VDC
		$V_C = 10.0$ VDC
	Comments:	Transistor voltages are indicative of a base-emitter open in the transistor or an open emitter resistor. Resistance check of R_E would isolate the fault to R_E.

Chapter 6:

Figure 6-41: Measured:
$V_B(1) = 1.73$ VDC $\quad V_B(2) = 1.73$ VDC $\quad$ Vout = 1.15 V
$V_C(1) = 5.41$ VDC $\quad V_C(2) = 5.40$ VDC
$V_E(1) = 980$ mVDC $\quad V_E(2) = 980$ mVDC
Vb(1) = 100 µV $\quad$ Vb(2) = 8.50 mV
Vc(1) = 8.49 mV $\quad$ Vc(2) = 1.15 V
Ve(1) = 0.13 µV $\quad$ Ve(2) = 10.3 µV
Comments: No-fault circuit measurements.

Figure 6-41a: Measured: Same as Figure 6-41.
Comments: No fault.

Figure 6-41b: Measured:
$V_B(1) = 1.73$ VDC $\quad V_B(2) = 1.73$ VDC $\quad$ Vout = 0 V
$V_C(1) = 5.41$ VDC $\quad V_C(2) = 5.41$ VDC
$V_E(1) = 980$ mVDC $\quad V_E(2) = 980$ mVDC
Vb(1) = 100 µV $\quad$ Vb(2) = 0.06 µV
Vc(1) = 18.4 mV $\quad$ Vc(2) = 0.09 µV
Ve(1) = 0.12 µV $\quad$ Ve(2) = 0.01 µV
Comments: Normal DC voltages with no AC signal coupling into the second stage is indicative of C3 open.

Figure 6-41c: Measured:
$V_B(1) = 1.73$ VDC $\quad V_B(2) = 1.73$ VDC $\quad$ Vout = 52.9 mV
$V_C(1) = 5.41$ VDC $\quad V_C(2) = 5.41$ VDC
$V_E(1) = 980$ mVDC $\quad V_E(2) = 980$ mVDC
Vb(1) = 100 µV $\quad$ Vb(2) = 11.6 mV
Vc(1) = 11.6 mV $\quad$ Vc(2) = 52.9 mV
Ve(1) = 0.13 µV $\quad$ Ve(2) = 11.3 mV
Comments: Greatly reduced gain in second stage is indicative of C4 open.

Figure 6-41d: Measured:
$V_B(1) = 1.73$ VDC $\quad V_B(2) = 1.75$ VDC $\quad$ Vout = 0 V
$V_C(1) = 5.41$ VDC $\quad V_C(2) = 10.0$ VDC
$V_E(1) = 980$ mVDC $\quad V_E(2) = 0$ VDC
Vb(1) = 100 µV $\quad$ Vb(2) = 11.7 mV
Vc(1) = 11.7 mV $\quad$ Vc(2) = 0.00 µV
Ve(1) = 0.12 µV $\quad$ Ve(2) = 0.00 µV
Comments: Collector of Q2 at supply voltage is indicative of a collector-emitter open in Q2.

Chapter 7:

Figure 7-13: Measured:
$V_B = 1.85$ VDC
$A_V = 117$ $\quad$ Output distorted
Comments: No-fault circuit measurements.

Figure 7-13a: Measured:
$V_B = 3.34$ VDC
$A_V = 156$ $\quad$ Clipped
Comments: The higher base voltage is indicative of R2 open, resulting in a base-biased circuit. The gain is meaningless due to the clipped output.

Figure 7-13b: Measured: V_B = 812 mVDC
                            A_V = 212   Clipped
                Comments: The base voltage approximately one diode drop above ground is indicative of a shorted emitter resistor or bypass capacitor. Resistance or current measurements will isolate the fault to C2. The gain is meaningless due to the clipped output.

Figure 7-13c: Measured: Same as Figure 7-13.
                Comments: No fault.

Chapter 8:

Figure 8-17:   Measured: V_{GS} = -1.08 VDC
                            V_D = 10.1 VDC I_D = 4.94 mA
                            V_S = 1.09 VDC
                Comments: No-fault circuit measurements.

Figure 8-17a: Measured: Same as Figure 8-17.
                Comments: No fault.

Figure 8-17b: Measured: V_{GS} = 0 VDC
                            V_D = 0 VDC I_D = 0 mA
                            V_S = 0 VDC
                Comments: No drain current with the drain at ground is indicative of R_D open.

Figure 8-17c: Measured: V_{GS} = -3.00 VDC
                            V_D = 15.0 VDC I_D = 0.02 µA
                            V_S = 3.03 VDC
                Comments: No drain current with drain at supply voltage and higher source voltage is indicative of R_S open.

Chapter 9:

Figure 9-28:   Measured: Vin = 10.0 mV $V_G(2)$ = <100 µVDC   Vout = 562 mV
                            $I_D(1)$ = 4.69 mA $V_g(2)$ = 75.0 mV
                            $V_D(1)$ = 4.97 VDC $I_D(2)$ = 4.69 mA
                Comments: No-fault circuit measurements.

Figure 9-28a: Measured: Same as Figure 9-28.
                Comments: No fault.

Figure 9-28b: Measured: Vin = 10.0 mV $V_G(2)$ = 2.56 VDC   Vout = 124 µV
                            $I_D(1)$ = 6.29 mA $V_g(2)$ = 552 µV
                            $V_D(1)$ = 2.56 VDC $I_D(2)$ = 6.25 mA
                Comments: DC drain voltage on Q1 and gate voltage on Q2 is indicative of C3 shorted.

Figure 9-28c: Measured: Vin = 10.0 mV $V_G(2)$ = 118 µVDC   Vout = 0.00 µV
                            $I_D(1)$ = 0.00 µA $V_g(2)$ = 0.00 µV
                            $V_D(1)$ = 12.0 VDC $I_D(2)$ = 4.69 mA
                Comments: No drain current through Q1 with drain at supply voltage is indicative of a drain-source open in Q1.

Figure 9-28d: Measured: V_{in} = 10.0 mV $V_G(2)$ = <100 μV V_{out} = 0.00 mV
                            $I_D(1)$ = 4.69 mA $V_g(2)$ = 75.0 mV
                            $V_D(1)$ = 4.97 VDC $I_D(2)$ = 0.00 μA
                                                      $V_D(2)$ = 0.00 μVDC
                Comments: No drain current and drain at ground is indicative of R5 open.

Chapter 10:

No circuits.

Chapter 11:

No circuits.

Chapter 12:

Figure 12-22:   Measured: V_{INV} = 100 mVDC
                            V_{OUT} = 2.23 VDC
                Comments: No-fault circuit measurements.

Figure 12-22a: Measured: Same as Figure 12-22.
                Comments: No fault.

Figure 12-22b: Measured: V_{INV} = <1 μVDC
                            V_{OUT} = 19.8 VDC
                Comments: Output at positive rail is indicative of Rf open.

Figure 12-26:   Measured: V_{IN} = 100 mVDC
                            V_{OUT} = 10 VDC
                Comments: No-fault circuit measurements.

Figure 12-26a: Measured: Same as Figure 12-26.
                Comments: No fault.

Figure 12-26b: Measured: V_{IN} = 100 mVDC
                            V_{OUT} = <1 μVDC
                Comments: Output near zero is indicative of Ri open.

Chapter 14:

Figure 14-27:   Measured: $V(1)$ = 3.00 VDC V_{OUT} = -8.84 VDC
                            $V(2)$ = 2.00 VDC
                            $V(3)$ = 8.00 VDC
                Comments: No-fault circuit measurements.

Figure 14-27a: Measured: $V(1)$ = 3.00 VDC V_{OUT} = -8.64 VDC
                            $V(2)$ = 2.00 VDC
                            $V(3)$ = 8.00 VDC
                Comments: With normal inputs, V_{OUT} value is indicative of R2 open.

Figure 14-27b: Measured: Same as Figure 14-27.
                Comments: No fault.

Figure 14-35:	Measured:	Linear ramp from 0 V to -4.8 V in 100 μs on output during input pulse HIGH time.
	Comments:	No-fault circuit measurements.
Figure 14-35a:	Measured:	Vout = 0 V
	Comments:	Output voltage is indicative of C shorted.
Figure 14-35b:	Measured:	Same as Figure 14-35
	Comments:	No-fault circuit measurements.
Figure 14-44:	Measured:	Vout clipped at ±8.57 V with I_{ZT} = 100 μA
	Comments:	No-fault circuit measurements.
Figure 14-44a:	Measured:	Vout clipped at -0.724 V and +7.837 V
	Comments:	Voltage measurements are indicative of D1 shorted.
Figure 14-44b:	Measured:	Vout clipped at ±2.31 V with I_{ZT} = 100 μA
	Comments:	Voltage measurements are indicative of Ri open.
Figure 14-44c:	Measured:	Same as Figure 14-44.
	Comments:	No-fault circuit measurements.

Figure 14-45: Measured:
V(1) = 1.00 VDC V_{OUT} = -1.80 VDC
V(2) = 0.5 VDC
V(3) = 0.2 VDC
V(4) = 0.1 VDC
Comments: No-fault circuit measurements.

Figure 14-45a: Measured:
V(1) = 1.00 VDC V_{OUT} = -20.0 VDC
V(2) = 0.5 VDC
V(3) = 0.2 VDC
V(4) = 0.1 VDC
Comments: Output voltage is indicative of R5 open.

Figure 14-45b: Measured: Same as Figure 14-45.
Comments: No-fault circuit measurements.

Chapter 15:

No circuits.

Chapter 16:

No circuits.

Chapter 17:

No circuits.

Chapter 18:

No circuits.

TUTORIAL.DOC

COPYRIGHT NOTICE

MicroSim, PSpice, and Probe are trademarks or registered trademarks of MicroSim Corporation. Windows and Windows95 are trademarks or registered trademarks of Microsoft Corporation.

ABOUT THIS TUTORIAL

This file presents a basic tutorial for the instructor and/or student to get "up and running" quickly with PSpice. The MicroSim schematic editor, PSpice and Probe programs are just some of the programs available in the evaluation software. Other programs, such as the PCB layout tools, are not related to this discussion and are thus not covered here. These three programs are all that are required to view and edit schematic files, run circuit simulations, and view analysis results. Along with the executable program files, the software also includes complete sets of the on-line MicroSim manuals, as well as symbol and part library files, and example files. This tutorial provides basic information useful for the first-time user of the programs. As the user gains experience with using the software, he or she should make use of the excellent on-line documentation provided which provides comprehensive coverage of the programs.

INSTALLING THE SOFTWARE

The first step is to install the software onto a fixed-disk computer system. Follow the installation instructions provided with the evaluation package. The package may be identified as "MicroSim evaluation software", or more recently as "MicroSim Design Lab evaluation software". Once the software is installed, it may be accessed either by clicking on the "Psched" (PSpice schematic editor), "PSpice" (simulator) or "Probe" (waveform analysis program) icons. On Windows 3.x systems, this will be under a newly created MicroSim program group. On Windows95 systems, these can be accessed via the START MENU / PROGRAMS / MICROSIM pull down menus, or the user can create "shortcuts" to the programs. In either case it would be a good idea to change the "startup directory" location for each of these programs to the "\ed5" directory (see the README.TXT file for details). This will allow for quicker access to the Electronic Devices, 5th Edition library, schematic and Probe files.

STARTING UP THE SCHEMATIC EDITOR PROGRAM

Click on the icon labeled PSCHED in the MicroSim program group, or from the Windows95 task bar, select: 'Start/Programs/MicroSim.../Schematics'.

When the schematic editor first starts, it loads default symbol library information. This takes a few seconds to load from disk. Once this operation is completed, a blank, gridded schematics page is displayed, along with the following "main menu":

File Edit Draw Navigate View Options Analysis Tools Markers Window Help

By default, a "button bar" is displayed below the main menu, and a "status bar" is displayed at the bottom of the screen. For the purposes of this tutorial, all commands and command sequences will use the pull down, cascading menus starting from the main menu. You can try out different options and menu selections as you wish. This tutorial will refer to the most important, most used commands and command sequences.

LOADING THE TUTORIAL SAMPLE SCHEMATIC SHEET

Using the mouse, select 'File/Open...' and this will display a dialog box from which files may be selected for opening. If the file "tutorial.sch" is in the dialog box, double-click on the icon to the left of the file name, or directly on the file name, to open the tutorial file. Otherwise, use the directory search boxes in the dialog box, to position to the 'ED5' directory. If the ED5 files were properly loaded on to drive C: for example, this would be at 'c:\ed5'.

GETTING FAMILIAR WITH THE 'VIEW' MENU OPTIONS... ZOOM IN, ZOOM OUT, AND REDRAW

Notice that the schematic sheet is, by default, zoomed in as much as possible to display the circuit. The entire sheet can be viewed by selecting: 'View/Entire Page'. You can zoom back by selecting 'View/Fit'. There are other useful commands available from the View dropdown menu you can learn later. One of the most important ones is 'View/Redraw', which will "clean up" any graphics boxes left on the display when you edit the schematic. Try these menu options for yourself to see how the program works.

GETTING FAMILIAR WITH THE 'EDIT' MENU OPTIONS

The 'Edit/...' menu is probably the most important submenu from the main menu. All edit commands are accomplished by first "selecting" a symbol or window in the schematic, and then applying editing functions. To select a single symbol, simply left-click on a symbol, and notice it will change color. You can also select a window for editing, by left-clicking at some point on the schematic, and then moving the mouse up and to the right, while continuing to hold down the left mouse button. A rectangular window box will be displayed while you make the window selection, and once you release the left mouse button, the selected window will change color to show which part of the schematic has been selected. To cancel the selection command, either on a single symbol or a window, simply left-click on the schematic anywhere there is an open space away from the symbol or window. Once the symbol or window is highlighted, you can apply various editing commands to the affected symbol(s). The most basic command is to move the highlighted symbol. This can be accomplished by left-clicking on any highlighted symbol, and while keeping the left mouse button depressed, moving the mouse to the desired location. The other commands are accessible by selecting: 'Edit/...' from the main menu, followed by a submenu choice. The most important choices are as follows:

Undelete Cut Copy Paste Delete Rotate Flip

These should be self-explanatory. You should experiment with all of these commands by picking various parts of the schematic to work on. Though there is no substitute for practice and experience in learning the tools, after a short while, you'll find the schematic editing tools to be very easy to use. The next section covers the saving and renaming of files, so you can try things out on the current schematic page without worrying about messing things up.

SAVING THE EDITED TUTORIAL FILE AS A PRACTICE FILE

You can save the edited file to a different file name. This will let you go back to the original tutorial file if you want, and demonstrates how to edit an existing file into a new one without losing the original one.

From the main menu, select: 'File/Save As...' and fill in the dialog box with a new name for the current file, for example, "practice.sch". Notice that the dialog box specifies that (.sch) will be the default extension for the file. You don't have to specify this extension, but you can if you want to. Once you do this, you'll notice that the schematic editor program window bar above the main menu will be updated to show the new working file name. If you simply use the 'File/Save' option, the file will be saved to the current file name loaded (i.e., "tutorial.sch"). To leave the schematic editor program altogether, select: 'File/Exit'. Try saving the file to a new name, then exiting the program. Then start up the schematic editor program again, this time, specifying "practice.sch" (or whatever you name you saved the file to) as the file to edit. You can continue the tutorial with this file re-load the default "tutorial.sch" file.

MORE EDITING: MOVING AND CHANGING DISPLAYED SYMBOL INFORMATION

All the symbols on the schematic have information describing values or other "attributes" of the symbol. For example, a simple resistor has two attributes displayed, the "reference designator", like R19, which distinguishes it from other resistors on the schematic, and the resistor value, like 100K, which says the resistor value is 100,000 ohms. To move these and other attributes, simply left-click on the attribute, and a selection box will appear around the attribute. Then you can left-click and hold on the attribute, while moving the mouse, to reposition the attribute. To change the value of the attribute, you must double-left-click on the attribute. This will bring up a dialog box for the component the attribute belongs to, and allow you to change the value of the attribute. Try clicking on the attributes for the resistor or voltage source on the tutorial schematic to get a feel for how this works. Another way to edit attributes or values associated with a symbol, is to double-left-click on the symbol itself. This will bring up a more complete dialog box, describing all of the attributes and values associated with the symbol. From this dialog box, you can change one, some, or all of the attributes for the symbol, before returning to the schematic sheet. Note that some attributes are "locked", in that they cannot be changed or displayed by the user. The symbol editing dialog box allows you to turn off the display of such attributes, if you wish. The symbol editing dialog boxes often contain many options. The most important ones are described herein. You can learn about the other ones as you gain experience using the software.

STILL MORE EDITING: RETRIEVING A PART FROM ONE OF THE SYMBOL LIBRARIES

Another basic editing function is to retrieve a part from one of the symbol libraries using the schematic editor Parts Browser. From the main menu select: 'Draw/Get New Part ...' and notice that a dialog box appears. From this dialog box, a full list of available components is displayed (in a scrolling list), along with several "button" choices, like CLOSE, PLACE, PLACE AND CLOSE, HELP, LIBRARIES and ADVANCED. Selecting ADVANCED opens a more expanded dialog box, complete with a mini-screen that displays the currently selected symbol. This helps you select the right symbol among many potential ones that are perhaps difficult to distinguish by name or number alone. You can experiment with the various options available here, but most often you will simply need to enter the correct symbol name in the 'Part Name' field. This field is highlighted as the default data entry field when the dialog box is first opened. As you type in the first few letters or numbers of the part to be retrieved, the selection list automatically "zooms" down the alphabetical symbol list, helping to make the selection process easier. When the proper symbol has been located, simply left-click on the 'PLACE AND CLOSE' box to return to the schematic with the chosen symbol already selected. This process is much easier to do in practice than to describe in words. With a little practice, you'll see how easy it is to choose components from the libraries and place them on the schematic sheet. The HELP box choice is a good source for more detailed information on using the parts Browser. The browser is set up to let you place more than one instance of the selected symbol as you wish. Terminate the command by right-clicking the mouse. Try selecting a few parts and placing them on the schematic. You can always re-load the schematic to dispose of any unwanted changes.

GETTING WIRED!

Of course, placing parts on the schematic is only part of the picture. Wires must be interconnected between the parts to describe the circuit connections between the parts. This is done by selecting: 'Draw/Wire' from the main menu. The cursor turns into a "pencil" icon, which you move to the starting point of the wire you wish to draw. This is usually a device pin or terminal, such as an opamp terminal or an end of a resistor. You then left-click on the terminal and move the mouse to the end point of the wire, left-clicking again. This draws the wire segment, but still leaves the editor in a wire-drawing mode, so that you can continue to draw the wire with several right-angle turns (wires can only be drawn orthogonally, with right-angle bends). When you are finished drawing the wire, simply right-click the mouse, to leave the wire drawing mode. You can delete a wire segment by left-clicking on any wire segment (the segment will then highlight in the "selection" color), and then press the delete key or select 'Edit/Delete'. You can assign a "name" or "label" to any wire by double left-clicking on a segment, which brings up a wire label dialog box. This has the effect of naming the entire circuit node, even though only one segment is highlighted. To see this, try clicking on another segment attached to the same node, and notice that the dialog box brings up the already-assigned name. When the Probe program is run, that node can be referred to by the name assigned on the schematic. For example, if the node is labeled OUT, then the voltage at that node can be displayed in Probe as the trace "v(out)". Notice that there is, for the most part, no case-sensitivity in PSpice or Probe. A label can be deleted simply by left-clicking on the label to highlight it, then using the delete key or 'Edit/Delete' from the main menu.

RUNNING A SIMULATION

All of the schematic editor functions described so far help you create, modify, load and save schematic files. Now it's time to explore the real power of PSpice, selecting ANALYSIS options, running the PSpice simulator, and viewing output results in Probe. Start by reloading the schematic file, "tutorial.sch". From the main menu, select 'Analysis/Simulate'. Notice that the software first generates a "netlist", which is simply a text-based circuit description file based on the schematic, used by PSpice to simulate the program. Once the netlisting is complete, the PSpice simulation program begins executing. While this program is running, a dialog box describing the circuit simulation is displayed. Upon completion, the Probe waveform analysis program is automatically started up, eventually opening up a dialog box with the message "The requested display does not exist". Click OK in the dialog box response area. This message comes up because, the schematic file includes a directive to automatically display the "last Probe session" when Probe is run. The first time Probe is run, however, there is no "last display" to work with. This is a normal message you will see from time to time, when a simulation is first run. You will see later, that it is a useful feature to have the program automatically display the last session's waveforms. It is a great timesaver when you find you are making iterative changes to the schematic and re-running a simulation several times. The place where you decide how Probe will run upon running a simulation is in the 'Analysis/Probe Setup...' menu selection from the schematic editor program. When you select this option, a dialog box opens with a few self-explanatory Probe options.

At this point, the Probe program window is the "active" window, with the schematic editor and PSpice windows being in the background. Switch back to the schematic editor window for a moment, by pressing the "ALT" and "TAB" keys simultaneously (Windows 3.x), or by clicking on the task bar (Windows95). This procedure demonstrates how you can have both the schematic editor program and the Probe program open at the same time, a useful feature of the software.

Getting back to the discussion on selecting Probe setup options, the following are recommended for most circuit files:

- Auto-Run Probe after simulations
- Restore last Probe session, or show all markers, if you are using markers
- Collect data at all nodes, except for subcircuit data

From the schematic editor, you can force the Probe program to run by selecting 'Analysis/Run Probe'. This is useful if you choose for some reason, not to auto-run Probe, or if you happened to close the Probe program and you want to re-start it.

One last important menu option under the ANALYSIS main menu option, is 'Analysis/Setup...'. This option is used to select which circuit analysis options you wish to simulate, and allows you to specify many parameters to control the simulation. The most important of the submenu choices here are: AC Sweep..., DC Sweep... and Transient... Occasionally, it is also important to select options under the Options... submenu. The on-line documentation provides excellent, comprehensive descriptions about these various analysis options. The limited space and scope of this tutorial cannot cover these options in the detail they deserve, so the reader is asked to look into these topics for his or herself. Suffice it to simply say,

- The AC Sweep Analysis allows you to simulate the response of the circuit to AC signals, such as from the 60Hz power line, a signal generator, oscillators, etc. For this analysis, the independent axis variable is Frequency.
- The DC Sweep Analysis allows you to simulate the response of the circuit from the standpoint of constant-level dc voltages and currents, such as from batteries and stable voltage and current sources. It does, however, allow you to analyze the effect of how the circuit response varies as you would vary the level or levels of the applied dc sources. For example, you might want to find the effect of how the output level of a voltage regulator circuit varies, as the dc input level is varied. For this analysis, the independent axis variable is DC Volts or Amperes.
- The Transient Analysis allows you to simulate the response of the circuit to time-varying (or constant) signals, as time progresses from some fixed starting time until some specified ending time. For this analysis, the independent axis variable is Time.

Depending on which analysis is chosen for simulation (you may choose more than one), you will need to specify such parameters as starting and ending frequency, source voltage or current, or time, the increment type (linear, by octave or by decade), step interval, and other factors. The help descriptions for these various analyses types provides all the information you need to select the best options for your particular requirements. See the section on using the on-line HELP utilities which comes later in the tutorial.

SELECTING WAVEFORM "TRACES" FOR DISPLAY

Switch back to the Probe window to resume the example session. The remainder of this basic tutorial will cover some of the most important menu selection options available in the Probe program, the post-simulation waveform display and analysis program. Notice that the menu structure is very similar to that displayed in the schematic editor program. The following list shows the main menu options available from within the Probe program:

File Edit Trace Plot View Tools Window Help

The File, View, Window and Help menu options are similarly structured and have similar functions, to the menu choices of the same name in the schematic editor program. The most important menu options other than these, are the Trace, Plot and Tools submenus. Let's look briefly at each of these submenus and their corresponding subfunctions.

From the main menu, select 'Trace/Add...'. Notice that a dialog box opens up, displaying a table of available nodes or "trace expressions". For example, various node voltages and device currents are displayed, like "V(A)" and "I(R1)". Notice, also, that several listing options are checked (selected), such as "Analog", "Digital", "Voltages" and "Currents", and that some are not selected, such as "Alias Names" and "Internal Subcircuit Nodes". In general, the default selections are adequate for looking at any node voltages or branch currents you would be interested in. If you were only interested in node voltages, you could turn off (uncheck the box) for all the options except "Analog" and "Voltages". PSpice and Probe can handle analog and digital signals, thus an option is provided for excluding one or the other from the list of available "traces" here. Finally, note that at the bottom of the dialog box is a data entry box prefaced with the words: "Trace Command:". You can specify one or more traces to be displayed by either explicitly typing the trace expression you want (like "V(A)", without the quotes), or you can simply click on the desired trace expression within the dialog box list. This will automatically put the expression on the Trace Command data entry box. If you accidentally specify an incorrect trace, or the same trace more than once, you can either backspace directly in the entry box, or simply select the "Cancel" button option, and re-do the command. For practice, click on the traces labeled "V(A)" and "I(R1)", and then select the "OK" button. The dialog box will disappear, and the two traces will be displayed. Notice that the V(A) trace (a sinusoid) is clearly displayed, but the I(R1) trace looks like a flat line at zero on the y-axis. You should also note that the independent variable axis, the x-axis, shows "Time" from 0s to 40ms. This demonstrates a common occurrence in using Probe with a single plot window, in that some traces can be "dwarfed" when plotted alongside other traces of very different magnitudes. The remedy for this situation is to put different traces on different plots, or at least to change the y-axis settings.

==
MODIFYING THE PLOT TO IMPROVE THE DISPLAY
==

Select the following menu choices to improve the display of the two traces:

- Left-Click once on the trace label "I(R1)" at the bottom of the Probe window. The label should turn colors to the "selection" color. This indicates the trace is selected for some following edit operation.
- Press the "Delete" key on the keyboard. The display should be re-drawn with only the V(A) trace visible.
- Select 'Plot/Add Plot' from the main menu. The display should split into two plot windows, with the bottom window showing the V(A) trace and the top window being blank, with "SEL>>" on the left. This indicates that the top window is "selected" for further editing.
- Select 'Trace/Add...' from the main menu, and then select I(R1) from the table. Close the dialog box by clicking on "OK".

Notice that the top window now shows a much better view of the current through resistor R1 as a function of time. The trace makes sense, too, because the current through the resistor is sinusoidal during the positive phase of the input voltage, where the diode is forward biased and conducting, and the current is essentially zero during the negative phase, where the diode is reverse biased, and therefore, blocking current flow.

Another useful means of controlling the displayed data is to provide "user defined" settings for the axis ranges. With the top plot window still selected, choose 'Plot/Y Axis Settings...' from the main menu. Notice that a dialog box appears, allowing you to specify an "automatic" or "user defined" range, "log" or "linear" scales, axis number, and axis title. For now, click on the "user defined" option, and set the minimum and maximum range values to -1 and 1, respectively. Click the OK button to finish the operation. Notice that the displayed trace for I(R1) now looks like a flat line. This explains what happened at first when there was just one plot window (the default). The Probe program must select a Y-axis range large enough to display the largest-magnitude trace the user requested. As you can see, it is indeed useful to be able to plot multiple traces each in their own plot windows. Finally, if you select 'Plot/Delete Plot' from the main menu, the currently selected plot (the one with "SEL>>" displayed to the left of the plot) will be removed, along with any traces that are displayed in it.

==
EVALUATING A "GOAL FUNCTION" EXPRESSION
==

Sometimes it is worthwhile to have the Probe program tell you the numeric value of a trace expression, rather than to display the trace in a plot form. For example, you might want to know what the maximum value of a voltage is without having to figure it out for yourself by examining the plotted trace. The Probe program has built-in analysis tools for doing just this, generically referred to as "goal functions". They essentially provide functions to help you quickly and easily achieve an analysis "goal" you would otherwise have to accomplish by tediously analyzing the plotted waveforms. As an example, enter the following main menu selection: 'Trace/Eval Goal Function...', and enter the following in the dialog box at the 'Trace Command:' prompt: "max(i(r1))". Do not include the double quotes. Notice that the dialog box disappears and another box appears, showing:

    Goal Function Value
    max(i(r1))=3.48771e-010

This gives a precise result in an easy to read format, without having to zoom in on the plot or provide individual plot windows for each trace. An important note here is that, unlike a regular "trace" expression, like "i(r1)", the goal function must specify some "function" or operation to be performed on the trace expression. In this case, the "max()" function is specified, to return the maximum value of the trace that was found in the simulation. This is necessary because the goal function utility is designed to return a single numeric value. In the case where dc (time invariant) voltages or currents are involved, you can still use the "max()" function to return the value, although the maximum value happens to be the same as the constant value held throughout the simulation.

==
USING MORE COMPLEX TRACE AND GOAL FUNCTION "EXPRESSIONS"
==

Part of the real power of using the Probe trace plotting and goal function utilities, is the ability to mix and match "traces" with mathematical operations and constants. For example, to find the maximum instantaneous power dissipation in the resistor R1, you could make use of the following formula for computing power in a resistor:

    Power (watts) = Resistor Current (amps) * Resistor Current (amps) * Resistance (ohms)

For the purposes of this example, we know the resistor value is 1K from the schematic. Then we can select 'Plot/Add Plot', then 'Trace/Add...' from the main menu, and explicitly type in the following in the "Trace Command:" box (without the double quotes, of course): "i(r1)*i(r1)*1k". Note that the expression you enter is essentially case-insensitive. The trace will be displayed showing the instantaneous power dissipation in R1. You could also enter this same expression under 'Trace/Eval Goal Function...', but you would need to specify which goal you were looking for, that is, perhaps the maximum value or the minimum value, of the instantaneous power dissipation. The following expressions would be returned for our example:

    max(i(r1)*i(r1)*1k)=0.000137322   (about 137 microwatts)
    min(i(r1)*i(r1)*1k)=0

===
USING THE ON-LINE HELP UTILITIES
===

This completes the brief introduction to getting the schematic editor, PSpice and Probe programs installed and running. As was stated before, the on-line help utilities are easy to use, comprehensive, and well written. They are the best all-around bet for learning how to use the program, both when you are first starting out, and after you become more experienced and wish to learn more. From the main menu of either the schematic editor or Probe programs, select 'Help/(Menu Choice)'. You'll find you can access a table of contents, search for help on a particular topic or keyword, look up terms in a glossary, and use powerful indexing and search functions to locate specific and related topics of interest. The Help utilities are accessible as the last main menu choice from within both the schematic editor program, and the Probe program. Don't be afraid to experiment with new options and choices available to you, from within these programs. Good luck, and have fun!

EXAMPLES.DOC

This file presents a summary of the PSPICE circuit analysis results run on the example problems for Electronic Devices, 5th Edition. The student and/or instructor should start the schematics editor program, PSCHED, open a schematic file, simulate the file by running PSPICE, and then analyze the results by viewing waveform "traces" and "goal function" evaluations in PROBE. Most of the schematic files are set up to automatically run PROBE upon completion of each simulation. Pertinent waveforms will be automatically displayed once PROBE starts up, as predefined in the accompanying probe setup files. In the tables below, the *max()* functions are evaluated in PROBE by selecting TRACE/EVAL GOAL FUNCTION and then entering the function argument/expression in the dialog box that appears. For brevity, the values shown below are shown to the precision given for corresponding values given in the text. *For comparison purposes, the text's values are shown in brackets, [].* Where the simulated value(s) deviate significantly from those shown in the text, accompanying explantory text describes the causes of those differences. For some examples, there is also additional explanatory text describing special features about the schematic files used in those examples. Where indicated by the words *computed average of*, or *dc value of*, the average of the max and min values were computed to determine the answer for comparison to the text.

===
CHAPTER 1
===

No Circuits

===
CHAPTER 2
===

FG02-06

max(v(outa)) = **4.3V** [4.3V]
max(v(outb)) = **99.2V** [99.3V]

===

FG02-10

max(v(out)) = **54.2V** [54.3V]

R1 and R2 included to meet simulation requirements regarding "floating" nodes. All nodes must have some finite amount of resistance to circuit "ground", to satisfy the computation algorithms. Often, a very high-value or very low-value resistor in series or parallel with a circuit element will do the job without affecting the circuit response.

===

FG02-18

swingr(v(sec1),0,1) = **50Vpp** [50Vpp]
swingr(v(sec2),0,1) = **50Vpp** [50Vpp]
max(v(out))   = **24.3V** [24.3V]

R1 and R2 used again. See above. The swingr() function, computed over the interval of 0 sec to 1 sec, returns the effective pk-pk value of the argument.

===

FG02-30

dc value of v(out) = **14.4V** [14.3V]
swingr(v(out),0,1) = **0.929V** [1.13V]

The calculated value in the text is approximate. A more exact application of the theoretical equation yields an output pk-pk swing of 0.948Vpp.

===

FG02-38

min(v(out)) = **-0.77V** [-0.70V]
max(v(out)) = **9.09V** [9.09V]

FG02-44

```
min(v(out)) = -5.75V [-5.7V]
max(v(out)) =  7.73V [7.7V]
```

===

FG02-52

```
min(v(out)) = -47.1V [-47.3V]
max(v(out)) =  0.78V [0.7V]
```

===
CHAPTER 3
===

FG03-10

```
@Vin=4.86v:  max(v(out)) = 4.78V [4.76V]
@Vin=25.7v:  max(v(out)) = 5.28V [6.13V]
```

The text assumes the zener impedance is a constant 7 ohms, regardless of zener current. The PSPICE models more accurately reflect the dynamic zener impedance associated with "real" devices.

===

FG03-13

```
min(v(out)) = -12V [-12V]
```

===

FG03-17

```
min(v(outa)) =  -3.99V [-4.0V]
max(v(outa)) =   5.77V [5.8V]
min(v(outb)) = -15.7V  [-15.7V]
max(v(outb)) =   6.93V [6.9V]
```

===
CHAPTER 4
===

FG04-08

```
max(ib(q1)) =   430uA [430uA]
max(ic(q1)) =  64.5mA [64.5mA]
max(ie(q1)) = -64.9mA [64.9mA]
max(vc(q1)) =   3.55V [3.55V]
max(vb(q1)) =    0.7V [0.7V]
max(v(c,b)) =   2.85V [2.85V]
```

This circuit file uses a special model to force Beta to 150 exactly.
The emitter current sign difference indicates current direction.

===

FG04-15

```
max(ic(q1)) = 9.87mA [9.8mA]
max(ib(q1)) = 219uA  [230uA]
```

This circuit file uses a special model to force Beta to 50 exactly.

===

FG04-24

```
min(v(c))    = 0.142V  [0.3V]
max(v(c))    = 9V
min(ic(q1))  = -47uA
max(ic(q1))  = 32.7mA
```

The text assumes Vce,sat = 0.3V. The PSPICE model saturates more tightly under these operating conditions. Also, with 47uA collector current, the transistor is effectively in "cutoff", whereas with 32.7mA current, it is effectively in "saturation".

==
CHAPTER 5
==

FG05-07

```
max(ib(q1)) = 197uA   [198uA]
max(ic(q1)) = 39.3mA  [39.6mA]
max(vc(q1)) = 7.02V   [6.93V ]
```

This circuit file uses a special model to force Beta to 200 exactly.

==

FG05-10

```
@BETA=100:  max(vc(q1a)) = 5.73V   [5.67V]
            max(ic(q1a)) = 11.2mA  [11.3mA]
@BETA=150:  max(vc(q1b)) = 2.59V   [2.48V ]
            max(ic(q1b)) = 16.8mA  [17.0mA]
```

This circuit file uses special models to force Beta to 100 and 150 exactly.

==

FG05-12

```
max(ie(q1))         = -1.78mA  [1.80mA]
max(ic(q1))         =  1.77mA  [1.80mA]
max(vc(q1)-ve(q1))  =  9.85V   [9.74V]
```

This circuit file uses a special model to force Beta to 150 exactly. The emitter current sign difference is due to PSPICE reflecting the direction of current flow.

==

FG05-16

```
max(vc(q1)) = -13.2V  [-13.1V]
max(ve(q1)) =  1.77V  [1.64V]
```

This circuit file uses a special model to force Beta to 100 exactly.

==

FG05-22

```
max(v(c,e)) = 2.74V   [1.95V]
max(ic(q1)) = 4.64mA  [5.16mA]
```

The PSPICE transistor model has a Vbe unequal to that which is assumed in the text. The text approximates the value and does not take Rin(base) into account. In the related exercise, which does take Rin(base) into account, the values calculated are closer to what the simulation results show. The more precise calculation yields:
Vce = 2.56V, Ic = 4.77mA

==

FG05-26

```
max(ic(q1)) = -2.22mA  [2.42mA]
max(v(e,c)) =  2.88V   [2.26V]
```

The PSPICE transistor model has a Vbe unequal to that which is assumed in the text. The text approximates the value and does not take Rin(base) into account. In the related exercise, which does take Rin(base) into account, the values calculated are closer to what the simulation results show. The more precise calculation yields:
Vec = 2.67V, Ic = 2.29mA.

The collector current sign difference is due to PSPICE reflecting the direction of current flow.

===

FG05-29

```
max(ic(q1)) = 832uA  [845uA]
max(v(c,e)) = 1.60V  [1.55V]
```

This circuit file uses a special model to force Beta to 100 exactly.

===
CHAPTER 6
===

FG06-24

```
dc value of vc(q1) = 4.92V    [4.74V]
swingr(v(out),0,1) = 223mVpp  [239mVpp]
```

The PSPICE transistor model has a Vbe unequal to that which is assumed in the text

===

FG06-31

```
Av = swingr(v(out),0,1)/swingr(v(in),0,1) = 0.991  [0.989]
```

This circuit file uses a special model to force Beta to 175 exactly.

===

FG06-35

```
Av = swingr(v(out),0,1)/swingr(v(in),0,1) = 71.2  [76.3]
```

The PSPICE transistor model has a Vbe unequal to that which is assumed in the text. The text approximates the value and does not take Rin(base) into account.

===

FG06-37

```
swingr(v(c1),0,1)  = 13.32mV
swingr(v(out),0,1) = 2.49V
Stage 1 Gain       = 66.5      [68.5]
Stage 2 Gain       = 187.3     [197]
Total Gain         = 12455.5   [13495]
```

The PSPICE transistor model has a Vbe unequal to that which is assumed in the text. The text approximates the value and does not take Rin(base) into account. This in turn leads to some discrepancy in the individual stage gains, and the overall gain. The swingr() function calculates peak-to-peak amplitude, over the interval 0 sec. to 1 sec. The Stage 1 and Stage 2 gains, and Total gain, are hand computed by taking the output swing divided by the input swing.

===
CHAPTER 7
===

FG07-10

```
Ic(sat) = max(ic(q1)) = 9.57mA  [8.97mA]
Vce(co) = max(v(c,e)) = 5.84V   [5.38V]
```

The PSPICE transistor model has a Vbe unequal to that which is assumed in the text. The text approximates the value and does not take Rin(base) into account.

===

FG07-13

```
Av = swingr(v(out),0,1)/swingr(v(in),0,1) = 103 [120]
```

The text's calculation assumes Re' = 5 ohms. The PSPICE transistor model doesn't precisely equate to this value, and cannot be directly set as a model parameter.

FG07-16

```
dc value of ic(q1) = 32.6mA  [35mA]
dc value of v(c,e) = 9.94V   [9.0V]
Power Diss.        = 324mW   [315mW]
Power Out          = 88mW    [101mW]
Efficiency         = 0.11    [0.12]
```

*The PSPICE transistor model has a Vbe unequal to that which is assumed in the text. The text approximates the value and does not take Rin(base) into account. Power dissipation is hand computed as Vce * Icc. Power out is hand computed as 0.5 * (Icc^2) * 165. Efficiency is hand computed as Power out / (Vcc * Icc).*

===

FG07-27

```
swingr(v(out),0,1) = 20Vpp [20Vpp]
```

===
CHAPTER 8
===

FG08-17

```
max(id(j1))         = 4.9mA   [5mA]
max(vg(j1)-vs(j1))  = -1.08V  [-1.1V]
max(vd(j1)-vs(j1))  = 9.0V    [8.9V]
```

The PSPICE model has Vgs(off)= -3V, Idss=12mA

===

FG08-19

```
max(id(j1))         = 5.87mA  [6mA]
max(vg(j1)-vs(j1))  = -881mV  [-882mV]
max(vd(j1))         = 6.13V   [6V]
```

Rs set to 150 ohms, Rd set to 1K ohms

===

FG08-24

```
max(id(j1)) = 1.57mA  [1.52mA]
max(vd(j1)) = 6.83V   [7V]
max(v(g))   = 1.54V   [1.54V]
max(v(s))   = 3.44V   [3.34V]
```

===

FG08-26

```
max(vg(j1)-vs(j1)) = -1.82V   [-1.8V]
max(id(j1))        =  1.76mA  [1.8mA]
```

===

FG08-45

```
max(vg(m1)-vs(m1)) =  3.13V   [3.13V]
max(vd(m1)-vs(m1)) = 11.25V   [11.2V]
```

===
CHAPTER 9
===

FG09-15

```
computed average of v(out) = 5.52V    [5.53V]
swingr(v(out),0,1)         = 2.93Vpp  [3.03Vpp]
```

===

FG09-19

```
computed average of v(d) = 7.6V     [8.4V]
swingr(v(out),0,1)       = 9.25Vpp  [9.31Vpp]
```

===

FG09-21

```
computed average of id(m1)  = 2.66mA   [2.65mA]
computed average of v(d,s)) = 6.22V    [6.26V]
swingr(v(out),0,1)          = 4.78Vpp  [4.89Vpp]
```

===

FG09-24

```
Av = max(v(out)/v(in)) = 0.893 [0.909]
```

===

FG09-27

```
swingr(v(out),0,1) = 2.72Vpp [2.83Vpp]
```

===
CHAPTER 10
===

FG10-15

```
max(db(v(out)))-3 = 34.33dB
```

*This trace is plotted vs. db(v(out)), showing an intersection at about **77.7Hz** [75.8Hz].*

===

FG10-29

```
max(db(v(out)))-3 = 32.52dB
```

*This trace is plotted vs. db(v(out)), showing an intersection at about **1.70MHz** [1.62MHz]. The discrepancy arises due to the model not explicitly allowing for specification of Cbe and Cbc directly, as is assumed in the text.*

===

FG10-39

max(db(v(out)))-3 = -48.5dB

*This trace is plotted vs. db(v(out)), showing an intersection at about **15.7Hz** [16.2Hz].*

===

FG10-41

max(db(v(out)))-6 = -58.2dB

*This trace is plotted vs. db(v(out)), showing an intersection at about **16.4Hz** [17.3Hz].*

===
CHAPTER 11
===

No Circuits

===
CHAPTER 12
===

FG12-22

Av = max(v(out)/v(in)) = **22.3** [22.3]

===

FG12-26

With Rf=220k, Av = max(v(out)/v(in)) = **-100** [-100,Rf=220k]

===

FG12-29

Av = max(v(out)/v(in)) = **23** [23.3]

The text's value is not as precise as the simulated value, due to round-off error in the text's calculation.

===

FG12-32

Av = max(v(out)/v(in)) = **-99.8** [-100]

===
CHAPTER 13
===

FG13-09

a) BW = 0dB crossing = **44.6kHz** [44.3kHz]
b) BW = 0dB crossing = **62.4kHz** [63.8kHz]

===
CHAPTER 14
===

FG14-03B

Vltp = **1.680V** [1.63V]
Vutp = **1.633V** [1.63V]

Probe display matches Fig. 14-4 in text.

===

FG14-09

Vltp = **-2.558V** [-2.5V]
Vutp = **+2.401V** [+2.5V]

Probe display matches text.

===

FG14-13

Vltp = **-2.594V** [-2.54V]
Vutp = **+2.595V** [+2.54V]

Probe display matches Fig. 14-14 trip points, but clipped v(out) shows a slightly greater Vpp. V(out) pk-pk differs due to non-ideal zener models.

===

FG14-24

max(v(out)) = **-12V** [-12V]

===

FG14-25

max(v(out)) = **-7V** [-7V]

===

FG14-26

max(v(out)) = **-2.5V** [-2.5V]

===

FG14-27

max(v(out)) = **-8.838V** [-8.84V]

===

FG14-35

Probe display matches Fig. 14-35(b) in text.

===
CHAPTER 15
===

FG15-29

max(v(out)) = **-0.155V** [-0.150V]

===

FG15-32

max(v(out)) = **-3.0V** [-3V]

This circuit file uses a special transistor model to approximate the one used in the text. The model parameter for saturation current had to be set as follows: Is=50nA. (The PSPICE model parameter Is roughtly equates to the conventional device parameter Iebo as mentioned in the text).

===
CHAPTER 16
===

FG16-11

max(db(v(out)))-3 = 1dB

*This trace is plotted vs. db(v(out)), showing an intersection at about **7.95kHz** [7.96kHz].*

FG16-19

f0 = **735Hz** [736Hz]
BW = **181Hz** [177Hz]

===

FG16-22

f0 = **7.24kHz** [7.23kHz]
BW = **220Hz**   [215Hz]

===

FG16-25

Probe display shows peaking at about **60.2Hz** [60Hz]

===
CHAPTER 17
===

FG17-12

f = 1/period(v(out)) = **15.9kHz** [15.9kHz]

===

FG17-14

f = 1/period(v(out)) = **6.494kHz** [6.5kHz]

Needed to set initial condition of Vout=1V for circuit to oscillate. Real-world parasitic circuit capacitances, noises, etc. would be sufficient to get real-world oscillator going.

===

FG17-30

a) R1=10k: f = 1/period(v(out)) = **8.264kHz** [8.25kHz]
b) R1=4.13k: f = 1/period(v(out)) = **19.867kHz** [20kHz]

===
CHAPTER 18
===

FG18-06

max(v(out)) = **10.2V** [10.2V]

===

TROUBLE.DOC

This file presents a summary of the PSPICE circuit analysis results run on the troubleshooting problems for Electronic Devices, 5th Edition. The PROBE files should be viewed by starting PROBE, reading the proper data file in, and then selecting TOOLS/DISPLAY CONTROL/LAST SESSION (RESTORE) to display the pertinent waveforms as predefined in the PROBE setup files. The values given below are from node voltage measurements obtained from the PROBE data files. The user should use the *swingr(v(trace),0,1)* GOAL FUNCTION expression format to return the pk-pk swing of the specified *trace*. This is how, for example, the ripple value was obtained for several of the problems. To compute the dc value of an ac signal, the user can use the *max()* and *min()* GOAL FUNCTION expressions, and then hand-compute the average of the results. The frequency of periodic waveforms can be computed by using the *1/period(v(trace))* GOAL FUNCTION expression, since the frequency is just the inverse of the period. Several problems ask for the gain to be computed, Av. This can be obtained by using the GOAL FUNCTION expression *swingr(v(out),0,1)/swingr(v(in))* for ac signals, or the expression *max(v(out)/v(in))* for dc levels. The correct expression(s) to use should be self-evident upon viewing the waveforms involved while in the PROBE program.

==
CHAPTER 1
==

No Circuits

==
CHAPTER 2
==

FG02-68

a) **Fuse Open**   Vout = 0V, Vsec = 0V

   Open fuse makes output, secondary voltages zero.

b) **No Fault**   Vout(dc) = 21.1V, Vout(ripple) = 1.34Vpp @ 120Hz

   Normal circuit operation.

c) **D2 Open**   Vout(dc) = 20.0V, Vout(ripple) = 2.84Vpp @ 60Hz

   Frequency halves and ripple doubles due to "half wave" rectification.

==
CHAPTER 3
==

FG03-48

a) **Sec Win Open**   Vout = 0V, Vsec = 0V

   Open secondary makes output, secondary voltages zero.

b) **Rsurge Open**   Vout = 0V, Vsec = 24.3Vpp

   Output voltage zero since no current can flow through open resistor.

c) **No Fault**   Vout(dc) = 15.3V, Vout(ripple) = 121mVpp @ 120Hz

   Normal circuit operation.

d) **Zener Open**   Vout(dc) = 23.2V, Vout(ripple) = 930uVpp @ 120Hz

   With zener open, output drifts asymptotically towards peak secondary voltage.

CHAPTER 4

FG04-30

a) **No Fault**   Vb = 0.716V, Vc = 5.17V

    Normal circuit operation.

b) **Rc Open**   Vb = 0.582V, Vc = 5.64mV

    With Rc open, collector floats close to ground potential.

c) **Xtr C-E Open** Vb = 3.000V, Vc = 9.000V

    With C-E open, base and collector impedances look infinite.

The PSPICE model works out to have a Beta of about 165.

CHAPTER 5

FG05-31

a) **R1 Open**   Vc = 10V, Vb = 0V, Ve = 0V

    With R1 open, base is pulled to ground, no current can flow; thus Vc = Vcc, Ve = 0V.

b) **Xtr B-E Open** Vc = 10V, Vb = 3.2V, Ve = 0V

    With B-E open, no current can flow; thus Vc = Vcc, Ve = 0V.

c) **No Fault**   Vc = 5V, Vb = 3.1V, Ve = 2.4V

    Normal circuit operation.

d) **Re Open**   Vc = 10V, Vb = 3.2V, Ve = 0V

    With Re open, no current can flow; thus Vc = Vcc, Ve = 0V.

CHAPTER 6

FG06-41

a) **No Fault**
```
VC(1) =   5.20V, VB(1) =   1.69V, VE(1) =   1.03V   (DC Values)
Vc(1) =  17mVpp, Vb(1) = 282uVpp, Ve(1) =    0Vpp   (ac Values)
VC(2) =   5.12V, VB(2) =   1.69V, VE(2) =   1.03V   (DC Values)
Vc(2) = 2.90Vpp, Vb(2) = 17.1mVpp, Ve(2) = 11.3uVpp (ac Values)
Vout  = 2.90Vpp                                     (ac Value)
```

    Normal circuit operation.

b) **C3 Open**
```
VC(1) =   5.20V, VB(1) =   1.69V, VE(1) = 1.03V   (DC Values)
Vc(1) =  48mVpp, Vb(1) = 282uVpp, Ve(1) =  0Vpp   (ac Values)
VC(2) =   5.20V, VB(2) =   1.69V, VE(2) = 1.03V   (DC Values)
Vc(2) =    0Vpp, Vb(2) =    0Vpp, Ve(2) =  0Vpp   (ac Values)
Vout  =    0Vpp                                   (ac Value)
```

    With C3 open, no ac signal gets through to second stage; thus output is zero volts.

c) **C4 Open**
```
VC(1) =   5.20V, VB(1) =   1.69V, VE(1) = 1.03V   (DC Values)
Vc(1) =  30mVpp, Vb(1) = 282uVpp, Ve(1) =  0Vpp   (ac Values)
VC(2) =   5.20V, VB(2) =   1.69V, VE(2) = 1.03V   (DC Values)
Vc(2) = 141mVpp, Vb(2) =  30mVpp, Ve(2) = 30mVpp  (ac Values)
Vout  = 141mVpp                                   (ac Value)
```

    With C4 open, stage 2 gain is substantially reduced.

d) **Q2 C-E Open** VC(1) =   5.20V, VB(1) =   1.69V, VE(1) = 1.03V   (DC Values)
                   Vc(1) = 32mVpp, Vb(1) = 282uVpp, Ve(1) = 0Vpp   (ac Values)
                   VC(2) =   10.0V, VB(2) =   1.77V, VE(2) =   0V   (DC Values)
                   Vc(2) =   0Vpp, Vb(2) = 32mVpp, Ve(2) = 0Vpp   (ac Values)
                   Vout =   0Vpp   (ac Value)

   With Q2 C-E open, output essentially zero, Q2 collector = Vcc, Q2 emitter = 0V.

===
CHAPTER 7
===

FG07-13

a) **R2 Open**   Av = 31.3, Vb(dc) = 3.52V, Vb(ripple) = 20mVpp

   With R2 open, base bias is messed up, output is distorted, Vb much higher than usual.

b) **C2 Short** Av = 87.8, Vb(dc) = 0.74V, Vb(ripple) = 20mVpp

   With C2 short, gain is messed up, output is distorted, Vb a diode drop above ground.

c) **No Fault** Av = 103.2, Vb(dc) = 1.87V, Vb(ripple) = 20mVpp

   Normal circuit operation.

===
CHAPTER 8
===

FG08-17

a) **No Fault** Vd = 10.11V, Vg = 0V, Vs = 1.07V

   Normal circuit operation.

b) **Rd Open**   Vd =   0V, Vg = 0V, Vs =   0V

   With Rd open, no current flows; thus nodes all look like ground potential.

c) **Rs Open**   Vd =   15V, Vg = 0V, Vs =   3V

   With Rs open, no current flows; thus Vd = Vdd, Vs = 3V due to self-biasing.

The PSPICE model has different model parameters

===
CHAPTER 9
===

FG09-28

a) **No Fault** V(G2)=0.2Vppac;   0Vdc, AVG[Id(J1)]=4.64mA, AVG[Id(J2)]=4.65mA, Vout=1.487Vpp

   Normal circuit operation.

b) **C3 Short** V(G2)=0.0Vppac; 2.57Vdc, AVG[Id(J1)]=4.52mA, AVG[Id(J2)]=6.22mA, Vout= 257uVpp

   With C3 short, ac signal is destroyed, dc biasing of J2 is messed up.

c) **J1 D-S Open** V(G2)=0.0Vppac; 11uVdc, AVG[Id(J1)]=   0mA, AVG[Id(J2)]=4.64mA, Vout=   0Vpp

   With J1 D-S open, ac signal is destroyed, J1 drain current is zero.

d) **R5 Open**   V(G2)=0.2Vppac;-279uVdc, AVG[Id(J1)]=4.64mA, AVG[Id(J2)]=   0mA, Vout=2.56uVpp

   With R5 open, no J2 drain current can flow, output is essentially zero.

CHAPTER 10

No Circuits

CHAPTER 11

No Circuits

CHAPTER 12

FG12-22

a) **No Fault**   Vfb = 100mV, Vout = 2.23V

   Normal circuit operation.

b) **Rf Open**   Vfb = 46.5uV, Vout = 20V

   With Rf open, Vfb is pulled to ground, output drifts to positive rail voltage.

FG12-26

a) **No Fault**   Vfb = 0V, Vout = -10V

   Normal circuit operation.

b) **Ri Open**   Vfb = 0V, Vout = 0V

   With Ri open, circuit acts like simple voltage follower with input grounded.

CHAPTER 13

No Circuits

CHAPTER 14

FG14-27

a) **R2 Open**   Vout = -8.638V

   With R2 open, circuit develops the weighted sum of the +3V and +8V inputs only.

b) **No Fault**   Vout = -8.838V

   Normal circuit operation.

FG14-35

a) **C Short**   Vout = 0V

   With C short, circuit acts like simple voltage follower with input grounded.

b) **No Fault**   Vout ramps linearly from 0V to -5V in 100usec; stays at -5V thereafter

   Normal circuit operation.

FG14-44

a) **D1 Short**   Vout,min = -0.727V, Vout,max = +7.626V

   With D1 short, circuit clamps to a diode drop in one direction, zener voltage minus diode drop in other direction.

b) **Ri Open**   Vout,min = +1.884V, Vout,max = +1.884V

   With Ri open, circuit self-biases to a steady state.
   NOTE: Some operational amplifiers may exhibit oscillation, rather than a steady biased state.

c) **No Fault**   Vout,min = -8.362V, Vout,max = +8.362V

   Normal circuit operation.

===

FG14-45

a) **R5 Open**   Vout = -20V

   With R5 open, amplifier acts as a comparator and swings output to negative supply rail.

b) **No Fault**   Vout = -1.8V

   Normal circuit operation.

===
CHAPTER 15
===

No Circuits

===
CHAPTER 16
===

No Circuits

===
CHAPTER 17
===

No Circuits

===
CHAPTER 18
===

No Circuits

Test Item File

to accompany

ELECTRONIC DEVICES
Fifth Edition

and

ELECTRONIC DEVICES
Electron-Flow Version
Third Edition

by
Thomas Floyd

Prepared by
Osama Maarouf

Prentice Hall

Upper Saddle River, New Jersey   Columbus, Ohio

CONTENTS

1	Introduction to Semiconductors	239
2	Diode Applications	243
3	Special-Purpose Diodes	249
4	Bipolar Junction Transistors	254
5	Transistor Bias Circuits	260
6	Small-Signal Bipolar Amplifiers	265
7	Power Amplifiers	270
8	Field-Effect Transistors and Biasing	276
9	Small-Signal FET Amplifiers	281
10	Amplifier Frequency Response	286
11	Thyristor and Other Devices	291
12	Operational Amplifiers	296
13	Op-Amp Frequency Response, Stability, and Compensation	301
14	Basic Op-Amp Circuits	306
15	More Op-Amp Circuits	311
16	Active Filters	316
17	Oscillators and the Phase-Locked Loop	322
18	Voltage Regulators	328

Chapter 1: Introduction to Semiconductors

MULTIPLE CHOICE

1. A molecule is the smallest particle of an element that retains the characteristics of that element.
   a) true
   b) false

   Answer: b Difficulty: 2

2. A forward biased diode of a conducting germanium diode has a potential of about 0.7 V across it.
   a) true
   b) false

   Answer: b Difficulty: 2

3. Silicon doped with impurities is used in the manufacture of semiconductor devices.
   a) true
   b) false

   Answer: a Difficulty: 2

4. Reverse bias permits full current through a pn junction.
   a) true
   b) false

   Answer: b Difficulty: 2

5. Semiconductor material of the p-type has few free electrons.
   a) true
   b) false

   Answer: a Difficulty: 2

6. The dc voltages for a device to operate properly is called
   a) rectification.
   b) amplification.
   c) bias.
   d) a pn-junction.

   Answer: c Difficulty: 2

7. The majority carriers are the holes in a/an
   a) n-type semiconductor.
   b) p-type semiconductor.
   c) p-n junction semiconductor.
   d) none of the above

   Answer: a Difficulty: 2

Chapter 1: Introduction to Semiconductors

8. Semiconductor materials are those with
   a) conductive properties that are in between those of a conductor or an insulator.
   b) conductive properties that are very good.
   c) no conductive properties.
   d) a or b

   Answer: a Difficulty: 2

9. Voltage is defined as
   a) the force causing movement of electrons down a wire.
   b) the opposition to the movement of electrons.
   c) the ability of a device to store electrons.
   d) the movement of free electrons in a conductor.

   Answer: a Difficulty: 2

10. Capacitance can be defined as
    a) the force causing movement of electrons down a wire.
    b) the opposition to the movement of electrons.
    c) the ability of a device to store electrons.
    d) the movement of free electrons in a conductor.

    Answer: c Difficulty: 2

11. A current flows across the junction of a forward biased diode. This current is called
    a) forward bias current.
    b) reverse breakdown current.
    c) conventional current.
    d) reverse leakage current.

    Answer: a Difficulty: 2

12. A large current that flows in the opposite direction across a pn junction is called
    a) forward bias current.
    b) reverse breakdown current.
    c) conventional current.
    d) reverse leakage current.

    Answer: b Difficulty: 2

13. A small current that flows when a diode is reverse biased is called
    a) forward bias current.
    b) reverse breakdown current.
    c) conventional current.
    d) reverse leakage current.

    Answer: d Difficulty: 2

14. As the forward current through a forward biased diode decreases, the voltage across the diode
    a) increases.
    b) decreases.
    c) is relatively constant.
    d) increases and then decreases.

    Answer: c Difficulty: 2

15. Which statement best describes a semiconductor?
    a) A material with many free electrons.
    b) A material doped to have some free electrons.
    c) A material with few free electrons.
    d) none of these

    Answer: b Difficulty: 2

16. As the forward current through a silicon diode decreases, the internal resistance of the diode will
    a) increase.
    b) decrease.
    c) remain the same.
    d) either b or c

    Answer: a Difficulty: 2

17. A silicon diode measures a high value of resistance with the meter leads in both positions. The trouble, if any, is
    a) the diode is open.
    b) the diode is shorted to ground.
    c) the diode is internally shorted.
    d) the diode is ok.

    Answer: a Difficulty: 2

18. A silicon diode is reverse biased. The voltage measured to ground from the anode is _____, and the voltage to ground from the anode is _____.
    a) 16 V, 15.3 V
    b) -16 V, -16.7 V
    c) 0.2 V, -0.5 V
    d) 15.3 V, 16 V

    Answer: d Difficulty: 3

19. The forward voltage across a conducting silicon diode is about
    a) 1.3 V.
    b) 0.3 V.
    c) 0.7 V.
    d) -0.3 V.

    Answer: c Difficulty: 2

20. To change ac to pulsating dc. The best type of diode to use might be
    a) a Shockley diode.
    b) a zener diode.
    c) a rectifier diode.
    d) a photodiode.

    Answer: c Difficulty: 2

21. Avalanche is the rapid multiplication of current carriers in forward breakdown.
    a) true
    b) false

    Answer: b Difficulty: 2

Chapter 1:   Introduction to Semiconductors

22. An unknown type diode is in a circuit. The voltage measured across it was found to be 0.3 V. The diode is
   a) a silicon diode.
   b) a germanium diode.
   c) a transistor
   d) none of the above

   Answer: b Difficulty: 2

23. A reverse biased diode has the _____ connected to the positive side of the source, and the _____ connected towards the negative side of the source.
   a) cathode, anode
   b) cathode, base
   c) base, anode
   d) anode, cathode

   Answer: a Difficulty: 3

24. A silicon diode is forward biased. You measure the voltage to ground from the anode at _____ V, and the voltage from the cathode to ground at _____ V.
   a) 16 V, 32 V
   b) 2.3 V, 1.6 V
   c) 1.6 V, 2.3 V
   d) 0.3 V, 0 V

   Answer: b Difficulty: 3

25. The boundary between p-type material and n-type material is called
   a) a diode.
   b) a reverse-biased diode.
   c) a pn junction.
   d) a forward-biased diode.

   Answer: c Difficulty: 2

Chapter 2: Diode Applications

MULTIPLE CHOICE

1. A diode conducts currents when forward biased and blocks current when reverse biased.
   a) true
   b) false

   Answer: a Difficulty: 2

2. The larger the ripple voltage, the better the filter.
   a) true
   b) false

   Answer: b Difficulty: 2

3. Clamping circuits use capacitors and diodes to add a dc level to a waveform.
   a) true
   b) false

   Answer: a Difficulty: 2

4. The diode in a half-wave rectifier conducts for _____ of the input cycle.
   a) 0°
   b) 45°
   c) 90°
   d) 180°

   Answer: d Difficulty: 2

5. A full-wave bridge rectifier uses _____ diode(s) in a bridge circuit.
   a) 1
   b) 2
   c) 3
   d) 4

   Answer: d Difficulty: 2

6. A silicon diode is connected in series with 10 kΩ resistor and a 12 V battery. If the cathode of the diode is connected to the positive terminal of the battery, the voltage from the anode to the negative terminal of the battery is
   a) 0 V.
   b) 0.7 V.
   c) 11.3 V.
   d) 12 V.

   Answer: a Difficulty: 3

Chapter 2: Diode Applications

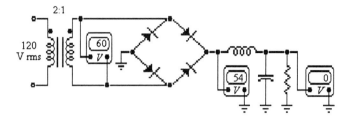

Figure 2-1

7. Refer to figure 2-1. If the voltmeter across the transformer secondary read 0 V, the probable trouble, if any, would be
   a) one of the diodes is open.
   b) the filter capacitor is shorted.
   c) the transformer secondary is open.
   d) the inductor is open.
   e) everything is normal.

   Answer: c Difficulty: 3

8. Refer to figure 2-1. In servicing this power supply, you notice that the ripple voltage is higher than normal and that the ripple frequency has changed to 60 Hz. The probable trouble is
   a) the filter capacitor has opened.
   b) the inductor has opened.
   c) a diode has shorted.
   d) a diode has opened.

   Answer: d Difficulty: 3

Figure 2-2

9. Refer to figure 2-2 (a). This oscilloscope trace indicates the output from
   a) a half-wave filtered rectifier.
   b) a full-wave rectifier with no filter and an open diode.
   c) a full-wave filtered rectifier.
   d) a full-wave filtered rectifier with an open diode.

   Answer: b Difficulty: 3

10. Refer to figure 2-2 (b). The trace on this oscilloscope indicates the output from
    a) a half-wave rectifier with no filter.
    b) a full-wave rectifier with no filter.
    c) a full-wave filtered rectifier.
    d) a full-wave filtered rectifier with an open diode.

    Answer: a Difficulty: 3

11. Refer to figure 2-2 (c). This is the output from
    a) a half-wave rectifier with no filter.
    b) a full-wave rectifier with no filter and an open diode.
    c) a full-wave filtered rectifier.
    d) a full-wave filtered rectifier with an open diode.

    Answer: c Difficulty: 3

12. Refer to figure 2-2 (d). This trace shows the output from
    a) a half-wave rectifier with no filter.
    b) a full-wave rectifier with no filter and an open diode.
    c) a full-wave filtered rectifier.
    d) a full-wave filtered rectifier with an open diode.

    Answer: d Difficulty: 3

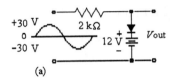
(a)

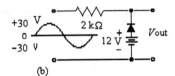
(b)

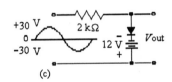
(c)

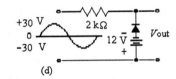
(d)

Figure 2-3

13. Refer to figure 2-3. These circuits are known as
    a) amplifiers.
    b) clippers.
    c) clampers.
    d) rectifiers.

    Answer: b Difficulty: 2

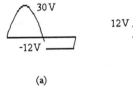
(a)

(b)

(c)

(d)

Figure 2-4

14. Which of the circuits in figure 2-3 will produce the signal in figure 2-4?
    a) (a)
    b) (b)
    c) (c)
    d) (d)

    Answer: d Difficulty: 2

Chapter 2: Diode Applications

15. Which of the circuits in figure 2-3 will produce the signal in figure 2-4 (b)?
    a) (a)
    b) (b)
    c) (c)
    d) (d)

    Answer: b Difficulty: 2

16. Which of the circuits in figure 2-3 will produce the signal in figure 2-4 (c)?
    a) (a)
    b) (b)
    c) (c)
    d) (d)

    Answer: a Difficulty: 2

17. Which of the circuits in figure 2-3 will produce the signal in figure 2-4 (d)?
    a) (a)
    b) (b)
    c) (c)
    d) (d)

    Answer: c Difficulty: 2

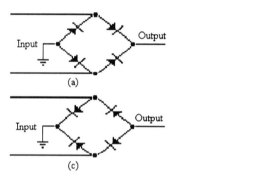

Figure 2-5

18. Refer to figure 2-5 (c). This rectifier arrangement
    a) will produce a positive output voltage.
    b) will produce a negative output voltage.
    c) is incorrectly connected.
    d) a or c

    Answer: b Difficulty: 2

19. Refer to figure 2-5 (d). This rectifier arrangement
    a) will produce a positive output voltage.
    b) will produce a negative output voltage.
    c) is incorrectly connected.
    d) none of the above

    Answer: c Difficulty: 2

20. A silicon diode has a voltage to ground of 117 V from the anode. The voltage to ground from the cathode is 117.7 V. The diode is
    a) open.
    b) shorted.
    c) forward biased.
    d) reverse biased.

    Answer: d Difficulty: 2

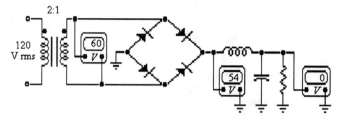

Figure 2-1

21. Refer to figure 2-1. The probable trouble, if any, indicated by these voltages
    a) is one of the diodes is open.
    b) is a diode is shorted.
    c) is an open transformer secondary.
    d) is the filter capacitor is shorted.
    e) is no trouble exists.

    Answer: d Difficulty: 3

22. Refer to figure 2-1. If the voltmeter across the transformer read 0 V, the probable trouble, if any, would be
    a) one of the diodes is open.
    b) is an open transformer secondary.
    c) is the filter capacitor is shorted.
    d) no trouble exists.

    Answer: c Difficulty: 3

Figure 2-2

23. Refer to figure 2-2. Which oscilloscope trace indicates the output from a full-wave rectifier with an open diode?
    a) (a)
    b) (b)
    c) (c)
    d) (d)

    Answer: d Difficulty: 3

Chapter 2: Diode Applications

24. The ripple frequency of a bridge rectifier is
    a) the same as the input frequency.
    b) double the input frequency.
    c) four times the input frequency.
    d) cannot be determined

    Answer: b Difficulty: 2

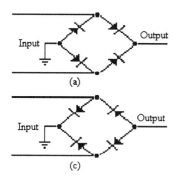
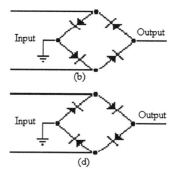

Figure 2-5

25. Refer to figure 2-5. Which diode arrangement is correct to supply a positive output voltage?
    a) (a)
    b) (b)
    c) (c)
    d) (d)

    Answer: a Difficulty: 2

Chapter 3: Special-Purpose Diodes

MULTIPLE CHOICE

1. The regulating ability of a zener diode depends upon its ability to operate in a breakdown condition.
   a) true
   b) false

   Answer: a Difficulty: 2

2. Dark Current is the amount of thermally generated forward current in a photodiode in the absence of light.
   a) true
   b) false

   Answer: b Difficulty: 2

3. A _____ diode maintains a constant voltage across it when operating in the breakdown condition.
   a) Silicon
   b) Germanium
   c) Zener
   d) None of the above

   Answer: c Difficulty: 2

4. A tunnel diode has _____ characteristic(s).
   a) an extremely narrow depletion region
   b) a negative resistance
   c) no breakdown effect
   d) All of the above

   Answer: b Difficulty: 2

5. Typically, the maximum V_F for an LED is between
   a) 0V and 1V
   b) 1V and 1.2V
   c) 1.2V and 3.2V
   d) 3.2V and 4V

   Answer: c Difficulty: 2

6. A 5.1 V zener has a resistance of 8 Ω. The actual voltage across its terminals when the current is 20 mA is
   a) 5.1 V.
   b) 100 mV.
   c) 5.26 V.
   d) 4.94 V.

   Answer: a Difficulty: 2

Chapter 3: Special-Purpose Diodes

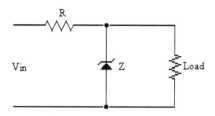

Figure 3-1

7. Refer to figure 3-1. If V_{IN} increases, V_R will
   a) increase.
   b) decrease.
   c) remain the same.
   d) cannot be determined

   Answer: a   Difficulty: 3

8. Refer to figure 3-1. If V_{RL} increases, I_Z will
   a) increase.
   b) decrease.
   c) remain the same.
   d) cannot be determined

   Answer: a   Difficulty: 3

9. Refer to figure 3-1. Measurements show that V_{RL} has increased. Which of the following faults, if any, could have caused this problem?
   a) R opens
   b) the zener shorts
   c) V_{IN} has decreased
   d) the zener opens

   Answer: d   Difficulty: 3

10. Refer to figure 3-1. If V_{RL} attempts to decrease, I_R will
    a) increase.
    b) decrease.
    c) remain the same.
    d) cannot be determined

    Answer: c   Difficulty: 2

11. Refer to figure 3-1. If the load current increases, I_R will _____ and I_Z will _____.
    a) remain the same, increase
    b) decrease, remain the same
    c) increase, remain the same
    d) remain the same, decrease

    Answer: b   Difficulty: 3

12. Refer to figure 3-1. If V_{IN} decreases, I_R will
    a) increase.
    b) decrease.
    c) remain the same.
    d) cannot be determined

    Answer: b Difficulty: 2

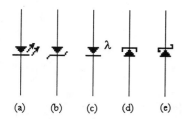

Figure 3-2

13. Refer to figure 3-2 (a). The symbol is for
    a) a zener diode.
    b) an LED.
    c) a Schottky diode.
    d) a photodiode.
    e) tunnel diode.

    Answer: b Difficulty: 2

14. Refer to figure 3-2 (b). The symbol is for
    a) a zener diode.
    b) an LED.
    c) a Schottky diode.
    d) a photodiode.
    e) tunnel diode.

    Answer: a Difficulty: 2

15. Refer to figure 3-2 (c). The symbol is for
    a) a zener diode.
    b) an LED.
    c) a Schottky diode.
    d) a photodiode.
    e) tunnel diode.

    Answer: d Difficulty: 2

16. Refer to figure 3-2 (d). The symbol is for
    a) a zener diode.
    b) an LED.
    c) a Schottky diode.
    d) a photodiode.
    e) tunnel diode.

    Answer: e Difficulty: 2

Chapter 3: Special-Purpose Diodes

17. Refer to figure 3-2 (e). The symbol is for
    a) a zener diode.
    b) an LED.
    c) a Schottky diode.
    d) a photodiode.
    e) tunnel diode.

    Answer: c Difficulty: 2

18. A varactor is a diode that
    a) varies its resistance with temperature.
    b) changes its capacitance with voltage.
    c) emits light when forward biased.
    d) switches very fast.
    e) exhibits an increase in reverse current with light intensity.

    Answer: b Difficulty: 2

19. A Schottky diode is a diode that
    a) varies its resistance with temperature.
    b) changes its capacitance with voltage.
    c) emits light when forward biased.
    d) switches very fast.
    e) exhibits an increase in reverse current with light intensity.

    Answer: d Difficulty: 2

20. A photodiode is a diode that
    a) varies its resistance with temperature.
    b) changes its capacitance with voltage.
    c) emits light when forward biased.
    d) switches very fast.
    e) exhibits an increase in reverse current with light intensity.

    Answer: e Difficulty: 2

21. An LED is being tested by placing it in a forward bias position across a 5 V dc supply. The correct conclusion would be
    a) nothing is wrong with the LED, go ahead and use it.
    b) your test was correct, but the LED was bad.
    c) your test was incorrect, and the LED is now bad.
    d) there is no way to test the LED. Put in a new one.

    Answer: c Difficulty: 3

22. A diode with a negative-resistance characteristic is needed. A correct selection might be
    a) a tunnel diode.
    b) a Gunn diode.
    c) a varactor diode.
    d) a Schottky diode.

    Answer: a Difficulty: 2

23. A 6.2 V zener is rated at 1 watt. The maximum safe current the zener can carry is
    a) 1.61 A.
    b) 161 mA.
    c) 16.1 mA.
    d) 1.61 mA.

    Answer: b Difficulty: 2

24. An LED is forward-biased. The diode should be on, but no light is showing. A possible trouble might be
    a) the diode is open.
    b) the series resistor is too small.
    c) none. The diode should be off if forward-biased.
    d) the power supply voltage is too high.

    Answer: a Difficulty: 3

25. The best type of diodes to use in a turning circuit is:
    a) an LED.
    b) a Schottky diode.
    c) a Gunn diode.
    d) a varactor.

    Answer: d Difficulty: 2

Chapter 4: Bipolar Junction Transistors

MULTIPLE CHOICE

1. BJT transistors have two pn junctions.
   a) true
   b) false

   Answer: a Difficulty: 2

2. A BJT transistor has the base-emitter junction reverse biased for proper operation.
   a) true
   b) false

   Answer: b Difficulty: 2

3. The ratio I_E/I_C is β_{dc}.
   a) true
   b) false

   Answer: b Difficulty: 2

4. Proper operation of a BJT requires that the base-collector junction should be reverse biased.
   a) true
   b) false

   Answer: a Difficulty: 2

5. The formula for I_C is, $I_C = I_E - I_B$
   a) true
   b) false

   Answer: a Difficulty: 2

6. A BJT has an I_B of 75 µA and a β_{dc} of 100. The value of I_C is:
   a) 175 µA
   b) 75 mA
   c) 10 mA
   d) 7.5 mA

   Answer: d Difficulty: 2

7. A certain transistor has an I_C = 12 mA and an I_B = 125 µA. β_{dc} is:
   a) 150
   b) 15
   c) 96
   d) 12

   Answer: c Difficulty: 2

8. Normal operation of an npn BJT requires the base to be _____ with respect to the emitter, and _____ with respect to the collector.
   a) positive, negative
   b) positive, positive
   c) negative, positive
   d) negative, negative

   Answer: a   Difficulty: 2

9. A transistor amplifier has an input voltage of 67 mV and an output voltage of 2.48 V. The voltage gain is:
   a) 67
   b) 37
   c) 27
   d) 17

   Answer: b   Difficulty: 2

10. A 22 mV signal is applied to the base of a properly biased transistor that has an $r_e = 7$ and an $R_C = 12\ k\Omega$. The output voltage at the collector is:
    a) 22 mV
    b) 17.1 V
    c) 7 V
    d) 3.77 V

    Answer: d   Difficulty: 2

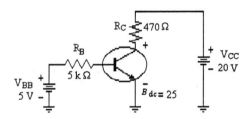

Figure 4-1

11. Refer to figure 4-1. This circuit is operating
    a) in cutoff.
    b) in saturation.
    c) normally.
    d) incorrectly because the bias voltages are wrong.

    Answer: c   Difficulty: 3

12. Refer to figure 4-1. The value of I_B is:
    a) 8.6 mA
    b) 860 μA
    c) 1 mA
    d) 0.7 μA

    Answer: b   Difficulty: 2

Chapter 4: Bipolar Junction Transistors

13. Refer to figure 4-1. If the value of V_{BB} were increased to 10 V, the transistor would be
    a) cut off.
    b) saturated.
    c) operating ok.
    d) cannot be determined

    Answer: b Difficulty: 3

14. Refer to figure 4-1. If this transistor is operating in saturation, minimum value of $I_{C(sat)}$ flowing is:
    a) 9.4 mA
    b) 4.26 mA
    c) 28.6 mA
    d) 42.6 mA

    Answer: d Difficulty: 3

15. Refer to figure 4-1. Assume that this circuit is operating in cutoff. The measurement, if any, that would confirm this assumption is:
    a) $V_{BE} = 0.7$ V
    b) $V_{CE} = 8$ V
    c) $V_{CE} = 20$ V
    d) $V_{CC} = 20$ V
    e) none of these

    Answer: c Difficulty: 3

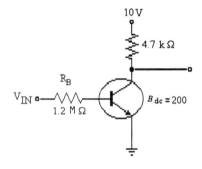

Figure 4-2

16. Refer to figure 4-2. The value of I_C at cutoff is:
    a) 0 mA
    b) 2.13 mA
    c) 10.65 µA
    d) 10 mA

    Answer: a Difficulty: 2

17. Refer to figure 4-2. If the value of the collector resistor is increased to 6.8 kΩ, the new value of $I_{C(sat)}$ is:
    a) 2.13 mA
    b) .68 mA
    c) 1.47 mA
    d) 0 mA

    Answer: c   Difficulty: 2

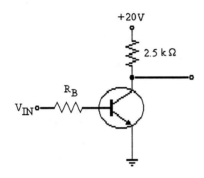

Figure 4-3

18. Refer to figure 4-3. If the collector resistor value is changed to 4.7 kΩ and β_{dc} = 200, $I_{C(sat)}$ would be:
    a) 4.26 mA
    b) 8 mA
    c) 4.26 μA
    d) 8.426 mA

    Answer: a   Difficulty: 2

19. Refer to figure 4-3. If the measure voltage from the collector to ground was 0 V, the transistor is operating in
    a) saturation.
    b) cutoff.
    c) normal.
    d) not enough data

    Answer: a   Difficulty: 2

20. Refer to figure 4-3. This circuit is saturated. To get the circuit to operate close to its linear range,
    a) R_B should be decreased.
    b) R_C should be decreased.
    c) V_{in} should be increased.
    d) R_B should be increased.

    Answer: d   Difficulty: 3

Chapter 4: Bipolar Junction Transistors

21. A 35 mV signal is applied to the base of a properly biased transistor with an $r_e = 8\ \Omega$ and $R_C = 1\ k\Omega$. The output signal voltage at the collector is
    a) 3.5 V.
    b) 28.57 V.
    c) 4.375 V.
    d) 4.375 mV.

    Answer: c Difficulty: 2

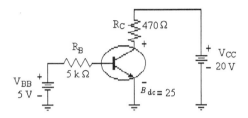

Figure 4-1

22. Refer to figure 4-1. The value of V_{CE} is:
    a) 9.9 V
    b) 9.2 V
    c) 0.7 V
    d) 19.3 V

    Answer: a Difficulty: 2

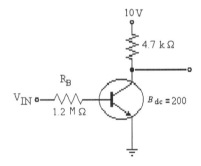

Figure 4-2

23. Refer to figure 4-2. The minimum value of I_B that will produce saturation is
    a) 0.25 mA.
    b) 5.325 µA.
    c) 1.065 µA.
    d) 10.65 µA.

    Answer: d Difficulty: 2

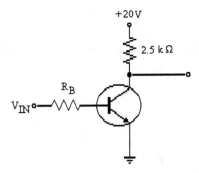

Figure 4-3

24. Refer to figure 4-3. The voltage V_{CE} was measured and found to be 20 V. The transistor is operating in
    a) saturation.
    b) cutoff.
    c) normal.
    d) not enough data

    Answer: b Difficulty: 2

25. Refer to figure 4-3. If V_{CE} is measured and is equal to nearly zero, the transistor is operating in
    a) cutoff.
    b) normally.
    c) saturation.
    d) cannot be determined

    Answer: c Difficulty: 3

Chapter 5: Transistor Bias Circuits

MULTIPLE CHOICE

1. Biasing a BJT amplifier means setting the dc voltages with the correct bias for proper operation.
   a) true
   b) false

   Answer: a Difficulty: 2

2. A transistor operating in saturation has very little current flowing.
   a) true
   b) false

   Answer: b Difficulty: 2

3. The base of fixed bias circuit arrangement provides good stability because the Q-point does not vary with temperature.
   a) true
   b) false

   Answer: b Difficulty: 2

4. Negative feedback in the collector-feedback circuit provides a more stable operation.
   a) true
   b) false

   Answer: a Difficulty: 2

5. The correct formula for finding the dc current gain is $\beta_{dc} = I_C/I_B$.
   a) true
   b) false

   Answer: a Difficulty: 2

6. A certain transistor in a fixed-bias circuit has these values, $I_B = 50$ µA, $\beta_{dc} = 125$, $V_{CC} = 18$ V, and $R_C = 1.2$ kΩ. V_C is:
   a) 0 V
   b) 7.5 V
   c) 10.5 V
   d) 18 V

   Answer: c Difficulty: 2

7. An indication of cutoff is that
   a) $I_C = I_{C(sat)}$.
   b) $V_{CE} = 0$ V.
   c) $V_{BE} = 0.7$ V.
   d) $V_{CE} = V_{CC}$.

   Answer: d Difficulty: 2

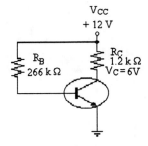

Figure 5-1

8. Refer to figure 5-1. This transistor is biased for _____ operation.
   a) saturation
   b) linear
   c) cutoff
   d) a or c

   Answer: b   Difficulty: 2

9. Refer to figure 5-1. The voltage on the base of this silicon transistor is
   a) 0.3 V.
   b) 0 V.
   c) 12 V.
   d) 11.3 V.
   e) 0.7 V.

   Answer: e   Difficulty: 2

10. Refer to figure 5-1. If β_{dc} = 100, the minimum value of I_B that would cause this transistor to saturate is
    a) 100 µA.
    b) 50 µA.
    c) 1 mA.
    d) 0.1 mA.

    Answer: a   Difficulty: 2

11. Refer to figure 5-1. If V_C is increased to 9 V, the change that is correct to do is to
    a) increase the value of R_B.
    b) replace the transistor with one with a higher β_{dc}.
    c) decrease the value of R_B.
    d) increase the value of R_C.

    Answer: a   Difficulty: 3

Chapter 5:   Transistor Bias Circuits

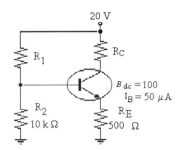

Figure 5-2

12. Refer to figure 5-2. The value of R_C that will produce a value of $V_C = 10$ V is
    a) 2.2 kΩ.
    b) 2 kΩ.
    c) 1 kΩ.
    d) 500 Ω.

    Answer: b   Difficulty: 3

13. Refer to figure 5-2. If the transistor were replaced with a transistor whose $\beta_{dc} = 200$, the change that might occur is:
    a) V_C would increase to near 20 V
    b) V_C would decrease to near 0 V
    c) I_B would increase significantly
    d) V_C would change a small amount

    Answer: d   Difficulty: 3

14. Refer to figure 5-2. If $V_C = 10$ V, the minimum value of I_B that would cause saturation is:
    a) 10 mA
    b) 8 mA
    c) 80 µA
    d) 100 µA

    Answer: c   Difficulty: 3

15. Refer to figure 5-2. The purpose for R_1 and R_2 is
    a) to form an upper limit for the base voltage.
    b) to stabilize the operating point with negative feedback.
    c) to develop the output voltage.
    d) to maintain V_{BE} at 0.7 V.

    Answer: a   Difficulty: 3

16. Refer to figure 5-2. The purpose of R_C is
    a) to form an upper limit for the base voltage.
    b) to stabilize the operating point with negative feedback.
    c) to develop the output voltage.
    d) to maintain V_{BE} at 0.7 V.

    Answer: c   Difficulty: 2

17. Refer to figure 5-2. The purpose of R_E is
    a) to form an upper limit for the base voltage.
    b) to stabilize the operating point with negative feedback.
    c) to develop the output voltage.
    d) to maintain V_{BE} at 0.7 V.

    Answer: b Difficulty: 2

18. Two important easily measured values that determine if a transistor amplifier is operating correctly are:
    a) β_{dc} and I_B.
    b) I_C and V_C.
    c) V_C and V_{BE}.
    d) V_{BE} and I_E.

    Answer: c Difficulty: 2

19. Saturation and cutoff are operating conditions that are very useful when operating the transistor
    a) as a linear amplifier.
    b) as a switch.
    c) as a current amplifier.
    d) none of the above

    Answer: b Difficulty: 2

20. For linear operation, it is usual to set the Q-point so that
    a) $V_{CE} \partial V_{CC}$
    b) $V_{CE} \partial V_E$
    c) $V_{CE} \partial V_{CC}/4$
    d) $V_{CE} \partial V_{CC}/2$

    Answer: d Difficulty: 2

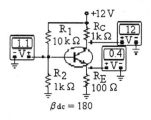
Figure 5-3 (a)

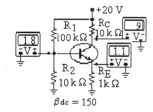
Figure 5-3 (b)

21. Refer to figure 5-3 (a). The most probable cause of trouble, if any, from these voltage measurements would be
    a) the base-emitter junction is open.
    b) R_E is open.
    c) a short from collector to emitter.
    d) no problems.

    Answer: b Difficulty: 3

Chapter 5: Transistor Bias Circuits

22. Refer to figure 5-3 (b). The most probable cause of trouble, if any, from these voltage measurements is
    a) the base-emitter junction is open.
    b) R_E is open.
    c) a short from collector to emitter.
    d) no problems.

    Answer: d Difficulty: 3

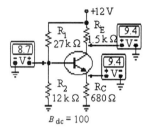

Figure 5-3 (c)

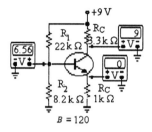

Figure 5-3 (d)

23. Refer to figure 5-3 (c). The most probable cause of trouble, if any, from these voltage measurements is
    a) the base-emitter junction is open.
    b) R_E is open.
    c) a short from collector to emitter.
    d) no problems.

    Answer: c Difficulty: 3

24. Refer to figure 5-3 (d). The most probable cause of trouble, if any, from these voltage measurements is
    a) the base-emitter junction is open.
    b) R_E is open.
    c) a short from collector to emitter.
    d) no problems.

    Answer: a Difficulty: 3

25. The most suitable biasing technique used is the:
    a) base-bias
    b) emitter-bias
    c) voltage divider-bias
    d) collector-bias

    Answer: c Difficulty: 2

Chapter 6: Small-Signal Bipolar Amplifiers

MULTIPLE CHOICE

1. A common-emitter amplifier has very high input impedance, high voltage gain, and high current gain.
   a) true
   b) false

   Answer: b Difficulty: 2

2. A high input impedance amplifier could be a Darlington pair.
   a) true
   b) false

   Answer: a Difficulty: 2

3. A common-collector amplifier is also known as an emitter follower.
   a) true
   b) false

   Answer: a Difficulty: 2

4. The total voltage gain, expressed as a ratio, of a multistage amplifier is the sum of the individual voltage gains.
   a) true
   b) false

   Answer: b Difficulty: 2

5. A common-base amplifier has a high current gain.
   a) true
   b) false

   Answer: b Difficulty: 2

6. A certain transistor has a dc emitter current of 25 mA. The value of r_e is
   a) 25 Ω.
   b) 2.5 Ω.
   c) 1.2 Ω.
   d) 1 Ω.

   Answer: d Difficulty: 2

Chapter 6: Small-Signal Bipolar Amplifiers

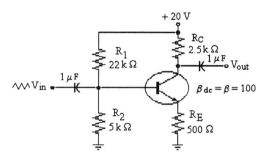

Figure 6-1

7. Refer to figure 6-1. The value of V_C is:
   a) 20 V
   b) 10 V
   c) 5 V
   d) 0 V

   Answer: c Difficulty: 2

8. Refer to figure 6-1. If an emitter bypass capacitor was added, the voltage gain
   a) would not change.
   b) would decrease.
   c) would increase.
   d) would decrease to zero.

   Answer: c Difficulty: 2

9. Refer to figure 6-1. If R_2 opened, V_{CE} would be
   a) 0 V.
   b) 20 V.
   c) 10 V.
   d) 4.8 V.

   Answer: a Difficulty: 3

10. Refer to figure 6-1. If R_2 opened, the value of I_C would be
    a) 6 mA.
    b) 6.67 mA.
    c) 8 mA.
    d) 10 mA.

    Answer: b Difficulty: 3

11. Refer to figure 6-1. If R_C opened, V_E would
    a) increase.
    b) decrease.
    c) remain the same.
    d) be undetermined

    Answer: b Difficulty: 2

12. Refer to figure 6-1. If the emitter-collector shorted, the voltage V_C would be
    a) 0 V.
    b) 20 V.
    c) 16.67 V.
    d) 3.33 V.

    Answer: d Difficulty: 2

13. Refer to figure 6-1. If the collector opened internally, the voltage on the collector would
    a) increase.
    b) decrease.
    c) remain the same.
    d) be undetrmined

    Answer: a Difficulty: 3

14. Refer to figure 6-1. If $V_E = 0$, the trouble might be that
    a) R_E is open.
    b) R_C is open.
    c) R_2 is open.
    d) R_1 is open.

    Answer: d Difficulty: 2

15. Refer to figure 6-1. If an emitter bypass capacitor was installed, the value of R_{in} would be
    a) 50 Ω.
    b) 175 Ω.
    c) 378 Ω.
    d) 500 Ω.

    Answer: c Difficulty: 2

16. Refer to figure 6-1. If an emitter bypass capacitor was installed, the new A_V would be
    a) 4.96.
    b) 125.
    c) 398.
    d) 600.

    Answer: d Difficulty: 2

Chapter 6: Small-Signal Bipolar Amplifiers

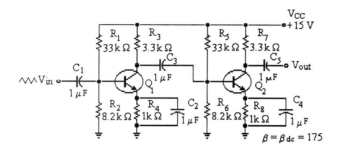

Figure 6-2

17. Refer to figure 6-2. If $A_{V1} = 75$ and $A_{V2} = 95$, A_{VT} would be:
    a) 75
    b) 95
    c) 1275
    d) 7125

    Answer: d Difficulty: 2

18. Refer to figure 6-2. When checking this amplifier, V_{out} was below normal. The trouble might be
    a) an open C_3.
    b) an open C_4.
    c) C_4 is shorted.
    d) C_1 is open.

    Answer: b Difficulty: 3

19. Refer to figure 6-2. If V_{B2} was higher than normal. The problem, if any, could be
    a) C_3 is shorted.
    b) R_3 is open.
    c) BE_1 is open.
    d) C_2 is open.

    Answer: a Difficulty: 3

20. Refer to figure 6-2. In servicing this amplifier V_{out} was found less than normal. The problem could be caused by
    a) an open C_3.
    b) an open C_2.
    c) an open base-emitter of Q_2.
    d) a shorted C_2.

    Answer: b Difficulty: 2

21. Refer to figure 6-2. The output signal from the first stage of this amplifier is 0 V. The trouble could be caused by
    a) an open C_4.
    b) an open C_2.
    c) an open base-emitter of Q_2.
    d) a shorted C_4.

    Answer: c Difficulty: 3

22. The best selection for a high input impedance amplifier is a:
    a) low gain common-emitter.
    b) common-base.
    c) common-collector.
    d) high gain common-emitter.

    Answer: c Difficulty: 2

23. The characteristic that is not of a common-base amplifier is:
    a) high input impedance
    b) current gain of 1
    c) medium voltage gain
    d) high output impedance

    Answer: a Difficulty: 2

24. The characteristic that is not of an emitter follower is:
    a) voltage gain of 1
    b) low input impedance
    c) low output impedance
    d) medium current gain

    Answer: b Difficulty: 2

25. The best choice for a very high power amplifier is a:
    a) common-collector.
    b) common-base.
    c) common-emitter.
    d) emitter-follower.

    Answer: c Difficulty: 2

Chapter 7: Power Amplifiers

MULTIPLE CHOICE

1. The class A amplifier is usually biased below cutoff.
   a) true
   b) false

   Answer: b Difficulty: 2

2. Darlington pair transistors are often used in power amplifiers because the input impedance is very low.
   a) 45°
   b) 90°
   c) 180°
   d) 360°

   Answer: b Difficulty: 2

3. A class B amplifier conducts _____ of the cycle.
   a) 45°
   b) 90°
   c) 180°
   d) 360°

   Answer: c Difficulty: 2

4. The class of amplifiers that is the most efficient and has the most distortion is class _____ amplifier
   a) A
   b) B
   c) C
   d) AB

   Answer: c Difficulty: 2

5. Push-pull amplifiers often use class _____ amplifiers.
   a) A
   b) B
   c) C
   d) AB

   Answer: b Difficulty: 2

6. If a class A amplifier has a voltage gain of 50 and a current gain of 75. The power gain would be
   a) 50.
   b) 75.
   c) 1500.
   d) 3750.

   Answer: d Difficulty: 2

7. If a class A amplifier has R_C = 4.7 kΩ and R_E = 1.5 kΩ and V_{CC} = 24 V, $I_{C(sat)}$ would be
   a) 5.1 mA.
   b) 16 mA.
   c) 3.87 mA.
   d) 0 mA.

   Answer: c Difficulty: 2

8. An application for an amplifier to operate in a linear mode is needed, the most likely choice would be a
   a) class A.
   b) class B.
   c) class C.
   d) class AB.

   Answer: a Difficulty: 2

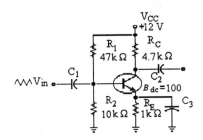

Figure 7-1

9. Refer to figure 7-1. If R_1 opened, and V_{in} at the base was large, V_{out} at the collector would
   a) increase.
   b) decrease.
   c) remain the same.
   d) distort.

   Answer: d Difficulty: 3

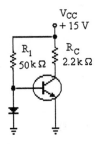

Figure 7-2

10. Refer to figure 7-2. If the diode opened, this amplifier would be operating as class
    a) A.
    b) B.
    c) C.
    d) AB.

    Answer: c Difficulty: 3

Chapter 7: Power Amplifiers

11. Refer to figure 7-2. The purpose of the diode is
    a) to bias the amplifier as class A.
    b) to bias the amplifier as class B.
    c) to bias the amplifier as class C.
    d) to bias the amplifier as class AB.

    Answer: b Difficulty: 2

12. A typical efficiency for a class A amplifier is about
    a) 25%.
    b) 50%.
    c) 75%.
    d) 100%.

    Answer: a Difficulty: 2

13. The amplifier with the most distortion would be a _____ amplifier
    a) class A.
    b) class B.
    c) class C.
    d) class AB.

    Answer: c Difficulty: 2

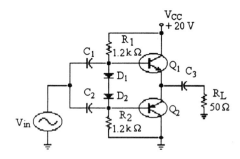

Figure 7-3

14. Refer to figure 7-3. The emitter voltage with respect to ground is
    a) 10.7 V.
    b) 9.3 V.
    c) 0 V.
    d) 10 V.

    Answer: d Difficulty: 2

15. Refer to figure 7-3. This amplifier only shows a positive alternation at the output. The possible trouble might be that
    a) C_3 is shorted.
    b) BE_1 is open.
    c) BE_2 is open.
    d) R_1 is open.

    Answer: c Difficulty: 3

16. Refer to figure 7-3. The dc voltage across R_L was measured at 10 V. A possible trouble, if any, might be
    a) C_1 is open.
    b) C_3 is shorted.
    c) R_1 is open.
    d) C_3 is open.

    Answer: b Difficulty: 3

17. Refer to figure 7-3. During the positive input alternation, Q_1 is _____ and Q_2 is _____.
    a) on, on
    b) on, off
    c) off, off
    d) off, on

    Answer: b Difficulty: 2

18. Refer to figure 7-3. The purpose for the diodes D_1 and D_2 is
    a) to apply equal signals to each transistor.
    b) to allow the correct bias voltages on the two bases.
    c) to maintain constant bias with temperature changes.
    d) all of the above

    Answer: d Difficulty: 3

19. Refer to figure 7-3. The two transistors are called ____ type
    a) same
    b) complementary
    c) npn
    d) pnp

    Answer: b Difficulty: 2

20. Refer to 7-3. This circuit is operating as a
    a) class A push-pull.
    b) class B push-pull.
    c) class C push-pull.
    d) class B.

    Answer: b Difficulty: 2

21. An application for a power amplifier to operate at radio frequencies is needed. The most likely choice would be a _____ amplifier.
    a) class A
    b) class B
    c) class C
    d) class AB

    Answer: c Difficulty: 2

Chapter 7:   Power Amplifiers

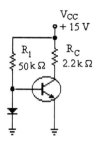

Figure 7-2

22. Refer to figure 7-2. The approximate voltages on the base, collector, and emitter, respectively, are
   a) 0.7 V, 6.8 V, 0 V.
   b) 0 V, 0 V, 0 V.
   c) 0.7 V, 15 V, 0 V.
   d) 0.7 V, 0 V, 15 V.

   Answer: c   Difficulty: 2

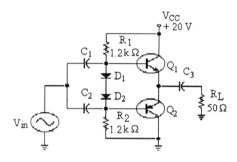

Figure 7-3

23. Refer to figure 7-3. If R_L shows a zero signal voltage on an oscilloscope, the problem might be
   a) C_3 is open.
   b) BE_1 is open.
   c) BE_2 is open.
   d) R_1 is open.

   Answer: a   Difficulty: 3

24. Refer to figure 7-3. If there was no output signal, and the measured dc voltage of Q_1 emitter was 0 V, the trouble might be
   a) D_1 is shorted.
   b) D_2 is shorted.
   c) R_1 is open.
   d) no trouble, everything is normal.

   Answer: c   Difficulty: 3

25. Refer to figure 7-3. Class AB amplifier is biased
    a) at cutoff.
    b) slightly above the center of the load line.
    c) slightly above cutoff.
    d) at the center of the load line.

    Answer: c Difficulty: 3

Chapter 8: Field-Effect Transistors and Biasing

MULTIPLE CHOICE

1. An FET has three terminals, source, drain, and gate.
   a) true
   b) false

   Answer: a Difficulty: 2

2. The JFET operates with a forward-biased gate-source pn junction.
   a) true
   b) false

   Answer: b Difficulty: 2

3. An E-MOSFET can be used as a switch.
   a) true
   b) false

   Answer: a Difficulty: 2

4. A D-MOFSET can operate with both positive and negative values of V_{GS}.
   a) true
   b) false

   Answer: a Difficulty: 2

5. Special care is required in handling a MOSFET.
   a) true
   b) false

   Answer: a Difficulty: 2

6. An n-channel JFET has a V_D = 8 V. V_{GS} = -5 V. The value of V_{DS} is
   a) 3 V.
   b) 8 V.
   c) -5 V.
   d) -3 V.

   Answer: a Difficulty: 2

7. Field effect transistors are also known as:
   a) one-charge carrier.
   b) two-charge carrier.
   c) three-charge carrier.
   d) none of the above

   Answer: a Difficulty: 2

8. The FET that has no physical channel is the:
   a) D MOSFET.
   b) E MOSFET.
   c) JFET.
   d) none of the above

   Answer: b Difficulty: 2

9. An FET that has no I$_{DSS}$ parameter is the:
   a) JFET
   b) DE MOSFET
   c) V MOSFET
   d) E MOSFET

   Answer: d Difficulty: 2

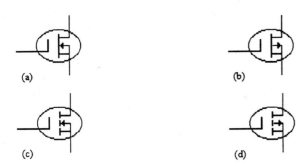

Figure 8-1

10. Refer to figure 8-1 (a). This symbol identifies
    a) a p-channel E MOSFET.
    b) an n-channel D MOSFET.
    c) a p-channel D MOSFET.
    d) an n-channel E MOSFET.

    Answer: b Difficulty: 2

11. Refer to figure 8-1 (b). This symbol identifies
    a) a p-channel E MOSFET.
    b) an n-channel D MOSFET.
    c) a p-channel D MOSFET.
    d) an n-channel E MOSFET.

    Answer: c Difficulty: 2

12. Refer to figure 8-1 (c). This symbol identifies
    a) a p-channel E MOSFET.
    b) an n-channel D MOSFET.
    c) a p-channel D MOSFET.
    d) an n-channel E MOSFET.

    Answer: d Difficulty: 2

13. Refer to figure 8-1 (d). This symbol identifies
    a) a p-channel E MOSFET.
    b) an n-channel D MOSFET.
    c) a p-channel D MOSFET.
    d) an n-channel E MOSFET.

    Answer: a Difficulty: 2

Chapter 8:   Field-Effect Transistors and Biasing

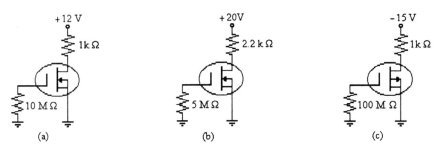

Figure 8-2

14. Refer to figure 8-2 (a). If I_D = 4 mA, the value of V_{DS} is:
    a) 12 V
    b) 8 V
    c) 4 V
    d) 0 V

    Answer: b   Difficulty: 2

15. Refer to figure 8-2 (b). If I_D = 4 mA, the value of V_{GS} is:
    a) 20 V
    b) 11.2 V
    c) 8.8 V
    d) 0 V

    Answer: d   Difficulty: 2

16. Refer to figure 8-2 (c). If I_D = 4 mA, the value of V_{DS} is:
    a) -11 V
    b) -14 V
    c) -15 V
    d) 0 V

    Answer: a   Difficulty: 3

17. A JFET manufacturers data sheet specifies $V_{GS(off)}$ = -8 V and I_{DSS} = 6 mA. The value of I_D when V_{GS} = -4 V would be:
    a) 6 ma
    b) 1.25 mA
    c) 1.5 mA
    d) 4 mA

    Answer: c   Difficulty: 3

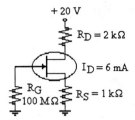

Figure 8-3

18. Refer to figure 8-3. The value of the voltage drop across R_D is:
    a) 20 V
    b) 12 V
    c) 6 V
    d) 3 V

    Answer: b Difficulty: 2

19. Refer to figure 8-3. This amplifier is biased for
    a) linear operation.
    b) pinch-off operation.
    c) saturation.
    d) operation as a switch.

    Answer: a Difficulty: 2

20. Refer to figure 8-3. In this circuit, V_{GS} is biased correctly for proper operation. This means that V_{GS} is
    a) positive.
    b) negative.
    c) either negative or positive.
    d) 0 V.

    Answer: b Difficulty: 3

21. Refer to figure 8-3. Calculate the value of V_D.
    a) 20 V
    b) 8 V
    c) 6 V
    d) 2 V

    Answer: b Difficulty: 2

22. Refer to figure 8-3. Calculate the value of V_{DS}.
    a) 0 V
    b) 2 V
    c) 4 V
    d) -2 V

    Answer: b Difficulty: 2

Chapter 8: Field-Effect Transistors and Biasing

23. For proper operation, an n-channel E-MOSFET should be biased so that V_{GS} is
    a) either positive or negative.
    b) negative.
    c) positive.
    d) -4 V.

    Answer: c Difficulty: 2

24. A good application for a V-MOSFET would be
    a) as a power amplifier.
    b) as a low power amplifier.
    c) as a low input impedance device.
    d) as a substitute for a diode.

    Answer: a Difficulty: 2

25. A V MOSFET device operates in
    a) the depletion mode.
    b) the enhancement mode.
    c) a JFET mode.
    d) in either enhancement or depletion mode.

    Answer: b Difficulty: 2

Chapter 9: Small-Signal FET Amplifiers

MULTIPLE CHOICE

1. The formula for the voltage gain of a common-source amplifier is R_D/g_m.
   a) true
   b) false

   Answer: b Difficulty: 2

2. Load resistance added to the output of an amplifier increases the voltage gain.
   a) true
   b) false

   Answer: b Difficulty: 2

3. The addition of a source bypass capacitor will increase the voltage gain.
   a) true
   b) false

   Answer: a Difficulty: 2

4. In an amplifier using a JFET, the gate current is 0.
   a) true
   b) false

   Answer: a Difficulty: 2

5. A common-source amplifier has a _____ phase shift between the input and the output.
   a) 45°
   b) 90°
   c) 180°
   d) 360°

   Answer: c Difficulty: 2

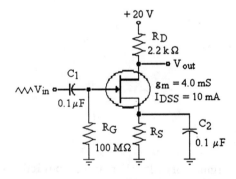

Figure 9-1

6. Refer to figure 9-1. Assuming midpoint biasing, if V_{GS} = -4 V, the value of R_S that will provide this value is:
   a) 600 Ω
   b) 1.2 kΩ
   c) 80 Ω
   d) 800 Ω

   Answer: d Difficulty: 2

Chapter 9: Small-Signal FET Amplifiers

7. Refer to figure 9-1. If V_{in} = 50 mV p-p, the output voltage is:
   a) 50 mV p-p
   b) 4.4 V p-p
   c) 0.044 V p-p
   d) 440 mV p-p

   Answer: d Difficulty: 3

8. Refer to figure 9-1. If the measured value of V_{out} was below normal, the problem might be one of the following
   a) R_D is open.
   b) C_2 is shorted.
   c) C_2 is open.
   d) V_{in} has increased.

   Answer: c Difficulty: 3

9. Refer to figure 9-1. If V_{in} = 1 V p-p, the output voltage V_{out} would be
   a) undistorted.
   b) clipped on the negative peaks.
   c) clipped on the positive peaks.
   d) 0 V.

   Answer: a Difficulty: 2

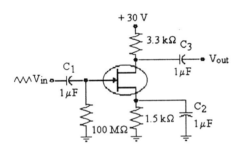

Figure 9-2

10. Refer to figure 9-2. If I_D = 6 mA, the value of V_{GS} is:
    a) 9 V
    b) -9 V
    c) -19.8 V
    d) -10.2 V

    Answer: b Difficulty: 2

11. Refer to figure 9-2. If g_m = 6500 µS and an input signal of 125 mV p-p is applied to the gate, the output voltage V_{out} is:
    a) 2.68 V p-p
    b) 0.8125 V p-p
    c) 1.625 V p-p
    d) 6.25 V p-p

    Answer: a Difficulty: 2

12. Refer to figure 9-2. If C_2 opened, the output signal would
    a) increase in value.
    b) decrease in value.
    c) not change.
    d) decrease and then increase.

    Answer: b Difficulty: 2

13. Refer to figure 9-2. If I_D = 4 mA, I_{DSS} = 16 mA, and $V_{GS}(off)$ = -8 V, V_{DS} would be:
    a) 19.2 V
    b) -6 V
    c) 10.8 V
    d) 30 V

    Answer: c Difficulty: 2

14. Refer to figure 9-2. If g_m = 4000 µS and a signal of 75 mV rms is applied to the gate, the p-p output voltage is:
    a) 990 mV
    b) 1.13 V p-p
    c) 2.8 V p-p
    d) 990 V p-p

    Answer: c Difficulty: 3

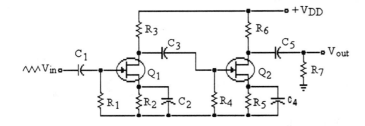

Figure 9-3

15. Refer to figure 9-3. If C_4 opened, the signal voltage at the drain of Q_2 would
    a) increase.
    b) decrease.
    c) remain the same.
    d) distort.

    Answer: b Difficulty: 2

16. Refer to figure 9-3. If R_7 were to increase in value, V_{out} would
    a) increase.
    b) decrease.
    c) remain the same.
    d) distort.

    Answer: a Difficulty: 3

Chapter 9:   Small-Signal FET Amplifiers

17. Refer to figure 9-3. If C_2 opened, V_{out} would
    a) increase.
    b) decrease.
    c) remain the same.
    d) distort.

    Answer: b Difficulty: 2

18. Refer to figure 9-3. If R_1 opened, V_{out} would
    a) increase.
    b) decrease.
    c) remain the same.
    d) distort.

    Answer: c Difficulty: 3

19. Refer to figure 9-3. If C_3 opened, V_{out} would
    a) increase.
    b) decrease.
    c) remain the same.
    d) distort.

    Answer: b Difficulty: 2

20. Refer to figure 9-3. If R_3 opened, V_{out} would
    a) increase.
    b) decrease.
    c) remain the same.
    d) distort.

    Answer: b Difficulty: 2

21. Refer to figure 9-3. If R_5 opened, V_{out} would
    a) increase.
    b) decrease.
    c) remain the same.
    d) distort.

    Answer: b Difficulty: 2

22. Refer to figure 9-3. If the source-drain of Q_2 shorted, the output signal from Q_1 would
    a) increase.
    b) decrease.
    c) remain the same.
    d) distort.

    Answer: c Difficulty: 3

23. Refer to figure 9-3. If $A_{V1} = 18$ and $A_{Vt} = 288$, the value of A_{V2} would be
    a) 5184.
    b) 18.
    c) 49.18.
    d) 16.

    Answer: d Difficulty: 2

24. Refer to figure 9-3. If C_4 opened, the signal voltage at the drain of Q_1 would
    a) increase.
    b) decrease.
    c) remain the same.
    d) distort.

    Answer: c Difficulty: 3

25. Refer to figure 9-3. If V_{in} was increased in amplitude a little, the signal voltage at the source of Q_2 would
    a) increase.
    b) decrease.
    c) remain the same.
    d) distort.

    Answer: c Difficulty: 3

Chapter 10: Amplifier Frequency Response

MULTIPLE CHOICE

1. Coupling and bypass capacitors limit the low-frequency response of an amplifier.
   a) true
   b) false

   Answer: a   Difficulty: 2

2. High-frequency response is limited by the internal capacitances of a transistor.
   a) true
   b) false

   Answer: a   Difficulty: 2

3. At the cutoff frequency, the output is down by 3 dB.
   a) true
   b) false

   Answer: a   Difficulty: 2

4. An octave of frequency change is a ten-times change.
   a) true
   b) false

   Answer: b   Difficulty: 2

5. The bandwidth is the sum of the two cutoff frequencies.
   a) true
   b) false

   Answer: b   Difficulty: 2

6. If an amplifier has an output voltage of 12.7 V p-p at the midpoint of the frequency range, the output voltage at the cutoff frequency would be
   a) 12.7 V p-p.
   b) 4.49 V p-p.
   c) 5.89 V p-p.
   d) 8.98 V p-p.

   Answer: d   Difficulty: 2

7. If an amplifier has an input signal voltage of 0.37 mV and an output voltage of 16.8 V, the voltage gain in dB would be
   a) 45.4 dB.
   b) 33.1 dB.
   c) 93.1 dB.
   d) 46.6 dB.

   Answer: c   Difficulty: 2

8. If an amplifier has a voltage gain of 54 dB, and an input signal of 22 mV, the output signal voltage would be
   a) 11 V.
   b) 55.3 V.
   c) 2.45 V.
   d) 24.5 V.

   Answer: a   Difficulty: 3

9. If an amplifier has a bandwidth of 47 kHz and a higher cutoff frequency of 104 kHz, the lower cutoff frequency would be
   a) 151 kHz.
   b) 57 kHz.
   c) 47 kHz.
   d) 104 kHz.

   Answer: b   Difficulty: 2

10. If an amplifier has an R_{in} = 950 Ω, and a coupling capacitor of value 3.3 ^{9}F, the approximate cutoff frequency would be
    a) 508 Hz.
    b) 50.8 kHz.
    c) 50.8 Hz.
    d) 5.08 Hz.

    Answer: c   Difficulty: 2

11. The fc of a certain RC network that has values of R = 470 Ω and C = 0.005 ^{9}F is
    a) 67.8 kHz.
    b) 425 kHz.
    c) 213 kHz.
    d) 12 kHz.

    Answer: a   Difficulty: 2

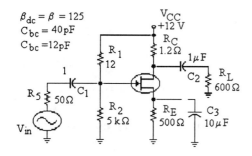

Figure 10-1

12. Refer to figure 10-1. Low frequency response is affected by
    a) R_C.
    b) C_{BE}.
    c) C_3.
    d) all of these.

    Answer: c   Difficulty: 2

Chapter 10: Amplifier Frequency Response

13. Refer to figure 10-1. High frequency response is affected by
    a) R_C.
    b) C_{BE}.
    c) C_3.
    d) all of these.

    Answer: b Difficulty: 2

14. Refer to figure 10-1. If the output voltage at the upper cutoff frequency was 7.19 V p-p, the output voltage that would be expected at the lower cutoff frequency is
    a) 5.08 V p-p.
    b) 7.19 V p-p.
    c) 10.17 V p-p.
    d) 2.11 V p-p.

    Answer: b Difficulty: 3

15. Refer to figure 10-1. The output voltage at f_{cl} = 22 mV. V_{out} at the midpoint frequency would be
    a) 22 mV.
    b) 17 mV.
    c) 31.1 mV.
    d) not enough data

    Answer: a Difficulty: 2

16. Refer to figure 10-1. The bandwidth of this amplifier is
    a) the sum of the upper and lower frequencies.
    b) the upper frequency divided by 0.707.
    c) the difference between the upper and lower frequencies.
    d) the lower frequency times 0.707.

    Answer: c Difficulty: 3

17. Refer to figure 10-1. The capacitance C_{bc} affects
    a) high-frequency response.
    b) low-frequency response.
    c) mid-range response.
    d) nothing.

    Answer: a Difficulty: 2

18. Refer to figure 10-1. A definite reduction in the output voltage is noticed. The trouble is
    a) C_3 has shorted.
    b) C_1 has opened.
    c) C_2 has opened.
    d) C_3 has opened.

    Answer: d Difficulty: 3

19. Refer to figure 10-1. The reduction in the output at very high frequencies is due to
    a) the negative feedback effect of R_E.
    b) the negative feedback effect of C_{bc}.
    c) the positive feedback effect of V_{BE}.
    d) R_L decreasing in value.

    Answer: b Difficulty: 2

20. Refer to figure 10-1. If the output voltage at f_{c1} = 12 mV, the output voltage at the midpoint frequency would be
    a) 12 mV.
    b) 12 mV p-p.
    c) 16.97 mV.
    d) 8.48 mV.

    Answer: c Difficulty: 2

21. Refer to figure 10-1. If R_L increases in value, the output voltage would
    a) increase.
    b) decrease.
    c) remain the same.
    d) cannot be determined.

    Answer: a Difficulty: 2

22. If an RC network has a roll-off of 40 dB per decade, the total attenuation between the output voltage in the mid-range of the pass-band compared to a frequency of 10f would be
    a) -3 dB.
    b) -20 dB.
    c) -23 dB.
    d) -43 dB.

    Answer: d Difficulty: 2

23. The cutoff frequency of a low pass filter occurs at
    a) -5 dB.
    b) -3 dB.
    c) +3 dB.
    d) -20 dB.

    Answer: b Difficulty: 2

24. A high pass filter may be used to
    a) pass low frequencies.
    b) pass high frequencies.
    c) pass frequencies between low and high.
    d) a or b

    Answer: b Difficulty: 2

Chapter 10: Amplifier Frequency Response

25. A roll-off of 20 dB per decade is equivalent to a roll-off of _____ per octave.
    a) 3 dB.
    b) 13 dB.
    c) 12 dB.
    d) 6 dB.

    Answer: d Difficulty: 2

Chapter 11: Thyristors and Other Devices

MULTIPLE CHOICE

1. The SCR is a device that can be triggered on by a pulse applied to the gate.
   a) true
   b) false

   Answer: a Difficulty: 2

2. A device that conducts current in only one direction is called a diac.
   a) true
   b) false

   Answer: b Difficulty: 2

3. A device that can be turned on or off by a gate pulse is called an SCS.
   a) true
   b) false

   Answer: a Difficulty: 2

4. A triac can be turned on by a pulse at the gate.
   a) true
   b) false

   Answer: a Difficulty: 2

5. A UJT is turned on by a negative pulse at the base.
   a) true
   b) false

   Answer: b Difficulty: 2

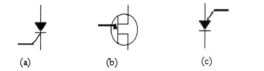

Figure 11-1

6. Refer to figure 11-1 (a). The symbol is for
   a) a triac.
   b) a UJT.
   c) a diac.
   d) a PUT.
   e) an SCR.

   Answer: e Difficulty: 2

Chapter 11: Thyristors and Other Devices

7. Refer to figure 11-1 (b). The symbol is for
   a) a triac.
   b) a UJT.
   c) a diac.
   d) a PUT.
   e) an SCR.

   Answer: b Difficulty: 2

8. Refer to figure 11-1 (c). The symbol is for
   a) a triac.
   b) a UJT.
   c) a diac.
   d) a PUT.
   e) an SCR.

   Answer: d Difficulty: 2

9. Refer to figure 11-1 (d). The symbol is for
   a) a triac.
   b) a UJT.
   c) a diac.
   d) a PUT.
   e) an SCR.

   Answer: c Difficulty: 2

10. Refer to figure 11-1 (e). The symbol is for
    a) a triac.
    b) a UJT.
    c) a diac.
    d) a PUT.
    e) an SCR.

    Answer: a Difficulty: 2

11. A good choice to trigger atriac would be:
    a) a UJT.
    b) an SCR.
    c) a diac.
    d) a Schockley diode.

    Answer: c Difficulty: 2

12. The best choice to operate a small variable speed ac motor is a/an:
    a) triac
    b) diac
    c) SCR
    d) UJT
    e) PUT

    Answer: a Difficulty: 2

13. The best choice to shut down a dc power supply in case of a high voltage condition is a(an)
   a) triac
   b) diac
   c) SCR
   d) UJT
   e) PUT

   Answer: c Difficulty: 3

14. A good choice to turn on a device at a particular voltage would be a/an:
   a) triac
   b) diac
   c) SCR
   d) UJT
   e) PUT

   Answer: e Difficulty: 2

15. The most likely device to be used in an oscillator is a/an
   a) triac
   b) diac
   c) SCR
   d) UJT
   e) PUT

   Answer: d Difficulty: 2

16. A typical use for an optical coupler might be
   a) to connect telephone lines to electronic equipment.
   b) to transfer signals to a fiber optic cable.
   c) to isolate one circuit from another.
   d) all of these.

   Answer: d Difficulty: 2

17. An SCS has a unique ability to
   a) be turned on or off with a pulse.
   b) be turned off only with a pulse.
   c) control a PUT.
   d) all of these

   Answer: a Difficulty: 2

18. If an SCR starts to conduct when a gate current is established, what will occur when the gate circuit is interrupted?
   a) The SCR will turn off.
   b) The SCR current will increase.
   c) The SCR will continue to conduct.
   d) The SCR gate current will increase.

   Answer: c Difficulty: 3

Chapter 11: Thyristors and Other Devices

19. An SCR will turn off when the voltage across it is
    a) increased to the supply voltage.
    b) decreased to near 0 V.
    c) timed out.
    d) decreased by the value of the gate voltage.

    Answer: b Difficulty: 2

20. A triac is used on ac because
    a) it conducts on both alternations.
    b) it is turned off when the ac voltage reaches zero.
    c) it can deliver more power to the load in a cycle.
    d) all of these

    Answer: d Difficulty: 2

21. A device is needed to trigger an SCR. A good one to use might be
    a) an SCR.
    b) a UJT.
    c) a Schockley diode.
    d) a PUT.

    Answer: b Difficulty: 3

22. The best device to be used to control a dc motor is
    a) triac.
    b) PUT.
    c) SCR.
    d) diac.

    Answer: c Difficulty: 2

23. An SCR is used to control the speed of a dc motor by _____ the _____ of the pulse delivered to the motor.
    a) varying, width
    b) increasing, amplitude
    c) decreasing, gate width
    d) none of these

    Answer: a Difficulty: 3

24. Which of the following applications would be likely to use a diac?
    a) a battery charger
    b) an oscillator
    c) a high frequency amplifier
    d) a lamp dimmer

    Answer: d Difficulty: 2

25. A light dimmer circuit using an SCR is tested and IG = 0mA was found. The light is still on. The trouble might be one of the following.
   a) The SCR is open.
   b) The switch is faulty.
   c) The gate circuit is shorted.
   d) This is normal, nothing is wrong.

   Answer: d Difficulty: 3

Chapter 12: Operational Amplifiers

MULTIPLE CHOICE

1. A good op-amp has high voltage gain, low output impedance, and high input impedance.
   a) true
   b) false

   Answer: a Difficulty: 2

2. An inverting amplifier has an input resistance equal to the input resistor.
   a) true
   b) false

   Answer: a Difficulty: 2

3. CMRR is the measure of an op-amps voltage gain for an inverting amplifier.
   a) true
   b) false

   Answer: b Difficulty: 2

4. All op-amp configurations must use negative feedback.
   a) true
   b) false

   Answer: b Difficulty: 2

5. A voltage follower has a very high input impedance, and is often used as a high voltage gain amplifier.
   a) true
   b) false

   Answer: b Difficulty: 2

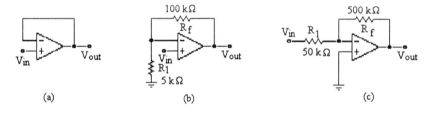

Figure 12-1

6. Refer to figure 12-1. Which circuit is the inverting amplifier?
   a) a
   b) b
   c) c
   d) none of the above

   Answer: c Difficulty: 2

7. Refer to figure 12-1. Which circuit is a voltage follower?
   a) a
   b) b
   c) c
   d) none of the above

   Answer: a Difficulty: 2

8. Refer to figure 12-1. Which circuit is the non-inverting amplifier?
   a) a
   b) b
   c) c
   d) none of the above

   Answer: b Difficulty: 2

9. Refer to figure 12-1. Which circuit has a voltage gain of 1?
   a) a
   b) b
   c) c
   d) none of the above

   Answer: a Difficulty: 2

10. See figure 12-1. Which circuit has an input impedance of about 5 kΩ?
    a) a
    b) b
    c) c
    d) none of the above

    Answer: d Difficulty: 3

11. Refer to figure 12-1. Which circuit has a voltage gain of 10?
    a) a
    b) b
    c) c
    d) none of the above

    Answer: c Difficulty: 2

12. Refer to figure 12-1. Which circuit has a voltage gain of 20?
    a) a
    b) b
    c) c
    d) none of the above

    Answer: d Difficulty: 2

13. Refer to figure 12-1 (a). If this circuit has a V_{in} = 12 V p-p, the value of V_{out} would be
    a) 20 V.
    b) -20 V.
    c) 8.48 V p-p.
    d) 12 V p-p.

    Answer: d Difficulty: 2

Chapter 12: Operational Amplifiers

14. Refer to figure 12-1 (b). If this circuit has a $V_{in} = 0.7$, V_{out} would be
    a) 14.7 V.
    b) -14.7 V.
    c) 14 V.
    d) 0 V.

    Answer: a Difficulty: 2

15. Refer to figure 12-1 (c). $V_{in} = -6$ V. The value of V_{out} is
    a) 60 V.
    b) -60 V.
    c) about -16 V.
    d) about 16 V.

    Answer: a Difficulty: 2

16. See figure 12-1. If these three circuits were connected as a multiple-stage amplifier, the total voltage gain would be
    a) 1.
    b) 10.
    c) 21.
    d) 210.

    Answer: d Difficulty: 2

17. Refer to figure 12-1 (c). If R_f is changed to 1 MΩ, the new Acl would be:
    a) 20
    b) -20
    c) 21
    d) -21

    Answer: b Difficulty: 2

18. Refer to figure 12-1 (c). If an amplifier with an input impedance of 12 kΩ and the same voltage gain is needed, the new value of R_f would be _____ and the new value of R_F would be _____.
    a) 10 kΩ, 100 kΩ
    b) 13.3 kΩ, 120 kΩ
    c) 12 kΩ, 108 kΩ
    d) 12 kΩ, 120 kΩ

    Answer: d Difficulty: 2

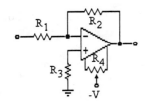

Figure 12-2

19. Refer to figure 12-2. This op-amp has a slew rate of 1.33 V/μs. How long would it take to change the output voltage from -12 V to +12 V?
   a) 18 μs
   b) 16 μs
   c) -18 μs
   d) 48 μs

   Answer: a Difficulty: 2

20. Refer to figure 12-2. Which components are used to set input impedance and voltage gain?
   a) R_4
   b) R_3
   c) R_1 and R_2
   d) R_3 and R_4

   Answer: c Difficulty: 2

21. Refer to figure 12-2. Which components are used for offset voltage compensation?
   a) R_4
   b) R_3
   c) R_1 and R_2
   d) R_2

   Answer: a Difficulty: 3

22. Refer to figure 12-2. Which components are used for bias current compensation?
   a) R_4
   b) R_3
   c) R_1 and R_2
   d) R_2

   Answer: b Difficulty: 2

23. Refer to figure 12-2. The purpose of R_1 and R_2 is
   a) for bias current compensation.
   b) for input offset voltage compensation.
   c) to set input impedance only.
   d) to set input impedance and voltage gain.

   Answer: d Difficulty: 2

Chapter 12: Operational Amplifiers

24. It takes an op-amp 22 μs to change its output from -15 V to +15 V. The slew rate for this amplifier is
    a) 1.36 V/μs.
    b) 0.68 V/μs.
    c) -0.68 V/μs.
    d) -1.36 V/μs.

    Answer: a Difficulty: 2

25. A voltage follower amplifier comes to you for service. You find the voltage gain to be 5.5 and the input impedance is 22 kΩ. The probable fault in this amplifier is, if any,
    a) the gain is too low for this type of amplifier.
    b) the input impedance is too high for this amplifier.
    c) nothing is wrong. The trouble must be somewhere else.
    d) cannot be determined

    Answer: d Difficulty: 3

Chapter 13: Op-Amp Frequency Response, Stability, and Compensation

MULTIPLE CHOICE

1. The open-loop gain of an op-amp is the voltage gain of a voltage follower.
   a) true
   b) false

   Answer: b Difficulty: 2

2. Negative feedback is when a resistor is placed in the feedback loop from the output to the inverting input of an op-amp.
   a) true
   b) false

   Answer: a Difficulty: 2

3. Op-amps have a large open-loop gain.
   a) true
   b) false

   Answer: a Difficulty: 2

4. Negative feedback applied to an op-amp will increase the bandwidth and decrease the voltage gain.
   a) true
   b) false

   Answer: a Difficulty: 2

5. For an op-amp to operate at high frequencies, it must have a low slew rate.
   a) true
   b) false

   Answer: b Difficulty: 2

6. A certain op-amp has a cutoff frequency of 550 Hz and a midrange voltage gain of 150,000. The open-loop gain at 300 Hz is
   a) 131.7.
   b) 1,317.
   c) 13,170.
   d) 131,700.

   Answer: d Difficulty: 2

7. An op-amp has a midrange voltage gain of 95,000 and a cutoff frequency of 150 Hz. The open-loop gain at 1.5 kHz is
   a) 94528.
   b) 90579.
   c) 89678.
   d) 87371.

   Answer: a Difficulty: 2

Chapter 13: Op-Amp Frequency Response, Stability, and Compensation

8. An RC network has an R = 6.8 kΩ and C = 0.002 μF. The cutoff frequency fc is
   a) 42.7 kHz.
   b) 11.7 MHz.
   c) 11.7 kHz.
   d) 5.85 kHz.

   Answer: c   Difficulty: 2

9. An RC network that has an f_c = 31.847 kHz is desired with a resistor value of 500 kΩ. What value of capacitor should be used?
   a) 100 μF
   b) 4.7 pF
   c) 100 pF
   d) 10 pF

   Answer: d   Difficulty: 3

10. An op-amp has an open-loop gain of 225,000. The gain in dB is:
    a) 53.5 dB
    b) 107 dB
    c) 200 dB
    d) 225,000 dB

    Answer: b   Difficulty: 2

11. A certain op-amp has a mid-range open-loop gain of 150 dB. The addition of negative feedback reduces this gain by 104 dB. The closed-loop voltage gain is
    a) 46 dB.
    b) 104 dB.
    c) 254 dB.
    d) 150 dB.

    Answer: a   Difficulty: 2

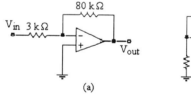 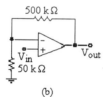

Figure 13-1

12. Refer to figure 13-1. The circuit that has a voltage gain of 1 is
    a) a
    b) b
    c) c
    d) none of these

    Answer: c   Difficulty: 2

13. Refer to figure 13-1. The circuit that has a midrange voltage gain of 11 is
    a) a
    b) b
    c) c
    d) none of these

    Answer: b Difficulty: 2

14. Refer to figure 13-1. The circuit that has a midrange voltage gain of 27.72 is
    a) a
    b) b
    c) c
    d) none of these

    Answer: d Difficulty: 2

15. Refer to figure 13-1 (b). The op-amp has a unity-gain bandwidth of 420 kHz. The bandwidth of the circuit is
    a) 15.75 kHz.
    b) 1.635 kHz.
    c) 1.575 kHz.
    d) none of these

    Answer: d Difficulty: 3

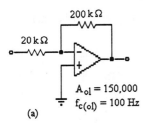 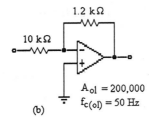

Figure 13-2

16. Refer to figure 13-2 (b). The circuit's bandwidth is:
    a) 83.3 HZ
    b) 83.3 KHZ
    c) 8.33 MHZ
    d) 83.3 MHZ

    Answer: b Difficulty: 2

17. Refer to figure 13-2 (a). The circuit's bandwidth is:
    a) 1.5 KHZ
    b) 15 KHZ
    c) 1.5 MHZ
    d) 15 MHZ

    Answer: c Difficulty: 2

Chapter 13: Op-Amp Frequency Response, Stability, and Compensation

18. Refer to figure 13-2 (a). $V_{in} = 0.5$ V. If the feedback resistor opens, V_{out} will
    a) increase to V_{sat}.
    b) decrease to $-V_{sat}$.
    c) remain the same.
    d) go to 0V.

    Answer: b Difficulty: 3

19. Refer to figure 13-2 (b). If the 10 kΩ resistor opens, the output voltage will
    a) increase to V_{sat}.
    b) decrease to $-V_{sat}$.
    c) decrease to V_{in}.
    d) none of these

    Answer: d Difficulty: 3

20. To increase the bandwidth of an op-amp and decrease the voltage gain, the following should be done.
    a) add positive feedback to the circuit.
    b) add frequency compensation.
    c) add phase-lag compensation.
    d) add negative feedback.

    Answer: d Difficulty: 2

21. If an amplifier has an upper critical frequency of 105 KHz and a lower critical frequency of 25 kHz. Its BW is
    a) 130 kHz.
    b) 80 kHz.
    c) 105 kHz.
    d) 25 kHz.

    Answer: b Difficulty: 2

22. The amplifier is stable when the closed-loop gain of an op amp intersects the open-loop response curve on a
    a) -20 dB/decade slope.
    b) 20 dB/decade slope.
    c) -6 dB/octave slope.
    d) a or c

    Answer: d Difficulty: 2

23. Compensation to an op-amp _____ bandwidth and _____ slew rate.
    a) reduces, increases
    b) increases, reduces
    c) reduces, reduces
    d) increases, increases

    Answer: a Difficulty: 3

24. The process of modifying the roll-off rate of an amplifier to ensure stability is
    a) roll-off.
    b) compensation.
    c) feedforward.
    d) none of the above

    Answer: a Difficulty: 2

25. Negative feedback added to an op-amp _____ the bandwidth and _____ the gain.
    a) increases, increases
    b) increases, decreases
    c) decreases, decreases
    d) decreases, increases

    Answer: b Difficulty: 3

Chapter 14: Basic Op-Amp Circuits

MULTIPLE CHOICE

1. An op-amp comparator has an output dependent upon the polarities of the two inputs.
   a) true
   b) false

   Answer: a   Difficulty: 2

2. The output voltage of a summing amplifier is proportional to the product of the input voltages.
   a) true
   b) false

   Answer: b   Difficulty: 2

3. Integration is a mathematical process for determining the area under a curve.
   a) true
   b) false

   Answer: a   Difficulty: 2

4. A square wave input to an op-amp integrator will produce a sine wave output.
   a) true
   b) false

   Answer: b   Difficulty: 2

5. Bounding allows the op-amp to have unlimited output voltage.
   a) true
   b) false

   Answer: b   Difficulty: 2

6. An op-amp has an open-loop gain of 100,000. V_{sat} = +/-12 V. A differential signal voltage of 150 µV p-p is applied between the inputs. What is the output voltage?
   a) 12 V
   b) -12 V
   c) 12 V p-p
   d) 24 V p-p

   Answer: d   Difficulty: 2

7. A summing amplifier can
   a) add dc voltages.
   b) add ac voltages.
   c) add dc to ac voltages.
   d) all of these

   Answer: d   Difficulty: 2

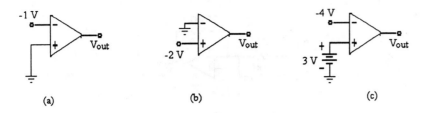

Figure 14-1

8. Refer to figure 14-1 (a). If V_{CC} = 15 V, the approximate output voltage is
   a) 1 V.
   b) -1 V.
   c) 13 V.
   d) -13 V.

   Answer: c Difficulty: 2

9. Refer to figure 14-1 (b). If V_{sat} = +/-12 V, the approximate output voltage is
   a) 12 V.
   b) -12 V.
   c) 2 V.
   d) -2 V.

   Answer: b Difficulty: 2

10. Refer to figure 14-1 (c). If V_{sat} = +/-10 V, the approximate value of V_{OUT} is
    a) -1 V.
    b) 1 V.
    c) -6 V.
    d) none of the above

    Answer: a Difficulty: 2

11. Refer to figure 14-1 (c). With the inputs shown, the output voltage would be
    a) 7 V.
    b) -7 V.
    c) $+V_{sat}$.
    d) $-V_{sat}$.

    Answer: c Difficulty: 2

Chapter 14: Basic Op-Amp Circuits

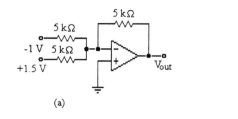
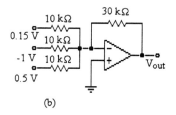

Figure 14-2

12. Refer to figure 14-2 (a). If a solder splash shorted the two ends of the feedback resistor to each other, the output voltage would be
    a) 0.5 V.
    b) -0.5 V.
    c) 0 V.
    d) $-V_{sat}$.

    Answer: c Difficulty: 3

13. Refer to figure 14-2 (b). A voltmeter placed from the inverting input to ground would read
    a) -0.925 V.
    b) -2.775 V.
    c) 2.775 V.
    d) ≈ 0 V.

    Answer: d Difficulty: 3

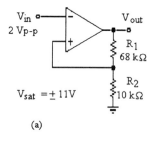
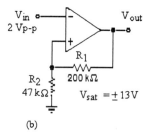

Figure 14-3

14. Refer to figure 14-3 (a). This circuit is known as
    a) a multivibrator.
    b) a zero level detector.
    c) a non-zero level detector.
    d) a non-inverting amplifier.

    Answer: c Difficulty: 2

15. Refer to figure 14-3 (b). This type of circuit will usually have
    a) a square wave output if the input is a sine wave.
    b) a triangle wave output.
    c) a ramp output for a square wave input.
    d) none of these

    Answer: a Difficulty: 2

16. Refer to figure 14-3 (b). The output voltage with the inputs as shown is
    a) $+V_{sat}$.
    b) $-V_{sat}$.
    c) 26 V_{p-p}.
    d) 17.06 V_{p-p}.

    Answer: c Difficulty: 3

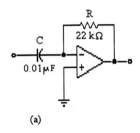

Figure 14-4

17. See figure 14-4. This circuit is known as
    a) a non-inverting amplifier.
    b) an integrator.
    c) a differentiator.
    d) a summing amplifier.

    Answer: b Difficulty: 2

18. Refer to figure 14-4. Which of these circuits is known as a differentiator?
    a) A
    b) B
    c) none of these

    Answer: a Difficulty: 2

19. Refer to figure 14-4 (b). A square wave input is applied to this amplifier. The output voltage is most likely to be
    a) a square wave.
    b) a triangle wave.
    c) a sine wave.
    d) no output.

    Answer: b Difficulty: 2

20. A Schmitt trigger is:
    a) a comparator with hysteresis.
    b) a comparator with one trigger point.
    c) a comparator with two trigger points.
    d) a and c

    Answer: d Difficulty: 2

Chapter 14: Basic Op-Amp Circuits

21. An op-amp has an open-loop gain of 90,000. $V_{sat} = +/-13$ V. A differential voltage of 0.1 V_{p-p} is applied between the inputs. The output voltage is
    a) 13 V.
    b) -13 V.
    c) 13 V_{p-p}.
    d) 26 V_{p-p}.

    Answer: d Difficulty: 3

22. The output of a Schmitt trigger is a
    a) triangle wave.
    b) sine wave.
    c) sawtooth.
    d) square wave.

    Answer: d Difficulty: 2

23. An integrated circuit
    a) uses a capacitor in its feedback circuit.
    b) for a step input voltage, it produces a ramp voltage at its output.
    c) uses an inductor in its feedback circuit.
    d) a and b

    Answer: d Difficulty: 2

24. A differential circuit
    a) uses a resistor in its feedback circuit.
    b) uses a capacitor in its feedback circuit.
    c) produces a ramp voltage at its output for a step input voltage.
    d) a and c

    Answer: a Difficulty: 2

25. Hysteresis voltage is defined as
    a) the voltage of the lower trigger point.
    b) the voltage of the upper trigger point.
    c) the difference in voltage between the upper and the lower trigger points.
    d) the sum of voltages of the upper and the lower trigger points.

    Answer: c Difficulty: 2

Chapter 15: More Op-Amp Circuits

MULTIPLE CHOICE

1. A basic instrumentation amplifier has three op-amps.
   a) true
   b) false

   Answer: a Difficulty: 2

2. One of the key characteristics of an instrumentation amplifier is its low input impedance.
   a) true
   b) false

   Answer: b Difficulty: 2

3. The voltage gain of an instrumentation amplifier is set with an external resistor.
   a) true
   b) false

   Answer: a Difficulty: 2

4. A basic isolation amplifier has two electrically isolated sections.
   a) true
   b) false

   Answer: b Difficulty: 2

5. Most isolation amplifiers use transformer coupling for isolation.
   a) true
   b) false

   Answer: a Difficulty: 2

6. OTA stands for operational transistor amplifier.
   a) true
   b) false

   Answer: b Difficulty: 2

7. A log amplifier has a JFET in the feedback loop.
   a) true
   b) false

   Answer: b Difficulty: 2

8. An antilog amplifier has a BJT in series with the input.
   a) true
   b) false

   Answer: a Difficulty: 2

Chapter 15: More Op-Amp Circuits

9. The main purpose of an instrumentation amplifier is to amplify common mode voltage.
   a) true
   b) false

   Answer: b Difficulty: 2

10. The OTA is a voltage-to-current amplifier.
    a) true
    b) false

    Answer: a Difficulty: 2

11. The OAT has a _____ input impedance and a _____ CMRR.
    a) high, low
    b) low, high
    c) high, high
    d) low, high

    Answer: c Difficulty: 2

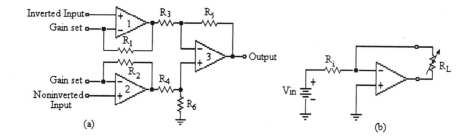

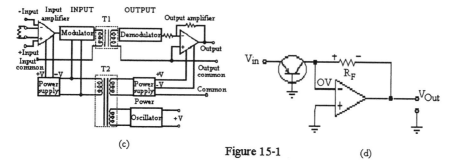

Figure 15-1

12. Refer to figure 15-1. Which of these circuits is known as an antilog amplifier?
    a) a
    b) b
    c) c
    d) d

    Answer: d Difficulty: 2

c) c
d) d

Answer: b Difficulty: 2

14. Refer to figure 15-1. Which of these circuits is known as an isolation amplifier?
    a) a
    b) b
    c) c
    d) d

Answer: c Difficulty: 2

15. Refer to figure 15-1. Which of these circuits is known as an instrumentation amplifier?
    a) a
    b) b
    c) c
    d) d

Answer: a Difficulty: 2

16. Refer to figure 15-1 (a). If $R_1 = R_2 = 30$ kΩ and the closed loop gain is 450, the value of the external gain-setting resistor R_G is
    a) 133.64 kΩ.
    b) 133.64 Ω.
    c) 13.364 Ω.
    d) none of the above

Answer: b Difficulty: 2

17. Refer to figure 15-1 (a). If $R_1 = R_2 = 28$ kΩ and $R_G = 100$ Ω, the A_{cl} would be
    a) 5.51.
    b) 55.1.
    c) 551.
    d) 550.

Answer: c Difficulty: 2

18. Refer to figure 15-1 (b). If $V_{in} = 5$ V and $R_{in} = 22$ kΩ, the current thru the load R_L would be
    a) 227.27 mA.
    b) .227 μA.
    c) 22.72 mA.
    d) 227.27 μA.

Answer: d Difficulty: 2

Chapter 15: More Op-Amp Circuits

19. Refer to figure 15-1 (d). If V_{in} = 200 mV, R_F = 52 k, and I_{EBO} ... would be
    a) 77.5 V.
    b) 7.75 mV.
    c) 7.75 V.
    d) 775 mV.

    Answer: c Difficulty: 2

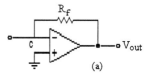

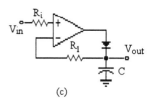

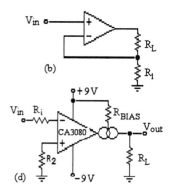

Figure 15-2

20. Refer to figure 15-2. Which of these circuits is known as a voltage-to-current converter?
    a) a
    b) b
    c) c
    d) d

    Answer: b Difficulty: 2

21. Refer to figure 15-2. Which of these circuits is known as a current-to-voltage converter?
    a) a
    b) b
    c) c
    d) d

    Answer: a Difficulty: 2

22. Refer to figure 15-2. Which of these circuits contains an OTA?
    a) a
    b) b
    c) c
    d) d

    Answer: d Difficulty: 2

23. Refer to figure 15-2. Which of these circuits is known as a peak detector?
    a) a
    b) b
    c) c
    d) d

    Answer: c Difficulty: 2

24. Refer to figure 15-2 (b). If R_L = 20 k, R_1 = 1.2 k, and V_{in} = 2.5 V, the load current I_L would be
    a) 20.83 mA.
    b) 2.083 mA.
    c) 2.083 A.
    d) 208.3 µA.

    Answer: b Difficulty: 2

25. Refer to figure 15-2 (d). If g_m = 25 mS and R_L = 25 kΩ, the voltage gain would be
    a) 625.
    b) 62.5.
    c) 6.25.
    d) not enough information

    Answer: a Difficulty: 2

Chapter 16: Active Filters

MULTIPLE CHOICE

1. The bandwidth of a band-pass filter is the difference between the two cutoff frequencies.
   a) true
   b) false

   Answer: a Difficulty: 2

2. Butterworth filters have a roll-off of 40 dB/decade and a widely varying output in the pass-band.
   a) true
   b) false

   Answer: b Difficulty: 2

3. A high-pass filter passes high frequencies easily and attenuates all others.
   a) true
   b) false

   Answer: a Difficulty: 2

4. A low-pass filter attenuates low frequencies.
   a) true
   b) false

   Answer: b Difficulty: 2

5. A band-reject filter passes all frequencies above and below a band.
   a) true
   b) false

   Answer: a Difficulty: 2

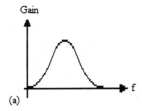
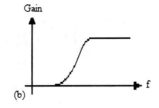
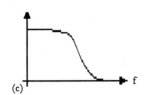
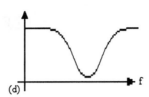

Figure 16-1

6. Refer to figure 16-1 (a). This is the frequency response curve for a
   a) low-pass filter.
   b) high-pass filter.
   c) band-pass filter.
   d) band-stop filter.

   Answer: c Difficulty: 2

7. Refer to figure 16-1 (b). This is the frequency response curve for a
   a) low-pass filter.
   b) high-pass filter.
   c) band-pass filter.
   d) band-stop filter.

   Answer: b Difficulty: 2

8. Refer to figure 16-1 (c). This is the frequency response curve for a
   a) low-pass filter.
   b) high-pass filter.
   c) band-pass filter.
   d) band-stop filter.

   Answer: a Difficulty: 2

9. Refer to figure 16-1 (d). This is the frequency response curve for a
   a) low-pass filter.
   b) high-pass filter.
   c) band-pass filter.
   d) band-stop filter.

   Answer: d Difficulty: 2

Chapter 16: Active Filters

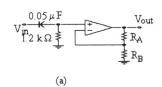
(a)

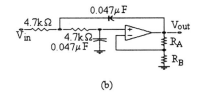
(b)

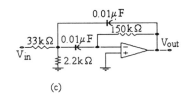
(c)

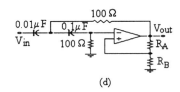
(d)

Figure 16-2

10. Refer to figure 16-2. Identify the active single-pole high-pass filter.
    a) a
    b) b
    c) c
    d) d

    Answer: a Difficulty: 2

11. Refer to figure 16-2. Identify the high-pass filter with a 40 dB/decade roll-off.
    a) a
    b) b
    c) c
    d) d

    Answer: d Difficulty: 2

12. Refer to figure 16-2. The low-pass filter with a 20 dB/decade roll-off is
    a) a.
    b) b.
    c) c.
    d) none of the above

    Answer: d Difficulty: 2

13. Refer to figure 16-2. The band-pass filter is
    a) a.
    b) b.
    c) c.
    d) d.

    Answer: c Difficulty: 2

14. Refer to figure 16-2. The low-pass filter with a roll-off of 40 db/decade is
    a) a.
    b) b.
    c) c.
    d) d.

    Answer: b Difficulty: 2

15. Refer to figure 16-2 (a). This circuit was checked for proper operation and f_C was correct but the voltage gain is 1. The cause of this problem might be
    a) the 1.2 kΩ resistor is open.
    b) the capacitor is shorted.
    c) R_A is open.
    d) R_B is open.

    Answer: d Difficulty: 3

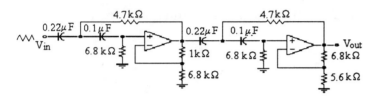

Figure 16-3

16. Refer to figure 16-3. This circuit is known as a _____ and the roll-off rate is _____.
    a) low-pass filter, 60 dB/decade
    b) high-pass filter, 20 dB/decade
    c) high-pass filter, 80 dB/decade
    d) band-pass filter, 80 dB/decade

    Answer: c Difficulty: 3

17. Refer to figure 16-3. The cutoff frequency for the first filter section is _____ the cutoff frequency for the second section.
    a) equal to
    b) higher than
    c) lower than
    d) none of these

    Answer: a Difficulty: 2

18. Refer to figure 16-3. This filter has a roll-off rate of
    a) 20 dB/decade.
    b) 40 dB/decade.
    c) 60 dB/decade.
    d) 80 dB/decade.

    Answer: b Difficulty: 2

Chapter 16: Active Filters

19. A high-pass filter has a cutoff frequency of 1.23 kHz. The bandwidth of this filter is
    a) 2.46 kHz.
    b) 1.23 kHz.
    c) 644 Hz.
    d) none of these

    Answer: d Difficulty: 2

20. A low-pass filter with a roll-off rate of 60 dB/decade is needed. The best combination to use is
    a) a 2-pole filter followed by another 2-pole.
    b) two single-pole filters in series.
    c) a 2-pole filter followed by a 1-pole.
    d) none of these

    Answer: c Difficulty: 2

21. A high-pass filter has R = 47 kΩ and C = 0.002 μF. The cutoff frequency is
    a) 1.694 kHz.
    b) 10.6 kHz.
    c) 3.39 Hz.
    d) none of these

    Answer: a Difficulty: 2

22. A pole is a network that contains
    a) a resistor and a capacitor.
    b) a resistor and an inductor.
    c) a capacitor and an inductor.
    d) two resistors and one inductor.

    Answer: a Difficulty: 2

23. A maximally flat frequency response is a common name for
    a) Chebyshev.
    b) bessel.
    c) Butterworth.
    d) Colpitts.

    Answer: c Difficulty: 2

24. An RC circuit produces a roll-off rate of
    a) -20 dB/decade.
    b) -6 dB/octave
    c) -40 dB/decade.
    d) a and b

    Answer: d Difficulty: 3

25. A low-pass filter has a cutoff frequency of 1.23 kHz. Determine the bandwidth of the filter.
   a) 2.46 kHz
   b) 1.23 kHz
   c) 644 Hz
   d) not enough information given

   Answer: b Difficulty: 3

Chapter 17: Oscillators and the Phase-Locked Loop

MULTIPLE CHOICE

1. To operate properly, an oscillator requires an external ac input signal.
   a) true
   b) false

   Answer: b Difficulty: 2

2. An oscillator can produce many types of outputs, such as sine, triangle, or square waves.
   a) true
   b) false

   Answer: a Difficulty: 2

3. Positive feedback is required for an oscillator to operate properly.
   a) true
   b) false

   Answer: a Difficulty: 2

4. Crystal oscillators are very stable.
   a) true
   b) false

   Answer: a Difficulty: 2

5. An RC phase-shift oscillator uses feedback from a tank circuit.
   a) true
   b) false

   Answer: b Difficulty: 2

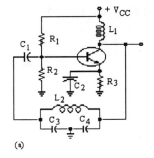
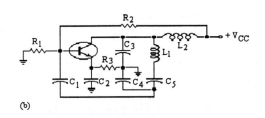
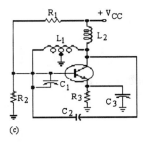

Figure 17-1

6. Refer to figure 17-1. Which of these circuits is known as a Clapp oscillator?
   a) a
   b) b
   c) c
   d) none of these

   Answer: b   Difficulty: 2

7. Refer to figure 17-1. Which of these circuits is known as a crystal oscillator?
   a) a
   b) b
   c) c
   d) none of these

   Answer: d   Difficulty: 2

8. Refer to figure 17-1. Which of these circuits is known as an Armstrong oscillator?
   a) a
   b) b
   c) c
   d) none of these

   Answer: d   Difficulty: 2

9. Refer to figure 17-1. Which of these circuits is known as a Colpitts oscillator?
   a) a
   b) b
   c) c
   d) none of these

   Answer: a   Difficulty: 2

Chapter 17: Oscillators and the Phase-Locked Loop

10. Refer to figure 17-1. Which of these circuits is known as a Hartley oscillator?
   a) a
   b) b
   c) c
   d) none of these

   Answer: c Difficulty: 2

11. Refer to figure 17-1 (a). The resonant frequency is determined by
   a) L_1, C_1.
   b) L_2, C_1, C_2.
   c) L_1, C_3, C_4.
   d) L_2, C_3, C_4.

   Answer: d Difficulty: 3

12. Refer to figure 17-1 (c). The main frequency determining components are
   a) L_2, C_2.
   b) L_1, C_1.
   c) L_1, C_2.
   d) L_2, C_1.

   Answer: c Difficulty: 2

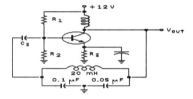

Figure 17-2

13. Refer to figure 17-2. If the 20 mH inductor were increased to 100 mH, the resonant frequency would
   a) increase.
   b) decrease.
   c) remain the same.
   d) cannot be determined

   Answer: b Difficulty: 2

14. Refer to figure 17-2. This circuit operates easily as a
   a) variable frequency oscillator.
   b) fixed frequency oscillator.
   c) a crystal oscillator.
   d) none of these

   Answer: b Difficulty: 3

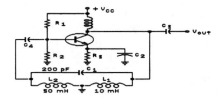

Figure 17-3

15. Refer to figure 17-3. This circuit is known as
    a) a Clapp oscillator.
    b) a Colpitts oscillator.
    c) an Armstrong oscillator.
    d) a Hartley oscillator.

    Answer: d Difficulty: 2

16. Refer to figure 17-3. This type of oscillator utilizes _____ feedback to control the oscillation. The voltage gain is _____.
    a) negative, low
    b) positive, high
    c) positive, low
    d) negative, high

    Answer: c Difficulty: 3

17. An op-amp differentiator with a linear ramp voltage as its input, will have _____ output
    a) dc.
    b) a square wave.
    c) a sine wave.
    d) a triangle wave.

    Answer: a Difficulty: 2

18. A very stable oscillator is needed to operate on a single frequency, a good choice might be
    a) a Hartley.
    b) a Colpitts.
    c) a crystal.
    d) a Clapp.

    Answer: c Difficulty: 2

Chapter 17: Oscillators and the Phase-Locked Loop

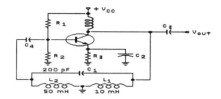

Figure 17-3

19. Refer to figure 17-3. If C_1 decreases in value, the resonant frequency will
    a) increase.
    b) decrease.
    c) remain the same.
    d) cannot be determined.

    Answer: a Difficulty: 2

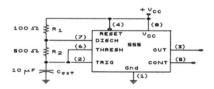

Figure 17-4

20. Refer to figure 17-4. If the value of V_{CC} = 5 V, the output voltage would be
    a) a square wave of 10 V_{p-p}.
    b) a square wave that varies between 0 V and 5 V.
    c) a sine wave.
    d) 5 V dc.

    Answer: b Difficulty: 2

21. Nonsinusoidal oscillators produce
    a) sine waves only.
    b) triangle waves only.
    c) square waves only.
    d) either b or c.

    Answer: d Difficulty: 2

22. The 555 timer contains
    a) 2 comparators.
    b) 3 comparators.
    c) 4 comparators.
    d) 5 comparators.

    Answer: b Difficulty: 2

23. The most stable type of oscillator is
    a) the Clapp oscillator.
    b) the Hartley oscillator.
    c) the Crystal oscillator.
    d) the Colpitts oscillator.

    Answer: c Difficulty: 2

24. Refer to figure 17-4. To reduce the duty cycle to less than 50%, the following circuit change would be necessary.
    a) Reduce the size of R_1.
    b) Reduce the size of R_2.
    c) Increase the size of R_1.
    d) Connect a diode in parallel with R_1.

    Answer: d Difficulty: 2

25. A circuit that can change the frequency of oscillation with an application of a dc voltage is sometimes called
    a) a voltage-controlled oscillator.
    b) a crystal oscillator.
    c) a Hartley oscillator.
    d) an astable multivibrator.

    Answer: a Difficulty: 2

Chapter 18: Voltage Regulators

MULTIPLE CHOICE

1. Switching regulators are very efficient.
   a) true
   b) false

   Answer: a   Difficulty: 2

2. A zener diode is sometimes used as a voltage regulator.
   a) true
   b) false

   Answer: a   Difficulty: 2

3. Line regulation is the percentage change in input voltage for a given change in output voltage.
   a) true
   b) false

   Answer: b   Difficulty: 2

4. In a shunt regulator, the control element is in series with the load.
   a) true
   b) false

   Answer: b   Difficulty: 2

5. Most voltage regulators include some kind of protection circuitry.
   a) true
   b) false

   Answer: a   Difficulty: 2

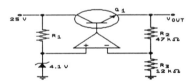

Figure 18-1(a)

6. Refer to figure 18-1 (a). If the zener had a voltage rating of 3.7 V, V_{out} would be
   a) 25 V.
   b) 20.2 V.
   c) 18.2 V.
   d) 7.1 V.

   Answer: c   Difficulty: 2

7. Refer to figure 18-1 (a). If a wire clipping were to short Q_1 emitter to collector, the problem that might result is
   a) R_2 would open.
   b) V_{OUT} would increase to 25 V.
   c) Q_1 would fail.
   d) the zener would open.

   Answer: b Difficulty: 3

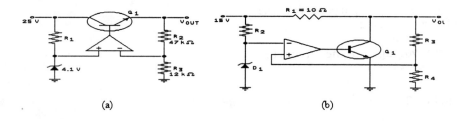

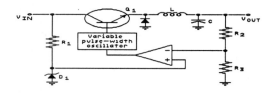

Figure 18-1

8. Refer to figure 18-1. Which of these circuits is known as a shunt regulator?
   a) (a)
   b) (b)
   c) (c)
   d) (a) or (b)

   Answer: b Difficulty: 2

9. Refer to figure 18-1. Which of these circuits is known as a step-up switching regulator?
   a) (a)
   b) (b)
   c) (c)
   d) none of these

   Answer: d Difficulty: 2

10. Refer to figure 18-1. Which of these circuits is known as a series regulator?
    a) (a)
    b) (b)
    c) (c)
    d) none of these

    Answer: a Difficulty: 2

Chapter 18: Voltage Regulators

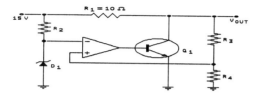

Figure 18-1(b)

11. Refer to figure 18-1 (b). The purpose for the op-amp is
    a) to supply a reference voltage.
    b) to sense the error signal.
    c) to limit the input voltage to the circuit.
    d) to amplify the error signal.

    Answer: d Difficulty: 2

12. Refer to figure 18-1 (b). An increase in V_{OUT} will cause Q_1
    a) to conduct less.
    b) to conduct the same.
    c) to conduct more.
    d) to open.

    Answer: c Difficulty: 3

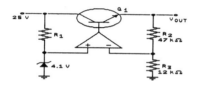

Figure 18-1(a)

13. Refer to figure 18-1 (a). To increase the current handling capability of this regulator, beyond the 5 A rating of the transistor, the reasonable thing to do would be:
    a) place another transistor in series with Q_1.
    b) increase the value of the zener diode.
    c) place another transistor in parallel with Q_1.
    d) change the values of R_2 and R_3.

    Answer: c Difficulty: 2

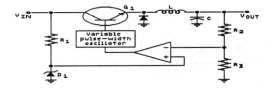

Figure 18-1(c)

14. Refer to figure 18-1 (c). If the output voltage tends to increase due to a decrease in load current, the transistor will conduct for _____ time each cycle.
   a) a longer
   b) a shorter
   c) the same
   d) exactly half the

   Answer: b Difficulty: 2

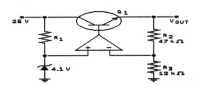

Figure 18-1(a)

15. Refer to figure 18-1 (a). This circuit is brought in for repair. The measured output voltage was 25 V under all load conditions. A possible cause of this symptom might be
   a) R_2 has opened.
   b) Q_1 base-emitter has opened.
   c) R_3 has opened.
   d) V_{IN} has decreased.

   Answer: a Difficulty: 3

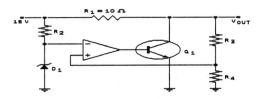

Figure 18-1(b)

16. Refer to figure 18-1 (b). If R_1 opened, V_{OUT} would
   a) increase.
   b) decrease.
   c) remain the same.
   d) cannot be determined

   Answer: b Difficulty: 2

Chapter 18: Voltage Regulators

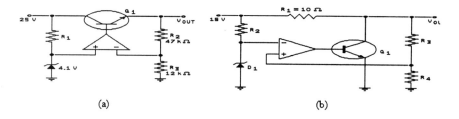

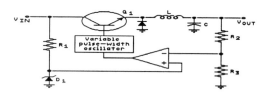

Figure 18-1

17. Refer to figure 18-1. In all of these circuits, the zener is used
    a) to sense the change in output voltage.
    b) as a reference voltage.
    c) to supply the op-amp with V_{CC}.
    d) to regulate the output voltage directly.

    Answer: b Difficulty: 2

18. Refer to figure 18-1. The circuit that will also regulate the output voltage when V_{IN} varies is
    a) (a)
    b) (b)
    c) (c)
    d) all of the above

    Answer: a Difficulty: 2

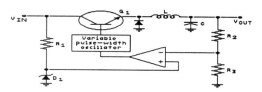

Figure 18-1(c)

19. Refer to figure 18-1 (c). This circuits operates at a _____ frequency and its efficiency is _____.
    a) low, low
    b) low, high
    c) high, high
    d) high, low

    Answer: c Difficulty: 2

332

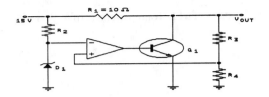

Figure 18-1(b)

20. Refer to figure 18-1 (b). The purpose for the diode D_1 is
    a) to supply a reference voltage.
    b) to amplify the error signal.
    c) to sense the error signal.
    d) to limit the input voltage to the circuit.

    Answer: a Difficulty: 2

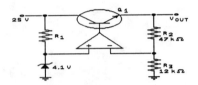

Figure 18-1(a)

21. Refer to figure 18-1 (a). If a solder splash shorted the ends of R_1 to each other, the result would be
    a) the op-amp would fail.
    b) that Q_1 would open.
    c) the output voltage would not change.
    d) the zener would fail.

    Answer: d Difficulty: 3

22. A voltage regulator with a no-load dc output of 15 V is connected to a load with a resistance of 12 Ω. If the load voltage decreases to 14.5 V, the percent regulation would be
    a) 96.7%.
    b) 3.33%.
    c) 3.45%.
    d) 100%.

    Answer: c Difficulty: 2

23. An advantage of a switching regulator is
    a) the filter components are small.
    b) the circuit is very efficient.
    c) voltages can be stepped-up or stepped-down.
    d) all of these
    e) none of these

    Answer: d Difficulty: 2

Chapter 18: Voltage Regulators

24. A voltage regulator has a no-load output of 18 V and a full load output of 17.3 V. The percent load regulation is
    a) 0.25%.
    b) 96.1%.
    c) 4.05%.
    d) 1.04%.

    Answer: c Difficulty: 2

25. A voltage regulator with a no-load output dc voltage of 12 V is connected to a load with a resistance of 10 Ω. If the load resistance decreases to 7.5 Ω, the load voltage will decrease to 10.9 V. The load current will be _____ and the percent load regulation is _____.
    a) 1.45 A, 90.8%
    b) 1.45 A, 9.17%
    c) 1.6 A, 90.8%
    d) 1.6 A, 9.17%

    Answer: b Difficulty: 2

Transparency Masters to Accompany

Electronic Devices
Fifth Edition

Electronic Devices: Electron-Flow Version
Third Edition

FIGURE 1-11
Creation of an electron-hole pair in an excited silicon atom. An electron in the conduction band is a free electron.

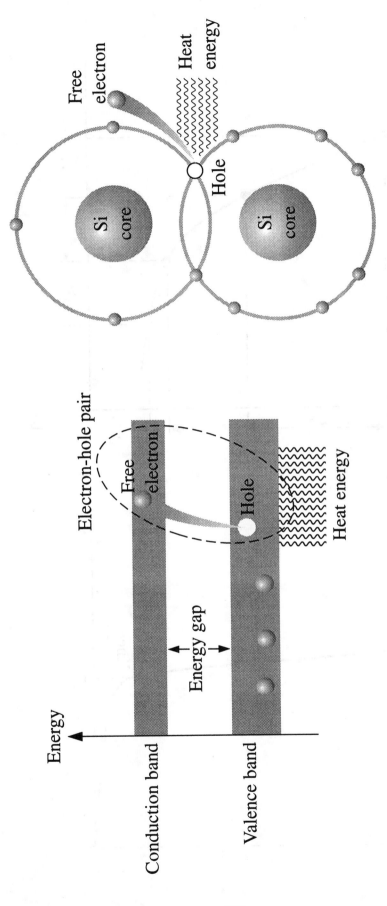

(a) Energy diagram

(b) Bonding diagram

Thomas L. Floyd
Electronic Devices, Fifth Edition
Electronic Devices: Electron-Flow Version, Third Edition

©1999 by Prentice-Hall, Inc.
Simon & Schuster/A Viacom Company
Upper Saddle River, New Jersey 07458
All rights reserved.

FIGURE 1-28

I-V characteristic curve for forward bias. Part (b) illustrates dynamic resistance.

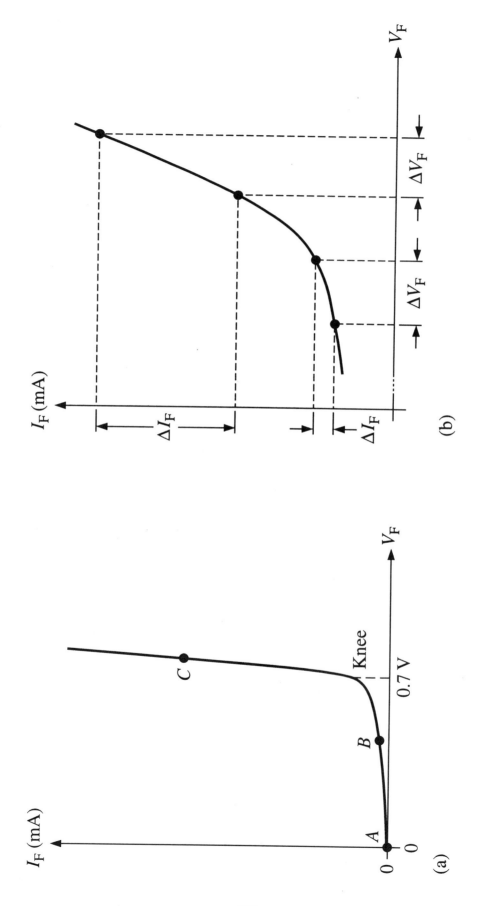

FIGURE 1-30
I-V characteristic curve for reverse bias.

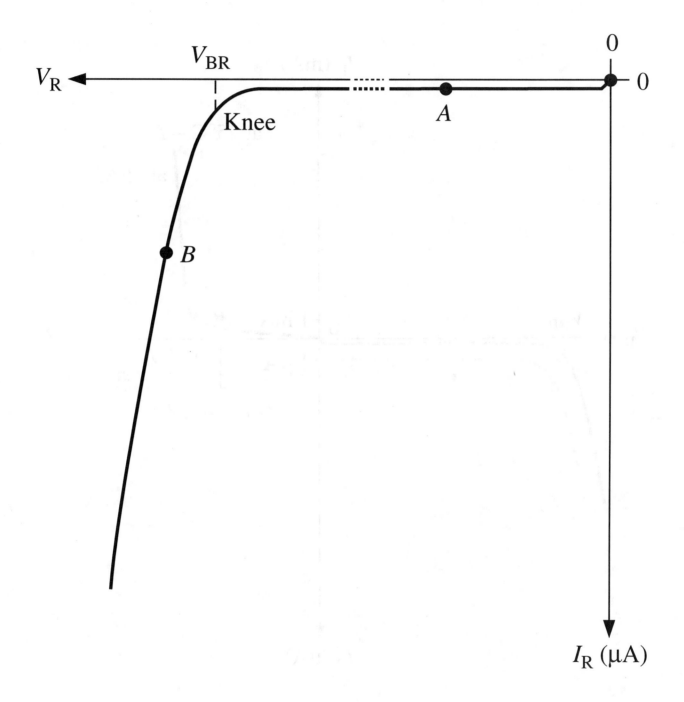

FIGURE 1-32
Temperature effect on the *I-V* characteristic of a *pn* junction. The 1 mA and 1 μA marks on the vertical axis are given as a basis for a relative comparison of the current scales.

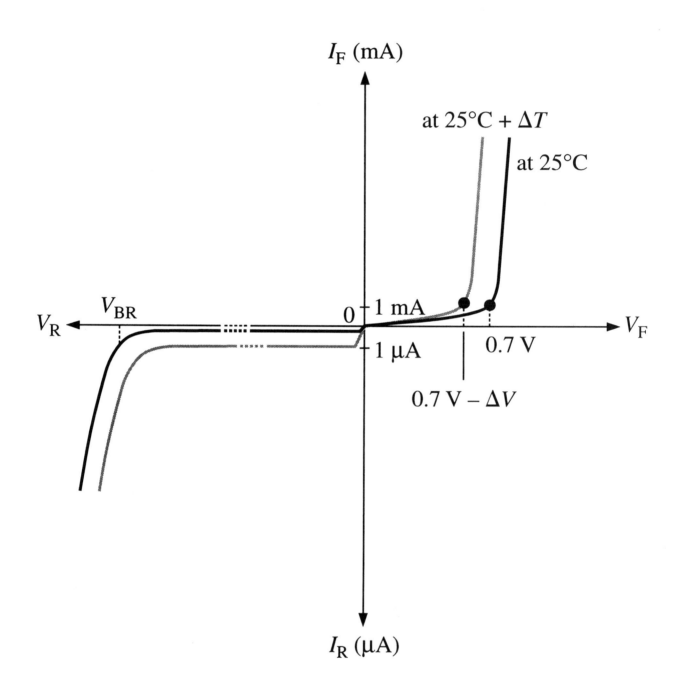

Thomas L. Floyd
Electronic Devices, Fifth Edition
*Electronic Devices: Electron-Flow
Version*, Third Edition

©1999 by Prentice-Hall, Inc.
Simon & Schuster/A Viacom Company
Upper Saddle River, New Jersey 07458
All rights reserved.

FIGURE 1-36*
The ideal model of a diode.

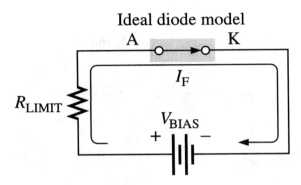

(a) Forward bias

(b) Reverse bias

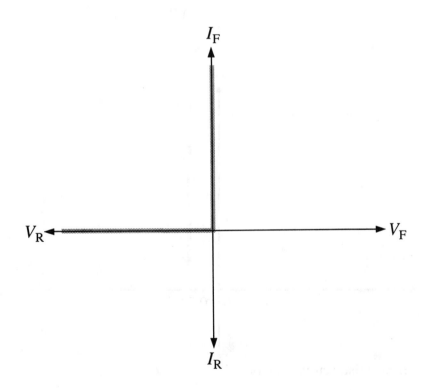

(c) Ideal characteristic curve

Thomas L. Floyd
Electronic Devices, Fifth Edition
*Current arrows indicate
 conventional flow.

©1999 by Prentice-Hall, Inc.
Simon & Schuster/A Viacom Company
Upper Saddle River, New Jersey 07458
All rights reserved.

FIGURE 1-37*
The practical model of a diode.

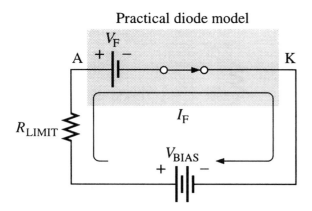
(a) Forward bias

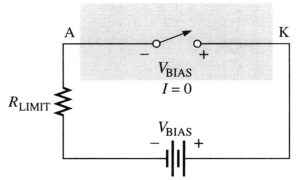
(b) Reverse bias

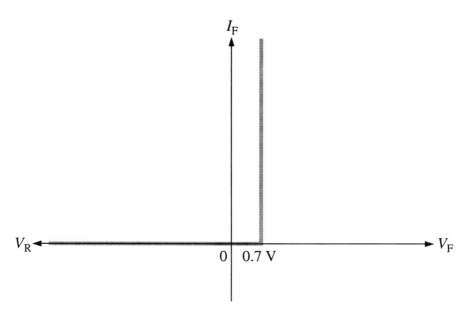
(c) Characteristic curve (silicon)

Thomas L. Floyd
Electronic Devices, Fifth Edition
*Current arrows indicate
 conventional flow.

©1999 by Prentice-Hall, Inc.
Simon & Schuster/A Viacom Company
Upper Saddle River, New Jersey 07458
All rights reserved.

FIGURE 1-38*
The complex model of a diode.

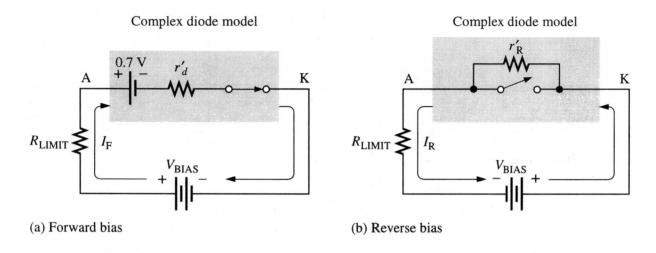

(a) Forward bias

(b) Reverse bias

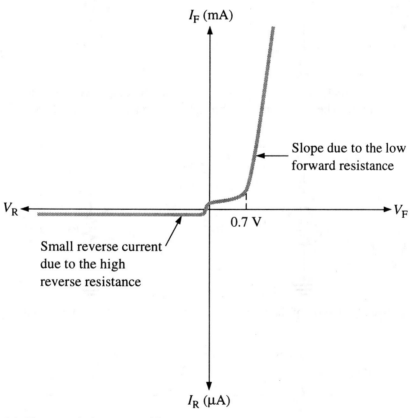

(c) Characteristic curve (silicon)

Thomas L. Floyd
Electronic Devices, Fifth Edition
*Current arrows indicate
   conventional flow.

©1999 by Prentice-Hall, Inc.
Simon & Schuster/A Viacom Company
Upper Saddle River, New Jersey 07458
All rights reserved.

FIGURE 2-2*
Half-wave rectifier operation. The diode is considered to be ideal.

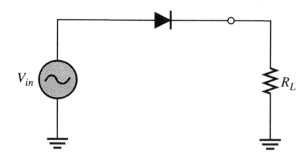

(a) A half-wave rectifier

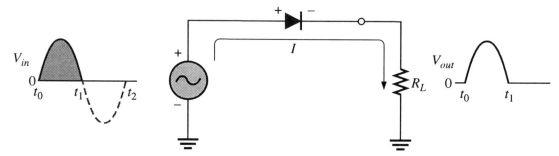

(b) During the positive alternation of the 60 Hz input voltage, the output voltage looks like the positive half of the input voltage. The current path is through ground back to the source.

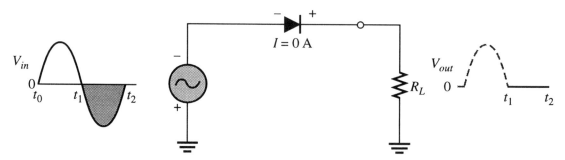

(c) During the negative alternation of the input voltage, the current is 0, so the output voltage is also 0.

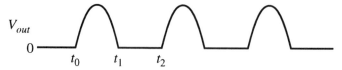

(d) 60 Hz half-wave output voltage for three input cycles

Thomas L. Floyd
Electronic Devices, Fifth Edition
*Current arrows indicate conventional flow.

©1999 by Prentice-Hall, Inc.
Simon & Schuster/A Viacom Company
Upper Saddle River, New Jersey 07458
All rights reserved.

FIGURE 2-14*
Basic operation of a full-wave center-tapped rectifier. Note that the current through the load resistor is in the same direction during the entire input cycle, so the output voltage always has the same polarity.

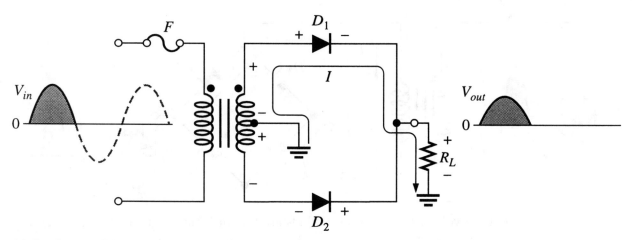

(a) During positive half-cycles, D_1 is forward-biased and D_2 is reverse-biased.

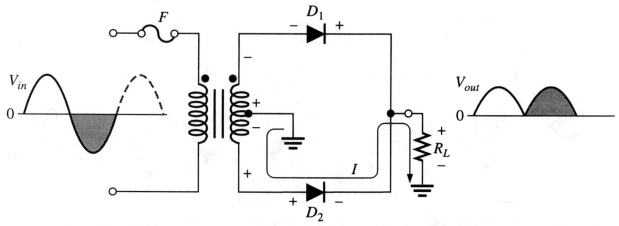

(b) During negative half-cycles, D_2 is forward-biased and D_1 is reverse-biased.

Thomas L. Floyd
Electronic Devices, Fifth Edition
*Current arrows indicate conventional flow.

©1999 by Prentice-Hall, Inc.
Simon & Schuster/A Viacom Company
Upper Saddle River, New Jersey 07458
All rights reserved.

FIGURE 2-20*

Operation of a full-wave bridge rectifier.

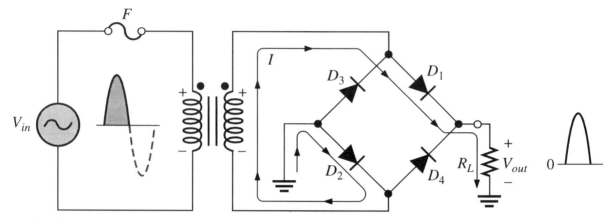

(a) During positive half-cycle of the input, D_1 and D_2 are forward-biased and conduct current. D_3 and D_4 are reverse-biased.

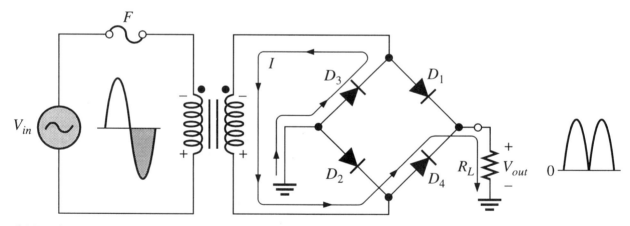

(b) During negative half-cycle of the input, D_3 and D_4 are forward-biased and conduct current. D_1 and D_2 are reverse-biased.

Thomas L. Floyd
Electronic Devices, Fifth Edition
*Current arrows indicate
 conventional flow.

©1999 by Prentice-Hall, Inc.
Simon & Schuster/A Viacom Company
Upper Saddle River, New Jersey 07458
All rights reserved.

FIGURE 2-25*
Operation of a half-wave rectifier with a capacitor filter.

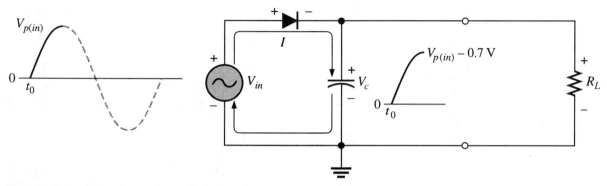

(a) Initial charging of capacitor (diode is forward-biased) happens only once when power is turned on.

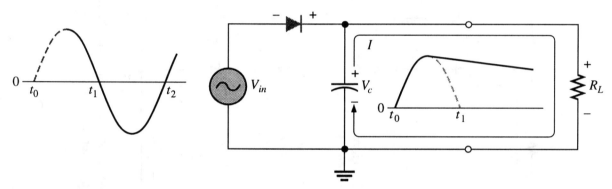

(b) The capacitor discharges through R_L after peak of positive alternation when the diode is reverse-biased. This discharging occurs during the portion of the input voltage indicated by the solid curve.

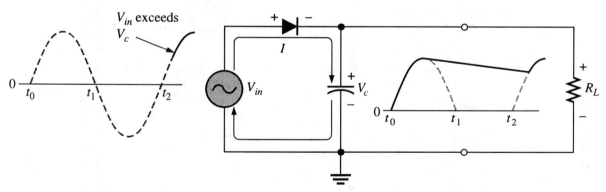

(c) The capacitor charges back to peak of input when the diode becomes forward-biased. This charging occurs during the portion of the input voltage indicated by the solid curve.

Thomas L. Floyd
Electronic Devices, Fifth Edition
*Current arrows indicate conventional flow.

©1999 by Prentice-Hall, Inc.
Simon & Schuster/A Viacom Company
Upper Saddle River, New Jersey 07458
All rights reserved.

FIGURE 2-37*
Examples of diode limiters (clippers).

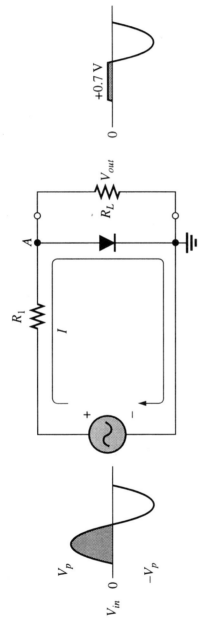

(a) Limiting of the positive alternation. The diode is forward-biased during the positive alternation (above 0.7 V) and reverse-biased during the negative alternation.

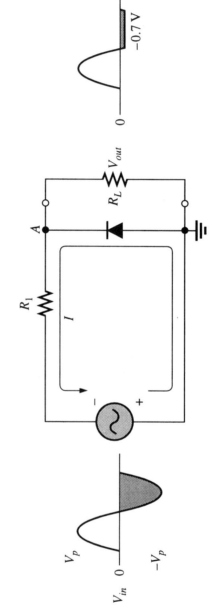

(b) Limiting of the negative alternation. The diode is forward-biased during the negative alternation (below −0.7 V) and reverse-biased during the positive alternation.

Thomas L. Floyd
Electronic Devices, Fifth Edition
*Current arrows indicate conventional flow.

©1999 by Prentice-Hall, Inc.
Simon & Schuster/A Viacom Company
Upper Saddle River, New Jersey 07458
All rights reserved.

FIGURE 2-49*
Positive clamper operation.

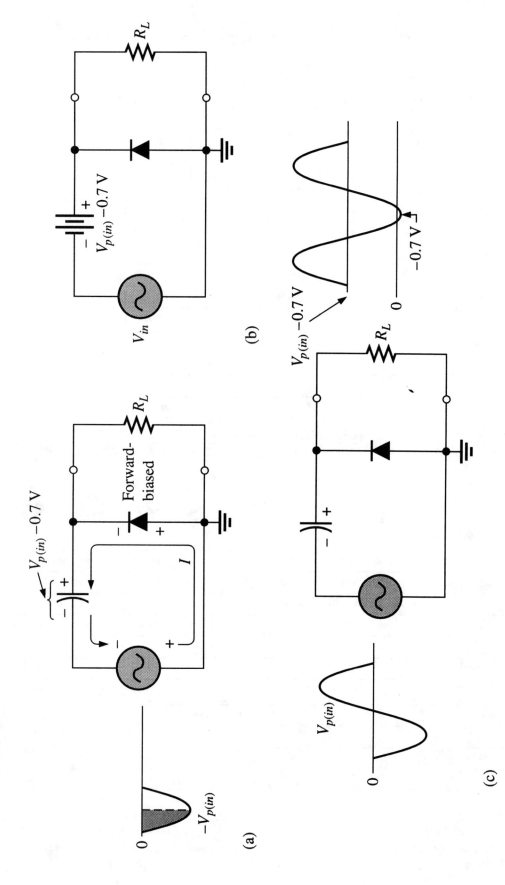

Thomas L. Floyd
Electronic Devices, Fifth Edition
*Current arrows indicate conventional flow.

©1999 by Prentice-Hall, Inc.
Simon & Schuster/A Viacom Company
Upper Saddle River, New Jersey 07458
All rights reserved.

FIGURE 2-60
A selection of rectifier diodes based on maximum ratings of I_O, I_{FSM}, and V_{RRM}.

V_{RRM} (Volts)	I_O, Average Rectified Forward Current (Amperes)					
	1.0	1.5	3.0			6.0
	59-03 (DO-41) Plastic	59-04 Plastic	60-01 Metal	267-03 Plastic	267-02 Plastic	194-04 Plastic
50	1N4001	1N5391	1N4719	MR500	1N5400	MR750
100	1N4002	1N5392	1N4720	MR501	1N5401	MR751
200	1N4003	1N5393 MR5059	1N4721	MR502	1N5402	MR752
400	1N4004	1N5395 MR5060	1N4722	MR504	1N5404	MR754
600	1N4005	1N5397 MR5061	1N4723	MR506	1N5406	MR756
800	1N4006	1N5398	1N4724	MR508		MR758
1000	1N4007	1N5399	1N4725	MR510		MR760
I_{FSM} (Amps)	30	50	300	100	200	400
T_A @ Rated I_O (°C)	75	$T_L = 70$	75	95	$T_L = 105$	60
T_C @ Rated I_O (°C)						
T_J (Max) (°C)	175	175	175	175	175	175

V_{RRM} (Volts)	I_O, Average Rectified Forward Current (Amperes)									
	12	20	24	25	30	40	50	25	35	40
	245A-02 (DO-203AA) Metal	339-02 Plastic	193-04 Plastic	43-02 (DO-21) Metal	42A-01 (DO-203AB) Metal	43-04 Metal		309A-03	309A-02	
50	MR1120 1N1199,A,B	MR2000	MR2400	MR2500	1N3491	1N3659	1N1183A	MR5005	MDA2500	MDA3500
100	MR1121 1N1200,A,B	MR2001	MR2401	MR2501	1N3492	1N3660	1N1184A	MR5010	MDA2501	MDA3501
200	MR1122 1N1202,A,B	MR2002	MR2402	MR2502	1N3493	1N3661	1N1186A	MR5020	MDA2502	MDA3502	MDA4002
400	MR1124 1N1204,A,B	MR2004	MR2404	MR2504	1N3495	1N3663	1N1188A	MR5040	MDA2504	MDA3504	MDA4004
600	MR1126 1N1206,A,B	MR2006	MR2406	MR2506			1N1190A		MDA2506	MDA3506	MDA4006
800	MR1128	MR2008		MR2508					MDA2508	MDA3508	MDA4008
1000	MR1130	MR2010		MR2510					MDA2510	MDA3510	
I_{FSM} (Amps)	300	400	400	400	300	400	800	600	400	400	800
T_A @ Rated I_O (°C)											
T_C @ Rated I_O (°C)	150	150	125	150	130	100	150	150	55	55	35
T_J (Max) (°C)	190	175	175	175	175	175	190	195	175	175	175

Thomas L. Floyd
Electronic Devices, Fifth Edition
Electronic Devices: Electron-Flow Version, Third Edition

©1999 by Prentice-Hall, Inc.
Simon & Schuster/A Viacom Company
Upper Saddle River, New Jersey 07458
All rights reserved.

FIGURE 2-72
Power supply preliminary schematic.

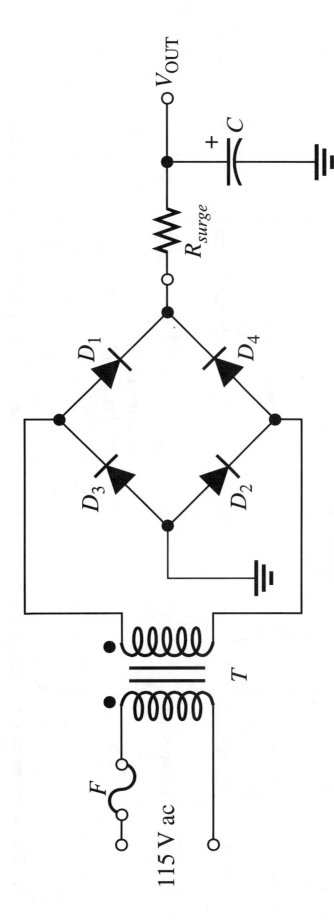

FIGURE 3-2
General diode V-I characteristic.

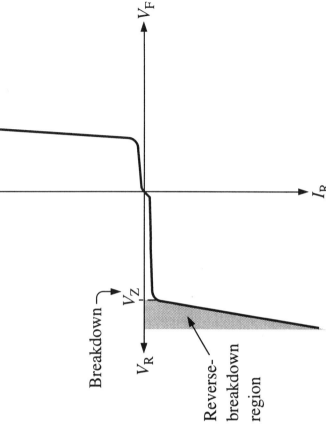

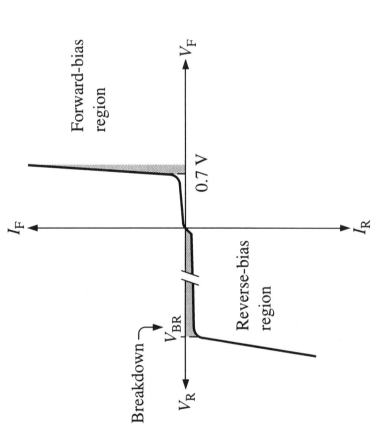

(a) The normal operating regions for a rectifier diode are shown as shaded areas.

(b) The normal operating region for a zener diode is shaded.

Thomas L. Floyd
Electronic Devices, Fifth Edition
Electronic Devices: Electron-Flow Version, Third Edition

 ©1999 by Prentice-Hall, Inc.
Simon & Schuster/A Viacom Company
Upper Saddle River, New Jersey 07458
All rights reserved.

FIGURE 3-3

Reverse characteristic of a zener diode. V_Z is usually specified at the zener test current, I_{ZT}, and is designated V_{ZT}.

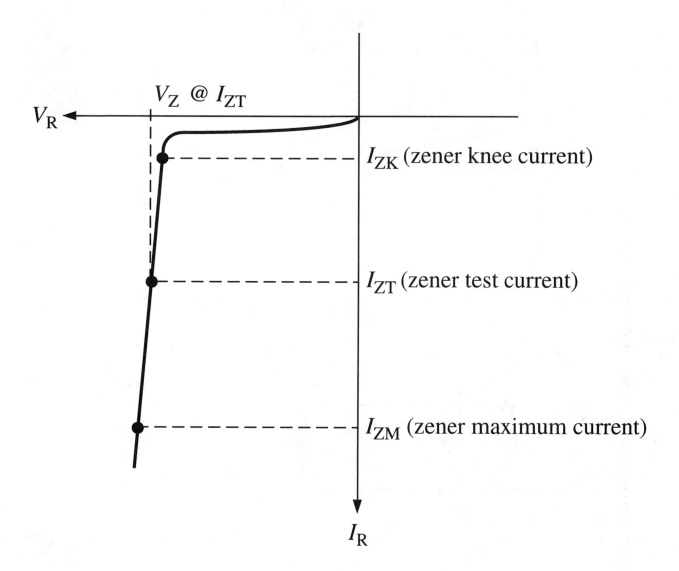

FIGURE 3-4
Zener diode equivalent circuit models and the characteristic curve illustrating Z_Z.

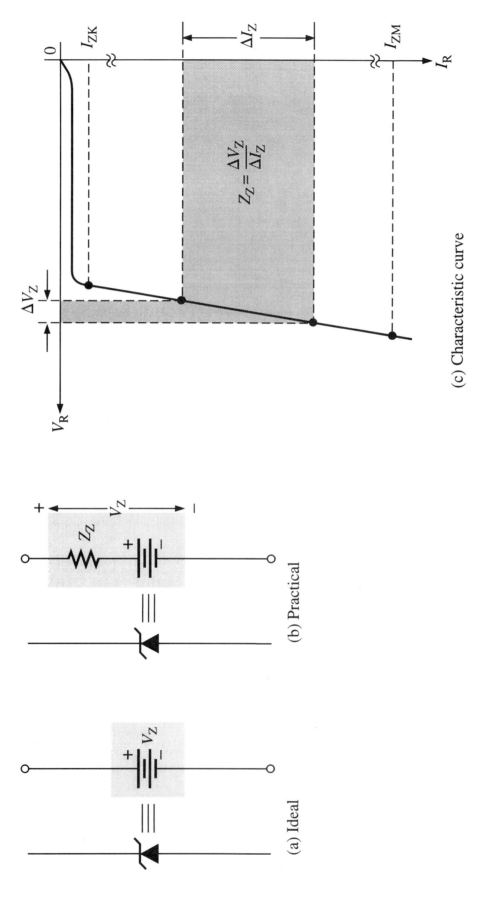

FIGURE 3-7
Partial data sheet for the 1N4728-1N4764 series 1 W zener diodes.

Maximum Ratings

Rating	Symbol	Value	Unit
DC power dissipation @ $T_A = 50°C$	P_D	1.0	Watt
Derate above 50°C		6.67	mW/C°
Operating and storage junction Temperature range	T_J, T_{stg}	−65 to +200	°C

Electrical Characteristics ($T_A = 25°C$ unless otherwise noted) $V_F = 1.2$ V max, $I_F = 200$ mA for all types.

JEDEC Type No. (Note 1)	Nominal Zener Voltage V_Z @ I_{ZT} Volts	Test Current I_{ZT} mA	Maximum Zener Impedance			Leakage Current	
			Z_{ZT} @ I_{ZT} Ohms	Z_{ZK} @ I_{ZK} Ohms	I_{ZK} mA	I_R µA Max	V_R Volts
1N4728	3.3	76	10	400	1.0	100	1.0
1N4729	3.6	69	10	400	1.0	100	1.0
1N4730	3.9	64	9.0	400	1.0	50	1.0
1N4731	4.3	58	9.0	400	1.0	10	1.0
1N4732	4.7	53	8.0	500	1.0	10	1.0
1N4733	5.1	49	7.0	550	1.0	10	1.0
1N4734	5.6	45	5.0	600	1.0	10	2.0
1N4735	6.2	41	2.0	700	1.0	10	3.0
1N4736	6.8	37	3.5	700	1.0	10	4.0
1N4737	7.5	34	4.0	700	0.5	10	5.0
1N4738	8.2	31	4.5	700	0.5	10	6.0
1N4739	9.1	28	5.0	700	0.5	10	7.0
1N4740	10	25	7.0	700	0.25	10	7.6
1N4741	11	23	8.0	700	0.25	5.0	8.4
1N4742	12	21	9.0	700	0.25	5.0	9.1
1N4743	13	19	10	700	0.25	5.0	9.9
1N4744	15	17	14	700	0.25	5.0	11.4
1N4745	16	15.5	16	700	0.25	5.0	12.2
1N4746	18	14	20	750	0.25	5.0	13.7
1N4747	20	12.5	22	750	0.25	5.0	15.2
1N4748	22	11.5	23	750	0.25	5.0	16.7
1N4749	24	10.5	25	750	0.25	5.0	18.2
1N4750	27	9.5	35	750	0.25	5.0	20.6
1N4751	30	8.5	40	1000	0.25	5.0	22.8
1N4752	33	7.5	45	1000	0.25	5.0	25.1
1N4753	36	7.0	50	1000	0.25	5.0	27.4
1N4754	39	6.5	60	1000	0.25	5.0	29.7
1N4755	43	6.0	70	1500	0.25	5.0	32.7
1N4756	47	5.5	80	1500	0.25	5.0	35.8
1N4757	51	5.0	95	1500	0.25	5.0	38.8
1N4758	56	4.5	110	2000	0.25	5.0	42.6
1N4759	62	4.0	125	2000	0.25	5.0	47.1
1N4760	68	3.7	150	2000	0.25	5.0	51.7
1N4761	75	3.3	175	2000	0.25	5.0	56.0
1N4762	82	3.0	200	3000	0.25	5.0	62.2
1N4763	91	2.8	250	3000	0.25	5.0	69.2
1N4764	100	2.5	350	3000	0.25	5.0	76.0

NOTE 1 — Tolerance and Type Number Designation. The JEDEC type numbers listed have a standard tolerance on the nominal zener voltage of ±10%. A standard tolerance of ±5% on individual units is also available and is indicated by suffixing "A" to the standard type number. C for ±2.0%, D for ±1.0%.

(a) Electrical characteristics

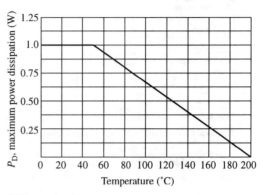

(b) Power derating

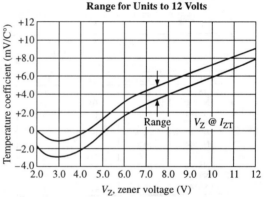

(c) Temperature coefficient

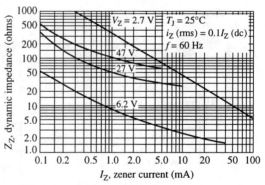

(d) Effect of zener current on zener impedance

Thomas L. Floyd
Electronic Devices, Fifth Edition
Electronic Devices: Electron-Flow Version, Third Edition

©1999 by Prentice-Hall, Inc.
Simon & Schuster/A Viacom Company
Upper Saddle River, New Jersey 07458
All rights reserved.

FIGURE 3-22
Partial data sheet for the 1N5139-1N5148 varactor diodes.

Maximum Ratings ($T_C = 25°C$ unless otherwise noted)

Rating	Symbol	Value	Unit
Reverse voltage	V_R	60	Volts
Forward current	I_F	250	mA
RF power input*	P_{in}	5.0	Watts
Device dissipation @ $T_A = 25°C$ Derate above 25°C	P_D	400 2.67	mW mW/C°
Device dissipation @ $T_C = 25°C$ Derate above 25°C	P_C	2.0 13.3	Watts mW/C°
Junction temperature	T_J	+175	°C
Storage temperature range	T_{stg}	−65 to +200	°C

*The RF power input rating assumes that an adequate heatsink is provided.

Electrical Characteristics ($T_A = 25°C$ unless otherwise noted)

Characteristic	Symbol	Min	Typ	Max	Unit
Reverse breakdown voltage ($I_R = 10$ μA dc)	$V_{(BR)R}$	60	70	−	V dc
Reverse voltage leakage current ($V_R = 55$ V dc, $T_A = 25°C$) ($V_R = 55$ V dc, $T_A = 150°C$)	I_R	− −	− −	0.02 20	μA dc
Series inductance ($f = 250$ MHz, $L \approx 1/16''$)	L_S	−	5.0	−	nH
Case capacitance ($f = 1.0$ MHz, $L \approx 1/16''$)	C_C	−	0.25	−	pF
Diode capacitance temperature coefficient ($V_R = 4.0$ V dc, $f = 1.0$ MHz)	TC_C	−	200	300	ppm/C°

Device	C_T, Diode Capacitance $V_R = 4.0$ V dc, $f = 1.0$ MHz pF			Q, Figure of Merit $V_R = 4.0$ V dc $f = 50$ MHz	TR, Tuning Ratio C_4/C_{60} $f = 1.0$ MHz	
	Min	Typ	Max	Min	Min	Typ
1N5139	6.1	6.8	7.5	350	2.7	2.9
1N5140	9.0	10	11	300	2.8	3.0
1N5141	10.8	12	13.2	300	2.8	3.0
1N5142	13.5	15	16.5	250	2.8	3.0
1N5143	16.2	18	19.8	250	2.8	3.0
1N5144	19.8	22	24.2	200	3.2	3.4
1N5145	24.3	27	29.7	200	3.2	3.4
1N5146	29.7	33	36.3	200	3.2	3.4
1N5147	36.1	39	42.9	200	3.2	3.4
1N5148	42.3	47	51.7	200	3.2	3.4

(a) Electrical characteristics

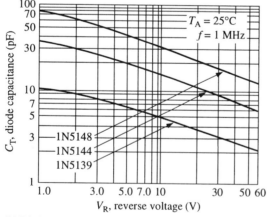

(b) Diode capacitance

(c) Figure of merit

Thomas L. Floyd
Electronic Devices, Fifth Edition
Electronic Devices: Electron-Flow Version, Third Edition

©1999 by Prentice-Hall, Inc.
Simon & Schuster/A Viacom Company
Upper Saddle River, New Jersey 07458
All rights reserved.

FIGURE 3-31
Partial data sheet for an MLED81 IR light-emitting diode.

Maximum Ratings

Rating	Symbol	Value	Unit
Reverse voltage	V_R	5	Volts
Forward current — continuous	I_F	100	mA
Forward current — peak pulse	I_F	1	A
Total power dissipation @ $T_A = 25°C$ Derate above 25°C	P_D	100 2.2	mW mW/C°
Ambient operating temperature range	T_A	−30 to +70	°C
Storage temperature	T_{stg}	−30 to +80	°C
Lead soldering temperature, 5 seconds max, 1/16 inch from case	—	260	°C

Electrical Characteristics ($T_A = 25°C$ unless otherwise noted)

Characteristic	Symbol	Min	Typ	Max	Unit
Reverse leakage current ($V_R = 3$ V)	I_R	—	10	—	nA
Reverse leakage current ($V_R = 5$ V)	I_R	—	1	10	μA
Forward voltage ($I_F = 100$ mA)	V_F	—	1.35	1.7	V
Temperature coefficient of forward voltage	ΔV_F	—	−1.6	—	mV/K
Capacitance ($f = 1$ MHz)	C	—	25	—	pF

Optical Characteristics ($T_A = 25°C$ unless otherwise noted)

Characteristic	Symbol	Min	Typ	Max	Unit
Peak wavelength ($I_F = 100$ mA)	λp	—	940	—	nm
Spectral half-power bandwidth	$\Delta\lambda$	—	50	—	nm
Total power output ($I_F = 100$ mA)	ϕe	—	16	—	mW
Temperature coefficient of total power output	$\Delta\phi e$	—	−0.25	—	%/K
Axial radiant intensity ($I_F = 100$ mA)	I_e	10	15	—	mW/sr
Temperature coefficient of axial radiant intensity	ΔI_e	—	−0.25	—	%/K
Power half-angle	φ	—	±30	—	°

(a) Ratings and characteristics

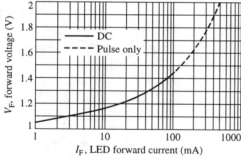

(b) LED forward voltage versus forward current

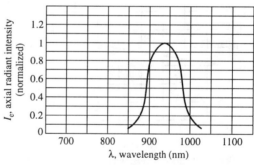

(c) Relative spectral emission

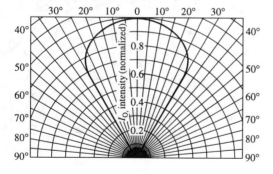

(d) Spatial radiation pattern

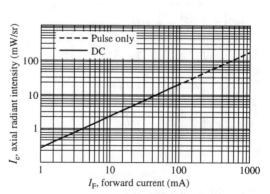

(e) Intensity versus forward current

Thomas L. Floyd
Electronic Devices, Fifth Edition
Electronic Devices: Electron-Flow Version, Third Edition

©1999 by Prentice-Hall, Inc.
Simon & Schuster/A Viacom Company
Upper Saddle River, New Jersey 07458
All rights reserved.

FIGURE 3-36
Partial data sheet for the MRD821 photodiode.

Maximum Ratings

Rating	Symbol	Value	Unit
Reverse voltage	V_R	35	Volts
Forward current — continuous	I_F	100	mA
Total power dissipation @ $T_A = 25°C$	P_D	150	mW
Derate above 25°C		3.3	mW/C°
Ambient operating temperature range	T_A	−30 to +70	°C
Storage temperature	T_{stg}	−40 to +80	°C
Lead soldering temperature, 5 seconds max, 1/16 inch from case	—	260	°C

Electrical Characteristics ($T_A = 25°C$ unless otherwise noted)

Characteristic	Symbol	Min	Typ	Max	Unit
Dark current ($V_R = 10$ V)	I_D	—	3	30	nA
Capacitance ($f = 1$ MHz, $V = 0$)	C_J	—	175	—	pF

Optical Characteristics ($T_A = 25°C$ unless otherwise noted)

Characteristic	Symbol	Min	Typ	Max	Unit
Wavelength of maximum sensitivity	λ_{max}	—	940	—	nm
Spectral range	$\Delta\lambda$	—	170	—	nm
Sensitivity ($\lambda = 940$ nm, $V_R = 20$ V)	S	—	50	—	$\mu A/mW/cm^2$
Temperature coefficient of sensitivity	ΔS	—	0.18	—	%/K
Acceptance half-angle	φ	—	±70	—	°
Short circuit current (Ev = 1000 lux)	I_S	—	50	—	μA
Open circuit voltage (Ev = 1000 lux)	V_L	—	0.3	—	V

(a) Ratings and characteristics

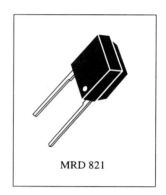
MRD 821

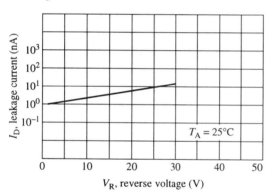

(b) Dark current versus reverse voltage

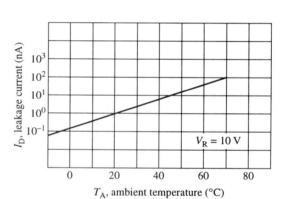

(c) Dark current versus temperature

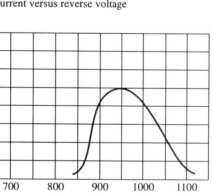

(d) Relative spectral sensitivity

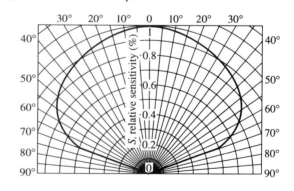

(e) Angular response

Thomas L. Floyd
Electronic Devices, Fifth Edition
Electronic Devices: Electron-Flow Version, Third Edition

©1999 by Prentice-Hall, Inc.
Simon & Schuster/A Viacom Company
Upper Saddle River, New Jersey 07458
All rights reserved.

FIGURE 3-52
Regulated power supply preliminary schematic.

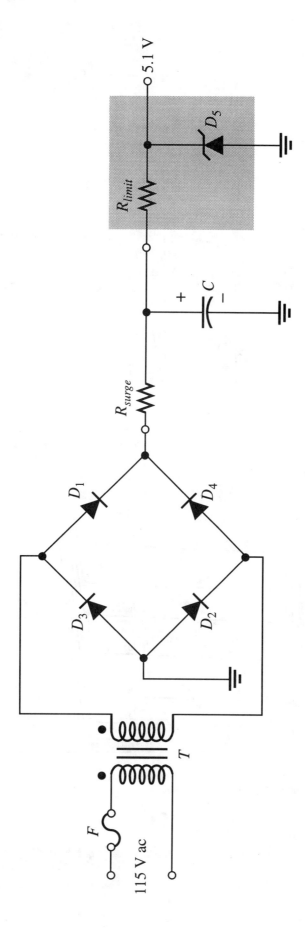

Thomas L. Floyd
Electronic Devices, Fifth Edition
Electronic Devices: Electron-Flow Version, Third Edition

©1999 by Prentice-Hall, Inc.
Simon & Schuster/A Viacom Company
Upper Saddle River, New Jersey 07458
All rights reserved.

FIGURE 4-9*
Collector characteristic curves.

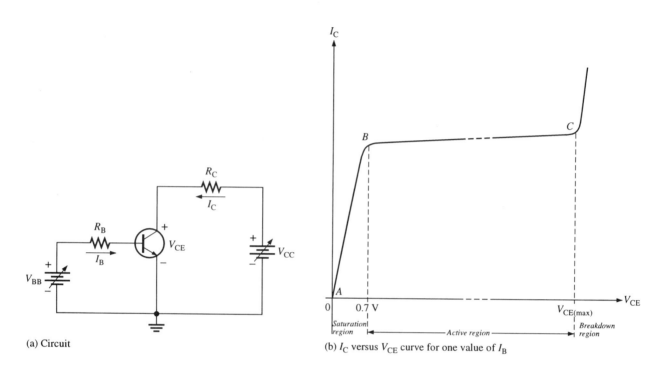

(a) Circuit

(b) I_C versus V_{CE} curve for one value of I_B

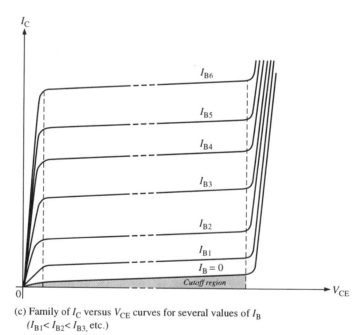

(c) Family of I_C versus V_{CE} curves for several values of I_B
($I_{B1} < I_{B2} < I_{B3}$, etc.)

Thomas L. Floyd
Electronic Devices, Fifth Edition
*Current arrows indicate conventional flow.

©1999 by Prentice-Hall, Inc.
Simon & Schuster/A Viacom Company
Upper Saddle River, New Jersey 07458
All rights reserved.

FIGURE 4-14
DC load line on a family of collector characteristic curves illustrating the cutoff and saturation conditions.

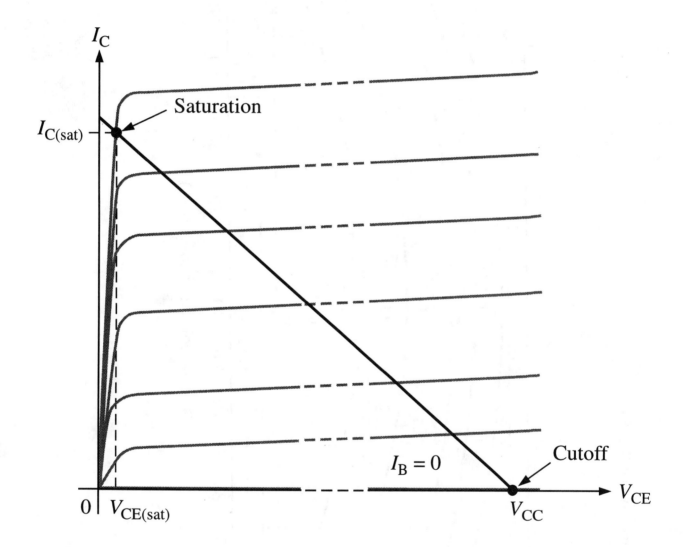

Thomas L. Floyd
Electronic Devices, Fifth Edition
Electronic Devices: Electron-Flow Version, Third Edition

©1999 by Prentice-Hall, Inc.
Simon & Schuster/A Viacom Company
Upper Saddle River, New Jersey 07458
All rights reserved.

FIGURE 4-16
Variation of β_{DC} with I_C for several temperatures.

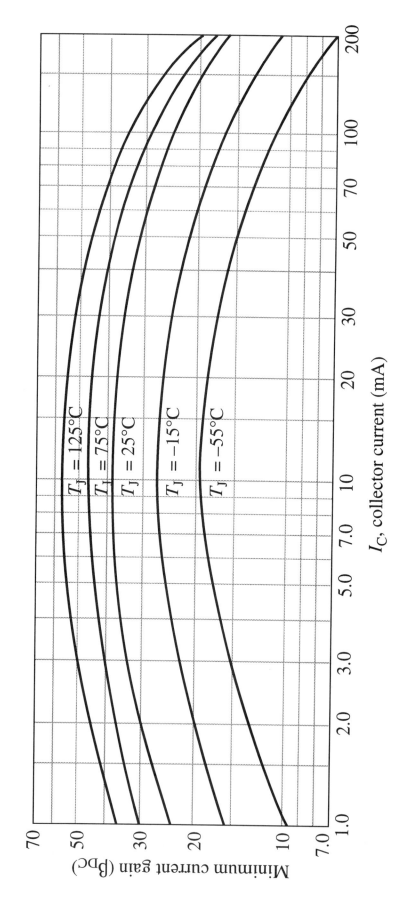

Thomas L. Floyd
Electronic Devices, Fifth Edition
Electronic Devices: Electron-Flow Version, Third Edition

©1999 by Prentice-Hall, Inc.
Simon & Schuster/A Viacom Company
Upper Saddle River, New Jersey 07458
All rights reserved.

FIGURE 4-17
Maximum power dissipation curve.

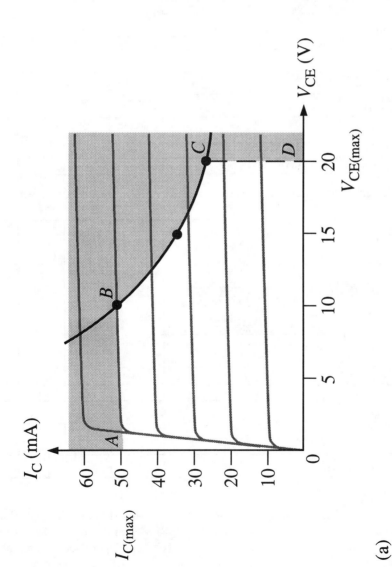

$P_{D(max)}$	V_{CE}	I_C
500 mW	5 V	100 mA
500 mW	10 V	50 mA
500 mW	15 V	33 mA
500 mW	20 V	25 mA

(b)

Thomas L. Floyd
Electronic Devices, Fifth Edition
Electronic Devices: Electron-Flow Version, Third Edition

©1999 by Prentice-Hall, Inc.
Simon & Schuster/A Viacom Company
Upper Saddle River, New Jersey 07458
All rights reserved.

FIGURE 4-42
Partial data sheet for the 2N3947 *npn* transistor.

2N3946
2N3947

General-Purpose Transistors

NPN Silicon

Maximum Ratings

Rating	Symbol	Value	Unit
Collector-Emitter voltage	V_{CEO}	40	V dc
Collector-Base voltage	V_{CBO}	60	V dc
Emitter-Base voltage	V_{EBO}	6.0	V dc
Collector current — continuous	I_C	200	mA dc
Total device dissipation @ $T_A = 25°C$ Derate above 25°C	P_D	0.36 2.06	Watts mW/C°
Total device dissipation @ $T_C = 25°C$ Derate above 25°C	P_D	1.2 6.9	Watts mW/C°
Operating and storage junction Temperature range	T_J, T_{stg}	−65 to +200	°C

Thermal Characteristics

Characteristic	Symbol	Max	Unit
Thermal resistance, junction to case	$R_{\theta JC}$	0.15	C°/mW
Thermal resistance, junction to ambient	$R_{\theta JA}$	0.49	C°/mW

Electrical Characteristics ($T_A = 25°C$ unless otherwise noted.)

Characteristic		Symbol	Min	Max	Unit
OFF Characteristics					
Collector-Emitter breakdown voltage ($I_C = 10$ mA dc)		$V_{(BR)CEO}$	40	–	V dc
Collector-Base breakdown voltage ($I_C = 10$ μA dc, $I_E = 0$)		$V_{(BR)CBO}$	60	–	V dc
Emitter-Base breakdown voltage ($I_E = 10$ μA dc, $I_C = 0$)		$V_{(BR)EBO}$	6.0	–	V dc
Collector cutoff current ($V_{CE} = 40$ V dc, $V_{OB} = 3.0$ V dc) ($V_{CE} = 40$ V dc, $V_{OB} = 3.0$ V dc, $T_A = 150°C$)		I_{CEX}	– –	0.010 15	μA dc
Base cutoff current ($V_{CE} = 40$ V dc, $V_{OB} = 3.0$ V dc)		I_{BL}	–	.025	μA dc
ON Characteristics					
DC current gain ($I_C = 0.1$ mA dc, $V_{CE} = 1.0$ V dc)	2N3946 2N3947	h_{FE}	30 60	– –	–
($I_C = 1.0$ mA dc, $V_{CE} = 1.0$ V dc)	2N3946 2N3947		45 90	– –	
($I_C = 10$ mA dc, $V_{CE} = 1.0$ V dc)	2N3946 2N3947		50 100	150 300	
($I_C = 50$ mA dc, $V_{CE} = 1.0$ V dc)	2N3946 2N3947		20 40	– –	
Collector-Emitter saturation voltage ($I_C = 10$ mA dc, $I_B = 1.0$ mA dc) ($I_C = 50$ mA dc, $I_B = 5.0$ mA dc)		$V_{CE(sat)}$	– –	0.2 0.3	V dc
Base-Emitter saturation voltage ($I_C = 10$ mA dc, $I_B = 1.0$ mA dc) ($I_C = 50$ mA dc, $I_B = 5.0$ mA dc)		$V_{BE(sat)}$	0.6 –	0.9 1.0	V dc
Small-Signal Characteristics					
Current gain — Bandwidth product ($I_C = 10$ mA dc, $V_{CE} = 20$ V dc, $f = 100$ MHz)	2N3946 2N3947	f_T	250 300	– –	MHz
Output capacitance ($V_{CB} = 10$ V dc, $I_E = 0, f = 100$ kHz)		C_{obo}	–	4.0	pF

Thomas L. Floyd
Electronic Devices, Fifth Edition
Electronic Devices: Electron-Flow Version, Third Edition

©1999 by Prentice-Hall, Inc.
Simon & Schuster/A Viacom Company
Upper Saddle River, New Jersey 07458
All rights reserved.

FIGURE 5-3*

Illustration of Q-point adjustments.

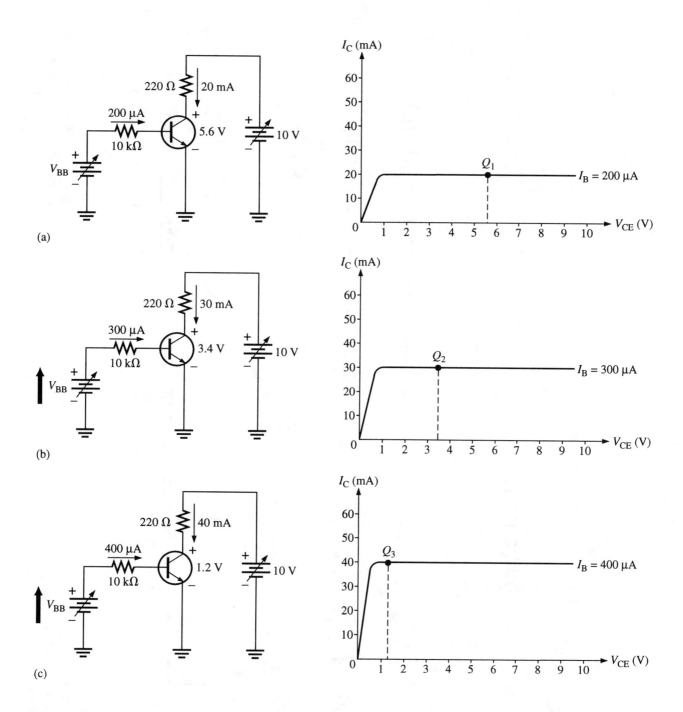

Thomas L. Floyd
Electronic Devices, Fifth Edition
*Current arrows indicate conventional flow.

©1999 by Prentice-Hall, Inc.
Simon & Schuster/A Viacom Company
Upper Saddle River, New Jersey 07458
All rights reserved.

FIGURE 5-4
The dc load line.

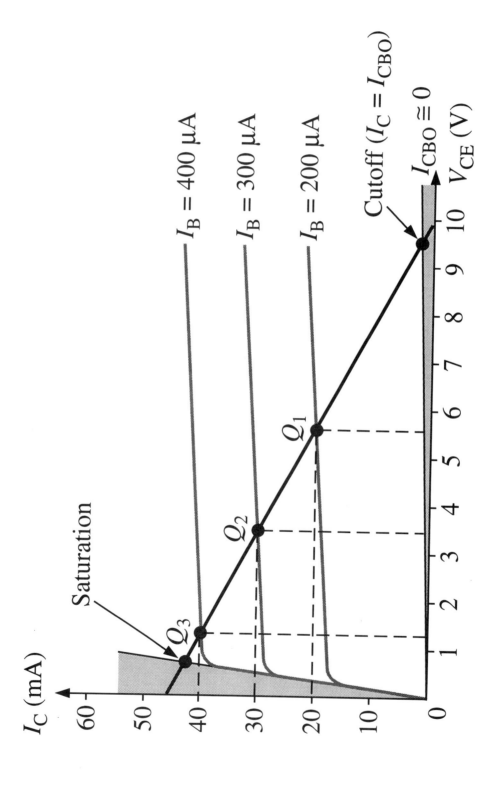

FIGURE 5-5
Variations in collector current and collector-to-emitter voltage as a result of a variation in base current. Notice that ac quantities are indicated by lowercase italic subscripts.

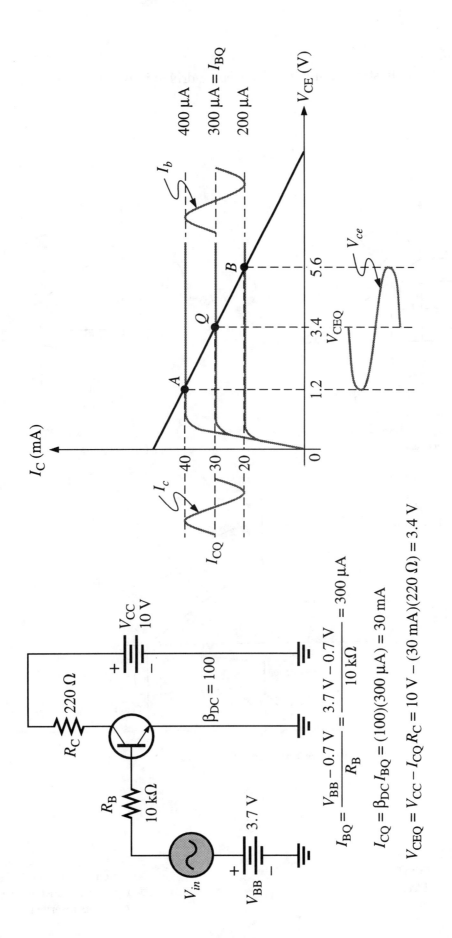

Thomas L. Floyd
Electronic Devices, Fifth Edition
Electronic Devices: Electron-Flow Version, Third Edition

©1999 by Prentice-Hall, Inc.
Simon & Schuster/A Viacom Company
Upper Saddle River, New Jersey 07458
All rights reserved.

FIGURE 5-6

Graphical load line illustration of a transistor being driven into saturation and cutoff.

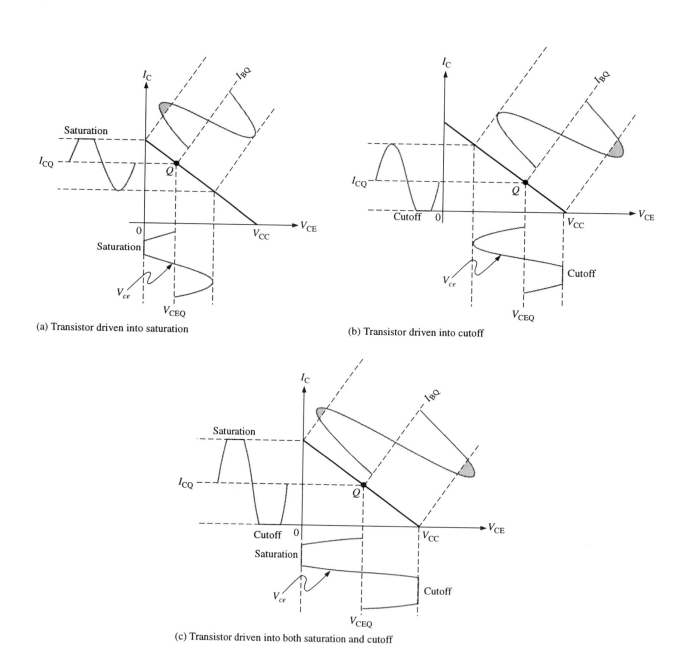

(a) Transistor driven into saturation

(b) Transistor driven into cutoff

(c) Transistor driven into both saturation and cutoff

Thomas L. Floyd
Electronic Devices, Fifth Edition
Electronic Devices: Electron-Flow Version, Third Edition

©1999 by Prentice-Hall, Inc.
Simon & Schuster/A Viacom Company
Upper Saddle River, New Jersey 07458
All rights reserved.

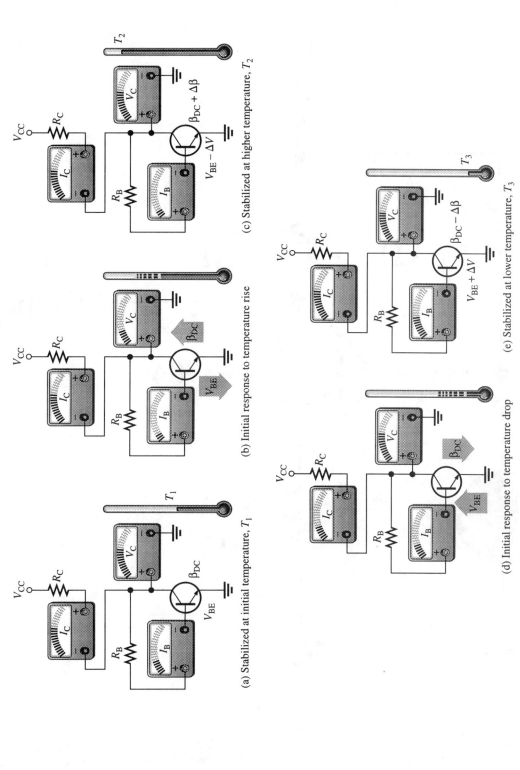

FIGURE 5-28
Illustration of collector-feedback stabilization of Q-point values over temperature.

FIGURE 5-35
Schematic of the temperature-to-voltage conversion circuit.

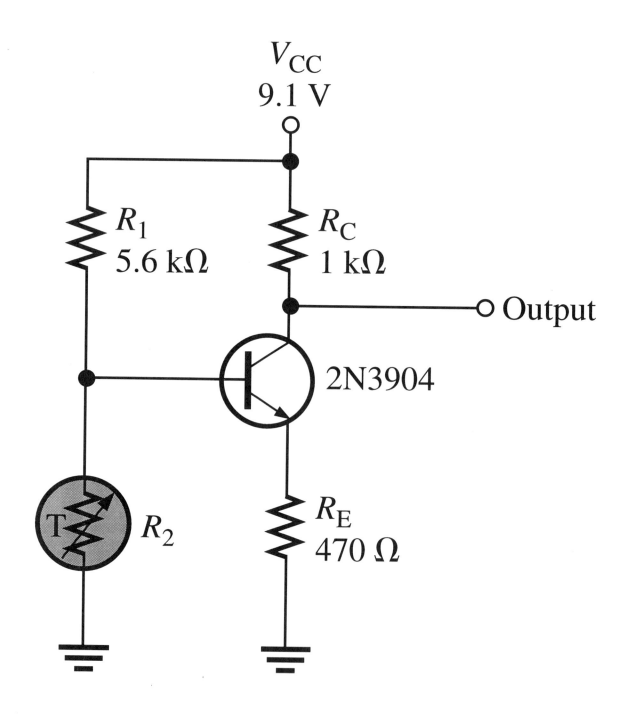

FIGURE 5-37
Power supply schematic.

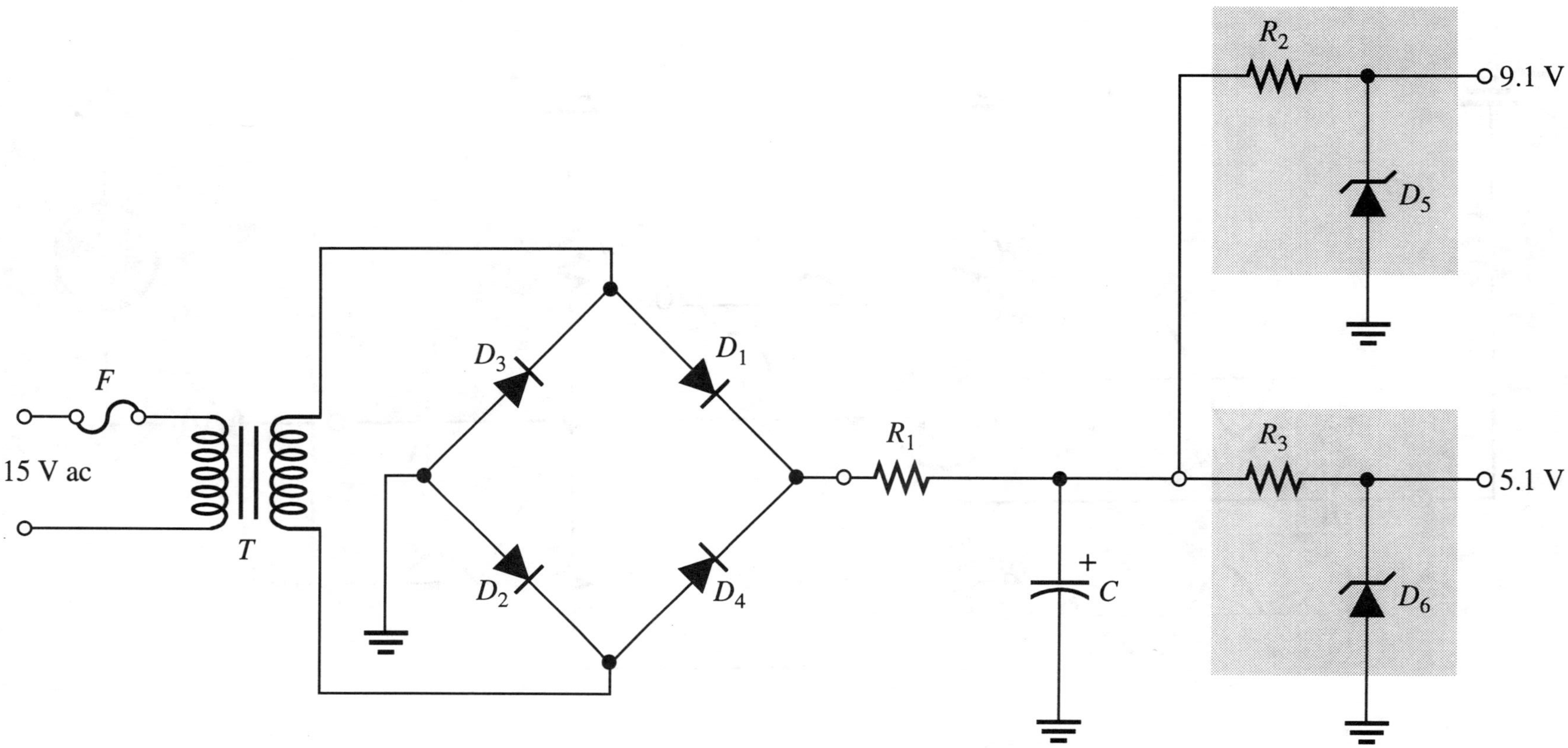

Thomas L. Floyd
Electronic Devices, Fifth Edition
Electronic Devices: Electron-Flow Version, Third Edition

© 1999 by Prentice-Hall, Inc.
Simon & Schuster/A Viacom Company
Upper Saddle River, New Jersey 07458
All rights reserved.

FIGURE 6-2
An amplifier with voltage-divider bias driven by an ac voltage source with an internal resistance, R_s.

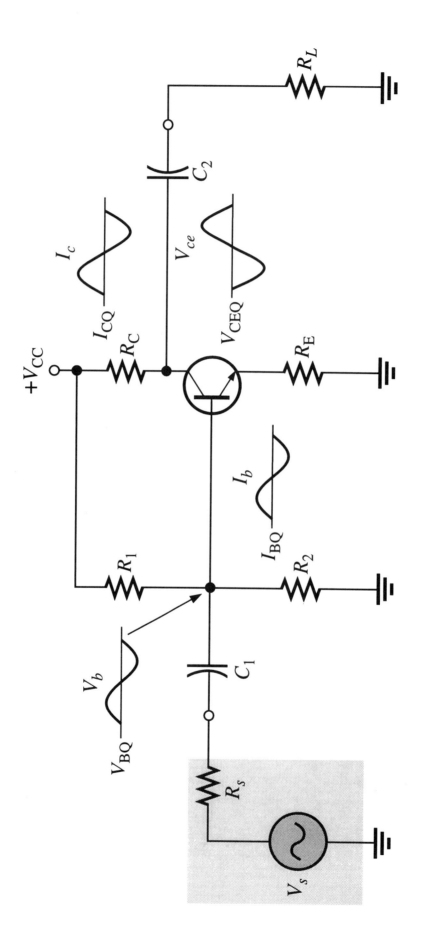

FIGURE 6–3
Graphical operation of the amplifier showing the variation of the base current, collector current, and collector-to-emitter voltage about their dc Q-point values. I_b and I_c are on different scales.

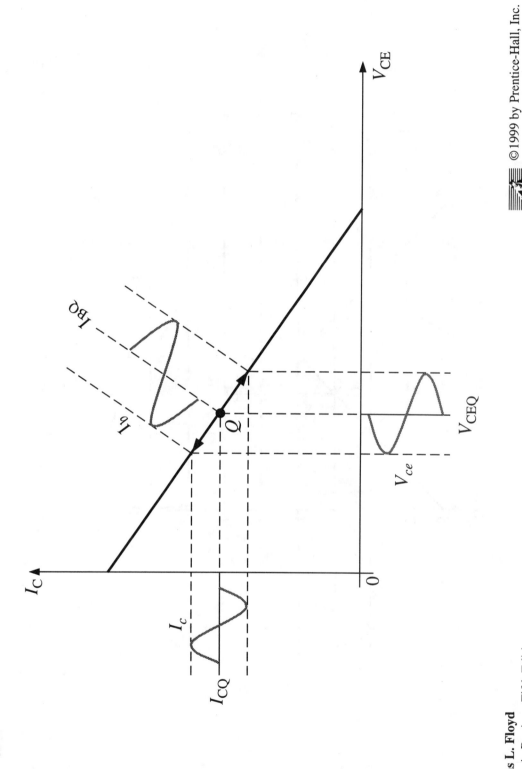

FIGURE 6-4

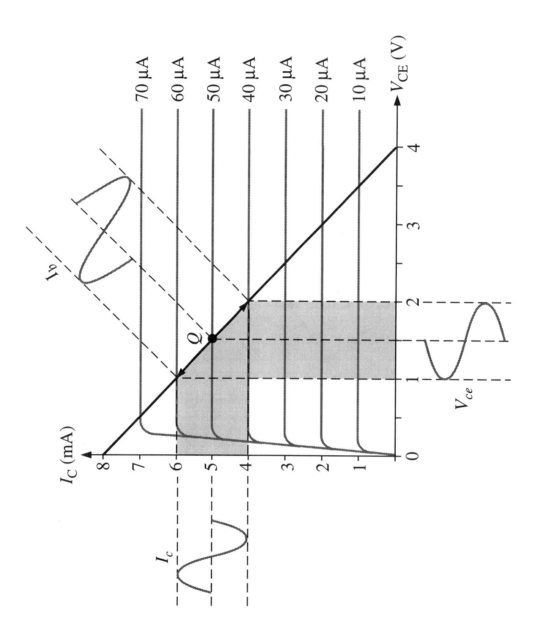

FIGURE 6-6*
AC equivalent circuits for defining h parameters using the common-emitter configuration.

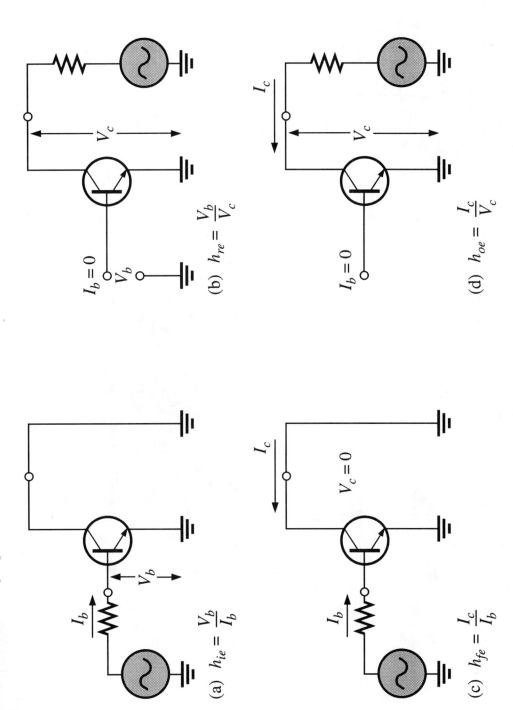

(a) $h_{ie} = \dfrac{V_b}{I_b}$

(b) $h_{re} = \dfrac{V_b}{V_c}$

(c) $h_{fe} = \dfrac{I_c}{I_b}$

(d) $h_{oe} = \dfrac{I_c}{V_c}$

Thomas L. Floyd
Electronic Devices, Fifth Edition
*Current arrows indicate conventional flow.

© 1999 by Prentice-Hall, Inc.
Simon & Schuster/A Viacom Company
Upper Saddle River, New Jersey 07458
All rights reserved.

FIGURE 6-8*

h-parameter equivalent circuits for the three amplifier configurations.

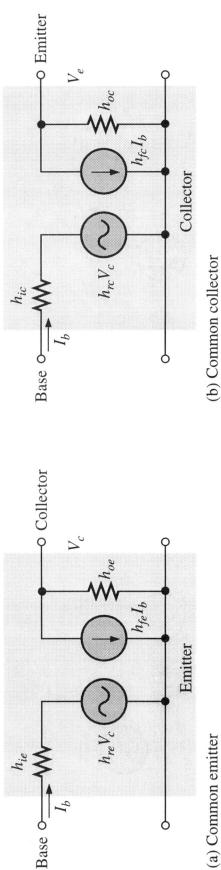

(a) Common emitter

(b) Common collector

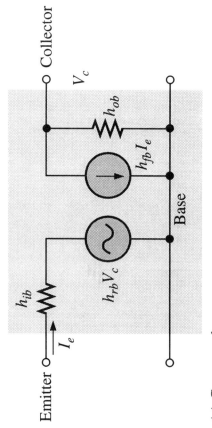

(c) Common base

Thomas L. Floyd
Electronic Devices, Fifth Edition
*Current arrows indicate conventional flow.

© 1999 by Prentice-Hall, Inc.
Simon & Schuster/A Viacom Company
Upper Saddle River, New Jersey 07458
All rights reserved.

FIGURE 6-19
Base circuit attenuation and overall gain.

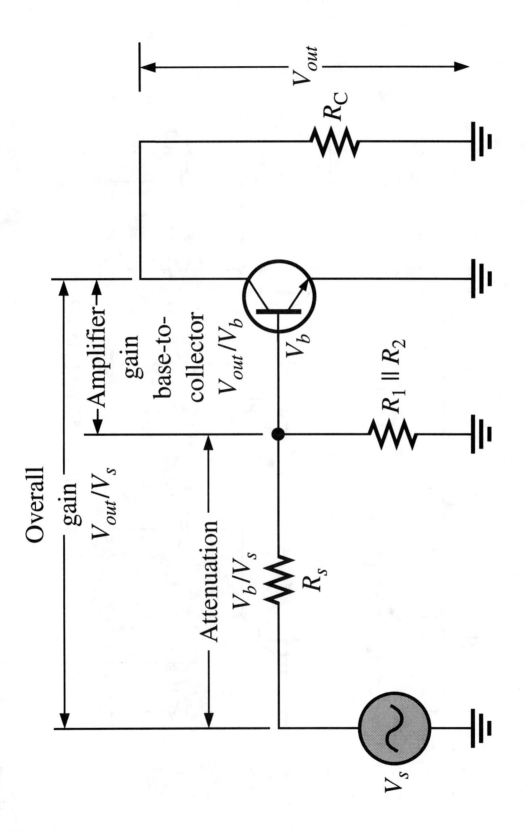

FIGURE 6-37
A two-stage common-emitter amplifier.

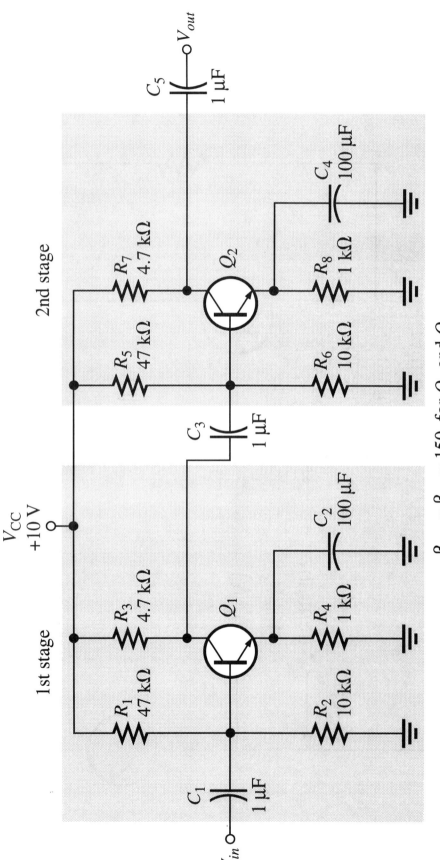

Thomas L. Floyd
Electronic Devices, Fifth Edition
Electronic Devices: Electron-Flow Version, Third Edition

© 1999 by Prentice-Hall, Inc.
Simon & Schuster/A Viacom Company
Upper Saddle River, New Jersey 07458
All rights reserved.

FIGURE 6-38
AC equivalent of first stage in Figure 6-37, showing loading from second stage input resistance.

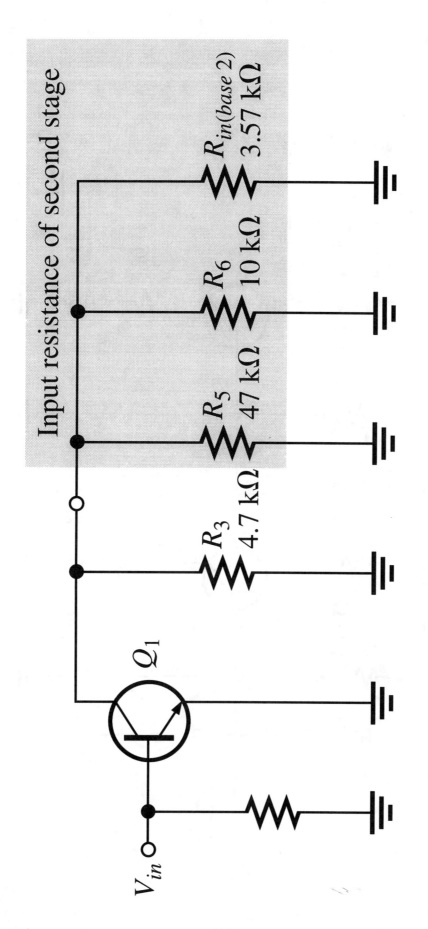

FIGURE 6-46
Schematic of the preamplifier circuit. Both transistors are 2N3904.

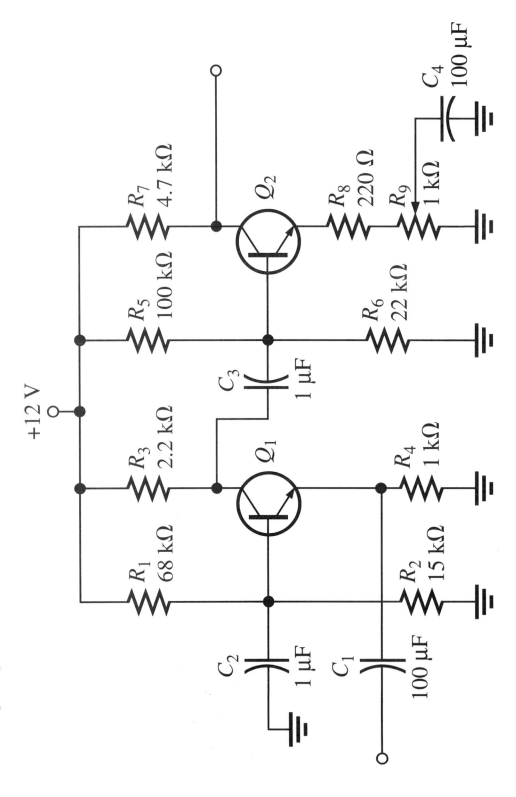

FIGURE 7-2
For maximum class A operation, the Q-point is centered on the ac load line.

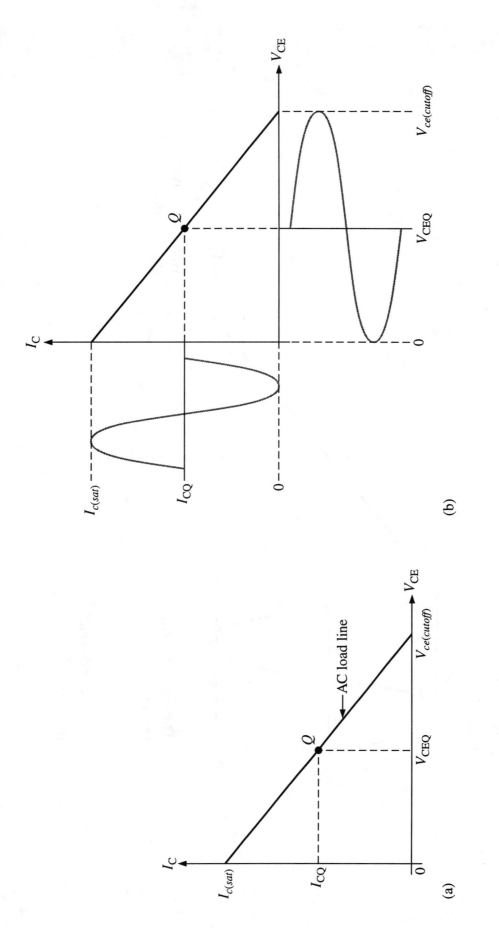

FIGURE 7–3
Waveforms are clipped at cutoff and saturation because the amplifier is overdriven (too large an input signal).

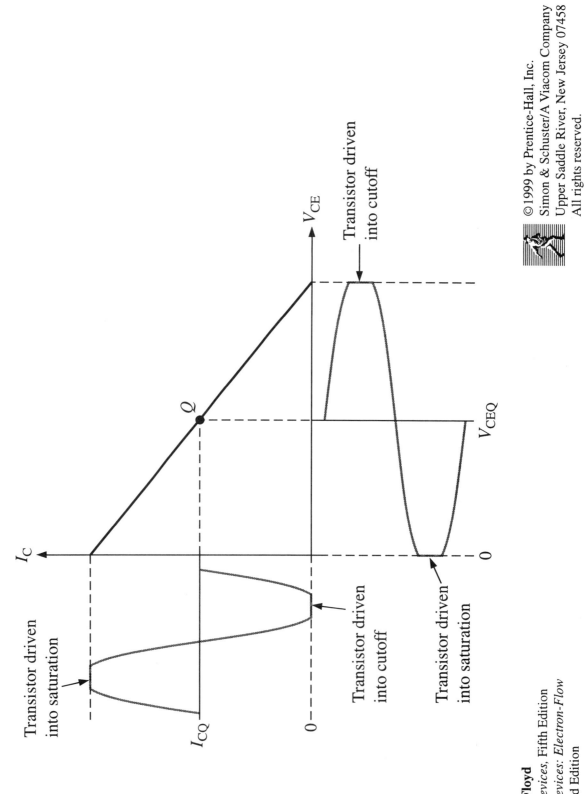

FIGURE 7-4
Q-point closer to cutoff.

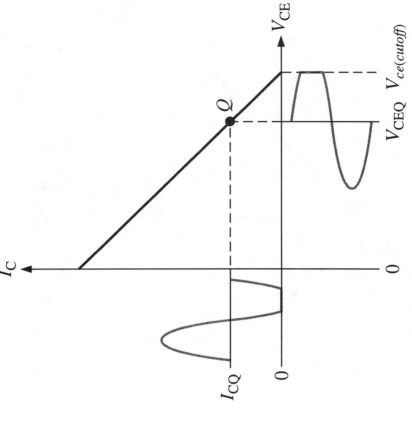

(a) Amplitude of V_{ce} and I_c limited by cutoff

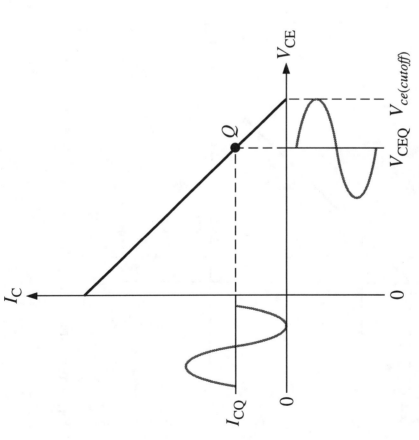

(b) Transistor driven into cutoff by a further increase in input amplitude

Thomas L. Floyd
Electronic Devices, Fifth Edition
Electronic Devices: Electron-Flow Version, Third Edition

©1999 by Prentice-Hall, Inc.
Simon & Schuster/A Viacom Company
Upper Saddle River, New Jersey 07458
All rights reserved.

FIGURE 7-5
Q-point closer to saturation.

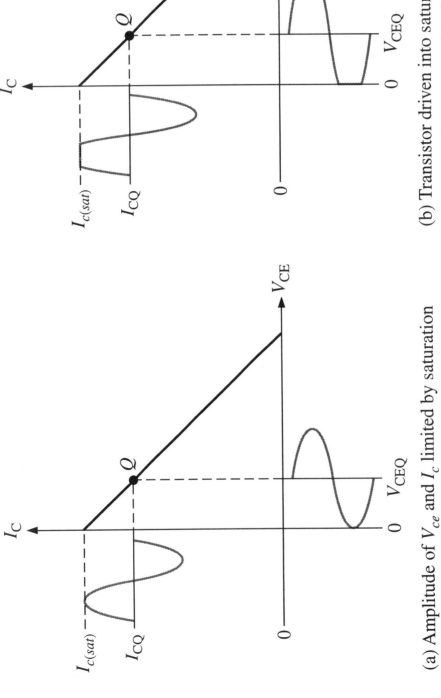

(a) Amplitude of V_{ce} and I_c limited by saturation

(b) Transistor driven into saturation by a further increase in input amplitude

Thomas L. Floyd
Electronic Devices, Fifth Edition
Electronic Devices: Electron-Flow Version, Third Edition

©1999 by Prentice-Hall, Inc.
Simon & Schuster/A Viacom Company
Upper Saddle River, New Jersey 07458
All rights reserved.

FIGURE 7–9
DC and ac load lines.

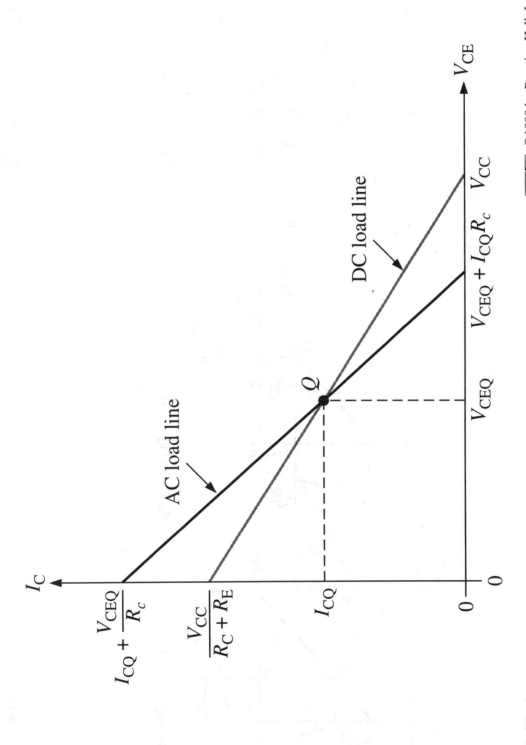

FIGURE 7–15
AC load line operation showing limitations of output voltage swings.

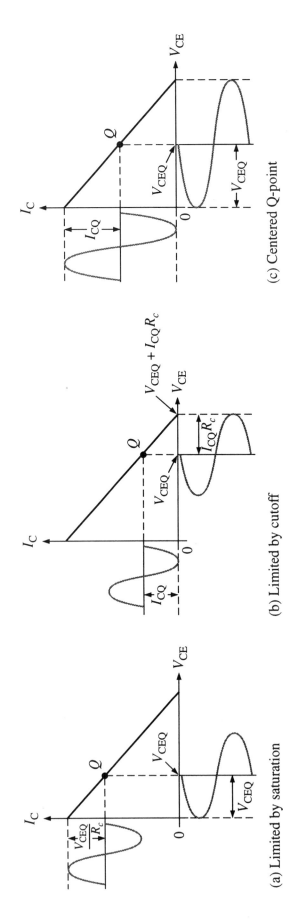

(a) Limited by saturation

(b) Limited by cutoff

(c) Centered Q-point

FIGURE 7-20
Class B push-pull ac operation.

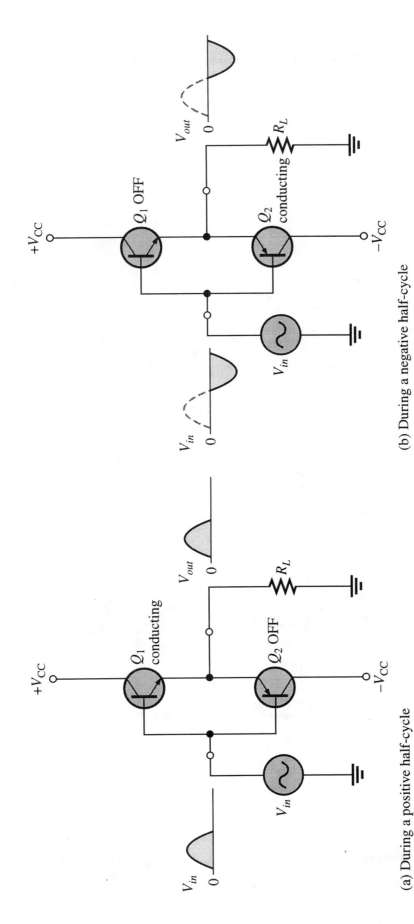

Thomas L. Floyd
Electronic Devices, Fifth Edition
Electronic Devices: Electron-Flow Version, Third Edition

©1999 by Prentice-Hall, Inc.
Simon & Schuster/A Viacom Company
Upper Saddle River, New Jersey 07458
All rights reserved.

FIGURE 7-26*
Ideal ac push-pull operation for maximum signal operation.

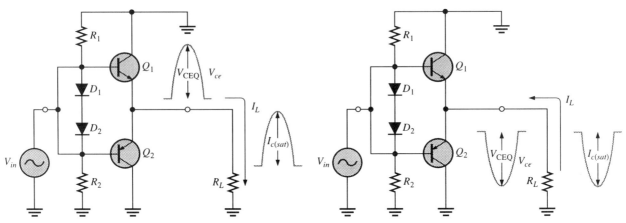

(a) Q_1 conducting with maximum signal output

(b) Q_2 conducting with maximum signal output

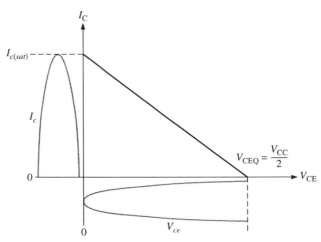

(c) AC load line for each transistor

Thomas L. Floyd
Electronic Devices, Fifth Edition
*Current arrows indicate
conventional flow.

©1999 by Prentice-Hall, Inc.
Simon & Schuster/A Viacom Company
Upper Saddle River, New Jersey 07458
All rights reserved.

FIGURE 7-35*
Resonant circuit action.

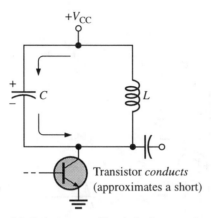

(a) *C* charges to $+V_{CC}$ at the input peak when transistor is conducting.

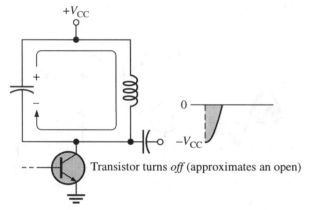

(b) *C* discharges to 0 volts.

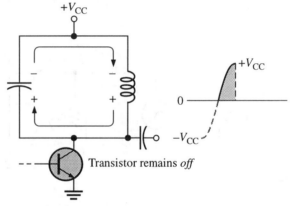

(c) *L* recharges *C* in opposite direction.

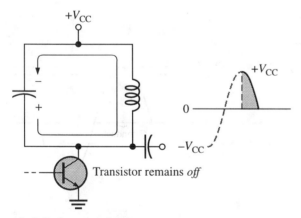

(d) *C* discharges to 0 volts.

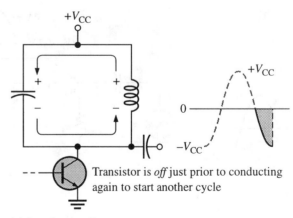

(e) *L* recharges *C*.

Thomas L. Floyd
Electronic Devices, Fifth Edition
*Current arrows indicate conventional flow.

©1999 by Prentice-Hall, Inc.
Simon & Schuster/A Viacom Company
Upper Saddle River, New Jersey 07458
All rights reserved.

FIGURE 7-38*
Clamper bias action.

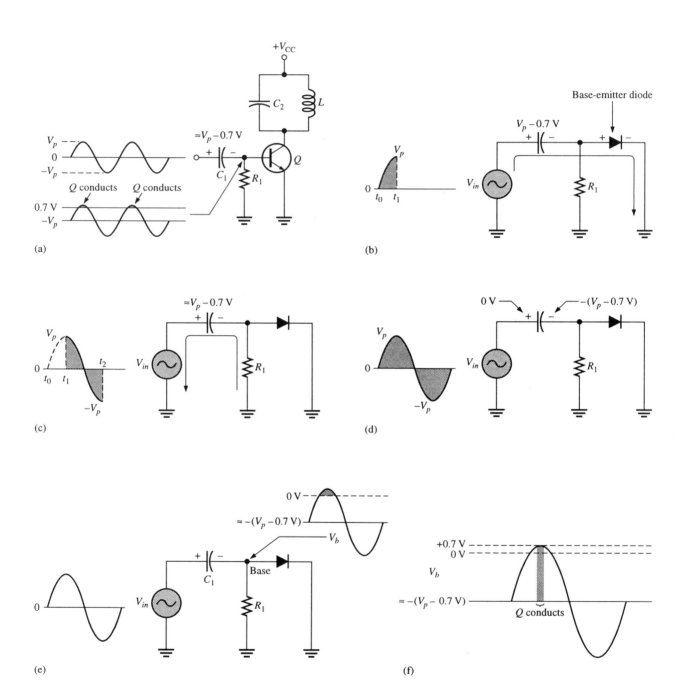

Thomas L. Floyd
Electronic Devices, Fifth Edition
*Current arrows indicate conventional flow.

©1999 by Prentice-Hall, Inc.
Simon & Schuster/A Viacom Company
Upper Saddle River, New Jersey 07458
All rights reserved.

FIGURE 7-42
Schematic of the power amplifier circuit.

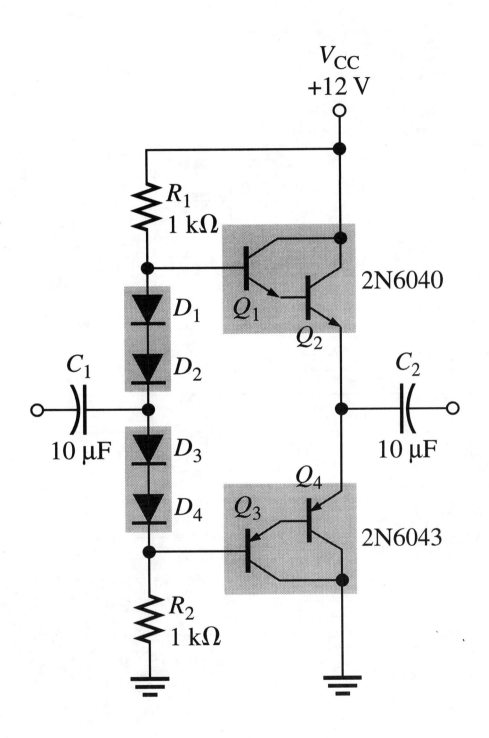

Thomas L. Floyd
Electronic Devices, Fifth Edition
*Electronic Devices: Electron-Flow
Version,* Third Edition

©1999 by Prentice-Hall, Inc.
Simon & Schuster/A Viacom Company
Upper Saddle River, New Jersey 07458
All rights reserved.

FIGURE 7-43
Partial data sheet for complementary darlington transistors 2N6040 (*npn*) and 2N6043 (*pnp*).

Plastic Medium-Power Complementary Silicon Transistors

... designed for general-purpose amplifier and low-speed switching applications.
- High DC current gain —
  $h_{FE} = 2500$ (Typ) @ $I_C = 4.0$ A dc
- Collector-Emitter sustaining voltage — @ 100 mA dc
  $V_{CEO(sus)} = 60$ V dc (Min) — 2N6040, 2N6043
  $= 80$ V dc (Min) — 2N6041, 2N6044
  $= 100$ V dc (Min) — 2N6042, 2N6045
- Low collector-emitter saturation voltage
  $V_{CE(sat)} = 2.0$ V dc (Max) @ $I_C = 4.0$ A dc — 2N6040,41,2N6043,44
  $= 2.0$ V dc (Max) @ $I_C = 3.0$ A dc — 2N6042, 2N6045
- Monolithic construction with built-in base-emitter shunt resistors

Darlington 8 ampere Complementary Silicon Power Transistors 60-80-100 VOLTS 75 WATTS

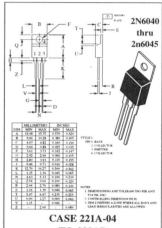

CASE 221A-04
TO-220AB

Maximum Ratings

Rating	Symbol	2N6040 2N6043 MJE6040 MJE6043	2N6041 2N6044 MJE6041 MJE6044	2N6042 2N6045 MJE6045	Unit
Collector-Emitter voltage	V_{CEO}	60	80	100	V dc
Collector-Base voltage	V_{CB}	60	80	100	V dc
Emitter-Base voltage	V_{EB}	←	5.0	→	V dc
Collector Current—Continuous Peak	I_C	←	8.0 16	→	A dc
Base current	I_B	←	120	→	mA dc
Total power dissipation @ $T_C = 25°C$ Derate above 25°C	P_D	←	75 0.60	→	Watts W/C°
Total power dissipation @ $T_A = 25°C$ Derate above 25°C	P_D	←	2.2 0.0175	→	Watts W/C°
Operating and storage junction, Temperature range	T_J, T_{stg}	←	−65 to +150	→	°C

Electrical Characteristics ($T_C = 25°C$ unless otherwise noted)

Characteristic	Symbol	Min	Max	Unit
DC current gain ($I_C = 4.0$ A dc, $V_{CE} = 4.0$ V dc) 2N6040,41,2N6043,44,MJE6040,41, MJE6043,44 ($I_C = 3.0$ A dc, $V_{CE} = 4.0$ V dc) 2N6042, 2N6045, MJE6045 ($I_C = 8.0$ A dc, $V_{CE} = 4.0$ V dc) All Types	h_{FE}	1000 1000 100	20,000 20,000 —	—
Collector-Emitter saturation voltage ($I_C = 4.0$ A dc, $I_B = 16$ mA dc) 2N6040,41,2N6043,44,MJE6040,41,MJE6043,44 ($I_C = 3.0$ A dc, $I_B = 12$ mA dc) 2N6042,2N6045,MJE6045 ($I_C = 8.0$ A dc, $I_B = 80$ mA dc) All Types	$V_{CE(sat)}$	— — —	2.0 2.0 4.0	V dc
Base-Emitter saturation voltage ($I_C = 8.0$ A dc, $I_B = 80$ mA dc)	$V_{CE(sat)}$	—	4.5	V dc
Base-Emitter on voltage ($I_C = 4.0$ A dc, $V_{CE} = 4.0$ V dc)	$V_{BE(on)}$	—	2.8	V dc

Dynamic Characteristics

Characteristic	Symbol	Min	Max	Unit
Small-signal current gain ($I_C = 3.0$ A dc, $V_{CE} = 4.0$ V dc, $f = 1.0$ MHz)	$|h_{fe}|$	4.0	—	
Output capacitance ($V_{CB} = 10$ V dc, $I_E = 0$, $f = 1.0$ MHz) 2N6040/2N6042, MJE6040 / 2N6043/2N6045, MJE6043/MJE6045	C_{ob}	— —	300 200	pF
Small-signal current gain ($I_C = 3.0$ A dc, $V_{CE} = 4.0$ V dc, $f = 1.0$ kHz)	h_{fe}	300	—	—

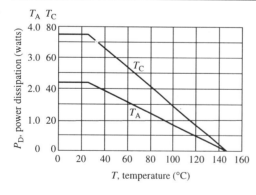

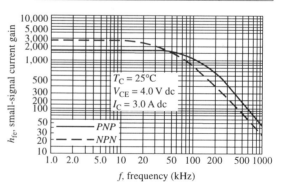

Thomas L. Floyd
Electronic Devices, Fifth Edition
Electronic Devices: Electron-Flow Version, Third Edition

©1999 by Prentice-Hall, Inc.
Simon & Schuster/A Viacom Company
Upper Saddle River, New Jersey 07458
All rights reserved.

FIGURE 8-3
Effects of V_{GS} on channel width, resistance, and drain current ($V_{GG} = V_{GS}$).

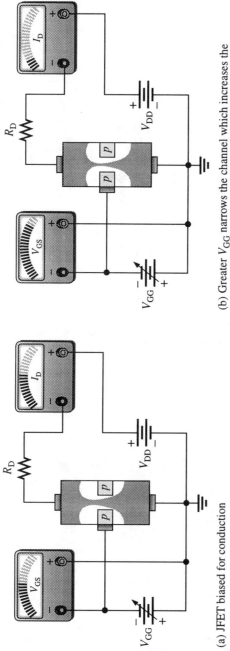

(a) JFET biased for conduction

(b) Greater V_{GG} narrows the channel which increases the resistance of the channel and decreases I_D.

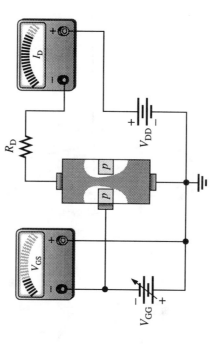

(c) Less V_{GG} widens the channel which decreases the resistance of the channel and increases I_D.

Thomas L. Floyd
Electronic Devices, Fifth Edition
Electronic Devices: Electron-Flow Version, Third Edition

©1999 by Prentice-Hall, Inc.
Simon & Schuster/A Viacom Company
Upper Saddle River, New Jersey 07458
All rights reserved.

FIGURE 8-5*
The drain characteristic curve of a JFET for $V_{GS} = 0$ showing pinch-off.

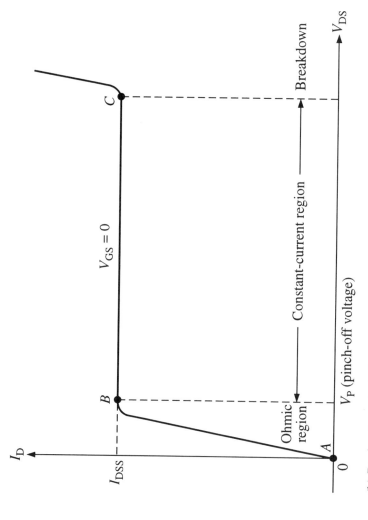

Thomas L. Floyd
Electronic Devices, Fifth Edition
*Current arrows indicate conventional flow.

©1999 by Prentice-Hall, Inc.
Simon & Schuster/A Viacom Company
Upper Saddle River, New Jersey 07458
All rights reserved.

FIGURE 8-6
JFET action that produces the characteristic curve for $V_{GS} = 0$ V.

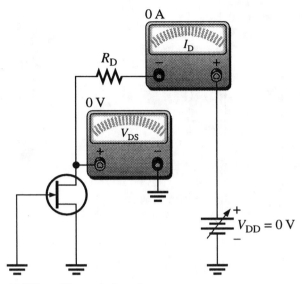

(a) When $V_{DS} = 0$, $I_D = 0$.

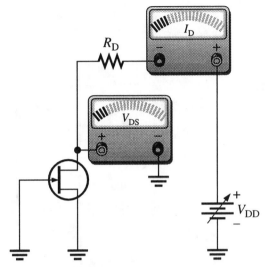

(b) I_D increases proportionally with V_{DS} in the ohmic region.

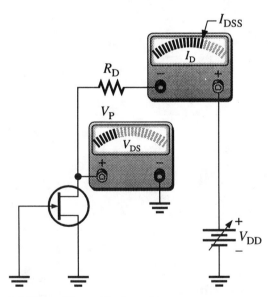

(c) When $V_{DS} = V_P$, $I_D = I_{DSS}$.

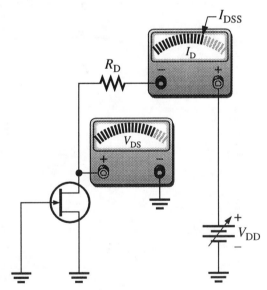

(d) As V_{DS} increases further, I_D remains at I_{DSS} unless breakdown occurs.

Thomas L. Floyd
Electronic Devices, Fifth Edition
Electronic Devices: Electron-Flow Version, Third Edition

©1999 by Prentice-Hall, Inc.
Simon & Schuster/A Viacom Company
Upper Saddle River, New Jersey 07458
All rights reserved.

FIGURE 8-7
Pinch-off occurs at a lower V_{DS} as V_{GS} is increased to more negative values.

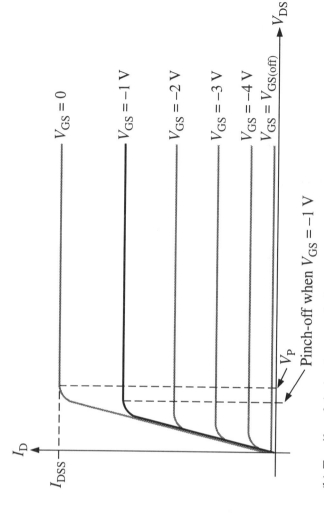

(a) JFET biased at $V_{GS} = -1$ V

(b) Family of drain characteristic curves

Thomas L. Floyd
Electronic Devices, Fifth Edition
Electronic Devices: Electron-Flow Version, Third Edition

©1999 by Prentice-Hall, Inc.
Simon & Schuster/A Viacom Company
Upper Saddle River, New Jersey 07458
All rights reserved.

FIGURE 8-8
V_{GS} controls I_D.

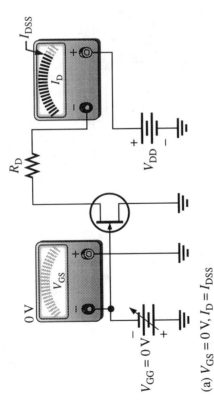

(a) $V_{GS} = 0\text{ V}$, $I_D = I_{DSS}$

(b) V_{GS} negative, I_D decreases

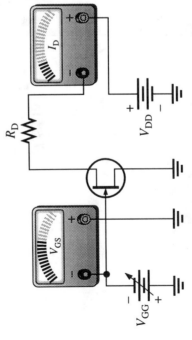

(c) I_D continues to decrease as V_{GS} is made more negative.

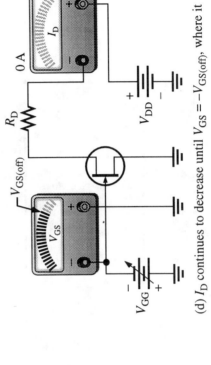

(d) I_D continues to decrease until $V_{GS} = -V_{GS(off)}$, where it becomes zero.

FIGURE 8-13
Example of the development of an *n*-channel JFET transfer characteristic curve (left) from the JFET drain characteristic curves (right).

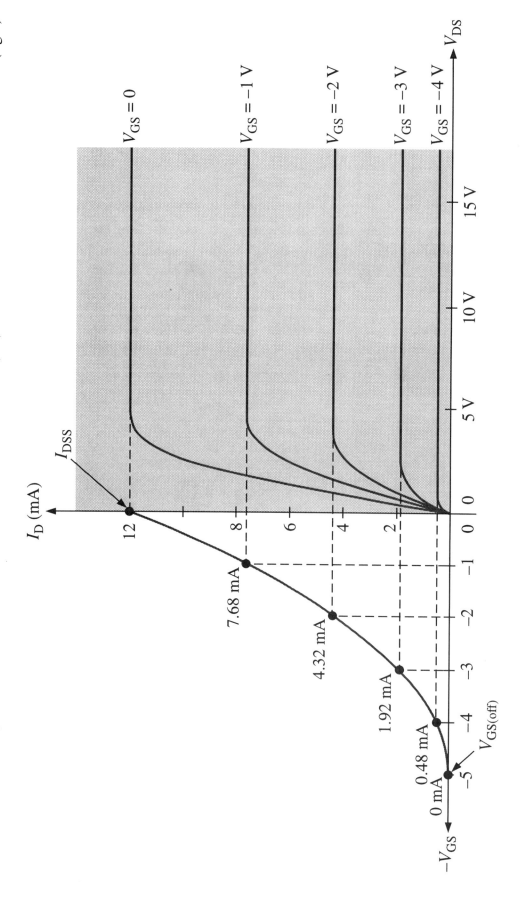

Thomas L. Floyd
Electronic Devices, Fifth Edition
Electronic Devices: Electron-Flow Version, Third Edition

©1999 by Prentice-Hall, Inc.
Simon & Schuster/A Viacom Company
Upper Saddle River, New Jersey 07458
All rights reserved.

FIGURE 8-14
JFET data sheet.

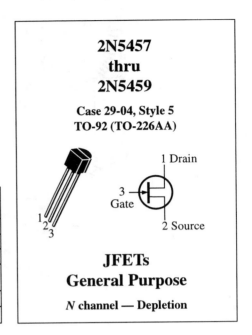

**2N5457
thru
2N5459**

Case 29-04, Style 5
TO-92 (TO-226AA)

**JFETs
General Purpose**

N channel — Depletion

Maximum Ratings

Rating	Symbol	Value	Unit
Drain-Source voltage	V_{DS}	25	V dc
Drain-Gate voltage	V_{DG}	25	V dc
Reverse gate-source voltage	V_{GSR}	−25	V dc
Gate current	I_G	10	mA dc
Total device dissipation @ T_A = 25°C Derate above 25°C	P_D	310 2.82	mW mW/C°
Junction temperature	T_J	125	°C
Storage channel temperature range	T_{stg}	−65 to +150	°C

Electrical Characteristics (T_A = 25°C unless otherwise noted.)

Characteristic		Symbol	Min	Typ	Max	Unit
OFF Characteristics						
Gate-Source breakdown voltage (I_G = −10 μA dc, V_{DS} = 0)		$V_{(BR)GSS}$	−25	−	−	V dc
Gate reverse current (V_{GS} = −15 V dc, V_{DS} = 0) (V_{GS} = −15 V dc, V_{DS} = 0, T_A = 100°C)		I_{GSS}	− −	− −	−1.0 −200	nA dc
Gate-Source cutoff voltage (V_{DS} = 15 V dc, I_D = 10 nA dc)	2N5457 2N5458 2N5459	$V_{GS(off)}$	−0.5 −1.0 −2.0	− − −	−6.0 −7.0 −8.0	V dc
Gate-Source voltage (V_{DS} = 15 V dc, I_D = 100 μA dc) (V_{DS} = 15 V dc, I_D = 200 μA dc) (V_{DS} = 15 V dc, I_D = 400 μA dc)	2N5457 2N5458 2N5459	V_{GS}	− − −	−2.5 −3.5 −4.5	− − −	V dc
ON Characteristics						
Zero-Gate-Voltage drain current (V_{DS} = 15 V dc, V_{GS} = 0)	2N5457 2N5458 2N5459	I_{DSS}	1.0 2.0 4.0	3.0 6.0 9.0	5.0 9.0 16	mA dc
Small-signal Characteristics						
Forward transfer admittance common source (V_{DS} = 15 V dc, V_{GS} = 0, f = 1.0 kHz)	2N5457 2N5458 2N5459	$\|y_{fs}\|$	1000 1500 2000	− − −	5000 5500 6000	μmhos or μS
Output admittance common source (V_{DS} = 15 V dc, V_{GS} = 0, f = 1.0 kHz)		$\|y_{os}\|$	−	10	50	μmhos or μS
Input capacitance (V_{DS} = 15 V dc, V_{GS} = 0, f = 1.0 MHz)		C_{iss}	−	4.5	7.0	pF
Reverse transfer capacitance (V_{DS} = 15 V dc, V_{GS} = 0, f = 1.0 MHz)		C_{rss}	−	1.5	3.0	pF

Thomas L. Floyd
Electronic Devices, Fifth Edition
Electronic Devices: Electron-Flow Version, Third Edition

©1999 by Prentice-Hall, Inc.
Simon & Schuster/A Viacom Company
Upper Saddle River, New Jersey 07458
All rights reserved.

FIGURE 8-30
Operation of *n*-channel D-MOSFET.

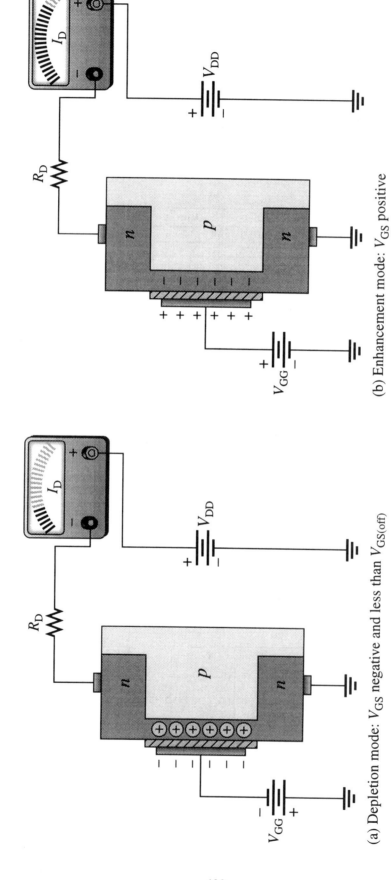

FIGURE 8-41
Data sheet for the 2N7008 *n*-channel E-MOSFET (TMOS construction).

Maximum Ratings

Rating	Symbol	Value	Unit
Drain-Source voltage	V_{DSS}	60	V dc
Drain-Gate voltage (R_{GS} = 1 MΩ)	V_{DGR}	60	V dc
Gate-Source voltage	V_{GS}	±40	V dc
Drain current			mA dc
Continuous	I_D	150	
Pulsed	I_{DM}	1000	
Total power dissipation @ $T_A = 25°C$	P_D	400	mW
Derate above 25°C		3.2	mW/C°
Operating and storage temperature range	T_J, T_{stg}	−55 to +150	°C

Thermal Characteristics

Thermal resistance junction to ambient	$R_{\theta JA}$	312.5	C°/W
Maximum lead temperature for soldering purposes, 1/16" from case for 10 seconds	T_L	300	°C

2N7008
Case 29-04, Style 22
TO-92 (TO-226AA)

TMOS FET Transistor

N channel — Enhancement

Electrical Characteristics ($T_C = 25°C$ unless otherwise noted.)

Characteristic	Symbol	Min	Max	Unit
OFF Characteristics				
Drain-Source breakdown voltage ($V_{GS} = 0$, $I_D = 100$ μA)	$V_{(BR)DSS}$	60	–	V dc
Zero gate voltage drain current	I_{DSS}			μA dc
($V_{DS} = 50$ V, $V_{GS} = 0$)		–	1.0	
($V_{DS} = 50$ V, $V_{GS} = 0$, $T_J = 125°C$)		–	500	
Gate-Body leakage current, forward ($V_{GSF} = 30$ V dc, $V_{DS} = 0$)	I_{GSSF}	–	−100	nA dc
ON Characteristics				
Gate threshold voltage ($V_{DS} = V_{GS}$, $I_D = 250$ μA)	$V_{GS(th)}$	1.0	2.5	V dc
Static drain-source on-resistance	$r_{DS(on)}$			Ohm
($V_{GS} = 5.0$ V dc, $I_D = 50$ A dc)		–	7.5	
($V_{GS} = 10$ V dc, $I_D = 500$ mA dc, $T_C = 125°C$)		–	13.5	
Drain-Source on-voltage	$V_{DS(on)}$			V dc
($V_{GS} = 5.0$ V, $I_D = 50$ mA)		–	1.5	
($V_{GS} = 10$ V, $I_D = 500$ mA)		–	3.75	
On-state drain current ($V_{GS} = 10$ V, $V_{DS} \geq 2.0 V_{D(on)}$)	$I_{D(on)}$	500	–	mA
Forward transconductance ($V_{DS} \geq 2.0 V_{DS(on)}$, $I_D = 200$ mA)	g_{fs}	80	–	μmhos or μS
Dynamic Characteristics				
Input capacitance	C_{iss}	–	50	pF
Output capacitance ($V_{DS} = 25$ V, $V_{GS} = 0$, $f = 1.0$ MHz)	C_{oss}	–	25	
Reverse transfer capacitance	C_{rss}	–	5.0	
Switching Characteristics				
Turn-On delay time ($V_{DD} = 30$ V, $I_D = 200$ mA,	t_{on}	–	20	ns
Turn-Off delay time $R_{gen} = 25$ ohms, $R_L = 150$ ohms)	t_{off}	–	20	

Thomas L. Floyd
Electronic Devices, Fifth Edition
Electronic Devices: Electron-Flow Version, Third Edition

©1999 by Prentice-Hall, Inc.
Simon & Schuster/A Viacom Company
Upper Saddle River, New Jersey 07458
All rights reserved.

FIGURE 8-52

Partial data sheet for the 2N3797 D-MOSFET.

Maximum Ratings

Rating	Symbol	Value	Unit
Drain-Source voltage	V_{DS}		V dc
2N3796		25	
2N3797		20	
Gate-Source voltage	V_{GS}	±10	V dc
Drain current	I_D	20	mA dc
Total device dissipation @ $T_A = 25°C$	P_D	200	mW
Derate above 25°C		1.14	mW/C°
Junction temperature range	T_J	+175	°C
Storage channel temperature range	T_{stg}	−65 to +200	°C

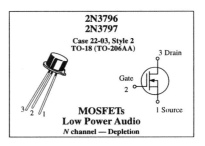

2N3796
2N3797
Case 22-03, Style 2
TO-18 (TO-206AA)
MOSFETs
Low Power Audio
N channel — Depletion

Electrical Characteristics ($T_A = 25°C$ unless otherwise noted.)

Characteristic		Symbol	Min	Typ	Max	Unit
OFF Characteristics						
Drain-Source breakdown voltage		$V_{(BR)DSX}$				V dc
($V_{GS} = -4.0$ V, $I_D = 5.0$ μA)	2N3796		25	30	–	
($V_{GS} = -7.0$ V, $I_D = 5.0$ μA)	2N3797		20	25	–	
Gate reverse current		I_{GSS}				pA dc
($V_{GS} = -10$ V, $V_{DS} = 0$)			–	–	1.0	
($V_{GS} = -10$ V, $V_{DS} = 0$, $T_A = 150°C$)			–	–	200	
Gate-Source cutoff voltage		$V_{GS(off)}$				V dc
($I_D = 0.5$ μA, $V_{DS} = 10$ V)	2N3796		–	−3.0	−4.0	
($I_D = 2.0$ μA, $V_{DS} = 10$ V)	2N3797		–	−5.0	−7.0	
Drain-Gate reverse current		I_{DGO}	–	–	1.0	pA dc
($V_{DG} = 10$ V, $I_S = 0$)						
ON Characteristics						
Zero-Gate-Voltage drain current	2N3796	I_{DSS}	0.5	1.5	3.0	mA dc
($V_{DS} = 10$ V, $V_{GS} = 0$)	2N3797		2.0	2.9	6.0	
On-State drain current	2N3796	$I_{D(on)}$	7.0	8.3	14	mA dc
($V_{DS} = 10$ V, $V_{GS} = +3.5$ V)	2N3797		9.0	14	18	
Small-Signal Characteristics						
Forward-transfer admittance		$|y_{fs}|$				μmhos
($V_{DS} = 10$ V, $V_{GS} = 0$, $f = 1.0$ kHz)	2N3796		900	1200	1800	or
	2N3797		1500	2300	3000	μS
($V_{DS} = 10$ V, $V_{GS} = 0$, $f = 1.0$ MHz)	2N3796		900	–	–	
	2N3797		1500	–	–	
Output admittance		$|y_{os}|$				μmhos
($V_{DS} = 10$ V, $V_{GS} = 0$, $f = 1.0$ kHz)	2N3796		–	12	25	or
	2N3797		–	27	60	μS
Input capacitance		C_{iss}				pF
($V_{DS} = 10$ V, $V_{GS} = 0$, $f = 1.0$ MHz)	2N3796		–	5.0	7.0	
	2N3797		–	6.0	8.0	
Reverse transfer capacitance		C_{rss}	–	0.5	0.8	pF
($V_{DS} = 10$ V, $V_{GS} = 0$, $f = 1.0$ MHz)						
Functional Characteristics						
Noise figure		NF	–	3.8	–	dB
($V_{DS} = 10$ V, $V_{GS} = 0$, $f = 1.0$ kHz, $R_S = 3$ megohms)						

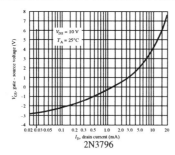
2N3796

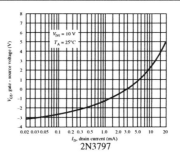
2N3797

Thomas L. Floyd
Electronic Devices, Fifth Edition
Electronic Devices: Electron-Flow Version, Third Edition

©1999 by Prentice-Hall, Inc.
Simon & Schuster/A Viacom Company
Upper Saddle River, New Jersey 07458
All rights reserved.

FIGURE 9-2
JFET characteristic curves.

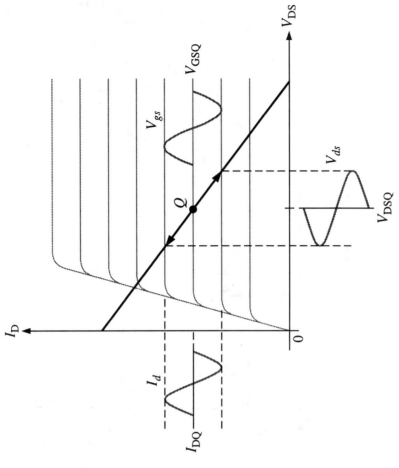

(a) JFET (n-channel) transfer characteristic curve showing signal operation

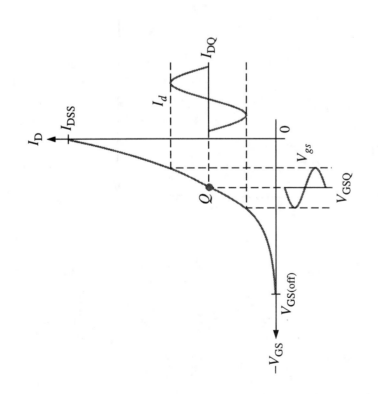

(b) JFET (n-channel) drain curves showing signal operation

Thomas L. Floyd
Electronic Devices, Fifth Edition
Electronic Devices: Electron-Flow Version, Third Edition

 ©1999 by Prentice-Hall, Inc.
Simon & Schuster/A Viacom Company
Upper Saddle River, New Jersey 07458
All rights reserved.

FIGURE 9-4
Depletion–enhancement operation of D-MOSFET shown on transfer characteristic curve.

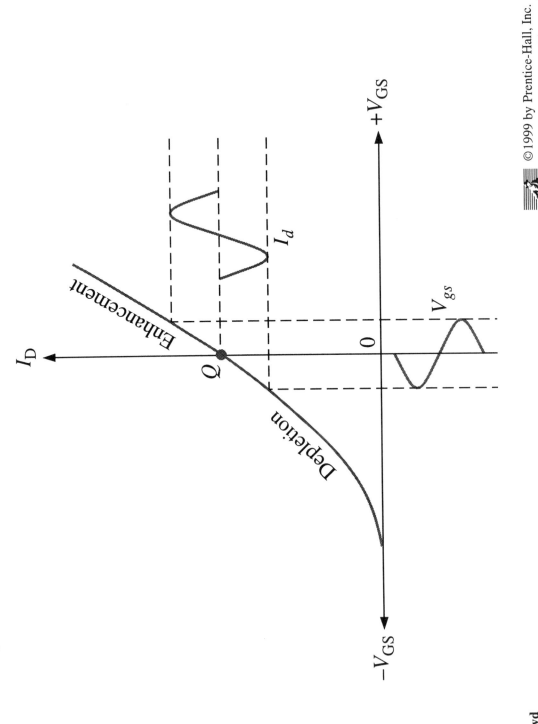

FIGURE 9-6
E-MOSFET (*n*-channel) operation shown on transfer characteristic curve.

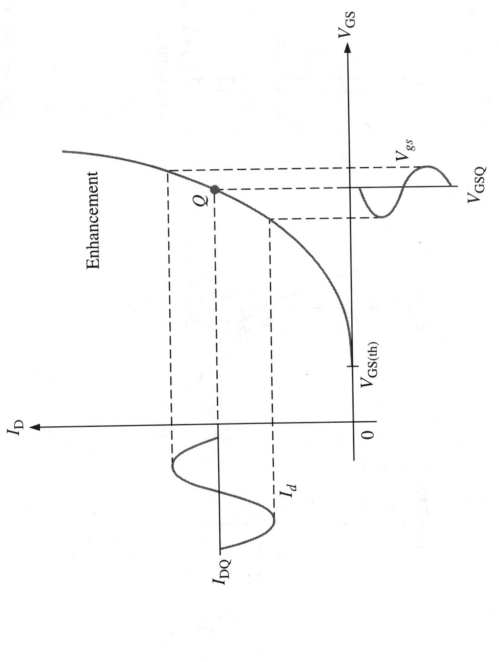

FIGURE 9-7

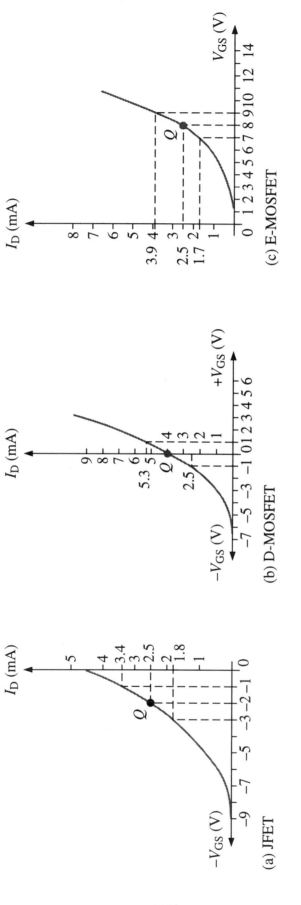

(a) JFET

(b) D-MOSFET

(c) E-MOSFET

Thomas L. Floyd
Electronic Devices, Fifth Edition
Electronic Devices: Electron-Flow Version, Third Edition

©1999 by Prentice-Hall, Inc.
Simon & Schuster/A Viacom Company
Upper Saddle River, New Jersey 07458
All rights reserved.

FIGURE 9-28
A two-stage FET amplifier circuit.

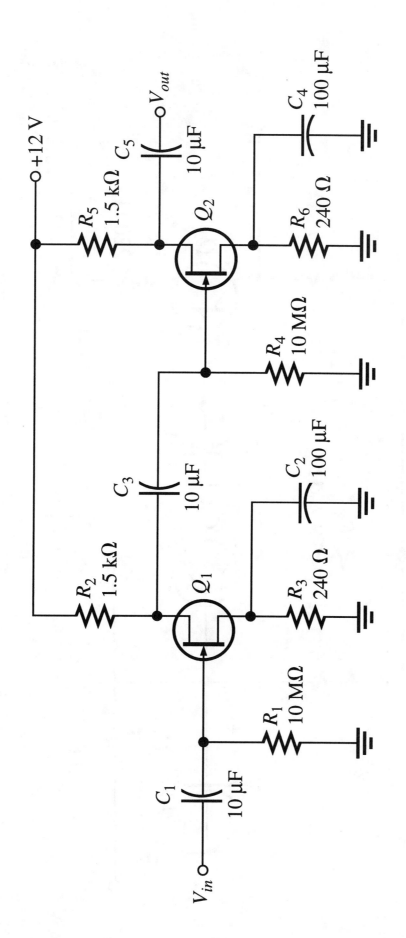

FIGURE 9-30
Bipolar transistor audio preamplifier. Both transistors are 2N3904. Assume $\beta_{DC} = \beta_{ac} = 100$.

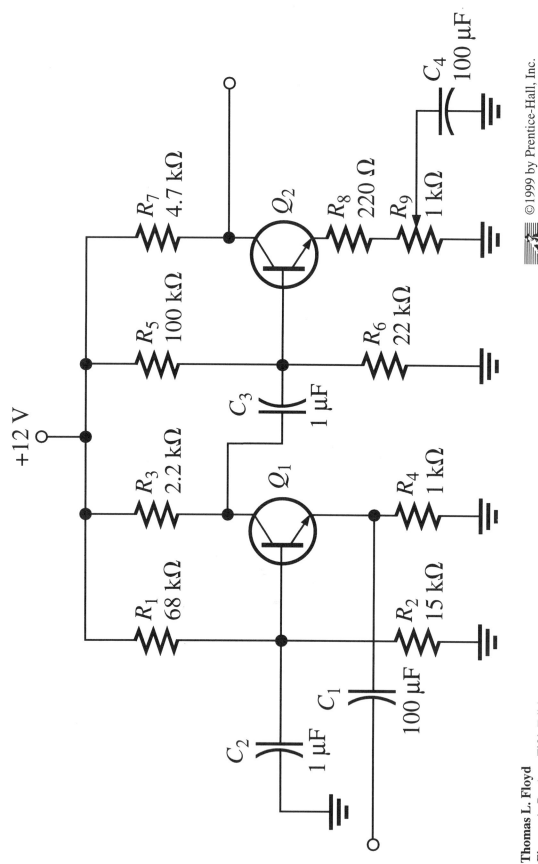

FIGURE 9-32
Partial data sheet for the 2N3797 D-MOSFET.

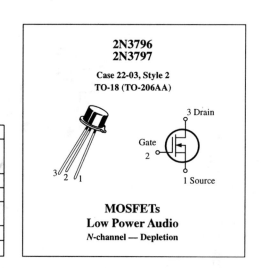

2N3796
2N3797

Case 22-03, Style 2
TO-18 (TO-206AA)

**MOSFETs
Low Power Audio**
N-channel — Depletion

Maximim Ratings

Rating	Symbol	Value	Unit
Drain-Source voltage	V_{DS}		V dc
2N3796		25	
2N3797		20	
Gate-Source voltage	V_{GS}	±10	V dc
Drain current	I_D	20	mA dc
Total device dissipation @ $T_A = 25°C$	P_D	200	mW
Derate above 25°C		1.14	mW/C°
Junction temperature	T_J	+175	°C
Storage channel temperature range	T_{stg}	−65 to +200	°C

Electrical Characteristics ($T_A = 25°C$ unless otherwise noted.)

Characteristic		Symbol	Min	Typ	Max	Unit
OFF Characteristics						
Drain-Source breakdown voltage		$V_{(BR)DSX}$				V dc
($V_{GS} = -4.0$ V, $I_D = 5.0$ μA)	2N3796		25	30	−	
($V_{GS} = -7.0$ V, $I_D = 5.0$ μA)	2N3797		20	25	−	
Gate reverse current		I_{GSS}				pA dc
($V_{GS} = -10$ V, $V_{DS} = 0$)			−	−	1.0	
($V_{GS} = -10$ V, $V_{DS} = 0$, $T_A = 150°C$)			−	−	200	
Gate-Source cutoff voltage		$V_{GS(off)}$				V dc
($I_D = 0.5$ μA, $V_{DS} = 10$ V)	2N3796		−	−3.0	−4.0	
($I_D = 2.0$ μA, $V_{DS} = 10$ V)	2N3797		−	−5.0	−7.0	
Drain-Gate reverse current		I_{DGO}				pA dc
($V_{DG} = 10$ V, $I_S = 0$)			−	−	1.0	
ON Characteristics						
Zero-gate-voltage drain current		I_{DSS}				mA dc
($V_{DS} = 10$ V, $V_{GS} = 0$)	2N3796		0.5	1.5	3.0	
	2N3797		2.0	2.9	6.0	
On-State drain current		$I_{D(on)}$				mA dc
($V_{DS} = 10$ V, $V_{GS} = +3.5$ V)	2N3796		7.0	8.3	14	
	2N3797		9.0	14	18	
Small-Signal Characteristics						
Forward transfer admittance		$|Y_{fs}|$				μmhos
($V_{DS} = 10$ V, $V_{GS} = 0$, $f = 1.0$ kHz)	2N3796		900	1200	1800	or
	2N3797		1500	2300	3000	μS
($V_{DS} = 10$ V, $V_{GS} = 0$, $f = 1.0$ MHz)	2N3796		900	−	−	
	2N3797		1500	−	−	
Output admittance		$|Y_{os}|$				μmhos or
($V_{DS} = 10$ V, $V_{GS} = 0$, $f = 1.0$ kHz)	2N3796		−	12	25	μS
	2N3797		−	27	60	
Input capacitance		C_{iss}				pF
($V_{DS} = 10$ V, $V_{GS} = 0$, $f = 1.0$ MHz)	2N3796		−	5.0	7.0	
	2N3797		−	6.0	8.0	
Reverse transfer capacitance		C_{rss}				pF
($V_{DS} = 10$ V, $V_{GS} = 0$, $f = 1.0$ MHz)			−	0.5	0.8	

Thomas L. Floyd
Electronic Devices, Fifth Edition
Electronic Devices: Electron-Flow Version, Third Edition

 ©1999 by Prentice-Hall, Inc.
Simon & Schuster/A Viacom Company
Upper Saddle River, New Jersey 07458
All rights reserved.

FIGURE 10–4
AC equivalent circuit for a bipolar amplifier showing effects of the internal capacitances C_{be} and C_{bc}.

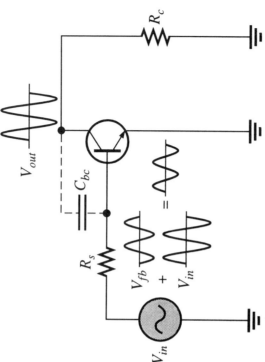

(a) Effect of C_{be}, where V_b is reduced by the voltage-divider action of R_s and $X_{C_{be}}$.

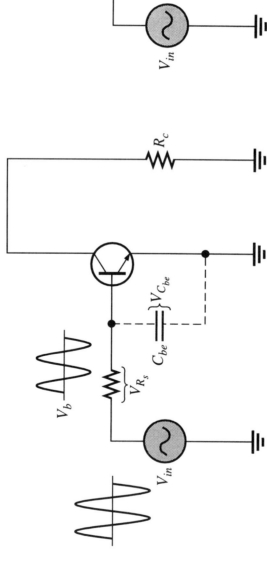

(b) Effect of C_{bc}, where part of V_{out} (V_{fb}) goes back through C_{bc} to the base and reduces the input signal because it is approximately 180° out of phase with V_{in}.

Thomas L. Floyd
Electronic Devices, Fifth Edition
Electronic Devices: Electron-Flow Version, Third Edition

 ©1999 by Prentice-Hall, Inc.
Simon & Schuster/A Viacom Company
Upper Saddle River, New Jersey 07458
All rights reserved.

FIGURE 10-5
Normalized voltage gain versus frequency curve.

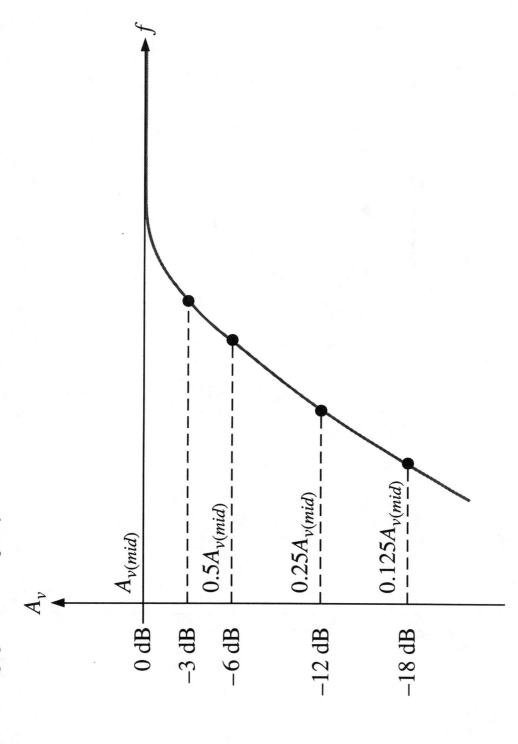

FIGURE 10-9
dB voltage gain versus frequency for the input RC circuit.

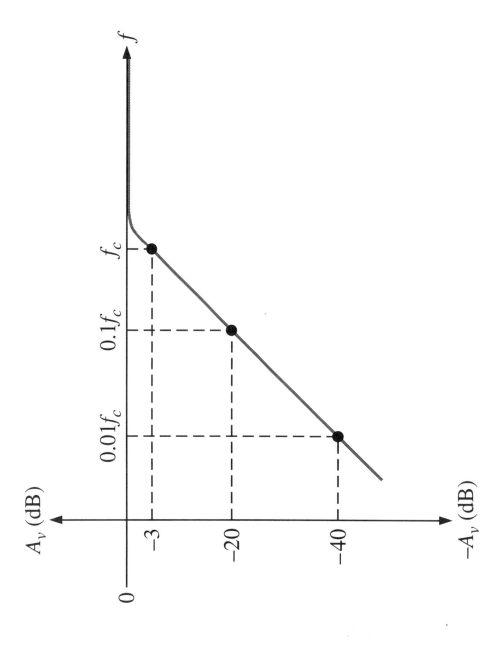

FIGURE 10-10
Phase angle versus frequency for the input RC circuit.

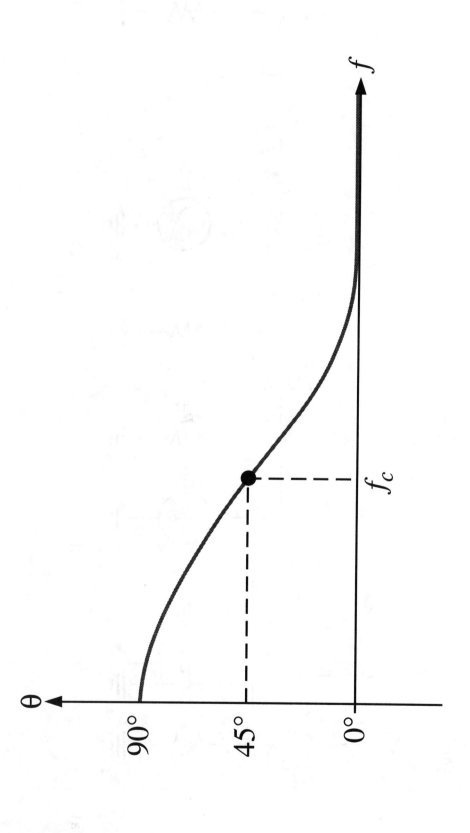

FIGURE 10-12
Development of the equivalent low-frequency output *RC* circuit.

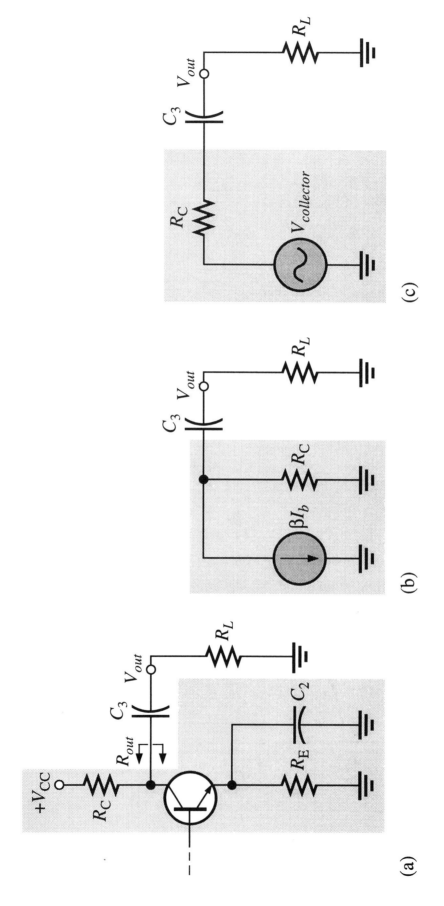

FIGURE 10-14*
Development of the equivalent bypass RC circuit.

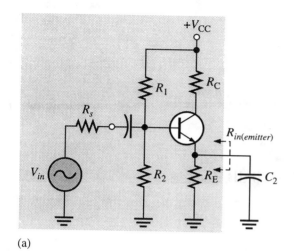

(a)

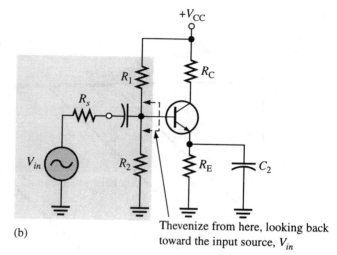

(b) Thevenize from here, looking back toward the input source, V_{in}

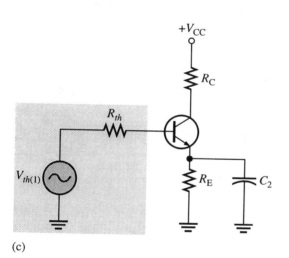

(c)

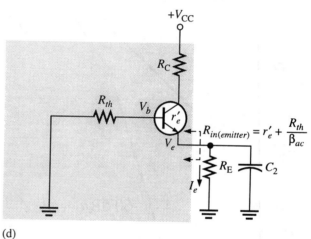

(d)

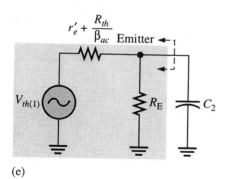

(e)

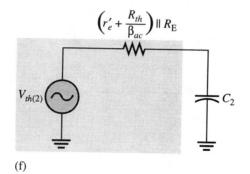

(f)

Thomas L. Floyd
Electronic Devices, Fifth Edition
*Current arrows indicate conventional flow.

©1999 by Prentice-Hall, Inc.
Simon & Schuster/A Viacom Company
Upper Saddle River, New Jersey 07458
All rights reserved.

FIGURE 10-17

Composite Bode plot of an amplifier response for three low-frequency *RC* circuits with different critical frequencies. Total response is shown by the curve.

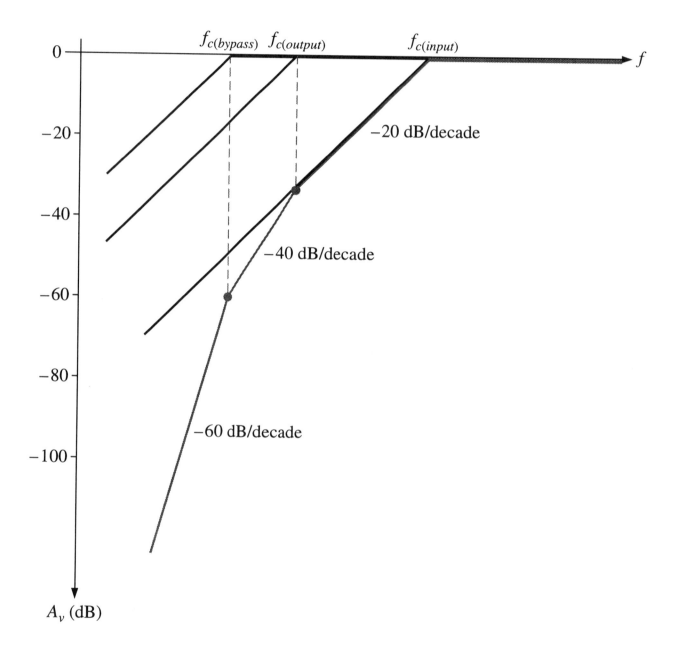

FIGURE 10-20
Ideal Bode plot for the total low-frequency response of the amplifier in Figure 10-19.

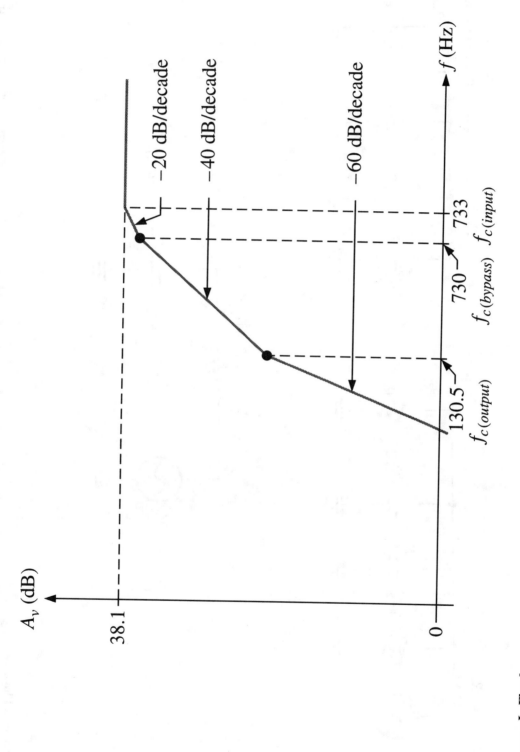

Thomas L. Floyd
Electronic Devices, Fifth Edition
Electronic Devices: Electron-Flow Version, Third Edition

©1999 by Prentice-Hall, Inc.
Simon & Schuster/A Viacom Company
Upper Saddle River, New Jersey 07458
All rights reserved.

FIGURE 10-28
Development of the equivalent high-frequency input *RC* circuit.

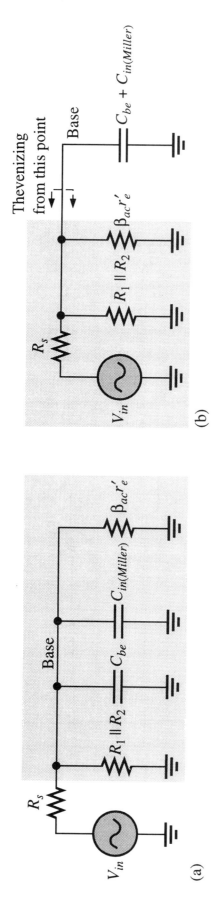
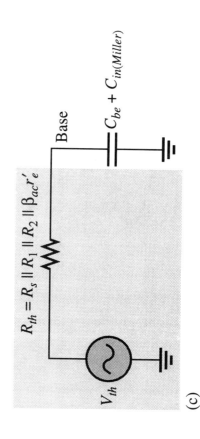

FIGURE 10-31*
Development of the equivalent high-frequency output RC circuit.

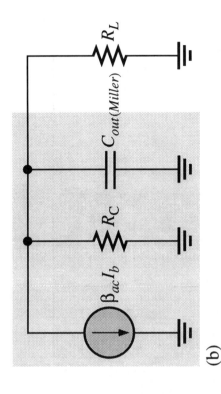
(a)

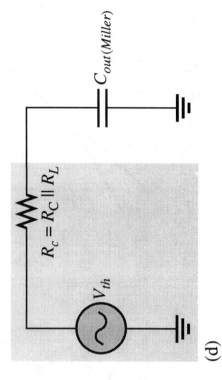
(b)

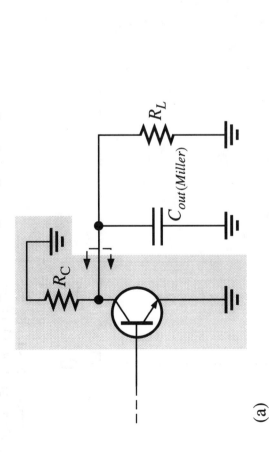
(c)

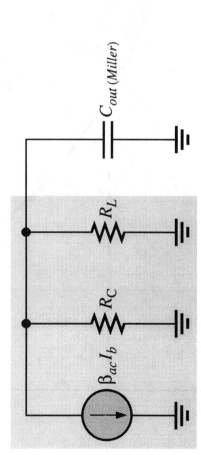
(d)

Thomas L. Floyd
Electronic Devices, Fifth Edition
*Current arrows indicate conventional flow.

©1999 by Prentice-Hall, Inc.
Simon & Schuster/A Viacom Company
Upper Saddle River, New Jersey 07458
All rights reserved.

FIGURE 10-35
Response curve illustrating the bandwidth of an amplifier.

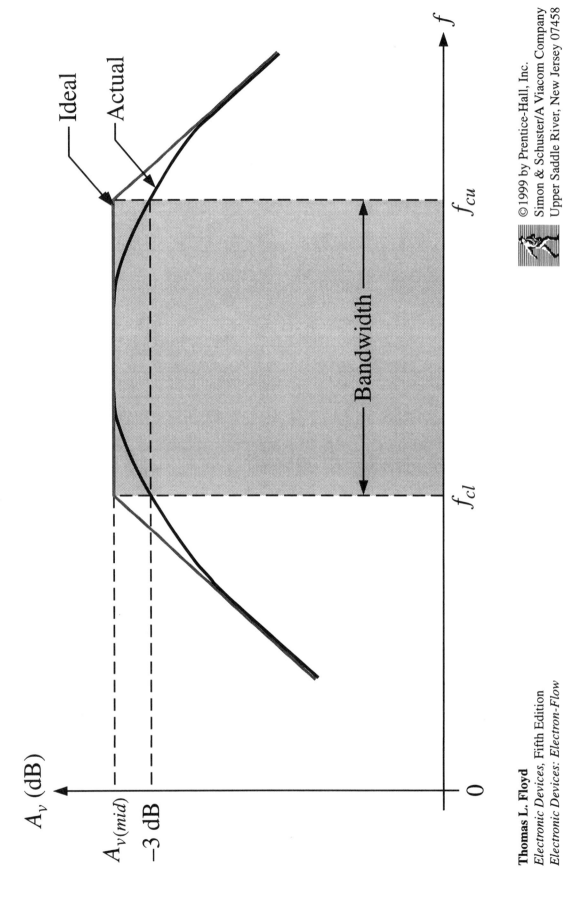

FIGURE 11-3*

Currents in a basic Shockley diode equivalent circuit.

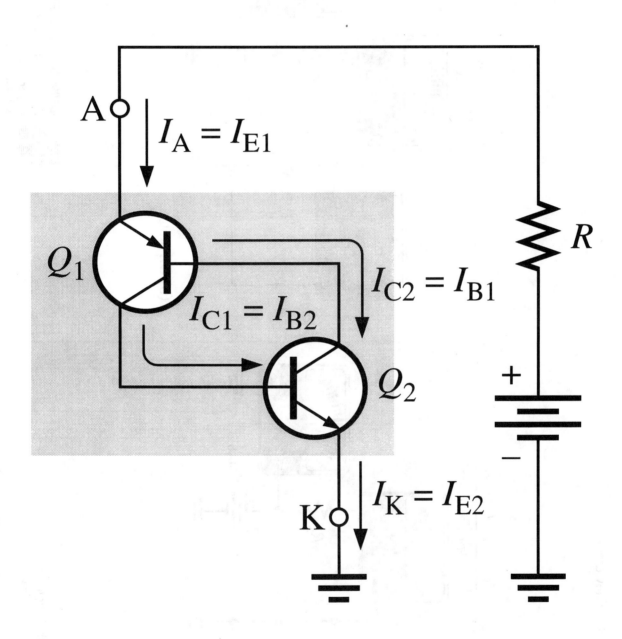

Thomas L. Floyd
Electronic Devices, Fifth Edition
*Current arrows indicate conventional flow.

©1999 by Prentice-Hall, Inc.
Simon & Schuster/A Viacom Company
Upper Saddle River, New Jersey 07458
All rights reserved.

FIGURE 11-5
On/off states of the Shockley diode.

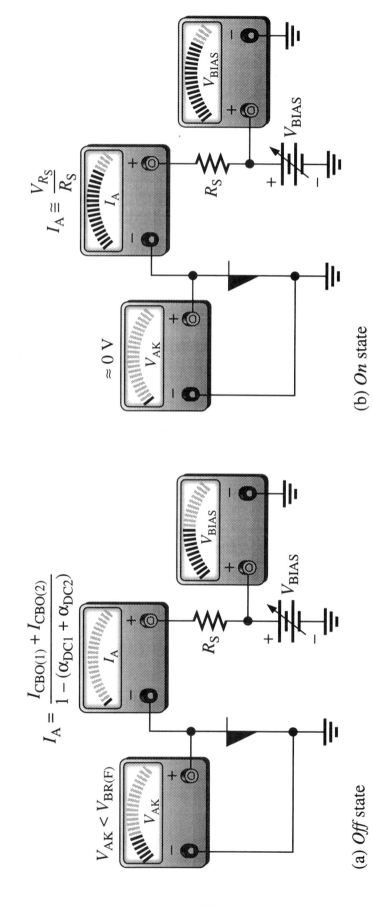

(a) *Off* state

(b) *On* state

FIGURE 11-10*
The SCR turn-on process with the switch equivalents shown.

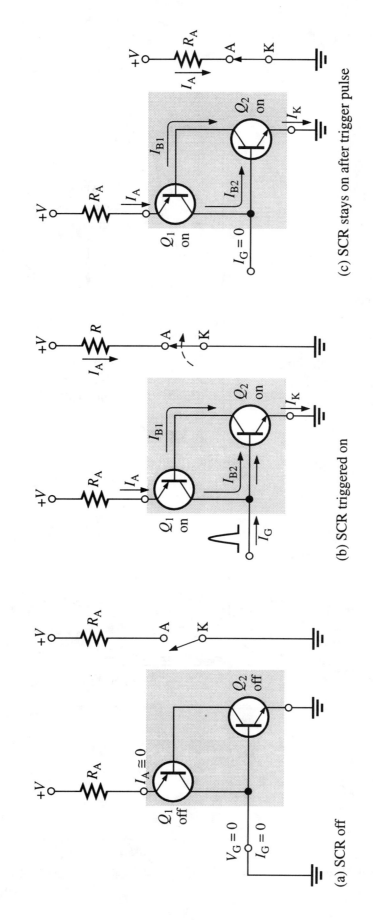

FIGURE 11-11
SCR characteristic curves.

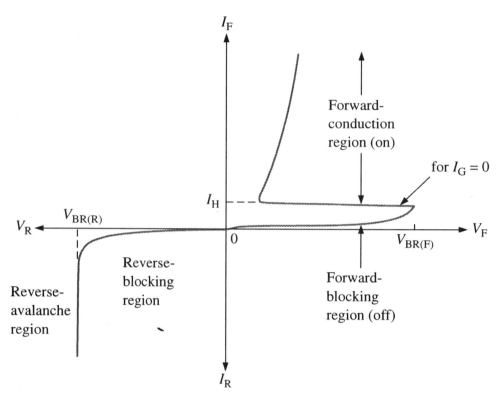

(a) For $I_G = 0$

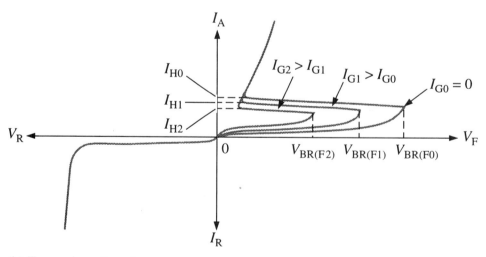

(b) For various I_G values

Thomas L. Floyd
Electronic Devices, Fifth Edition
Electronic Devices: Electron-Flow Version, Third Edition

©1999 by Prentice-Hall, Inc.
Simon & Schuster/A Viacom Company
Upper Saddle River, New Jersey 07458
All rights reserved.

FIGURE 11-16*
Operation of the phase-control circuit.

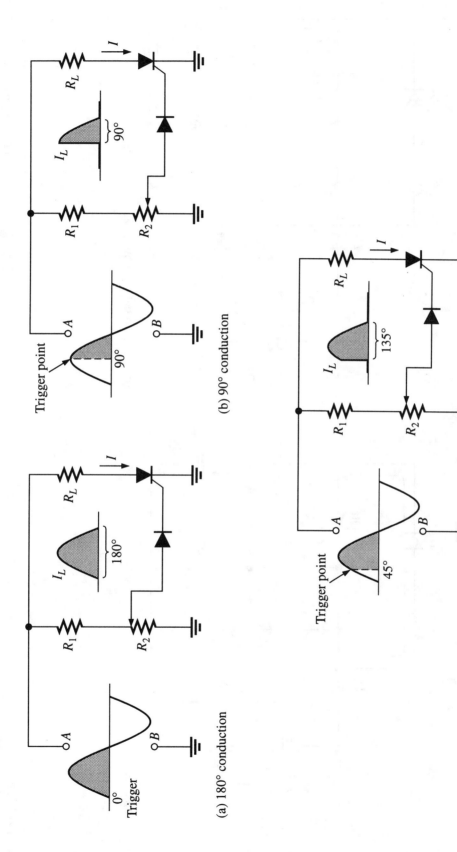

(a) 180° conduction

(b) 90° conduction

(c) 135° conduction

Thomas L. Floyd
Electronic Devices, Fifth Edition
*Current arrows indicate conventional flow.

©1999 by Prentice-Hall, Inc.
Simon & Schuster/A Viacom Company
Upper Saddle River, New Jersey 07458
All rights reserved.

FIGURE 11-17
Automatic back-up lighting circuit.

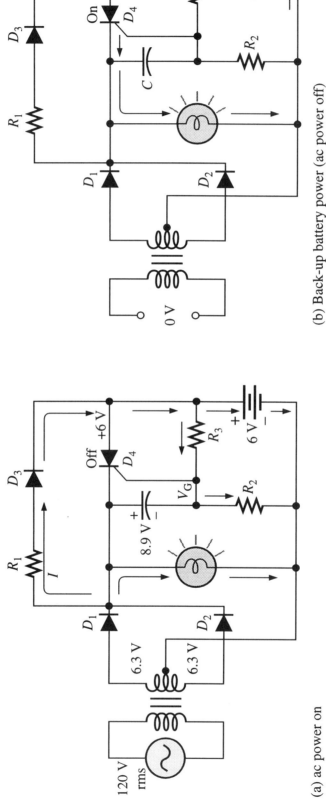

(a) ac power on

(b) Back-up battery power (ac power off)

Thomas L. Floyd
Electronic Devices, Fifth Edition
*Current arrows indicate conventional flow.

©1999 by Prentice-Hall, Inc.
Simon & Schuster/A Viacom Company
Upper Saddle River, New Jersey 07458
All rights reserved.

FIGURE 11-18
A basic SCR over-voltage protection circuit.

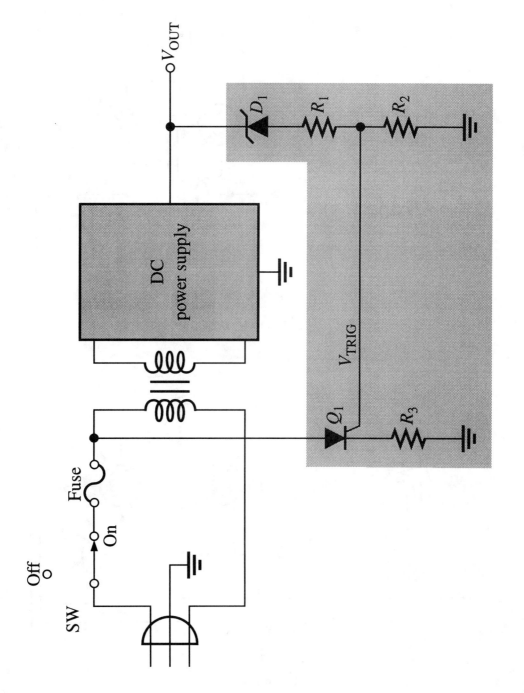

FIGURE 11-27*
Bilateral operation of a triac.

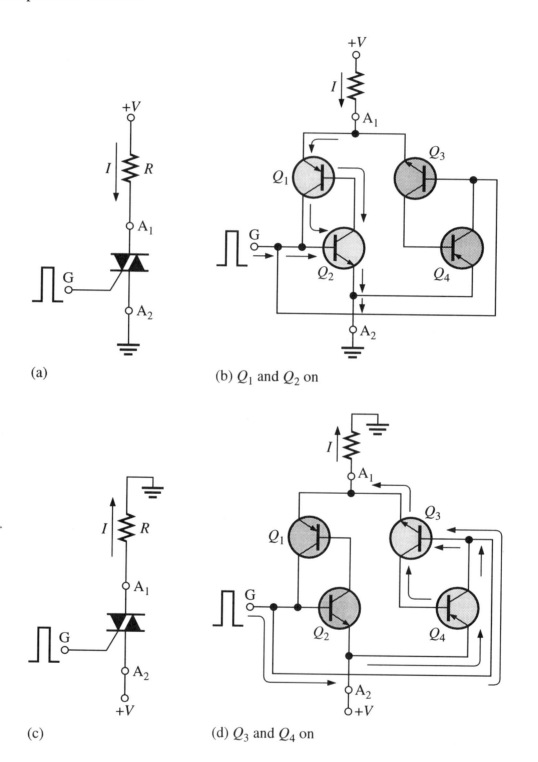

(a)

(b) Q_1 and Q_2 on

(c)

(d) Q_3 and Q_4 on

Thomas L. Floyd
Electronic Devices, Fifth Edition
*Current arrows indicate conventional flow.

©1999 by Prentice-Hall, Inc.
Simon & Schuster/A Viacom Company
Upper Saddle River, New Jersey 07458
All rights reserved.

FIGURE 11-39
PUT relaxation oscillator.

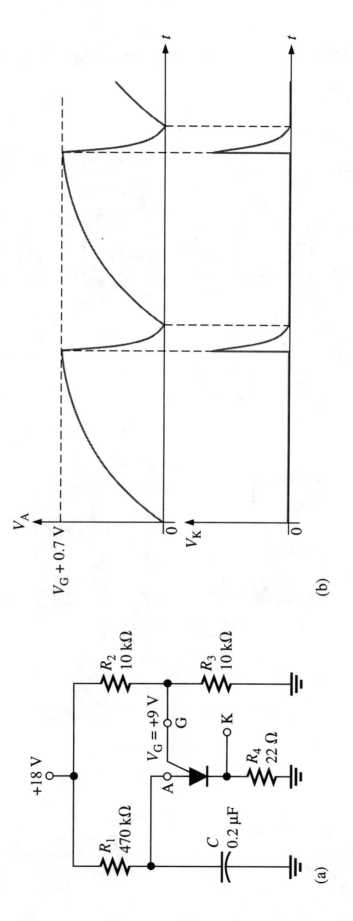

FIGURE 12-5
Basic operation of a differential amplifier (ground is zero volts) showing relative changes in currents and voltages.

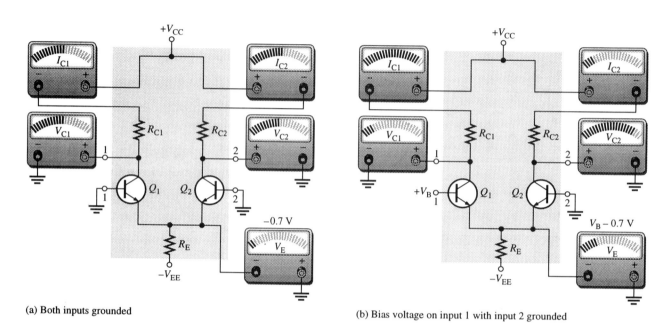

(a) Both inputs grounded

(b) Bias voltage on input 1 with input 2 grounded

(c) Bias voltage on input 2 with input 1 grounded

Thomas L. Floyd
Electronic Devices, Fifth Edition
Electronic Devices: Electron-Flow Version, Third Edition

©1999 by Prentice-Hall, Inc.
Simon & Schuster/A Viacom Company
Upper Saddle River, New Jersey 07458
All rights reserved.

FIGURE 12-6
Single-ended input operation of a differential amplifier.

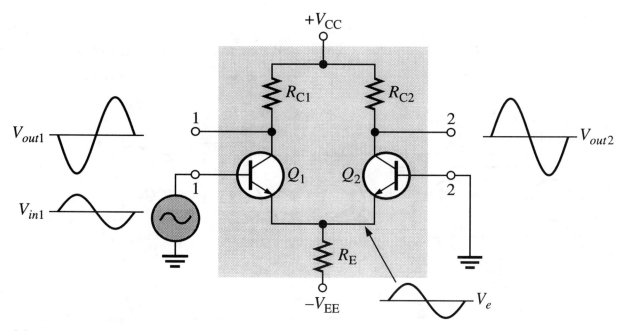

(a)

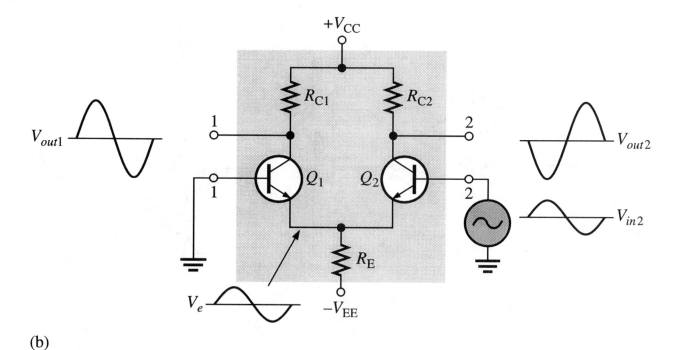

(b)

Thomas L. Floyd
Electronic Devices, Fifth Edition
Electronic Devices: Electron-Flow Version, Third Edition

©1999 by Prentice-Hall, Inc.
Simon & Schuster/A Viacom Company
Upper Saddle River, New Jersey 07458
All rights reserved.

FIGURE 12-10
Simplified internal circuit of a basic op-amp.

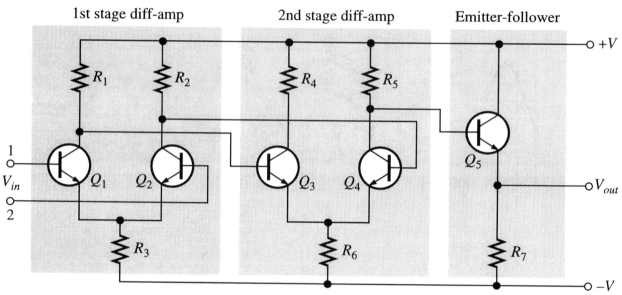

(a) Circuit

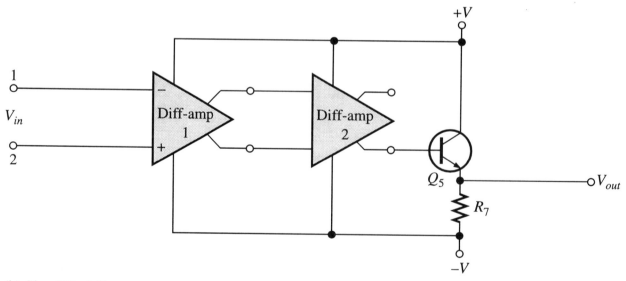

(b) Simplified diagram

Thomas L. Floyd
Electronic Devices, Fifth Edition
Electronic Devices: Electron-Flow Version, Third Edition

©1999 by Prentice-Hall, Inc.
Simon & Schuster/A Viacom Company
Upper Saddle River, New Jersey 07458
All rights reserved.

FIGURE 12-25*
Virtual ground concept and closed-loop voltage gain development for the inverting amplifier.

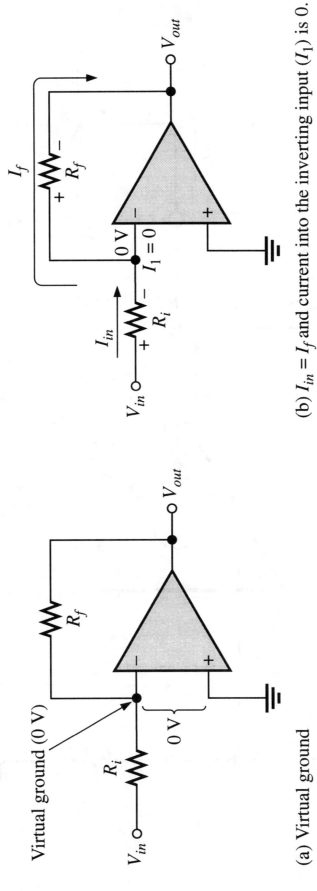

(a) Virtual ground

(b) $I_{in} = I_f$ and current into the inverting input (I_1) is 0.

Thomas L. Floyd
Electronic Devices, Fifth Edition
*Current arrows indicate conventional flow.

©1999 by Prentice-Hall, Inc.
Simon & Schuster/A Viacom Company
Upper Saddle River, New Jersey 07458
All rights reserved.

FIGURE 12-28*

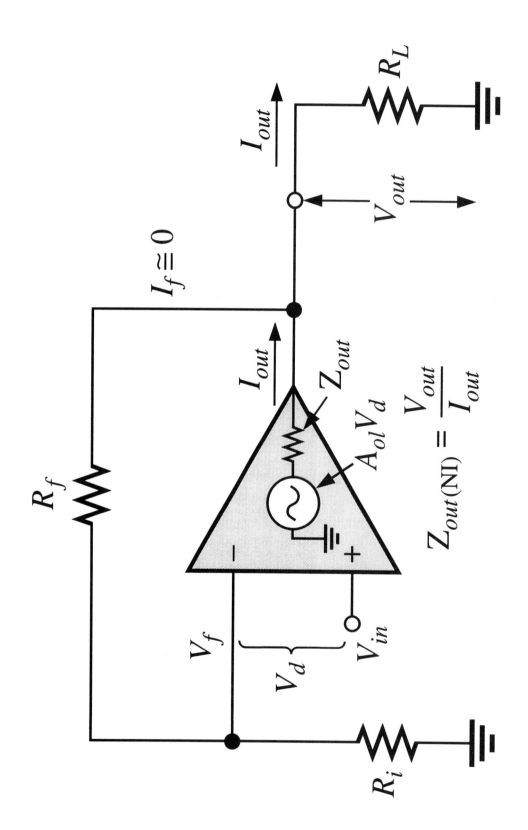

Thomas L. Floyd
Electronic Devices, Fifth Edition
*Current arrows indicate conventional flow.

FIGURE 12-44
Photocell/Amplifier schematic.

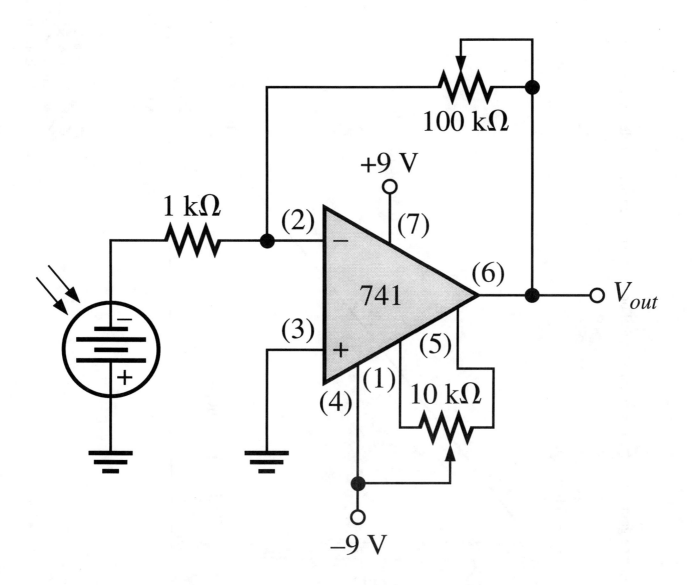

Thomas L. Floyd
Electronic Devices, Fifth Edition
*Electronic Devices: Electron-Flow
Version*, Third Edition

©1999 by Prentice-Hall, Inc.
Simon & Schuster/A Viacom Company
Upper Saddle River, New Jersey 07458
All rights reserved.

FIGURE 13-2
Ideal plot of open-loop voltage gain versus frequency for a typical op-amp. The frequency scale is logarithmic.

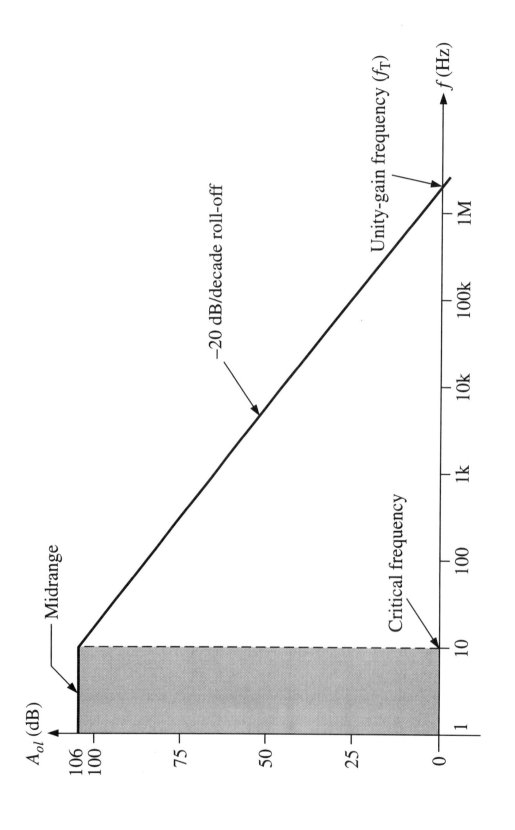

FIGURE 13-7
Op-amp open-loop frequency response.

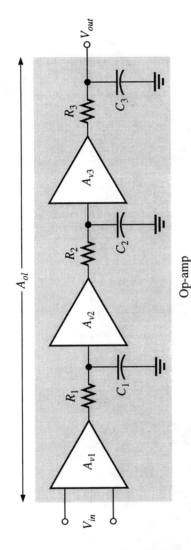

(a) Representation of an op-amp with three internal stages

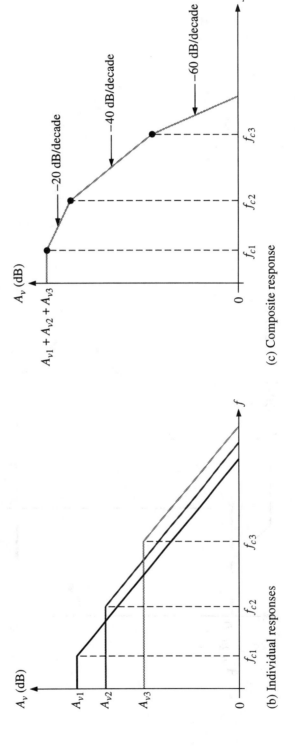

(b) Individual responses

(c) Composite response

FIGURE 13-8
Closed-loop gain compared to open-loop gain.

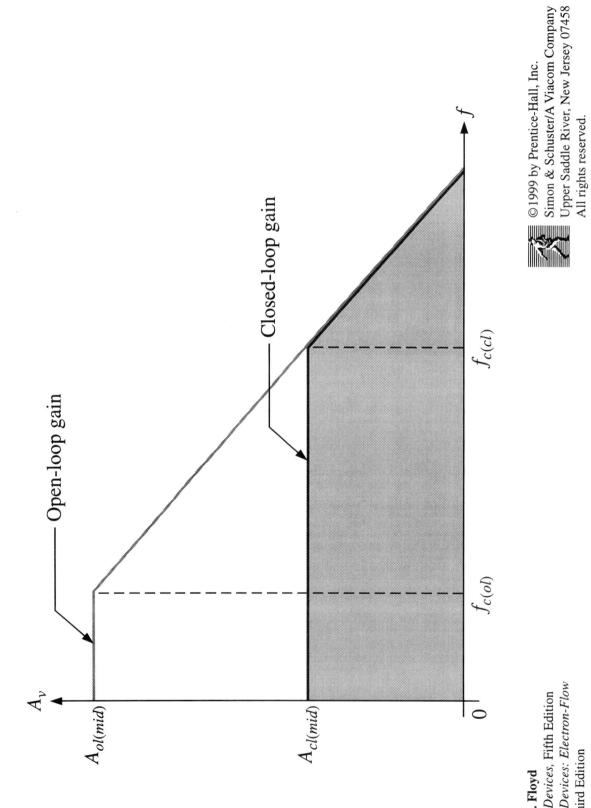

FIGURE 13-15
Bode plot illustrating the effect of phase compensation on open-loop gain of a typical op-amp.

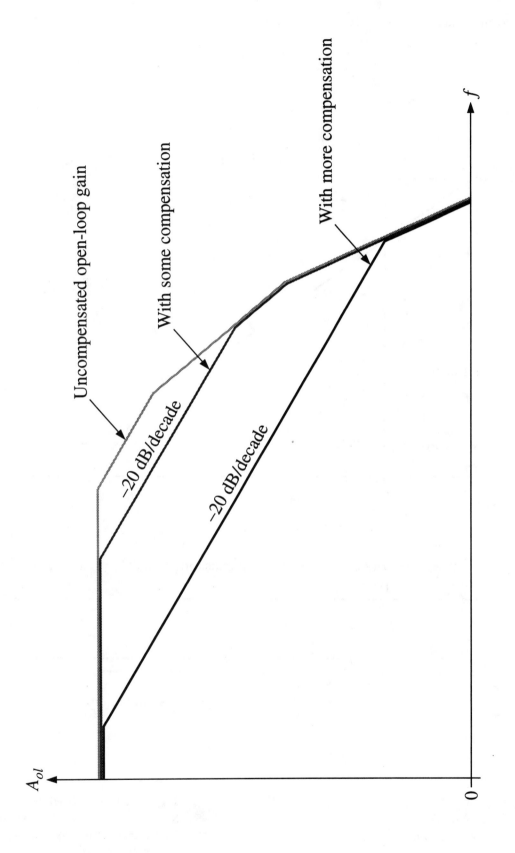

FIGURE 13-18
Example of compensated op-amp frequency response.

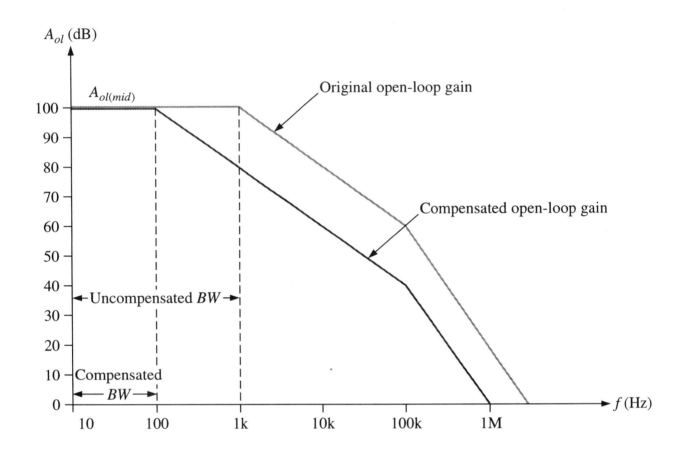

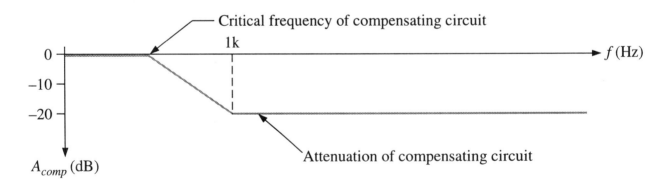

FIGURE 13-23
Example of single-capacitor compensation of an LM101A op-amp.

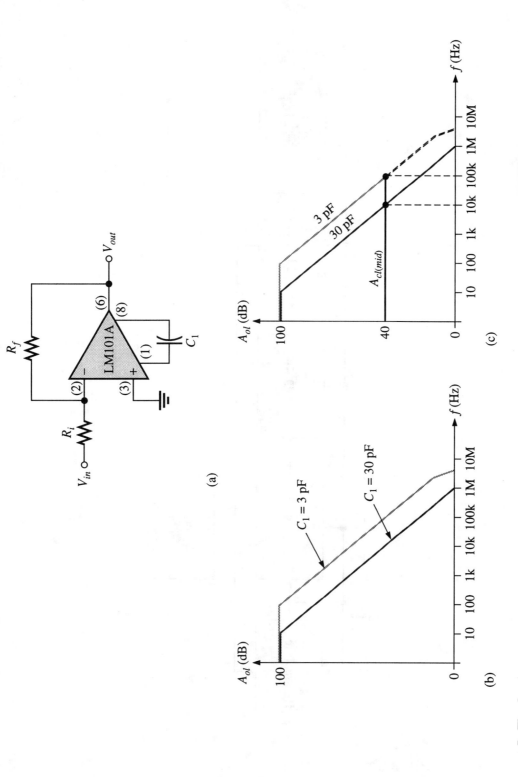

FIGURE 13-26
Block diagram of basic superheterodyne AM receiver.

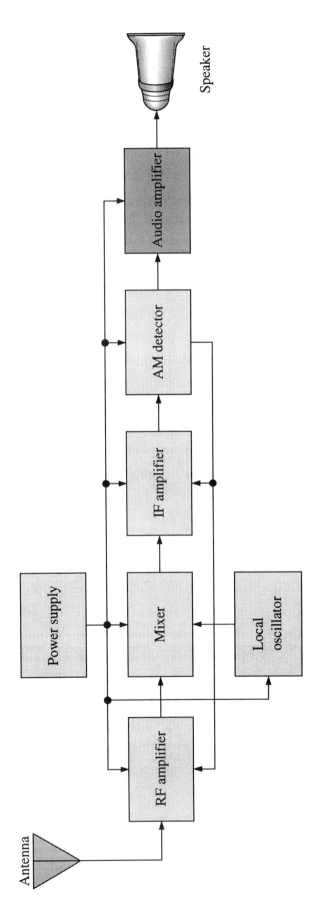

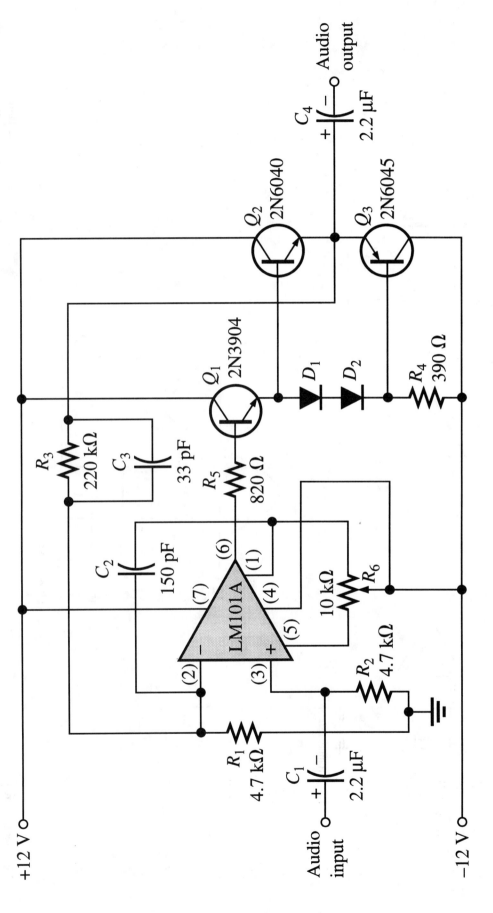

FIGURE 13-28
Audio amplifier schematic.

FIGURE 14-2
Nonzero-level detectors.

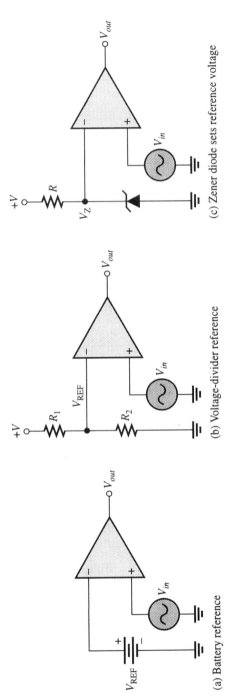

(a) Battery reference

(b) Voltage-divider reference

(c) Zener diode sets reference voltage

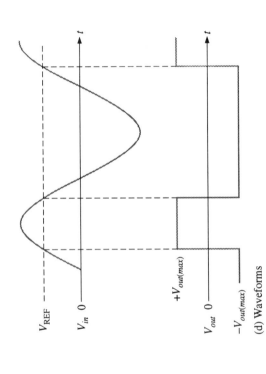

(d) Waveforms

FIGURE 14-8
Operation of a comparator with hysteresis.

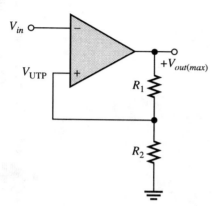

(a) Output at the maximum positive voltage

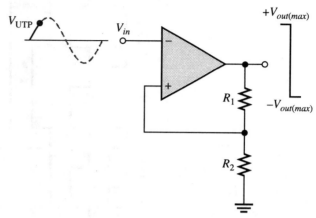

(b) Input exceeds UTP; output switches from the maximum positive voltage to the maximum negative voltage.

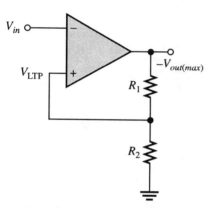

(c) Output at the maximum negative voltage

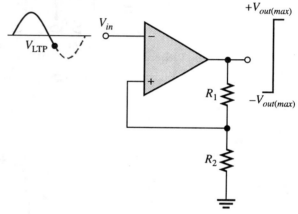

(d) Input goes below LTP; output switches from maximum negative voltage back to maximum positive voltage.

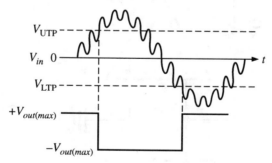

(e) Device triggers only once when UTP or LTP is reached; thus, there is immunity to noise that is riding on the input signal.

Thomas L. Floyd
Electronic Devices, Fifth Edition
Electronic Devices: Electron-Flow Version, Third Edition

©1999 by Prentice-Hall, Inc.
Simon & Schuster/A Viacom Company
Upper Saddle River, New Jersey 07458
All rights reserved.

FIGURE 14-29

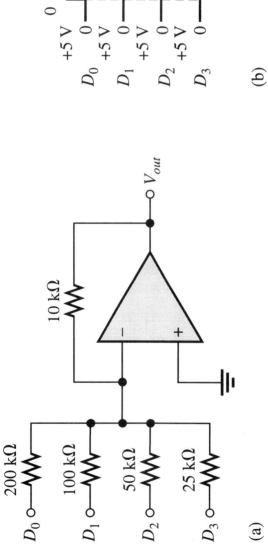

(a)

(b)

FIGURE 14-30

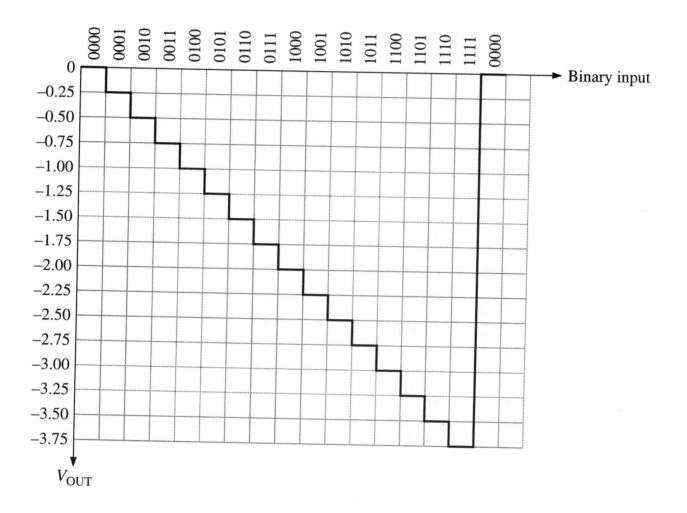

FIGURE 14-47
Block diagram of dual-slope analog-to-digital converter.

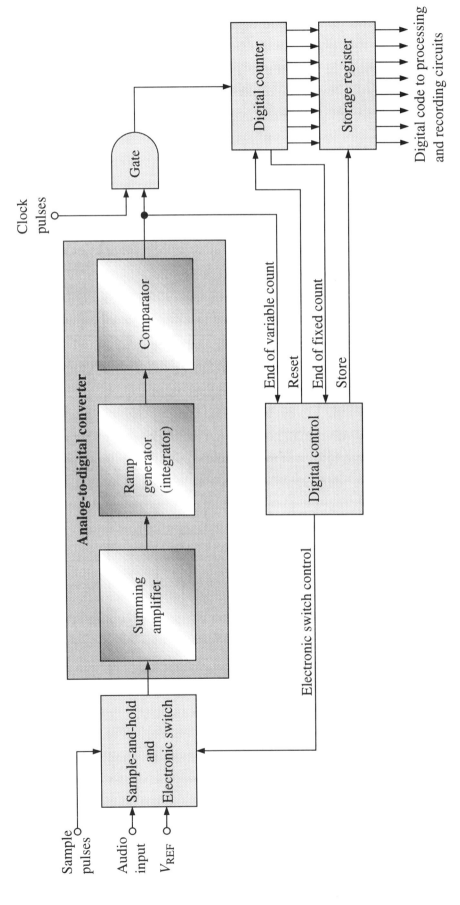

Thomas L. Floyd
Electronic Devices, Fifth Edition
Electronic Devices: Electron-Flow Version, Third Edition

©1999 by Prentice-Hall, Inc.
Simon & Schuster/A Viacom Company
Upper Saddle River, New Jersey 07458
All rights reserved.

FIGURE 14-49

During the fixed-time interval of the positive-going ramp, the sampled audio input is applied to the integrator. During the variable time interval of the fixed-slope negative-going ramp, the reference voltage is applied to the integrator. The counter controls the fixed time interval and is reset. Another count begins during the variable interval and the digital code in the counter at the end of this interval represents the sampled audio value.

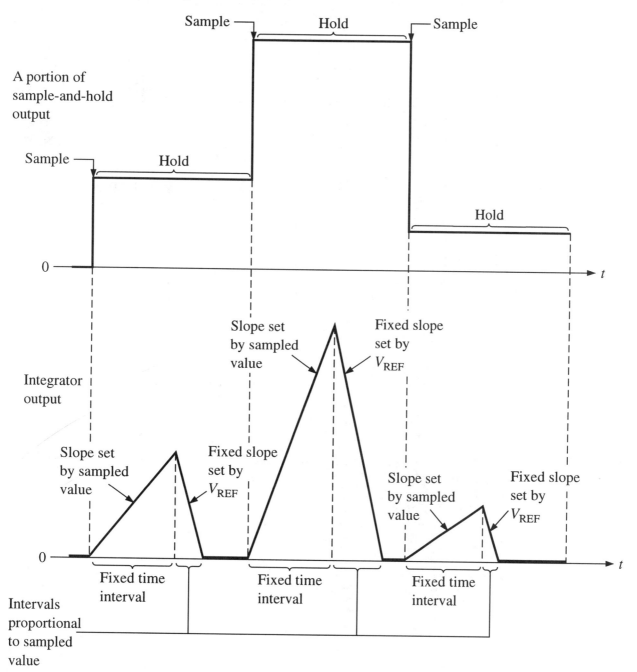

Thomas L. Floyd
Electronic Devices, Fifth Edition
Electronic Devices: Electron-Flow Version, Third Edition

©1999 by Prentice-Hall, Inc.
Simon & Schuster/A Viacom Company
Upper Saddle River, New Jersey 07458
All rights reserved.

FIGURE 14-51
Schematic of the ADC.

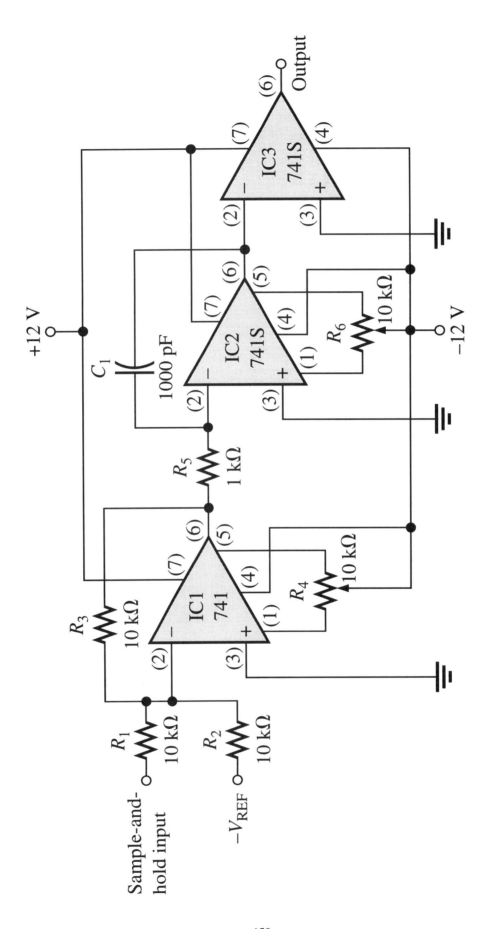

FIGURE 15-2

The instrumentation amplifier with the external gain-setting resistor R_G. Differential and common-mode signals are indicated.

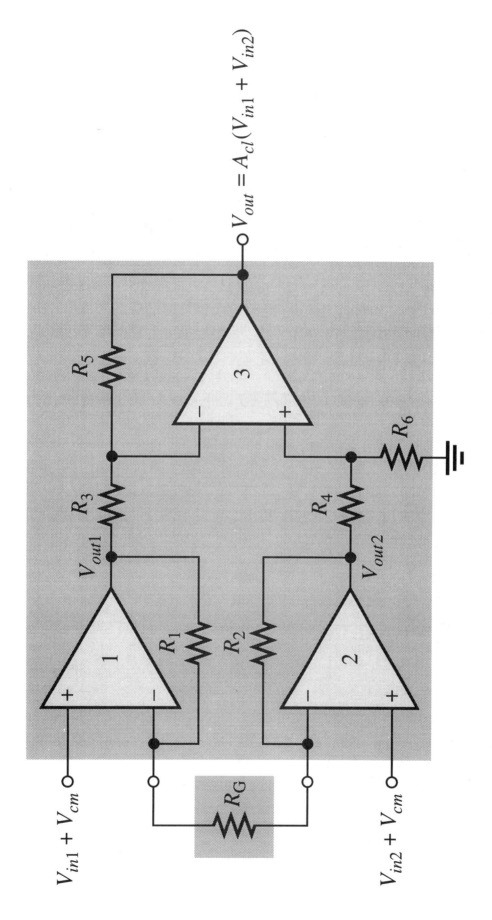

Thomas L. Floyd
Electronic Devices, Fifth Edition
Electronic Devices: Electron-Flow Version, Third Edition

©1999 by Prentice-Hall, Inc.
Simon & Schuster/A Viacom Company
Upper Saddle River, New Jersey 07458
All rights reserved.

FIGURE 15-8
Basic isolation amplifier block diagram.

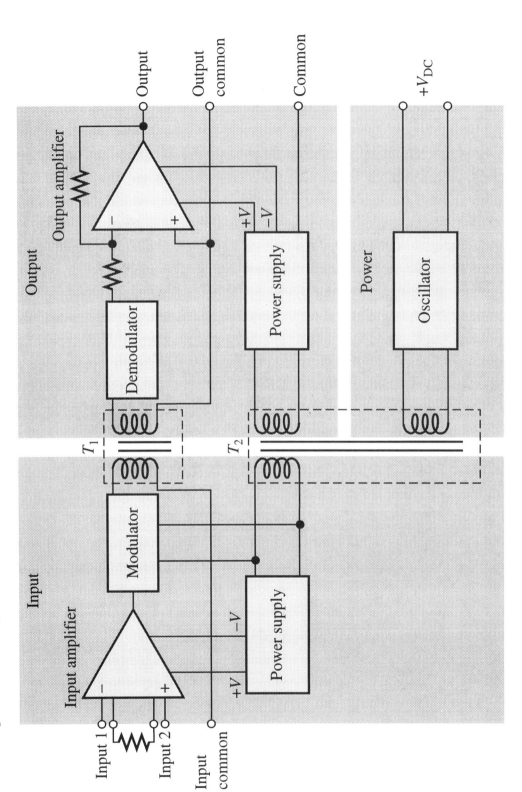

Thomas L. Floyd
Electronic Devices, Fifth Edition
Electronic Devices: Electron-Flow Version, Third Edition

©1999 by Prentice-Hall, Inc.
Simon & Schuster/A Viacom Company
Upper Saddle River, New Jersey 07458
All rights reserved.

FIGURE 15-10
The AD295 isolation amplifier.

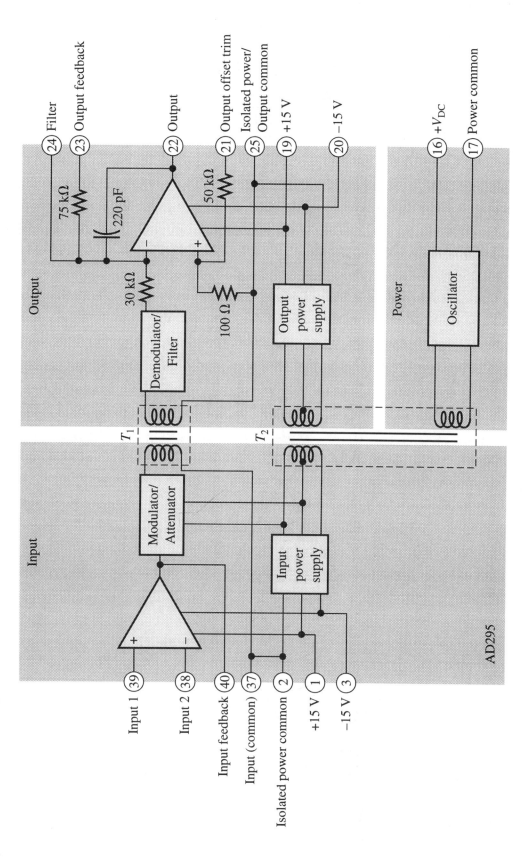

Thomas L. Floyd
Electronic Devices, Fifth Edition
Electronic Devices: Electron-Flow Version, Third Edition

©1999 by Prentice-Hall, Inc.
Simon & Schuster/A Viacom Company
Upper Saddle River, New Jersey 07458
All rights reserved.

FIGURE 15-22
The OTA as an amplitude modulator.

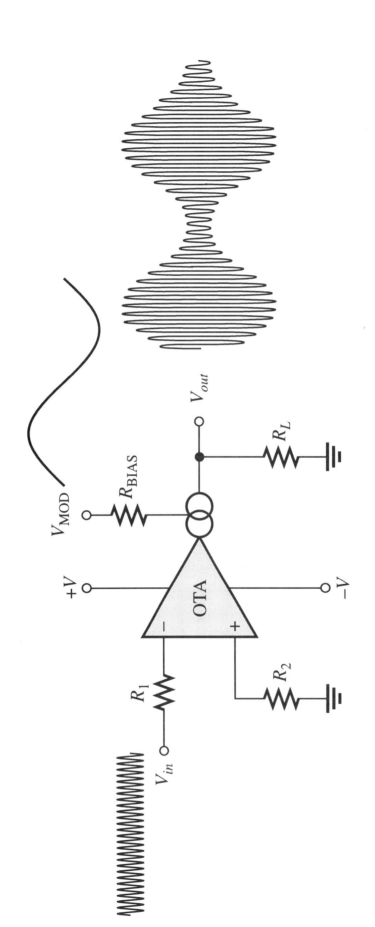

FIGURE 15-24

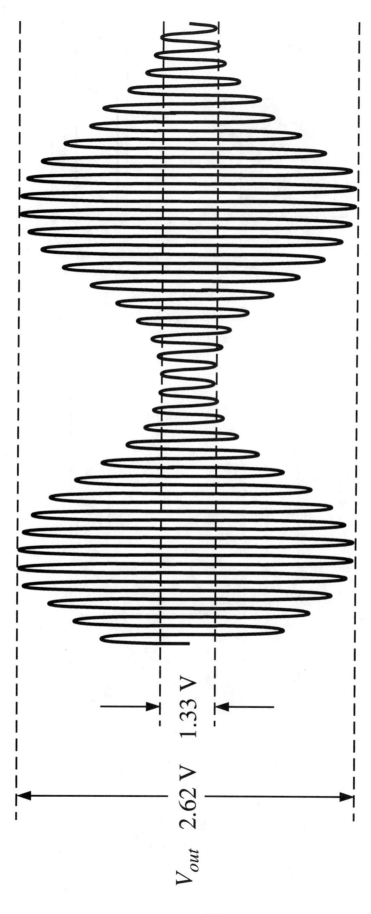

Thomas L. Floyd
Electronic Devices, Fifth Edition
Electronic Devices: Electron-Flow Version, Third Edition

©1999 by Prentice-Hall, Inc.
Simon & Schuster/A Viacom Company
Upper Saddle River, New Jersey 07458
All rights reserved.

FIGURE 15-38
Block diagram of the ECG system.

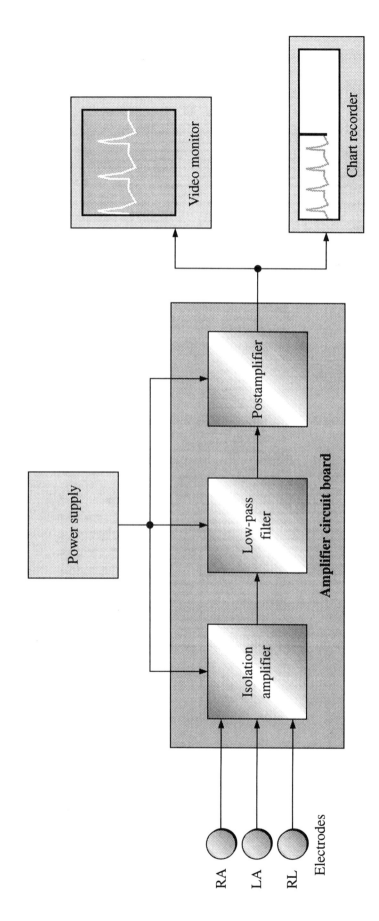

Thomas L. Floyd
Electronic Devices, Fifth Edition
Electronic Devices: Electron-Flow Version, Third Edition

©1999 by Prentice-Hall, Inc.
Simon & Schuster/A Viacom Company
Upper Saddle River, New Jersey 07458
All rights reserved.

FIGURE 15-40
Schematic of the amplifier board.

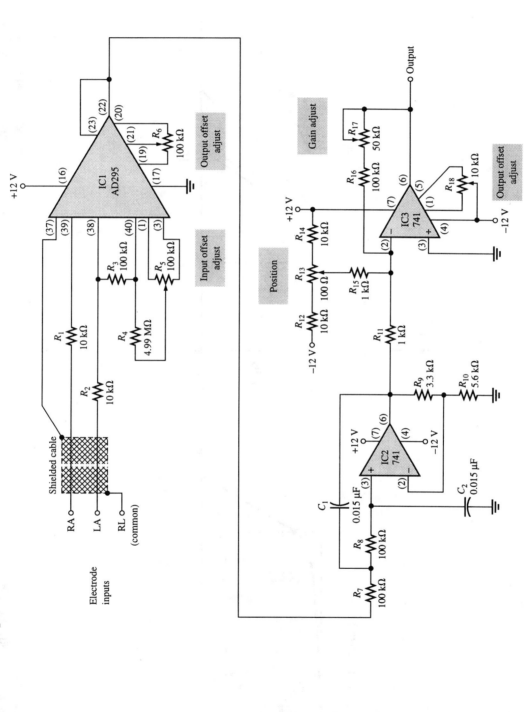

Thomas L. Floyd
Electronic Devices, Fifth Edition
Electronic Devices: Electron-Flow Version, Third Edition

©1999 by Prentice-Hall, Inc.
Simon & Schuster/A Viacom Company
Upper Saddle River, New Jersey 07458
All rights reserved.

FIGURE 16-1
Low-pass filter responses.

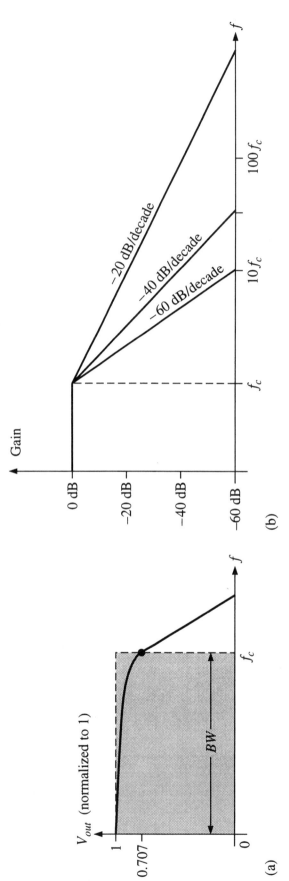

FIGURE 16-2
High-pass filter responses.

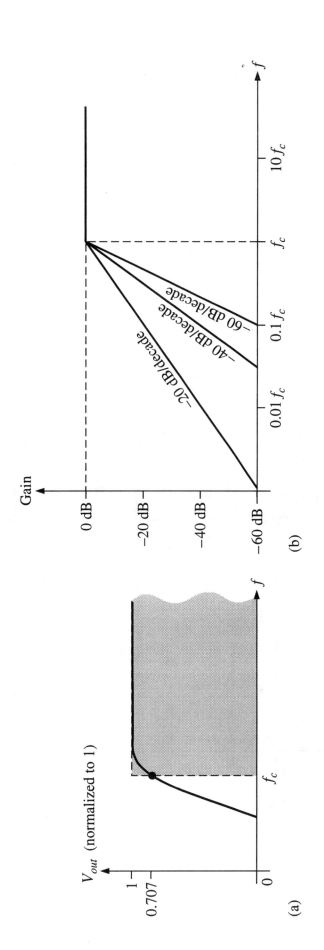

FIGURE 16-3
General band-pass response curve.

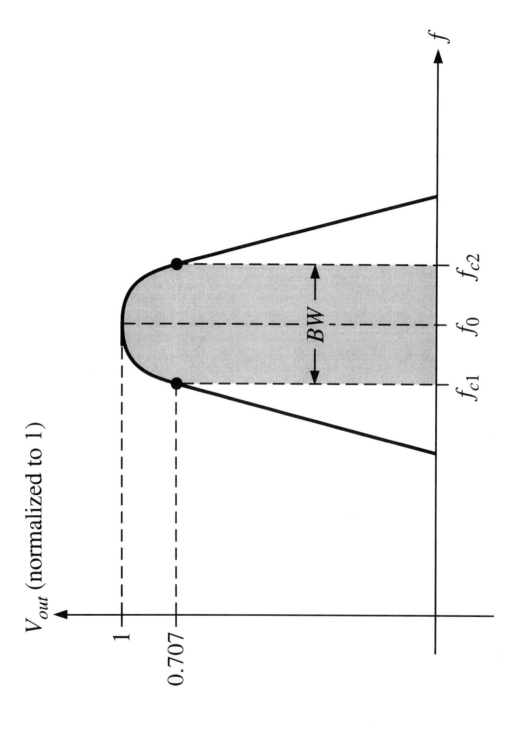

Thomas L. Floyd
Electronic Devices, Fifth Edition
Electronic Devices: Electron-Flow Version, Third Edition

© 1999 by Prentice-Hall, Inc.
Simon & Schuster/A Viacom Company
Upper Saddle River, New Jersey 07458
All rights reserved.

FIGURE 16-9
Single-pole active low-pass filter and response curve.

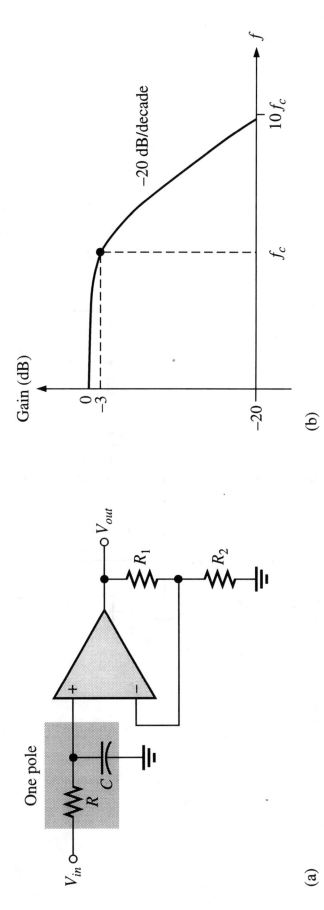

(a)

(b)

Thomas L. Floyd
Electronic Devices, Fifth Edition
Electronic Devices: Electron-Flow Version, Third Edition

©1999 by Prentice-Hall, Inc.
Simon & Schuster/A Viacom Company
Upper Saddle River, New Jersey 07458
All rights reserved.

FIGURE 16–12
Cascaded low-pass filters.

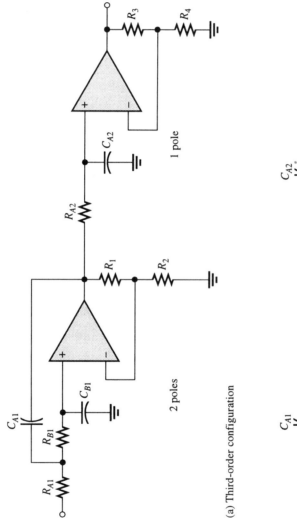

(a) Third-order configuration

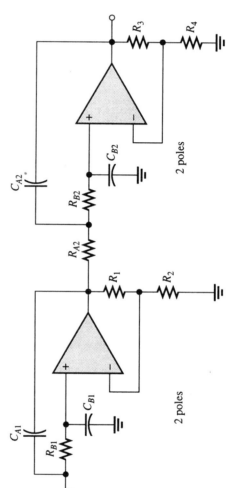

(b) Fourth-order configuration

Thomas L. Floyd
Electronic Devices, Fifth Edition
Electronic Devices: Electron-Flow Version, Third Edition

©1999 by Prentice-Hall, Inc.
Simon & Schuster/A Viacom Company
Upper Saddle River, New Jersey 07458
All rights reserved.

FIGURE 16-17
Band-pass filter formed by cascading a two-pole high-pass and a two-pole low-pass filter (it does not matter in which order the filters are cascaded).

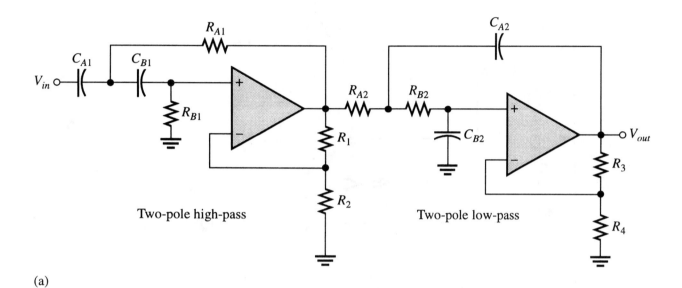

(a)

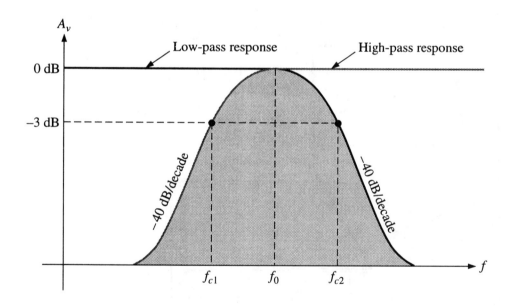

(b)

Thomas L. Floyd
Electronic Devices, Fifth Edition
Electronic Devices: Electron-Flow Version, Third Edition

©1999 by Prentice-Hall, Inc.
Simon & Schuster/A Viacom Company
Upper Saddle River, New Jersey 07458
All rights reserved.

FIGURE 16–20
State-variable band-pass filter.

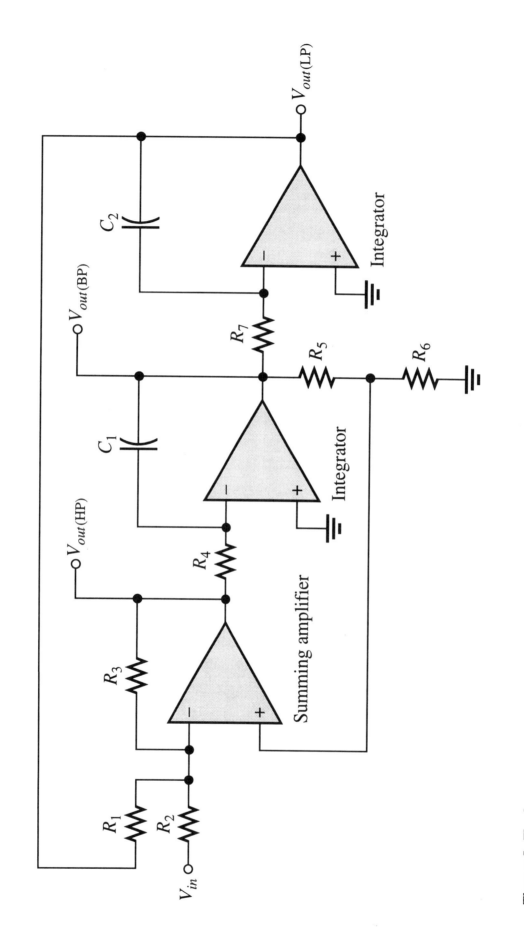

FIGURE 16-25

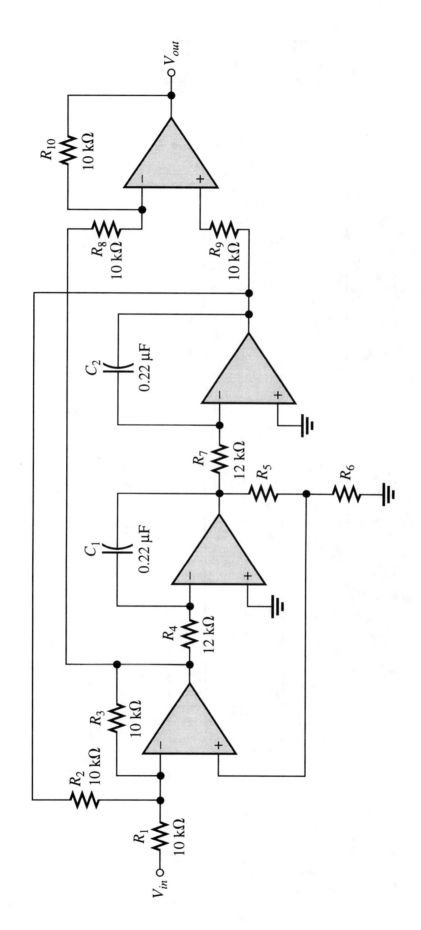

FIGURE 16-28
Basic block diagram of an FM receiver system.

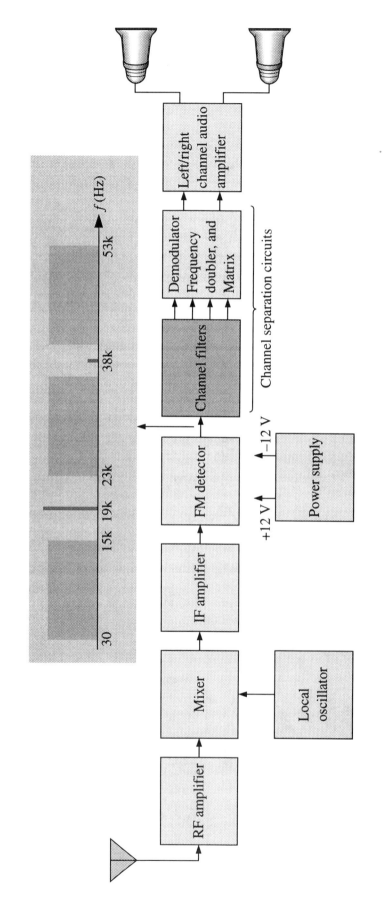

FIGURE 16-30
Channel separation circuits. The circuits on the filter board are shown in the four, large shaded blocks.

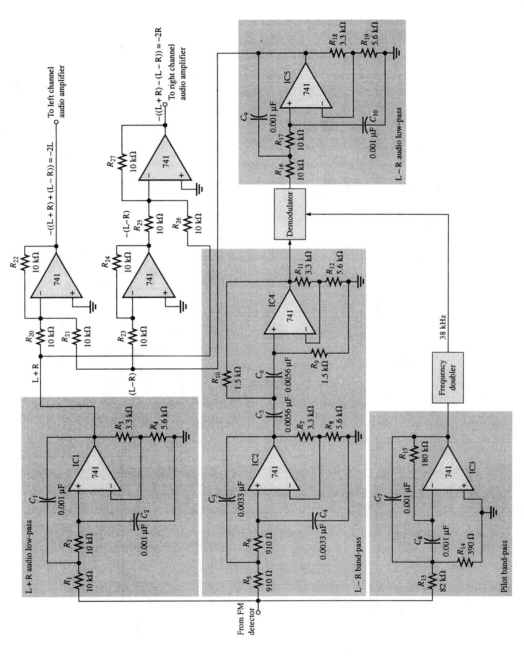

Thomas L. Floyd
Electronic Devices, Fifth Edition
Electronic Devices: Electron-Flow Version, Third Edition

© 1999 by Prentice-Hall, Inc.
Simon & Schuster/A Viacom Company
Upper Saddle River, New Jersey 07458
All rights reserved.

FIGURE 17-3
Positive feedback produces oscillation.

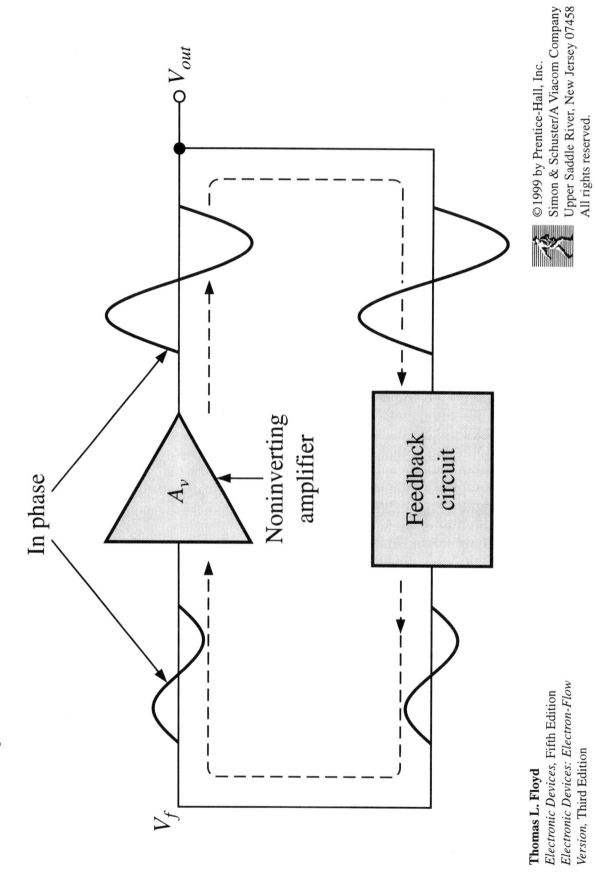

FIGURE 17-4
Conditions for oscillation.

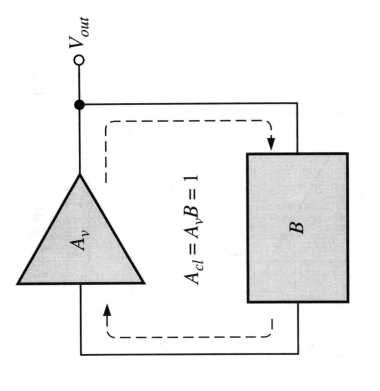

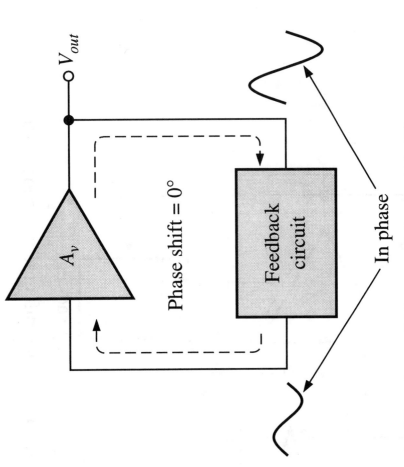

(a) The phase shift around the loop is 0°.

(b) The closed loop gain is 1.

©1999 by Prentice-Hall, Inc.
Simon & Schuster/A Viacom Company
Upper Saddle River, New Jersey 07458
All rights reserved.

Thomas L. Floyd
Electronic Devices, Fifth Edition
Electronic Devices: Electron-Flow Version, Third Edition

FIGURE 17-8
Conditions for oscillation.

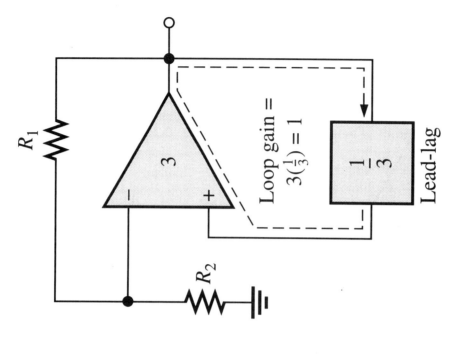

(b) The voltage gain around the loop is 1.

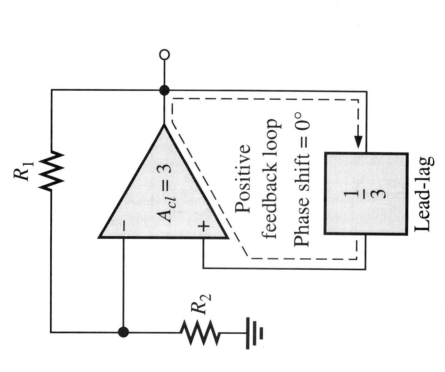

(a) The phase shift around the loop is 0°.

Thomas L. Floyd
Electronic Devices, Fifth Edition
Electronic Devices: Electron-Flow Version, Third Edition

 ©1999 by Prentice-Hall, Inc.
Simon & Schuster/A Viacom Company
Upper Saddle River, New Jersey 07458
All rights reserved.

FIGURE 17-22
A basic Clapp oscillator.

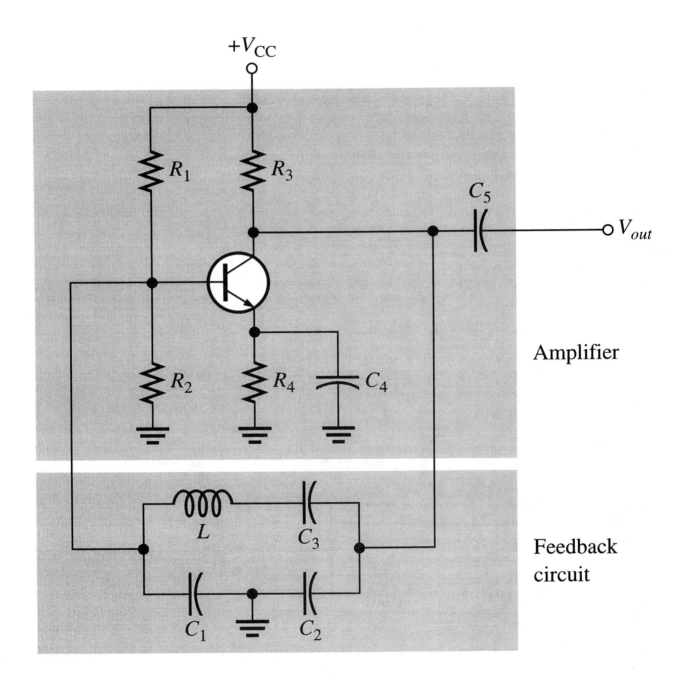

FIGURE 17-23
A basic Hartley oscillator.

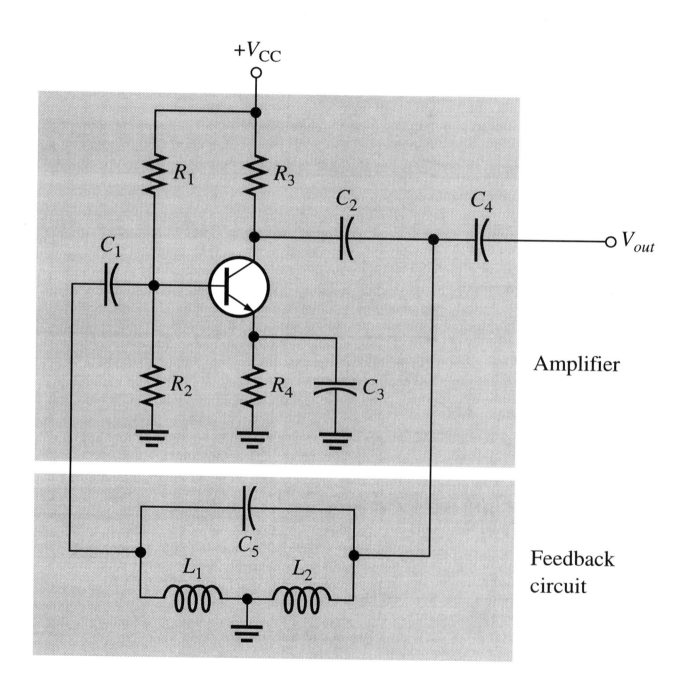

FIGURE 17-26
Basic crystal oscillators.

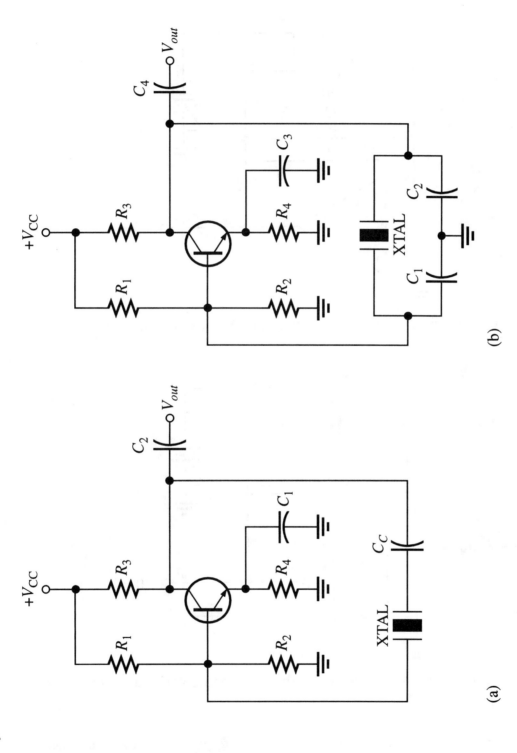

FIGURE 17–31*

Voltage-controlled sawtooth oscillator operation.

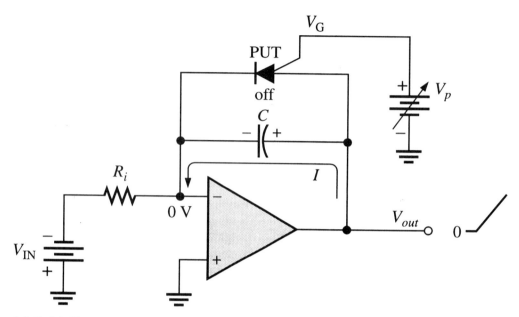

(a) Initially, the capacitor charges, the output ramp begins, and the PUT is off.

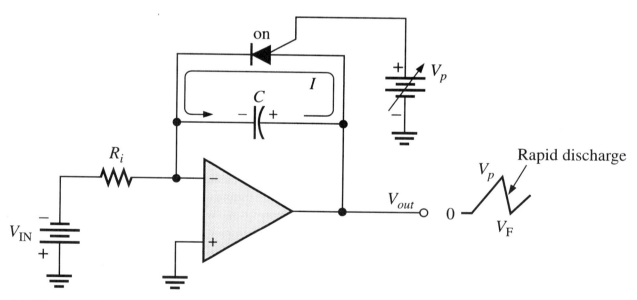

(b) The capacitor rapidly discharges when the PUT momentarily turns on.

Thomas L. Floyd
Electronic Devices, Fifth Edition
*Current arrows indicate conventional flow.

©1999 by Prentice-Hall, Inc.
Simon & Schuster/A Viacom Company
Upper Saddle River, New Jersey 07458
All rights reserved.

FIGURE 17-38*
Operation of the 555 timer in the astable mode.

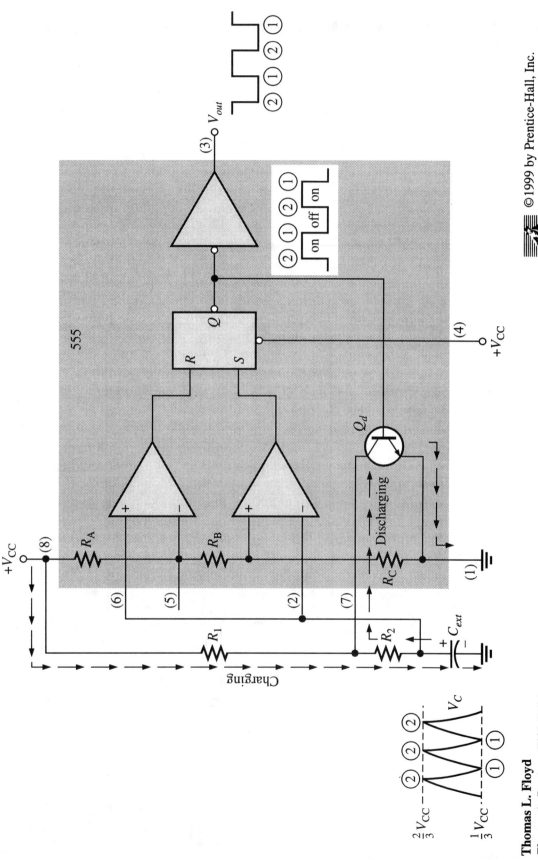

Thomas L. Floyd
Electronic Devices, Fifth Edition
*Current arrows indicate conventional flow.

©1999 by Prentice-Hall, Inc.
Simon & Schuster/A Viacom Company
Upper Saddle River, New Jersey 07458
All rights reserved.

FIGURE 17-39*

The addition of diode D_1 allows the duty cycle of the output to be adjusted to less than 50 percent by making $R_1 < R_2$.

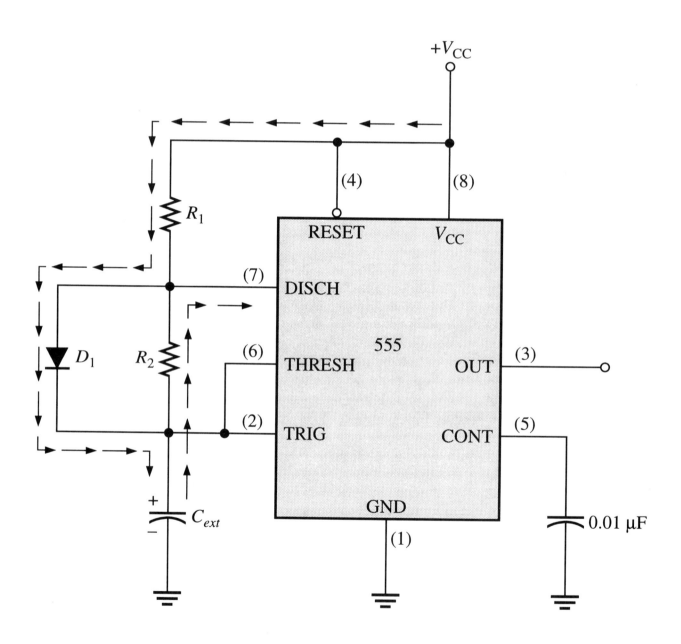

Thomas L. Floyd
Electronic Devices, Fifth Edition
*Current arrows indicate conventional flow.

©1999 by Prentice-Hall, Inc.
Simon & Schuster/A Viacom Company
Upper Saddle River, New Jersey 07458
All rights reserved.

FIGURE 17-48
Block diagram of the function generator.

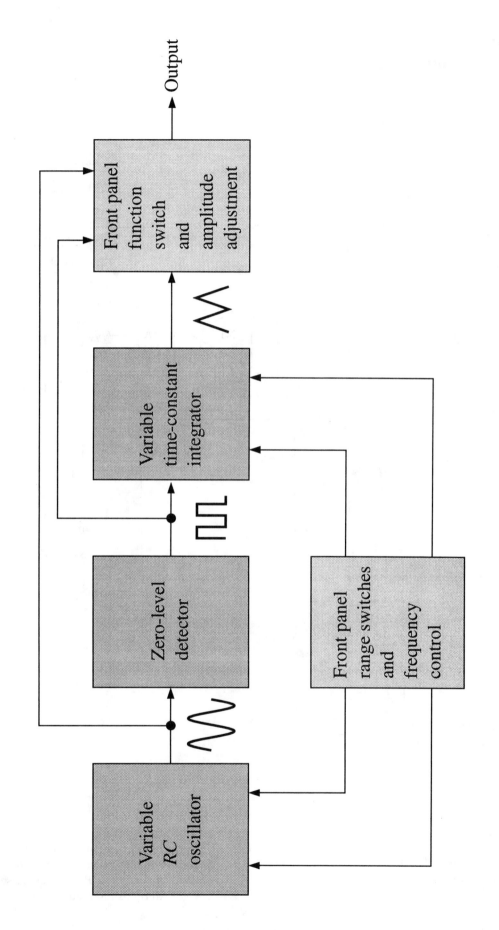

FIGURE 17–49
Schematic of the function generator.

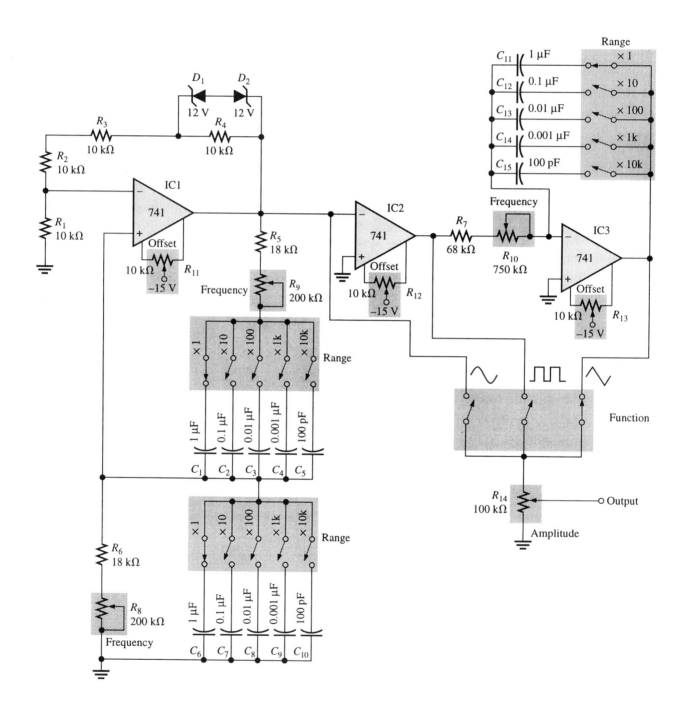

Thomas L. Floyd
Electronic Devices, Fifth Edition
*Electronic Devices: Electron-Flow
Version,* Third Edition

©1999 by Prentice-Hall, Inc.
Simon & Schuster/A Viacom Company
Upper Saddle River, New Jersey 07458
All rights reserved.

FIGURE 18-5

Illustration of series regulator action that keeps V_{OUT} constant when V_{IN} or R_L changes.

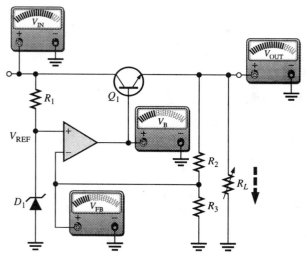

(a) When V_{IN} or R_L decreases, V_{OUT} attempts to decrease. The feedback voltage, V_{FB}, also attempts to decrease, and as a result, the op-amp's output voltage V_B attempts to increase, thus compensating for the attempted decrease in V_{OUT} by increasing the Q_1 emitter voltage. Changes in V_{OUT} are exaggerated for illustration.

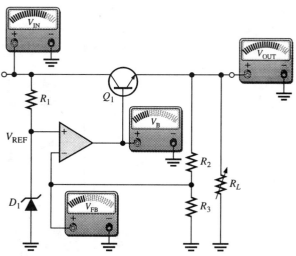

(b) When V_{IN} (or R_L) stabilizes at its new lower value, the voltages return to their original values, thus keeping V_{OUT} constant as a result of the negative feedback.

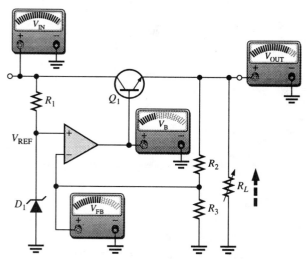

(c) When V_{IN} or R_L increases, V_{OUT} attempts to increase. The feedback voltage, V_{FB}, also attempts to increase, and as a result, V_B, applied to the base of the control transistor, attempts to decrease, thus compensating for the attempted increase in V_{OUT} by decreasing the Q_1 emitter voltage.

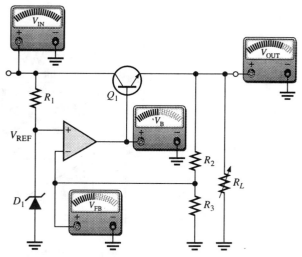

(d) When V_{IN} (or R_L) stabilizes at its new higher value, the voltages return to their original values, thus keeping V_{OUT} constant as a result of the negative feedback.

Thomas L. Floyd
Electronic Devices, Fifth Edition
Electronic Devices: Electron-Flow Version, Third Edition

©1999 by Prentice-Hall, Inc.
Simon & Schuster/A Viacom Company
Upper Saddle River, New Jersey 07458
All rights reserved.

FIGURE 18-13

Sequence of responses when V_{OUT} tries to decrease as a result of a decrease in R_L or V_{IN} (opposite responses for an attempted increase).

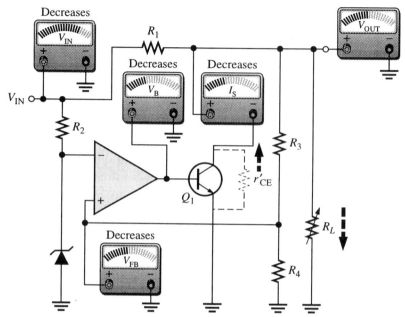

(a) Response to a decrease in V_{IN} or R_L

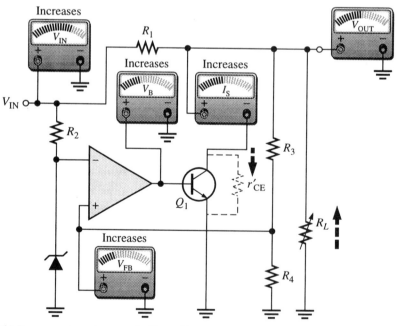

(b) Response to an increase in V_{IN} or R_L

Thomas L. Floyd
Electronic Devices, Fifth Edition
Electronic Devices: Electron-Flow Version, Third Edition

©1999 by Prentice-Hall, Inc.
Simon & Schuster/A Viacom Company
Upper Saddle River, New Jersey 07458
All rights reserved.

FIGURE 18–16

Switching regulator waveforms. The V_C waveform is for no inductive filtering to illustrate the charge and discharge action. L and C smooth V_C to a nearly constant level, as indicated by the dashed line for V_{OUT}.

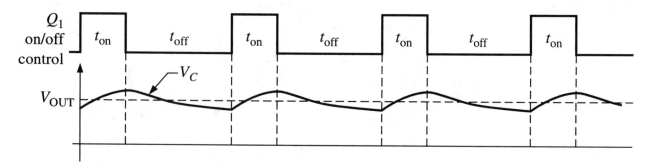

(a) V_{OUT} depends on the duty cycle.

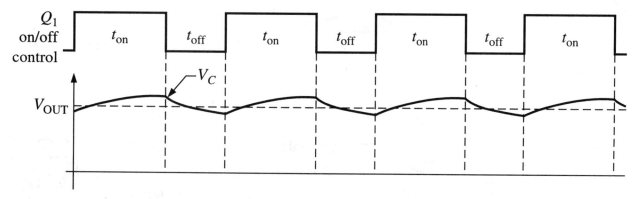

(b) Increase the duty cycle and V_{OUT} increases.

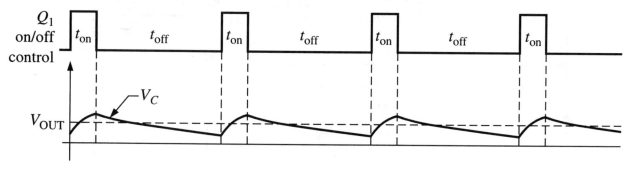

(c) Decrease the duty cycle and V_{OUT} decreases.

Thomas L. Floyd
Electronic Devices, Fifth Edition
Electronic Devices: Electron-Flow Version, Third Edition

©1999 by Prentice-Hall, Inc.
Simon & Schuster/A Viacom Company
Upper Saddle River, New Jersey 07458
All rights reserved.

FIGURE 18-17*
Regulating action of the basic step-down switching regulator.

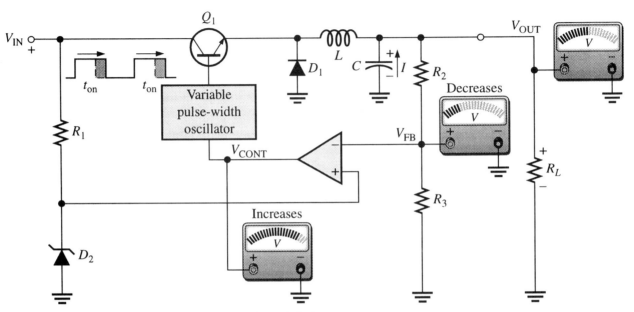

(a) When V_{OUT} attempts to decrease, the on-time of Q_1 increases.

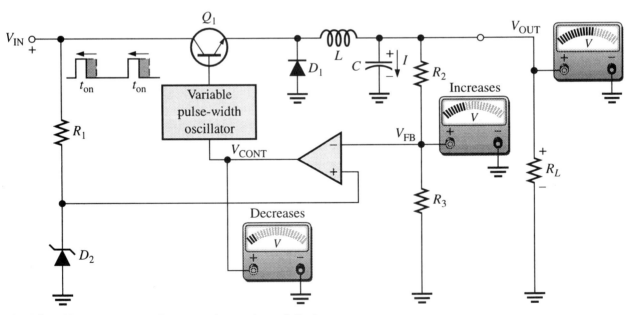

(b) When V_{OUT} attempts to increase, the on-time of Q_1 decreases.

Thomas L. Floyd
Electronic Devices, Fifth Edition
*Current arrows indicate
 conventional flow.

©1999 by Prentice-Hall, Inc.
Simon & Schuster/A Viacom Company
Upper Saddle River, New Jersey 07458
All rights reserved.

FIGURE 18-19*
Switching action of the basic step-up regulator.

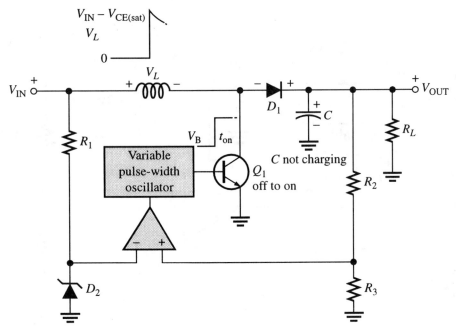

(a) When Q_1 is on

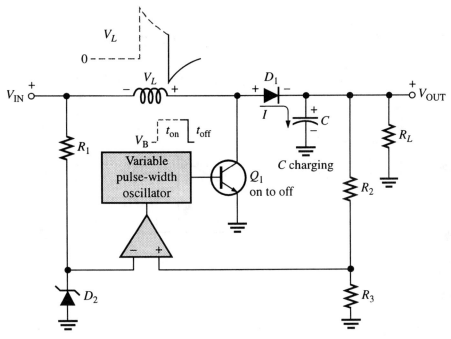

(b) When Q_1 turns off

Thomas L. Floyd
Electronic Devices, Fifth Edition
*Current arrows indicate conventional flow.

©1999 by Prentice-Hall, Inc.
Simon & Schuster/A Viacom Company
Upper Saddle River, New Jersey 07458
All rights reserved.

FIGURE 18-22*
Inverting action of the basic inverting switching regulator.

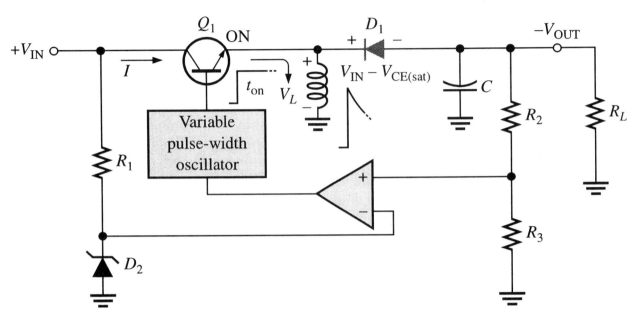

(a) When Q_1 is on, D_1 is reverse-biased.

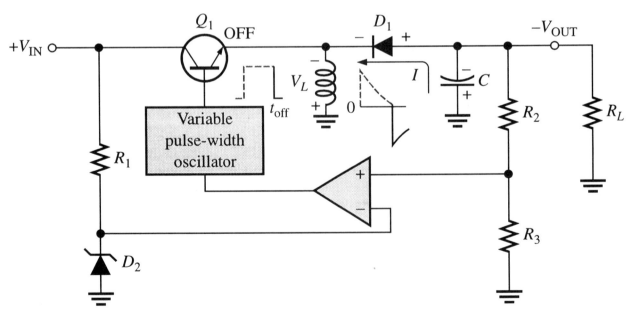

(b) When Q_1 turns off, D_1 forward biases.

Thomas L. Floyd
Electronic Devices, Fifth Edition
*Current arrows indicate
conventional flow.

©1999 by Prentice-Hall, Inc.
Simon & Schuster/A Viacom Company
Upper Saddle River, New Jersey 07458
All rights reserved.

FIGURE 18-34*
The current-limiting action of the regulator circuit.

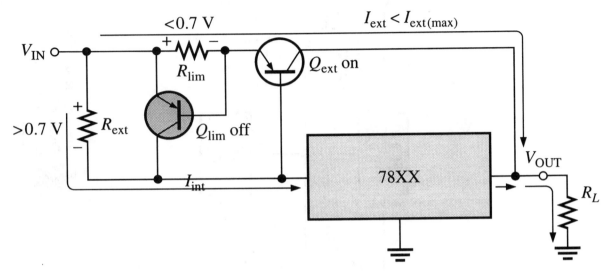

(a) During normal operation, when the load current is not excessive, Q_{lim} is off.

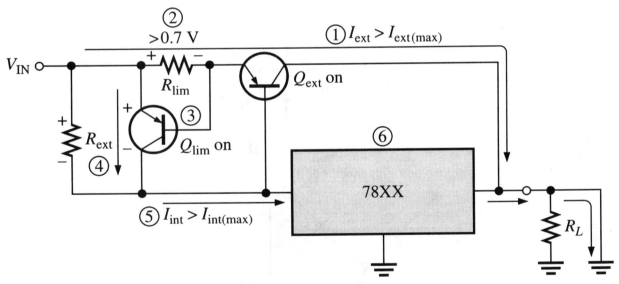

(b) When short occurs ①, the external current becomes excessive and the voltage across R_{lim} increases ② and turns on Q_{lim} ③, which then conducts current away from Q_{ext} and routes it through the regulator ④, causing the internal regulator current to become excessive ⑤ and to force the regulator into thermal shut down ⑥.

Thomas L. Floyd
Electronic Devices, Fifth Edition
*Current arrows indicate conventional flow.

©1999 by Prentice-Hall, Inc.
Simon & Schuster/A Viacom Company
Upper Saddle River, New Jersey 07458
All rights reserved.

FIGURE 18-41
The dual-polarity power supply schematic.

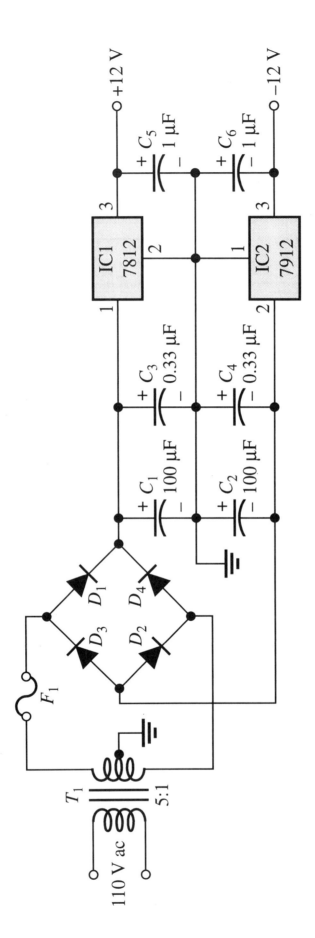